2/13

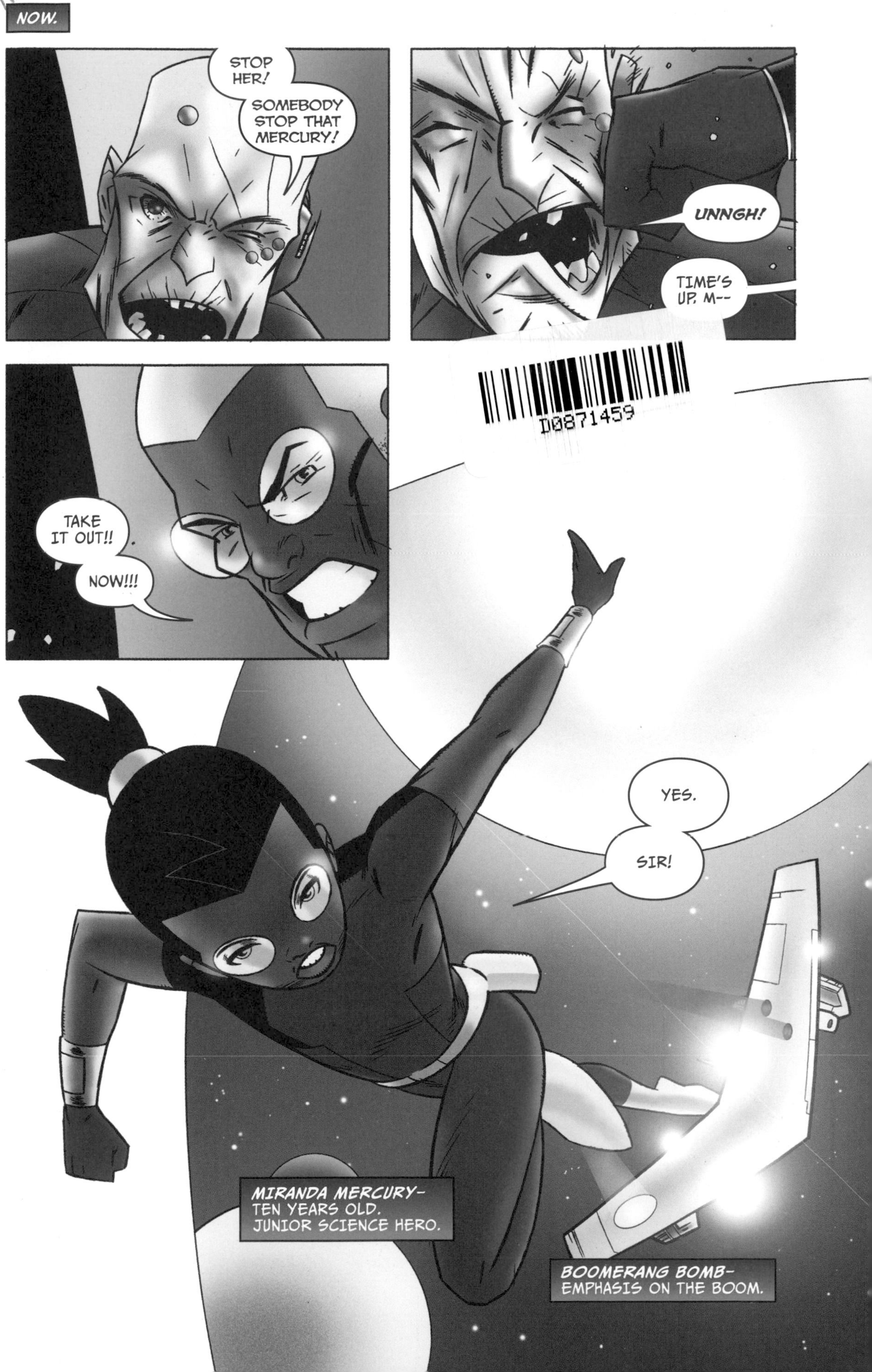
NOW.
STOP HER!
SOMEBODY STOP THAT MERCURY!
UNNGH!
TIME'S UP, M--
TAKE IT OUT!!
NOW!!!
YES.
SIR!
MIRANDA MERCURY- TEN YEARS OLD. JUNIOR SCIENCE HERO.
BOOMERANG BOMB- EMPHASIS ON THE BOOM.

ARE YOU READY, MIRANDA?

YES.

OOOH...

CONGRATULATIONS.

JAMES MERCURY—
INVENTOR. SCIENCE HERO.
GRANDPA.

MIRANDA MERCURY—
PAIN IS GAIN.

DOROTHY MERCURY—
PILOT. SCIENCE HERO.
DEVOTED TO JAMES
AND JUSTICE.

MARIE MERCURY—
INFANT. WAITING HER TURN.

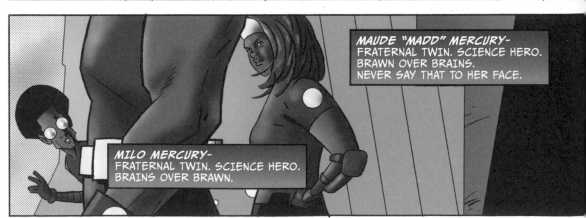

MAUDE "MADD" MERCURY—
FRATERNAL TWIN. SCIENCE HERO.
BRAWN OVER BRAINS.
NEVER SAY THAT TO HER FACE.

MILO MERCURY—
FRATERNAL TWIN. SCIENCE HERO.
BRAINS OVER BRAWN.

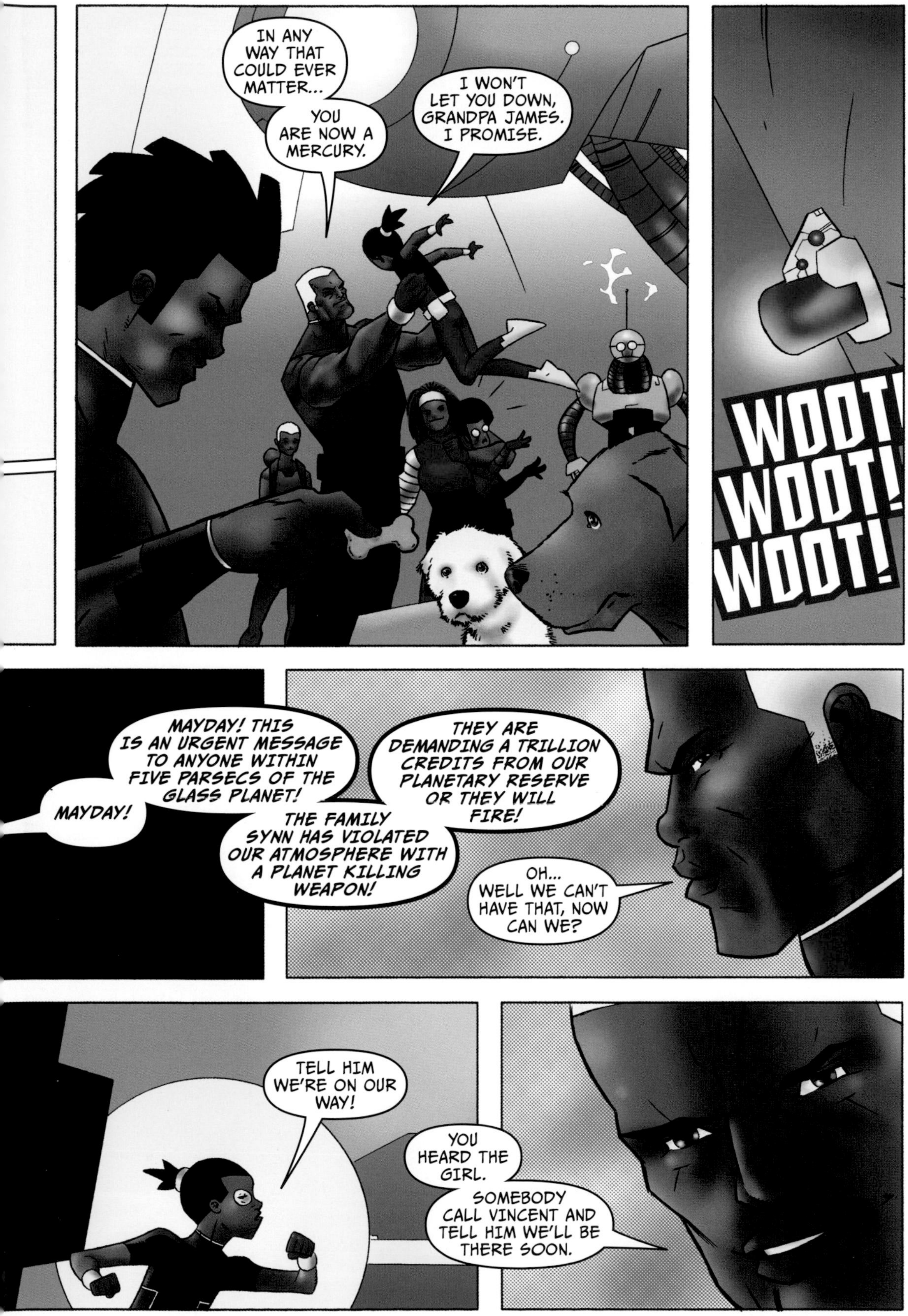
IN ANY WAY THAT COULD EVER MATTER...
YOU ARE NOW A MERCURY.
I WON'T LET YOU DOWN, GRANDPA JAMES. I PROMISE.
WOOT! WOOT! WOOT!
MAYDAY!
MAYDAY! THIS IS AN URGENT MESSAGE TO ANYONE WITHIN FIVE PARSECS OF THE GLASS PLANET!
THE FAMILY SYNN HAS VIOLATED OUR ATMOSPHERE WITH A PLANET KILLING WEAPON!
THEY ARE DEMANDING A TRILLION CREDITS FROM OUR PLANETARY RESERVE OR THEY WILL FIRE!
OH... WELL WE CAN'T HAVE THAT, NOW CAN WE?
TELL HIM WE'RE ON OUR WAY!
YOU HEARD THE GIRL.
SOMEBODY CALL VINCENT AND TELL HIM WE'LL BE THERE SOON.

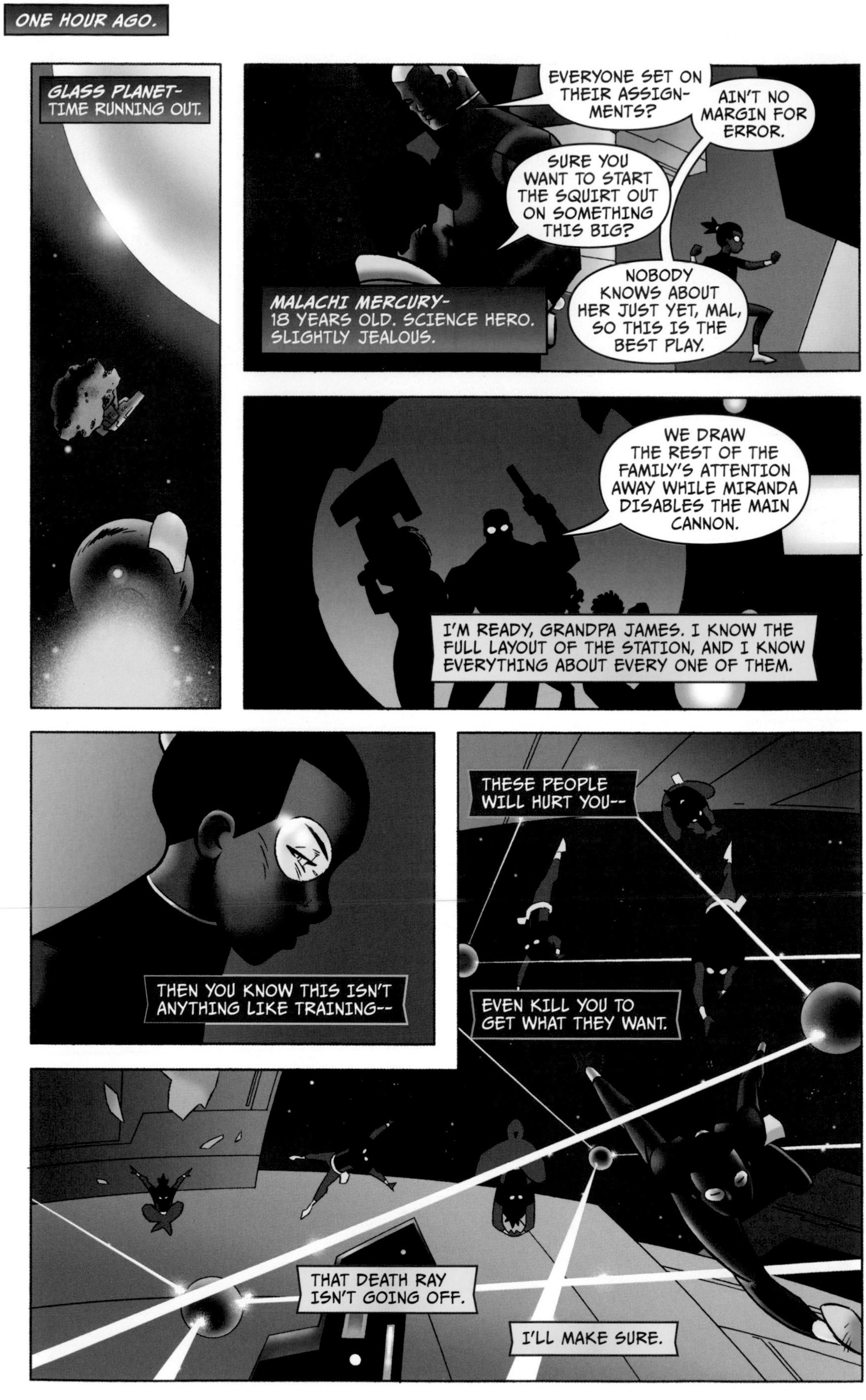
ONE HOUR AGO.
GLASS PLANET-
TIME RUNNING OUT.
EVERYONE SET ON THEIR ASSIGN-MENTS?
AIN'T NO MARGIN FOR ERROR.
SURE YOU WANT TO START THE SQUIRT OUT ON SOMETHING THIS BIG?
MALACHI MERCURY-
18 YEARS OLD. SCIENCE HERO. SLIGHTLY JEALOUS.
NOBODY KNOWS ABOUT HER JUST YET, MAL, SO THIS IS THE BEST PLAY.
WE DRAW THE REST OF THE FAMILY'S ATTENTION AWAY WHILE MIRANDA DISABLES THE MAIN CANNON.
I'M READY, GRANDPA JAMES. I KNOW THE FULL LAYOUT OF THE STATION, AND I KNOW EVERYTHING ABOUT EVERY ONE OF THEM.
THEN YOU KNOW THIS ISN'T ANYTHING LIKE TRAINING--
THESE PEOPLE WILL HURT YOU--
EVEN KILL YOU TO GET WHAT THEY WANT.
THAT DEATH RAY ISN'T GOING OFF.
I'LL MAKE SURE.

AND JUST WHO ARE YOU SUPPOSED TO BE?

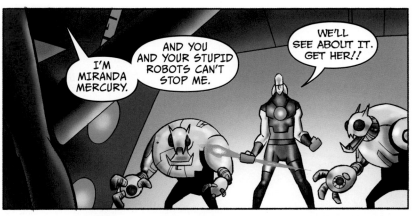

I'M MIRANDA MERCURY.

AND YOU AND YOUR STUPID ROBOTS CAN'T STOP ME.

WE'LL SEE ABOUT IT. GET HER!!

SILLY LITTLE GIRL-- I BUILT THEM MYSELF, YOU KNOW.

AND THEY'RE TOTALLY AWESOME!

I THINK YOU MEAN TOTALLY BROKEN, SYNN.

WHAT ELSE YOU GOT?

YOU'RE GONNA PAY FOR THAT, MERCURY!

YOU'RE GONNA PAY!!!

BROTHER SYNN– 12 YEARS OLD. BIG FOR HIS AGE. IN SOO MUCH TROUBLE IF HE LOSES A FIGHT WITH A TEN YEAR OLD.

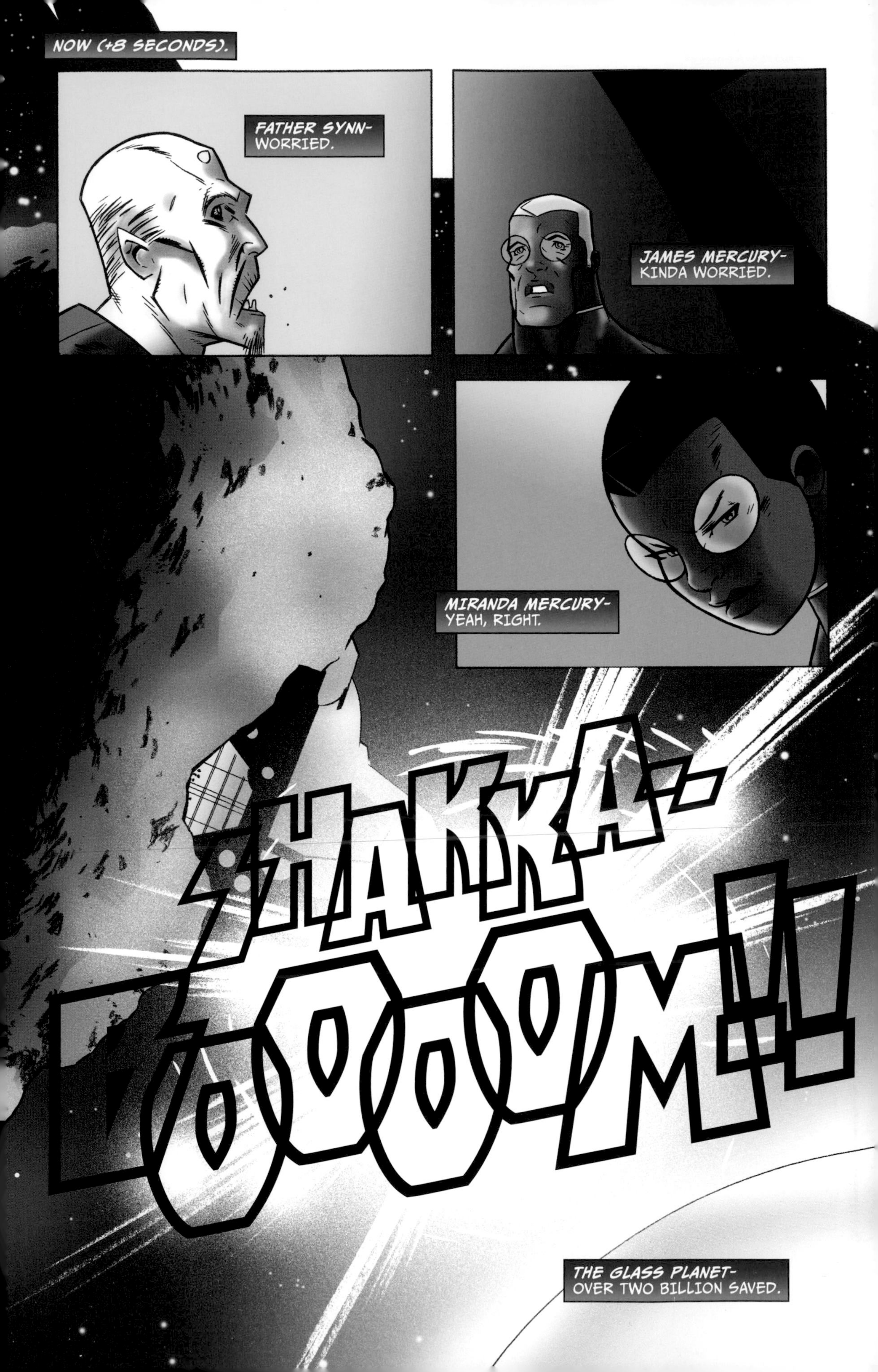

NOW (+8 SECONDS).
FATHER SYNN- WORRIED.
JAMES MERCURY- KINDA WORRIED.
MIRANDA MERCURY- YEAH, RIGHT.
SHAKKA-KOOOOM!!
THE GLASS PLANET- OVER TWO BILLION SAVED.

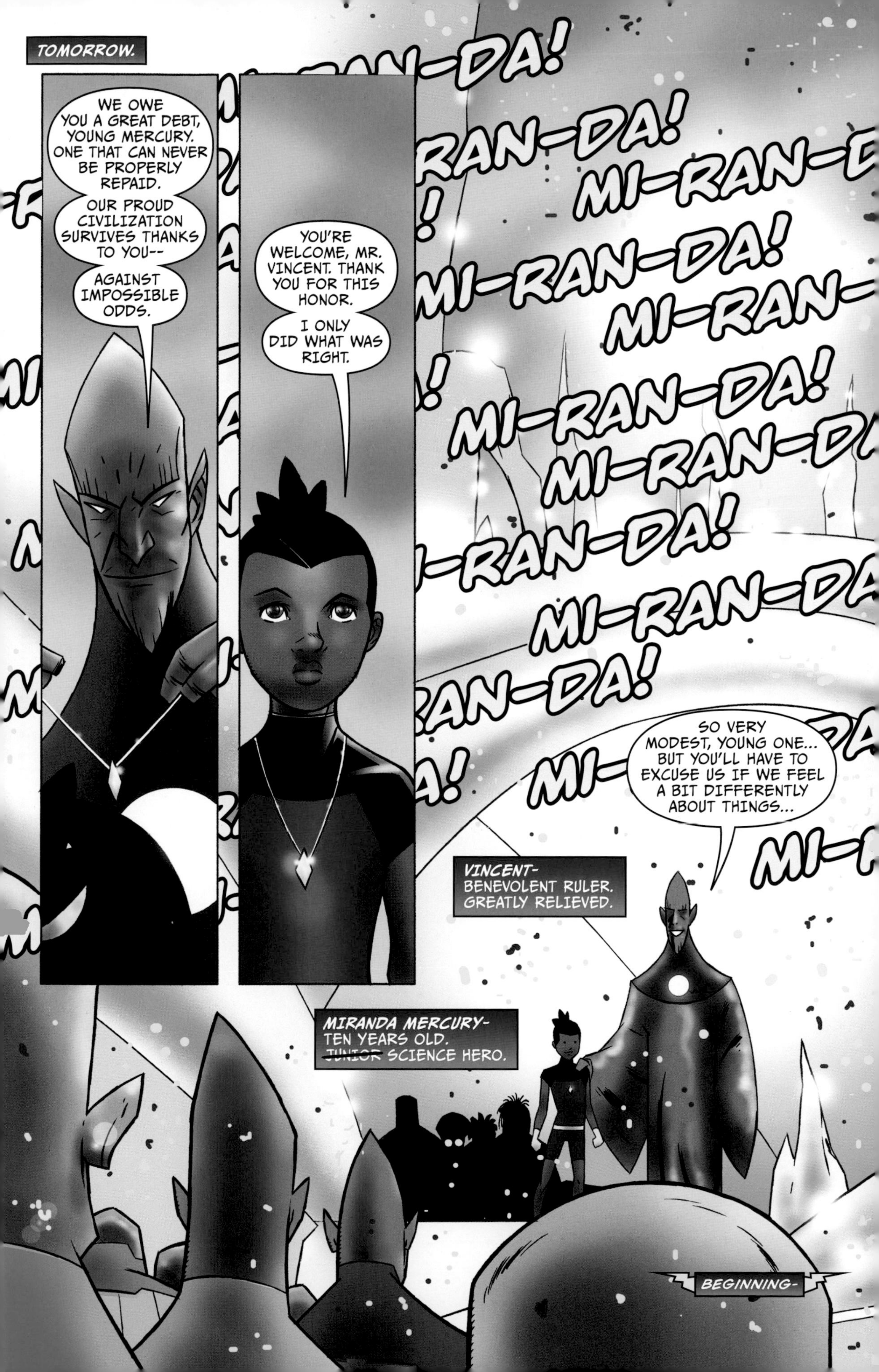
TOMORROW.
WE OWE YOU A GREAT DEBT, YOUNG MERCURY. ONE THAT CAN NEVER BE PROPERLY REPAID.
OUR PROUD CIVILIZATION SURVIVES THANKS TO YOU--
AGAINST IMPOSSIBLE ODDS.
YOU'RE WELCOME, MR. VINCENT. THANK YOU FOR THIS HONOR.
I ONLY DID WHAT WAS RIGHT.
MI-RAN-DA!
MI-RAN-DA!
MI-RAN-DA!
MI-RAN-DA!
MI-RAN-DA!
SO VERY MODEST, YOUNG ONE... BUT YOU'LL HAVE TO EXCUSE US IF WE FEEL A BIT DIFFERENTLY ABOUT THINGS...
VINCENT- BENEVOLENT RULER. GREATLY RELIEVED.
MIRANDA MERCURY- TEN YEARS OLD. ~~JUNIOR~~ SCIENCE HERO.
BEGINNING-

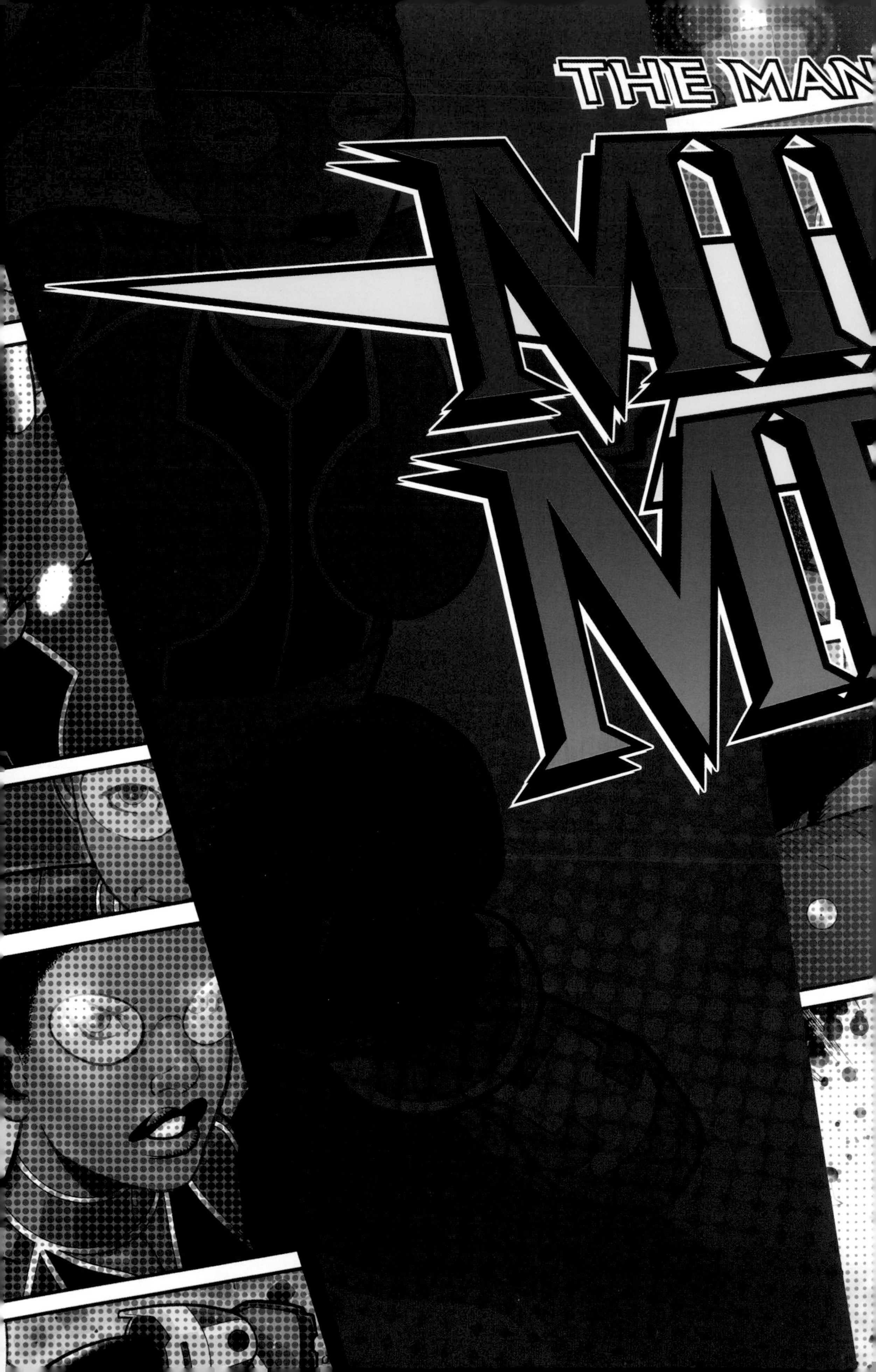
THE MAN

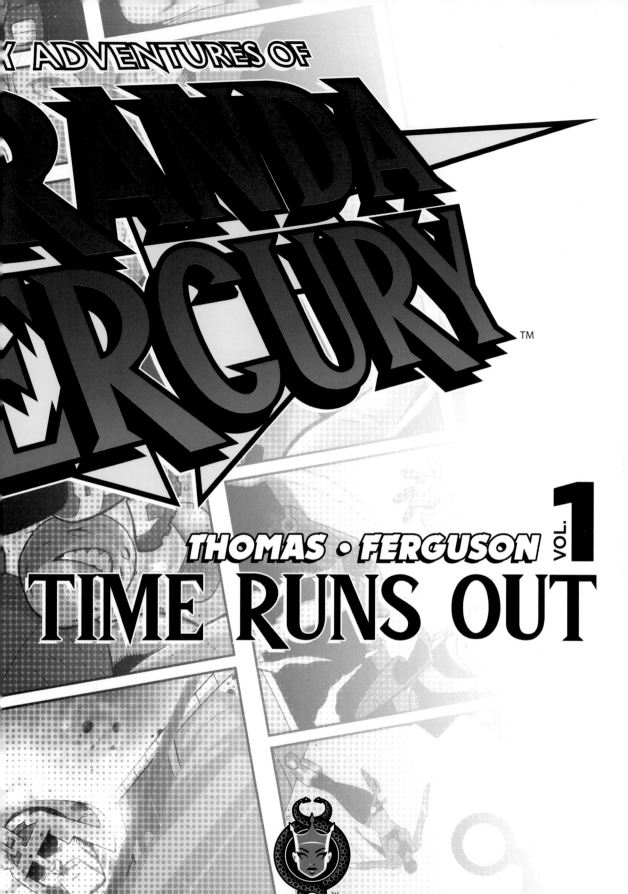

THE AMAZING ADVENTURES OF

RANDA MERCURY

™

THOMAS · FERGUSON VOL. 1
TIME RUNS OUT

ARCHAIA ENTERTAINMENT LLC
WWW.ARCHAIA.COM

WRITER/CREATOR
BRANDON THOMAS

PENCILER/CREATOR
LEE FERGUSON

INKER
MARC DEERING

LETTERER/PRODUCTION/DESIGN
MATTY RYAN

COLORISTS
LEE FERGUSON
FELIX SERRANO
JORDAN BOYD
CRAIG CERMAK
JAMES BROWN

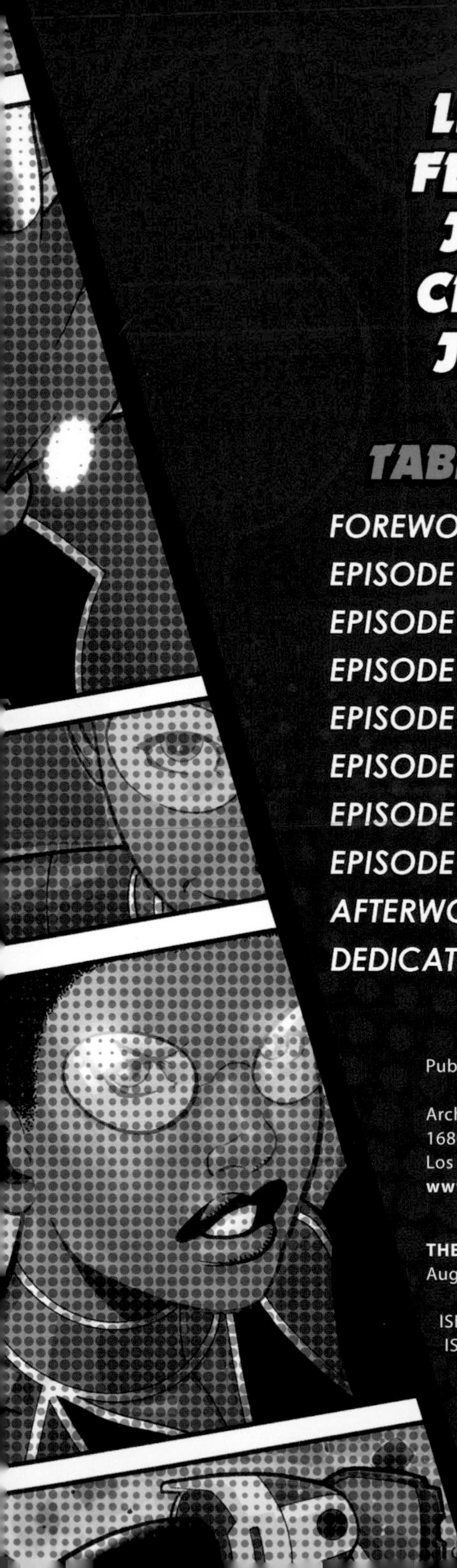

TABLE OF CONTENTS

Published by **Archaia**

Archaia Entertainment LLC
1680 Vine Street, Suite 912
Los Angeles, California, 90028, USA
www.archaia.com

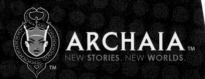

ARCHAIA™
NEW STORIES. NEW WORLDS.

THE MANY ADVENTURES OF MIRANDA MERCURY VOLUME ONE.
August 2011. FIRST PRINTING.

ISBN: 1-936393-05-0
ISBN 13: 978-1-936393-05-3

Printed in Korea.

FOREWORD

THIS IS THE OFFICIAL **MIRANDA MERCURY** " COMICBOOK CELEBRITY" INTRODUCTION
*(filling in for the "comicbook celebrity"... **Joe Casey**)*

First things first... "Miranda Mercury" is a cool ass name. So we're already starting out ahead of the game.

If there's one thing I can appreciate in a comicbook... it's energy. And this comicbook seems to have it. Hell, it's got energy to spare. From the ideas, to the characters, to the writing, to the art, to the coloring... there's a lot to dig here. A personal favorite is the pure storytelling bravura on display in Chapter Three (or issue #297, if you're really paying attention). But you'll get to that...

Brandon, Lee and Co. have been on a long journey to get this book into your hands. I know these guys, I've worked with them, I know what this book means to them. Comicbooks are, at best, an immediate form of entertainment creation. You're working at the speed of thought and inflicting your ideas and your craft on an audience at a speed that most entertainment media simply cannot match.

And then sometimes... it takes awhile. Unforeseen circumstances occur, life gets in the way, the world spins backwards... any number of things happen that can somehow delay the delivery of, as Brandon himself might say, the New Hotness. All I can really say about that is... some things are worth waiting for. Despite the obstacles placed before them -- much like the 36 movements it takes to solve a cosmic Rubik's Cube -- these guys did whatever it took to make sure their ideas, their blood, their sweat and everything else they've got is let loose in the big bad world. And that's something I can definitely appreciate.

There's a nice familiarity to the ideas in this comicbook. An appealing, sci-fi milieu complete with conflicted cosmic warriors and broken glass cities... a cool lead character with a quick wit and quick on the draw... colorful adversaries that challenge the hero on levels far beyond the physical... moments of true humanity that bring you closer to the characters... cliffhanger-styled stories that leave you breathless... these are tales of high adventures and you can tell the creators behind the music are putting everything and the kitchen sink into this book. Which is just the way I like it. But, as with anything, it's the mix that really sells it. They've got all the right ingredients, sure... but, damn, if they don't know how to bake a great cake.

I could go on, but your best bet is to simply sit back and let the experience of reading these stories for the first time wash over you. Hopefully, you'll have as good an experience as I had. And that's really what it's all about, isn't it...?

Not to mention... Miranda Mercury is a cool ass name. Sometimes that's all you need. But, in this book, a cool name is just the beginning...

Read on,
Joe Casey

*Joe Casey has been writing great comicbooks for almost 15 years and apparently sees no need to stop now. He's amassed a string of critically-acclaimed runs and collaborations, which include (but are not limited to) **Wildcats**, **Automatic Kafka**, **The Intimates**, **Mr. Majestic**, **Adventures of Superman**, **GØDLAND**, **Codeflesh**, and **Nixon's Pals**. Upcoming neo-classics include **Butcher Baker: The Righteous Maker**, **Doc Bizarre** and an expanded version of **Officer Downe**. Along with his Man of Action co-conspirators, he's also responsible for corrupting the minds of unsuspecting youth with the popular animated series' **Ben 10** and **Generator Rex**, currently airing on the Cartoon Network. Not to mention, he's a supervising producer/story editor on the upcoming **Ultimate Spider-Man** animated series premiering next year on Disney XD. He's written columns for CBR, plays rock 'n roll, and knows what he's talking about.*

Despite this laundry list of accomplishments, he remains incredibly modest... so much so that he got Brandon Thomas to write this bio...

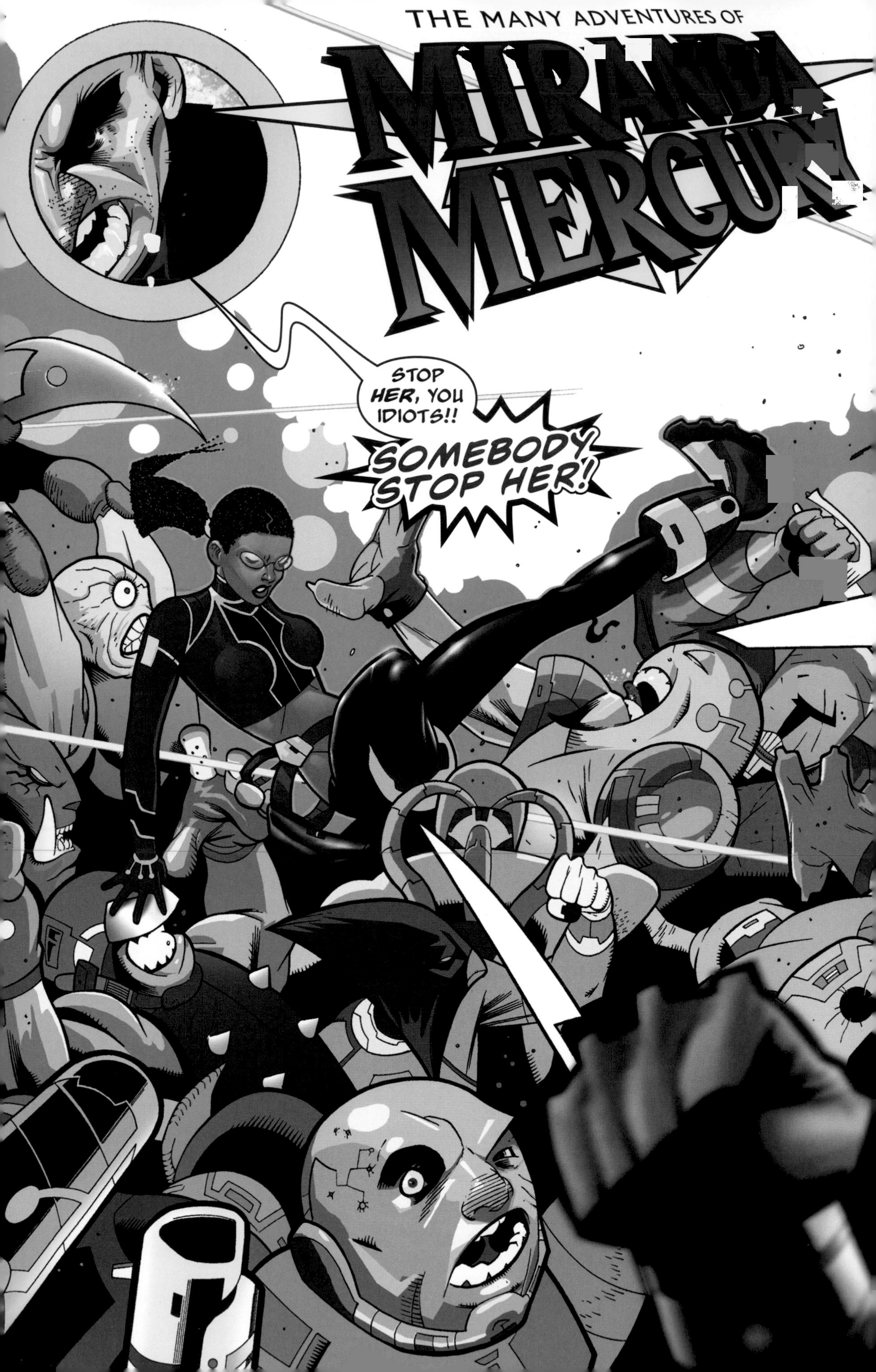
THE MANY ADVENTURES OF
MIRANDA MERCURY
STOP HER, YOU IDIOTS!!
SOMEBODY STOP HER!

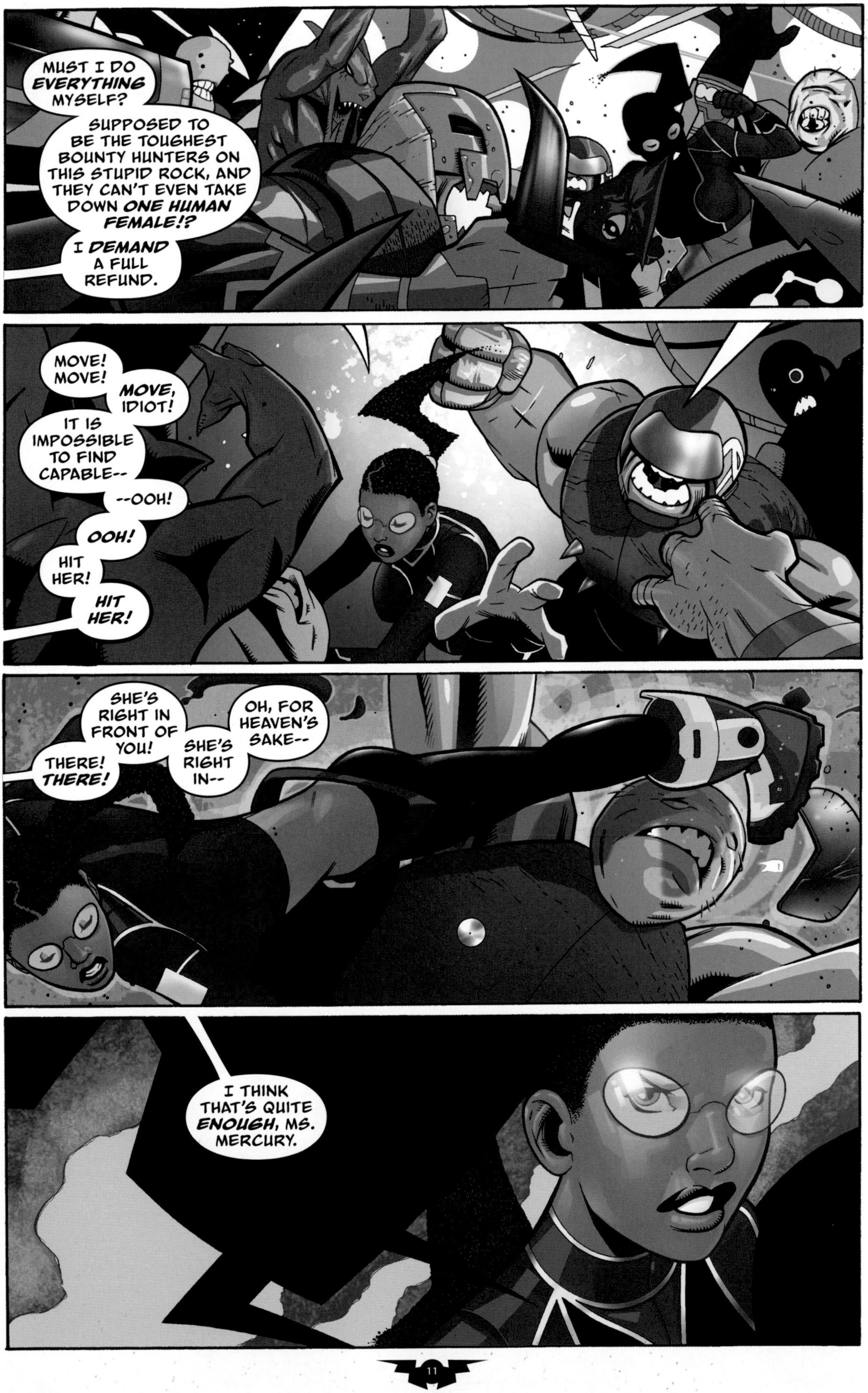
MUST I DO EVERYTHING MYSELF?
SUPPOSED TO BE THE TOUGHEST BOUNTY HUNTERS ON THIS STUPID ROCK, AND THEY CAN'T EVEN TAKE DOWN ONE HUMAN FEMALE!?
I DEMAND A FULL REFUND.
MOVE! MOVE!
MOVE, IDIOT!
IT IS IMPOSSIBLE TO FIND CAPABLE--
--OOH!
OOH!
HIT HER!
HIT HER!
SHE'S RIGHT IN FRONT OF YOU!
THERE! THERE!
SHE'S RIGHT IN--
OH, FOR HEAVEN'S SAKE--
I THINK THAT'S QUITE ENOUGH, MS. MERCURY.

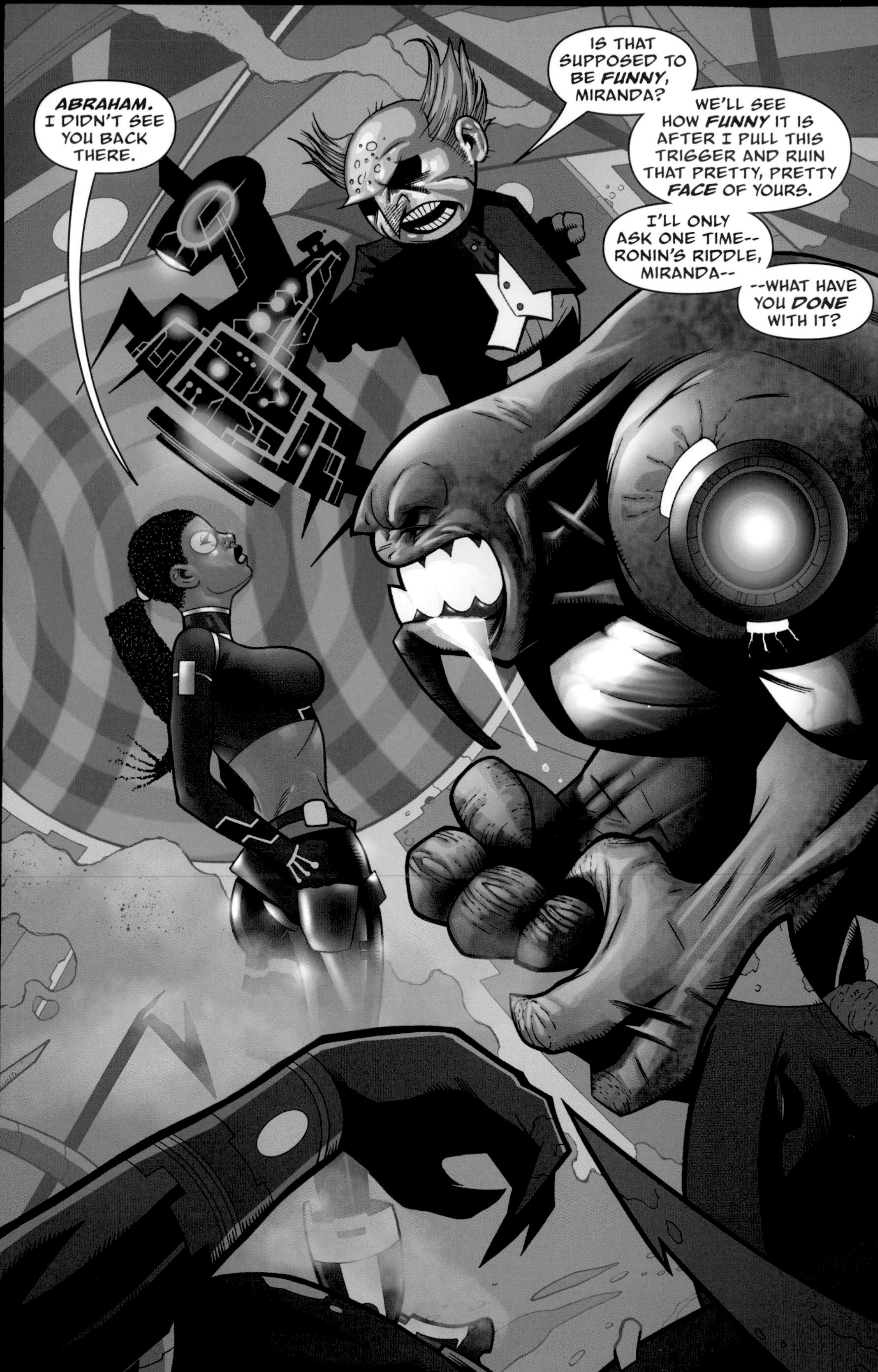
ABRAHAM. I DIDN'T SEE YOU BACK THERE.
IS THAT SUPPOSED TO BE FUNNY, MIRANDA?
WE'LL SEE HOW FUNNY IT IS AFTER I PULL THIS TRIGGER AND RUIN THAT PRETTY, PRETTY FACE OF YOURS.
I'LL ONLY ASK ONE TIME-- RONIN'S RIDDLE, MIRANDA--
--WHAT HAVE YOU DONE WITH IT?

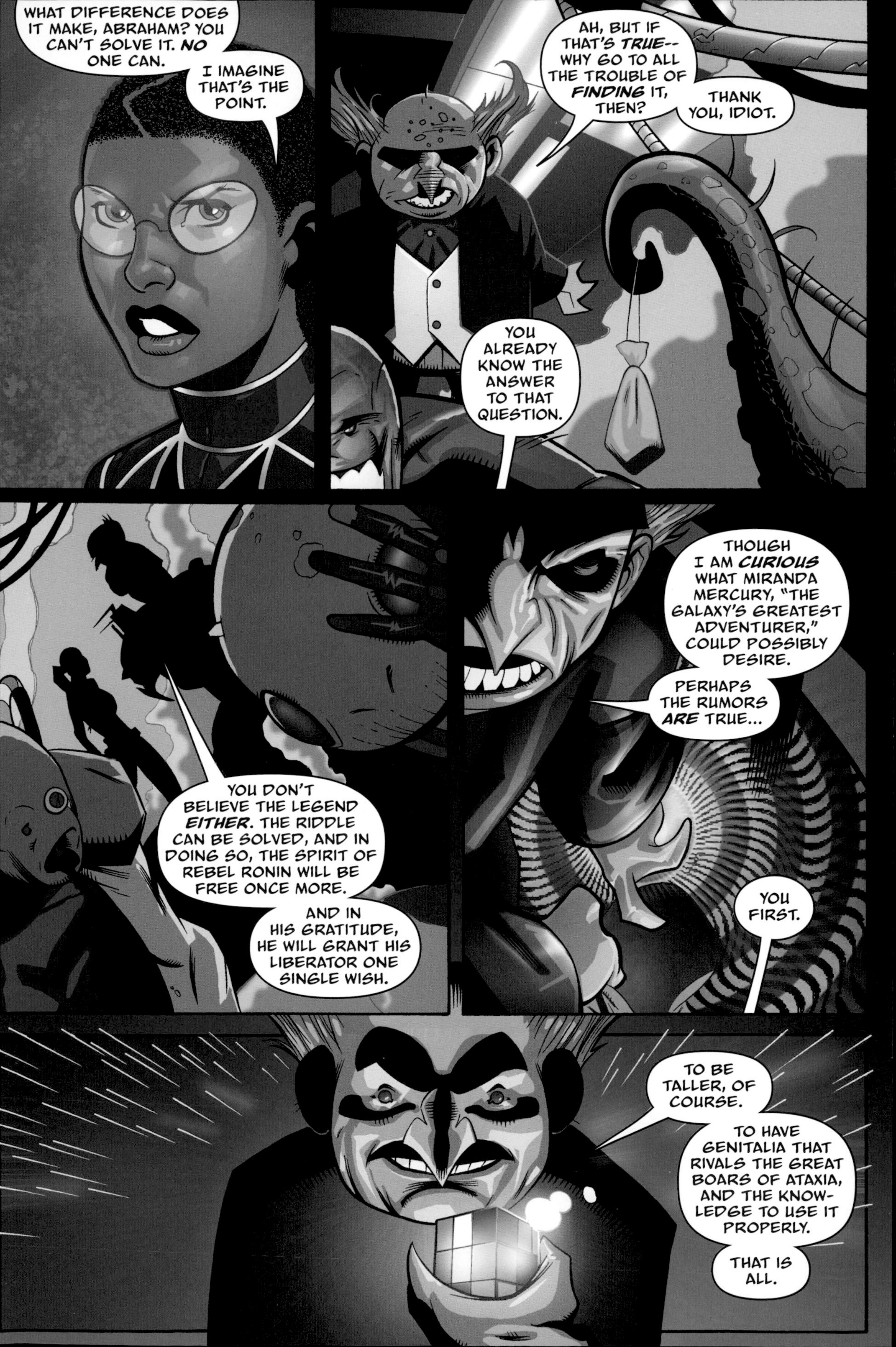
WHAT DIFFERENCE DOES IT MAKE, ABRAHAM? YOU CAN'T SOLVE IT. NO ONE CAN.
I IMAGINE THAT'S THE POINT.
AH, BUT IF THAT'S TRUE-- WHY GO TO ALL THE TROUBLE OF FINDING IT, THEN?
THANK YOU, IDIOT.
YOU ALREADY KNOW THE ANSWER TO THAT QUESTION.
YOU DON'T BELIEVE THE LEGEND EITHER. THE RIDDLE CAN BE SOLVED, AND IN DOING SO, THE SPIRIT OF REBEL RONIN WILL BE FREE ONCE MORE.
AND IN HIS GRATITUDE, HE WILL GRANT HIS LIBERATOR ONE SINGLE WISH.
THOUGH I AM CURIOUS WHAT MIRANDA MERCURY, "THE GALAXY'S GREATEST ADVENTURER," COULD POSSIBLY DESIRE.
PERHAPS THE RUMORS ARE TRUE...
YOU FIRST.
TO BE TALLER, OF COURSE.
TO HAVE GENITALIA THAT RIVALS THE GREAT BOARS OF ATAXIA, AND THE KNOW-LEDGE TO USE IT PROPERLY.
THAT IS ALL.

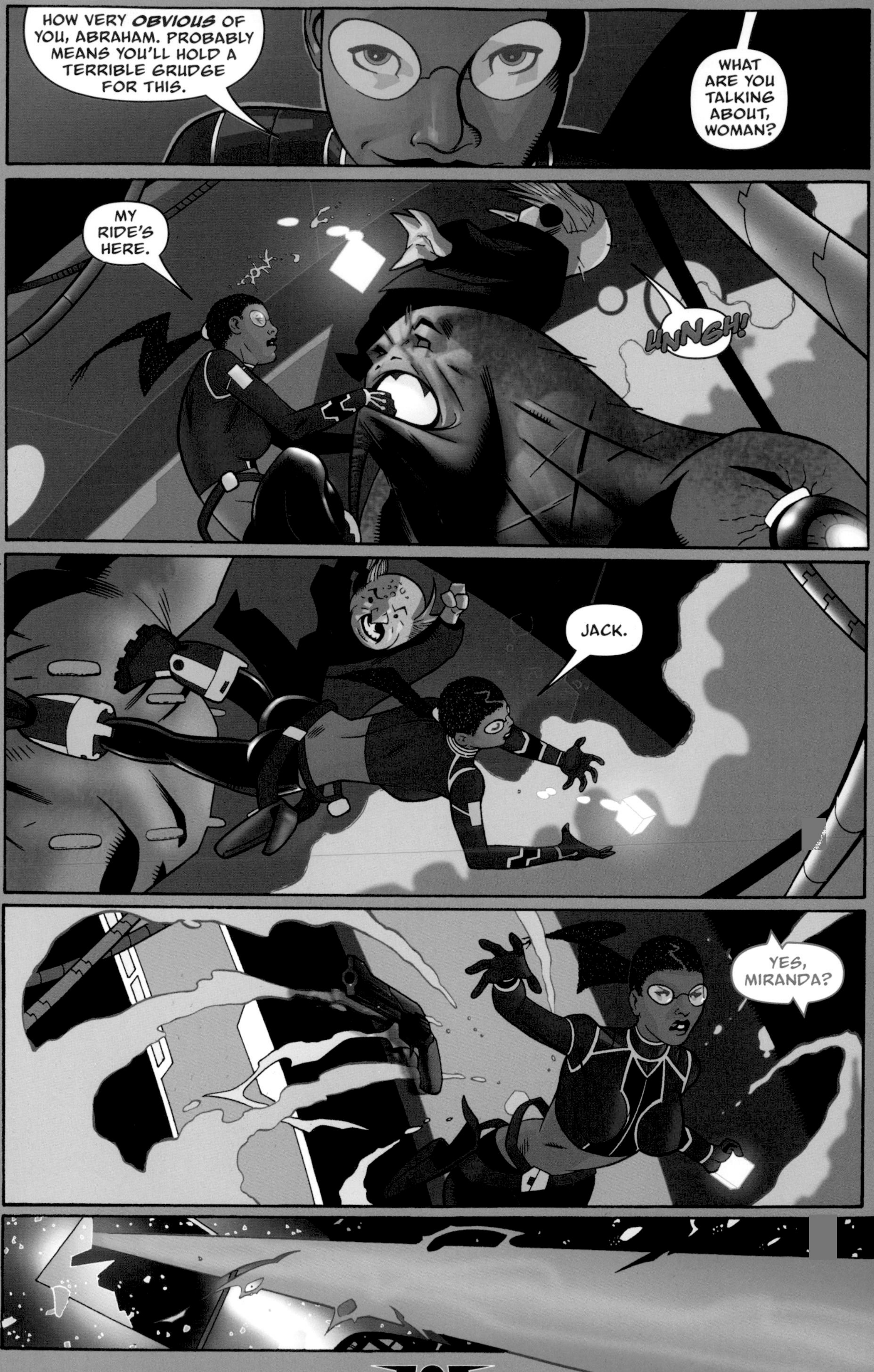
HOW VERY OBVIOUS OF YOU, ABRAHAM. PROBABLY MEANS YOU'LL HOLD A TERRIBLE GRUDGE FOR THIS.
WHAT ARE YOU TALKING ABOUT, WOMAN?
MY RIDE'S HERE.
UNNGH!
JACK.
YES, MIRANDA?

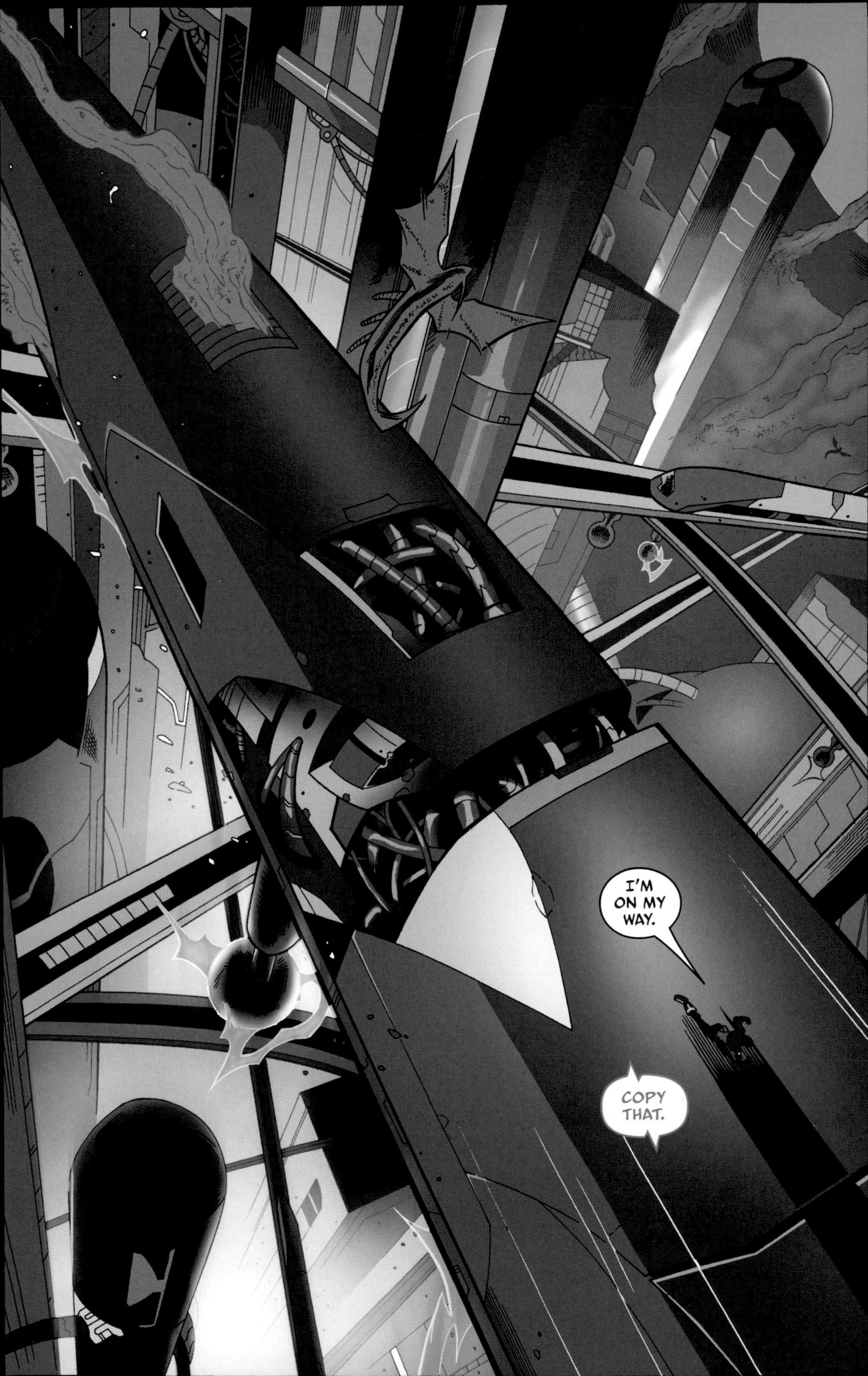
I'M ON MY WAY.
COPY THAT.

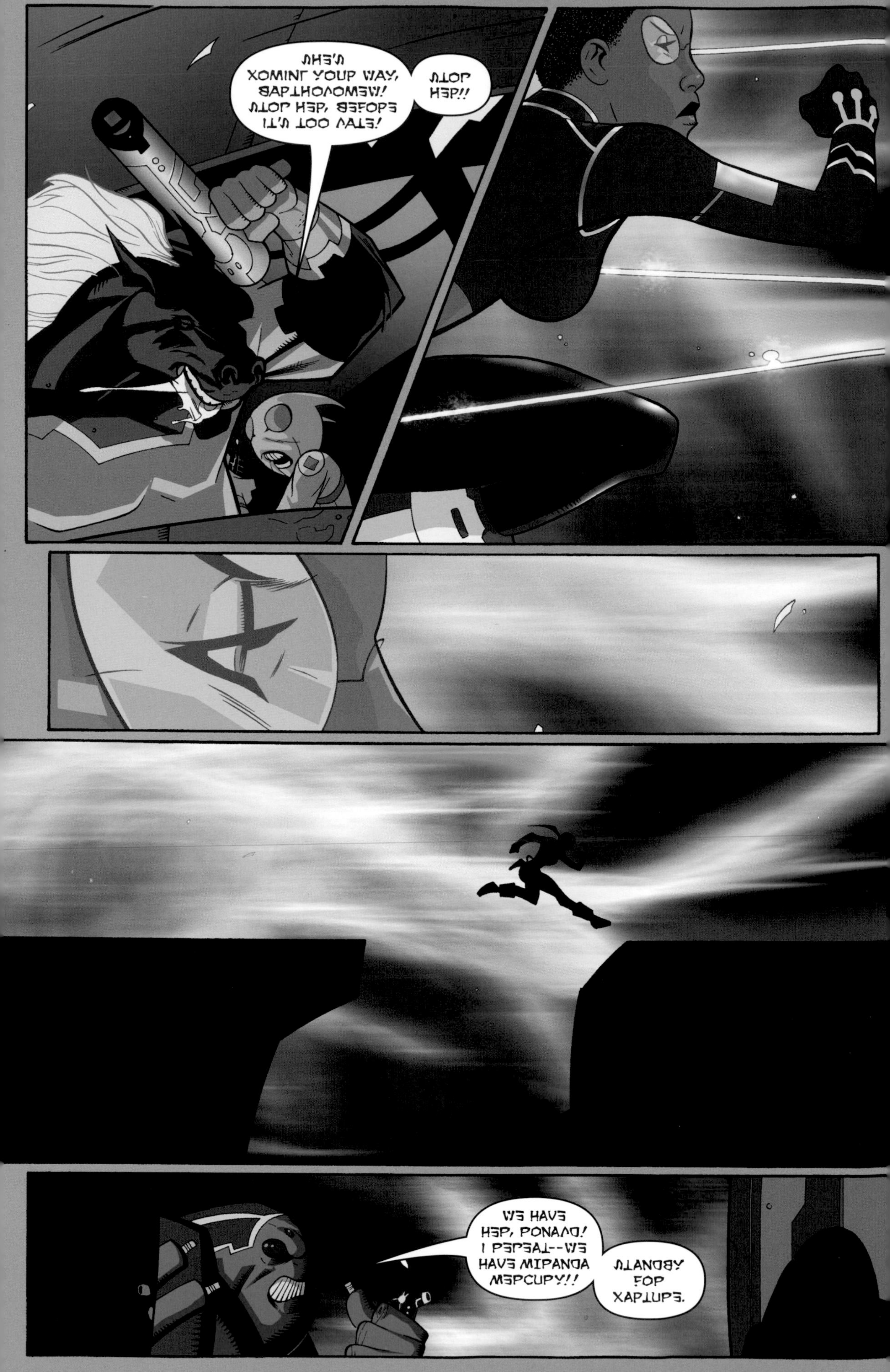
SHE'S COMING YOUR WAY, BARTHOLOMEW! STOP HER, BEFORE IT'S TOO LATE!
STOP HER!!
WE HAVE HER, RONALD! I REPEAT--WE HAVE MIRANDA MERCURY!!
STANDBY FOR CAPTURE.

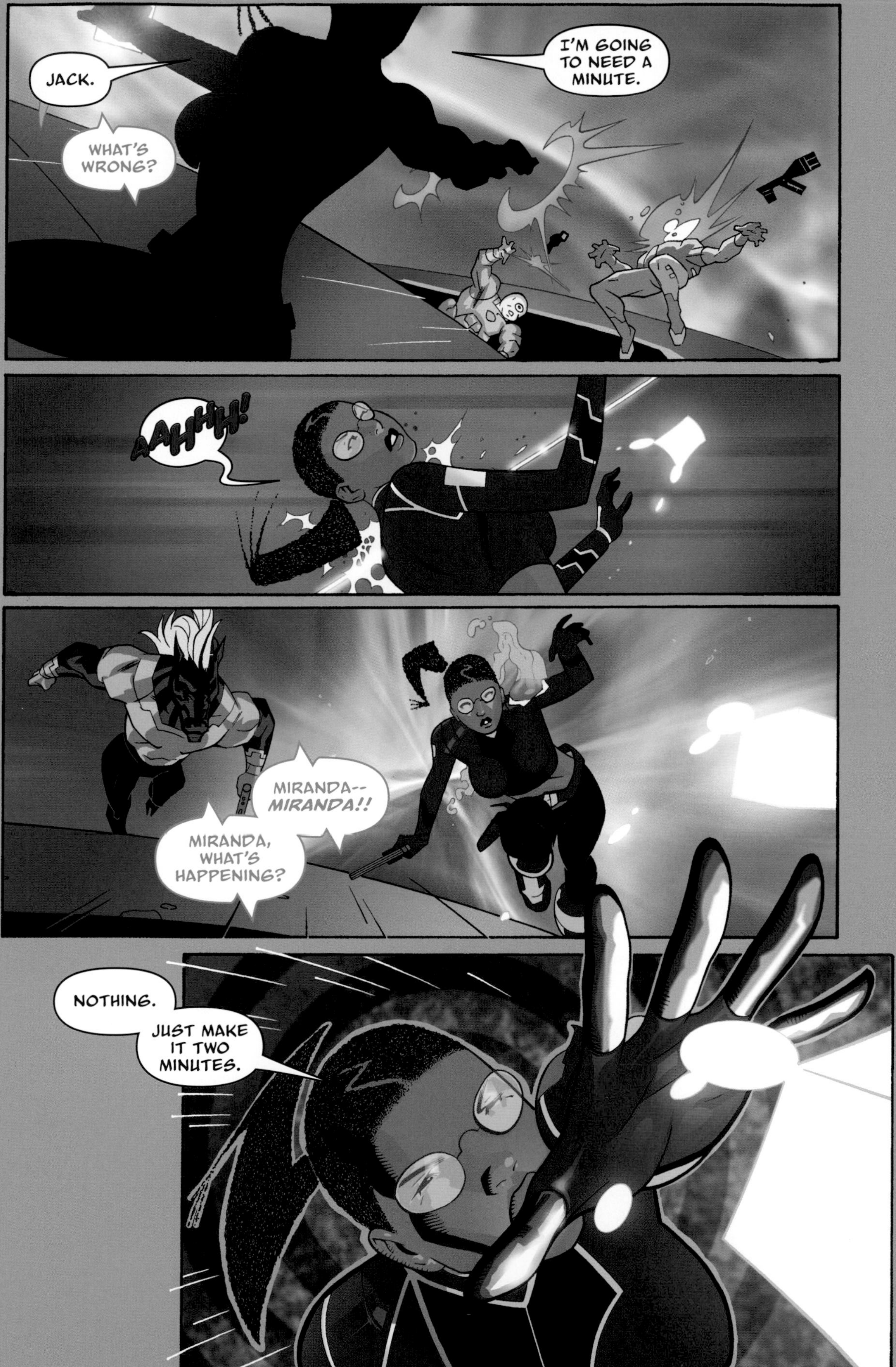
JACK.
I'M GOING TO NEED A MINUTE.
WHAT'S WRONG?
AAHHH!
MIRANDA-- MIRANDA!!
MIRANDA, WHAT'S HAPPENING?
NOTHING.
JUST MAKE IT TWO MINUTES.

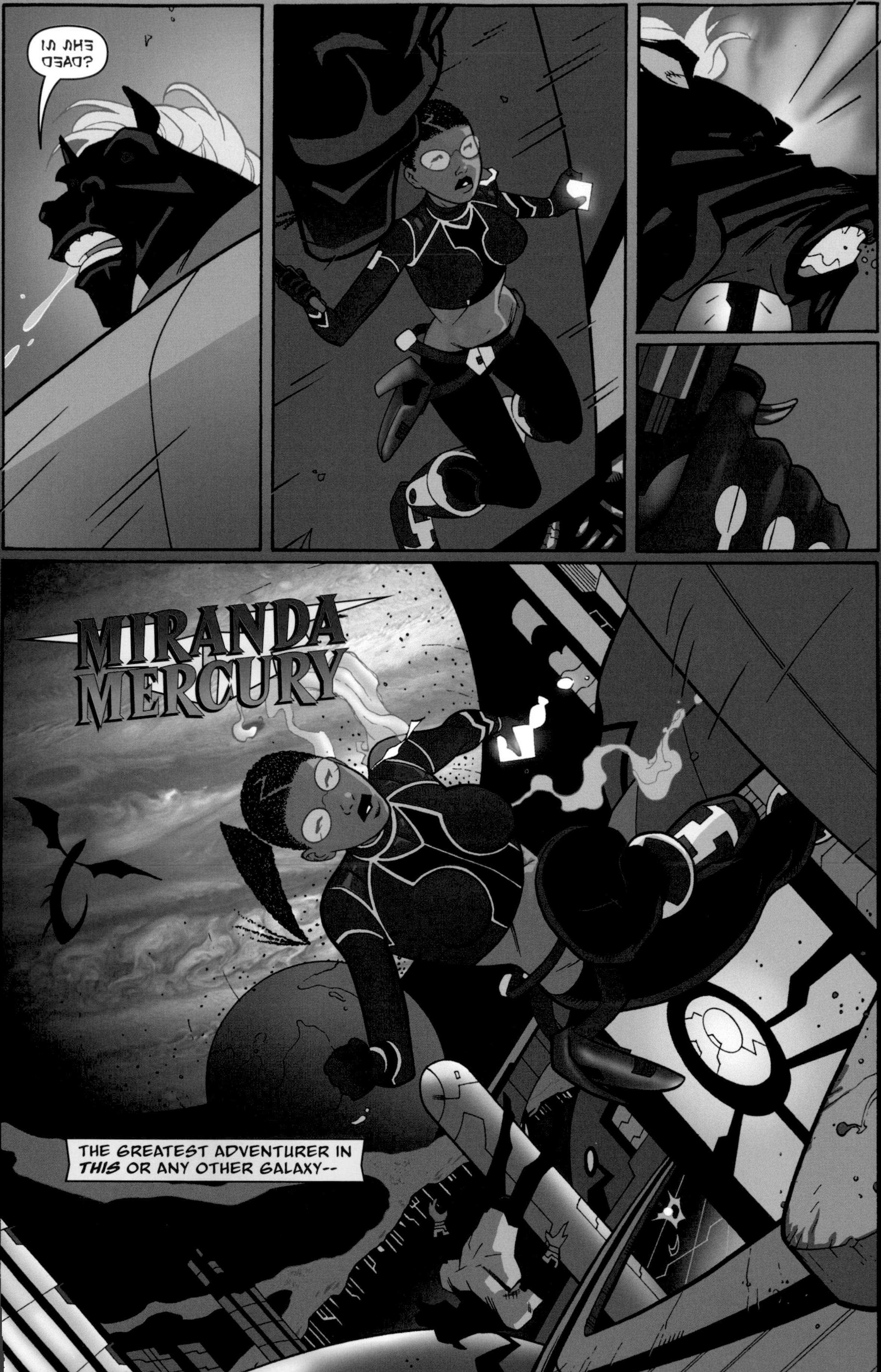

MIRANDA MERCURY
THE GREATEST ADVENTURER IN *THIS* OR ANY OTHER GALAXY--

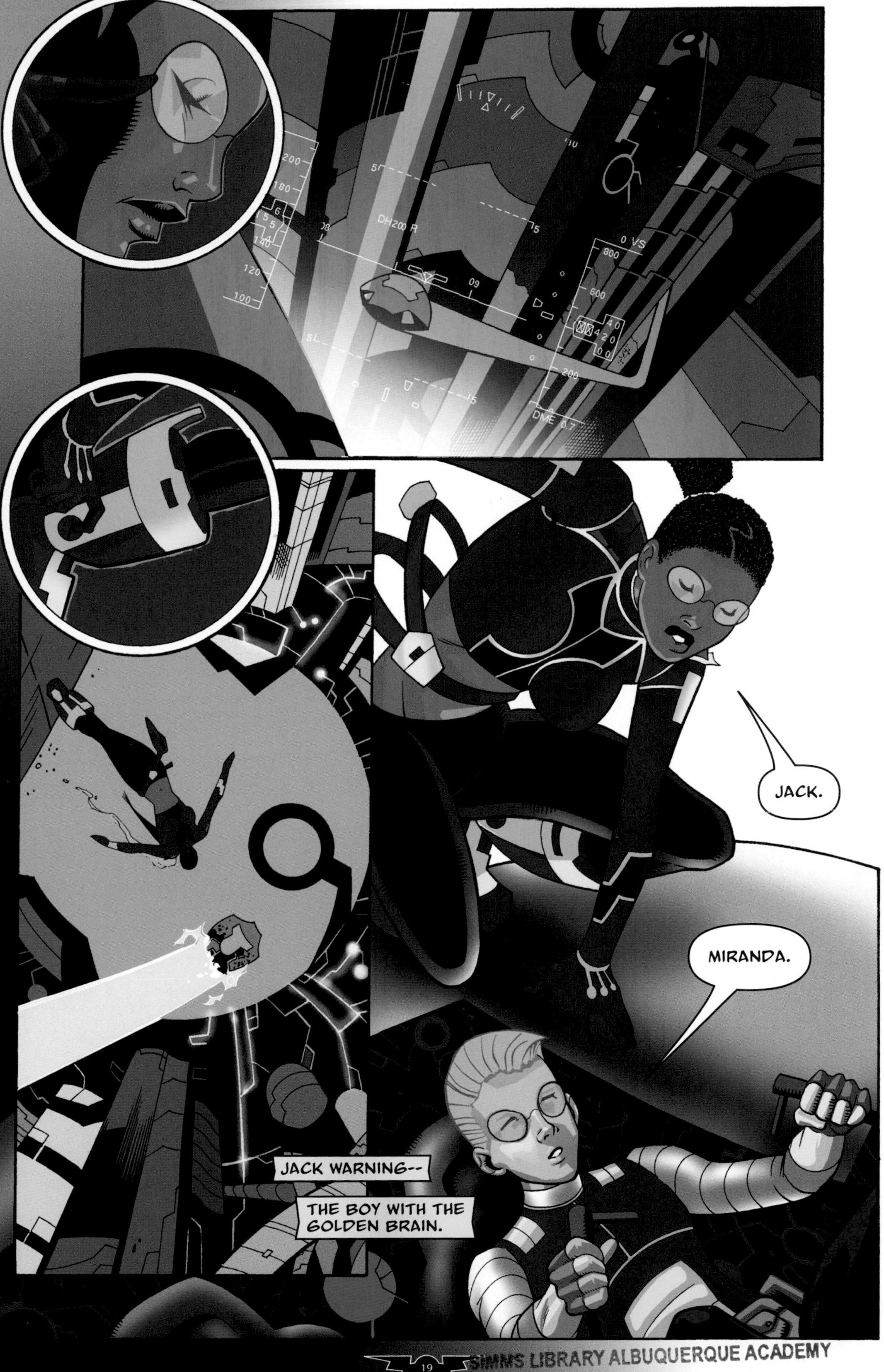
JACK.
MIRANDA.
JACK WARNING--
THE BOY WITH THE GOLDEN BRAIN.

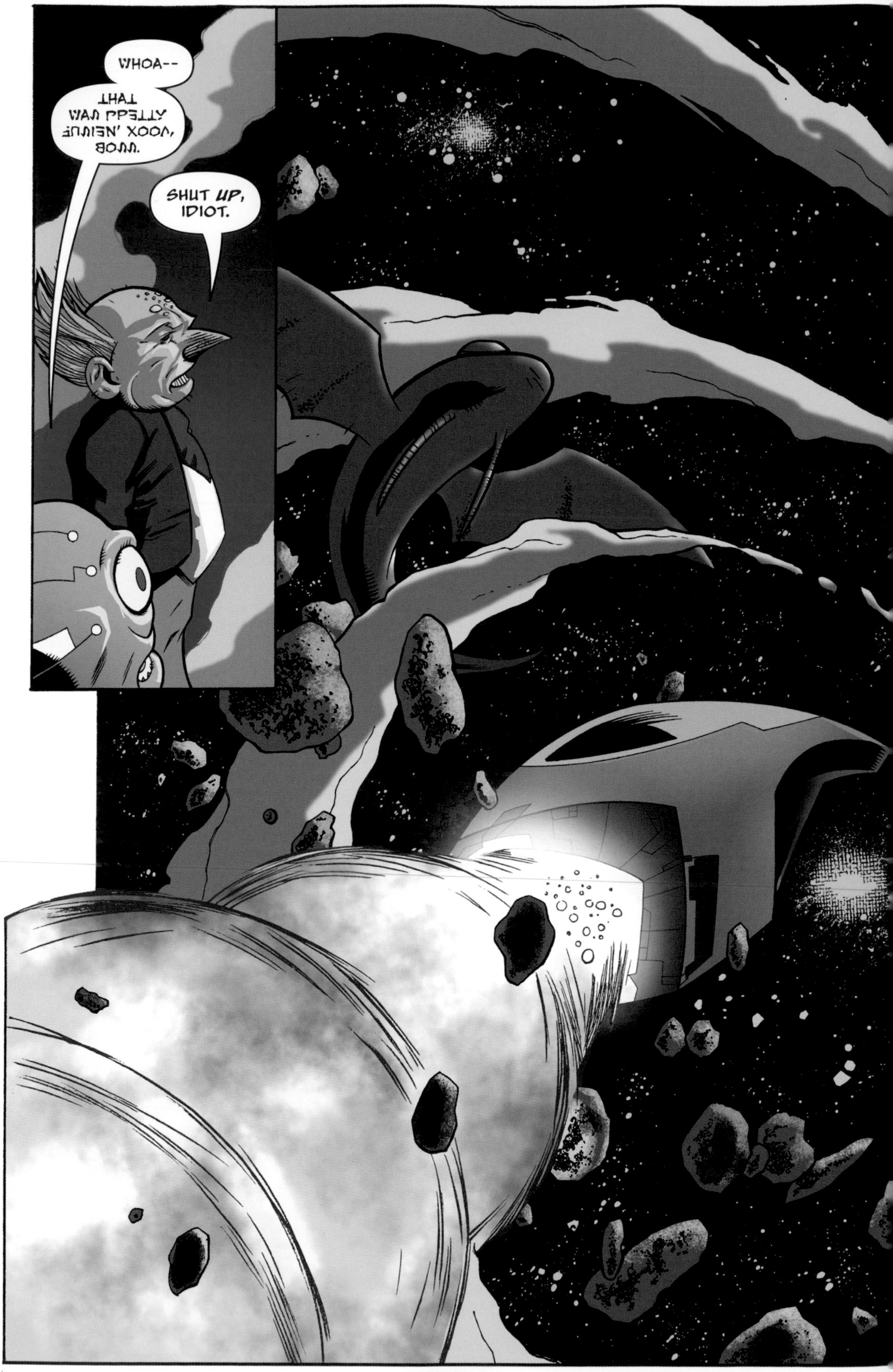
WHOA--
THAT WAS PRETTY
BOSS.
SHUT UP, IDIOT.

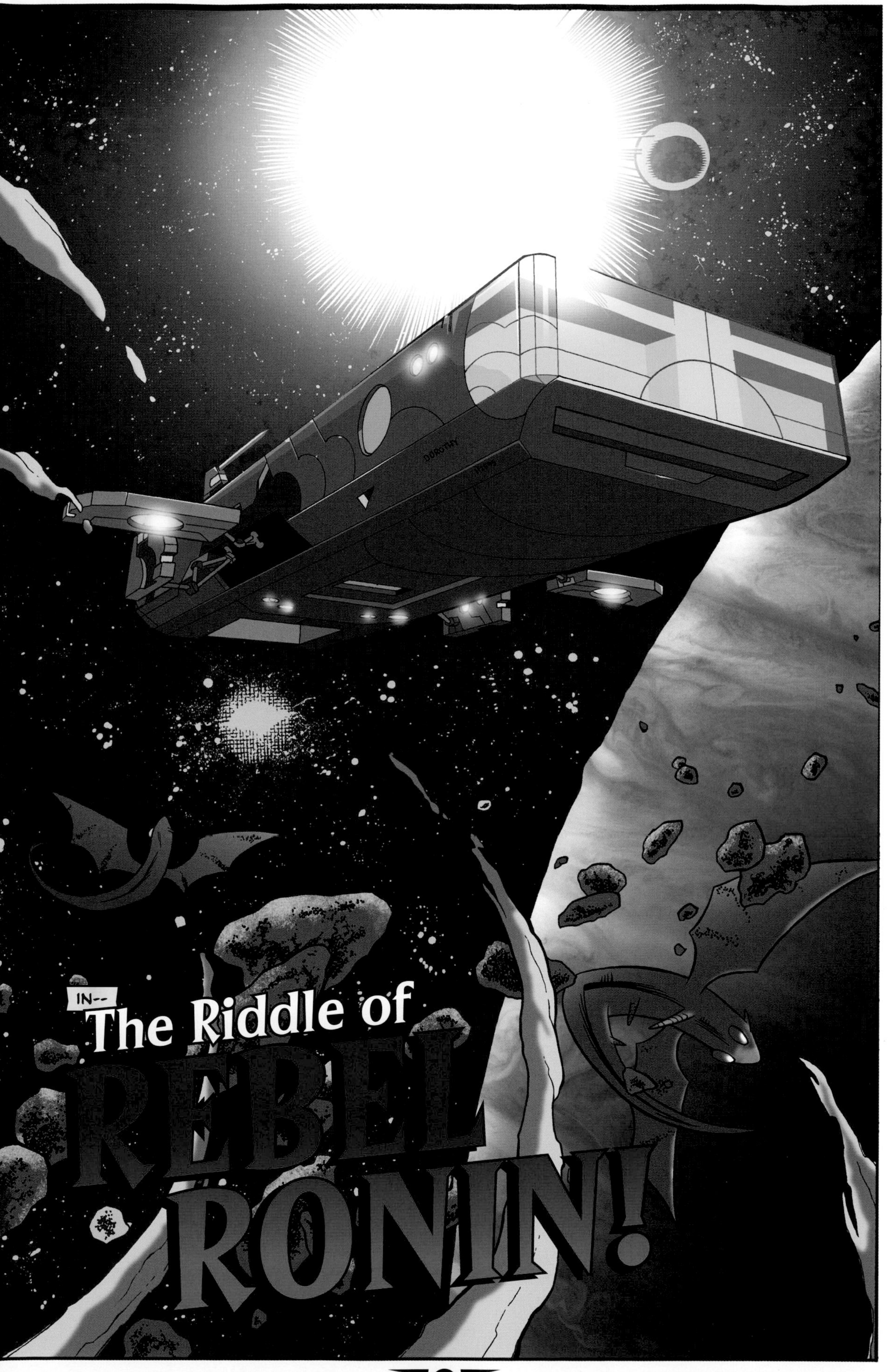
IN--
The Riddle of
REBEL
RONIN!

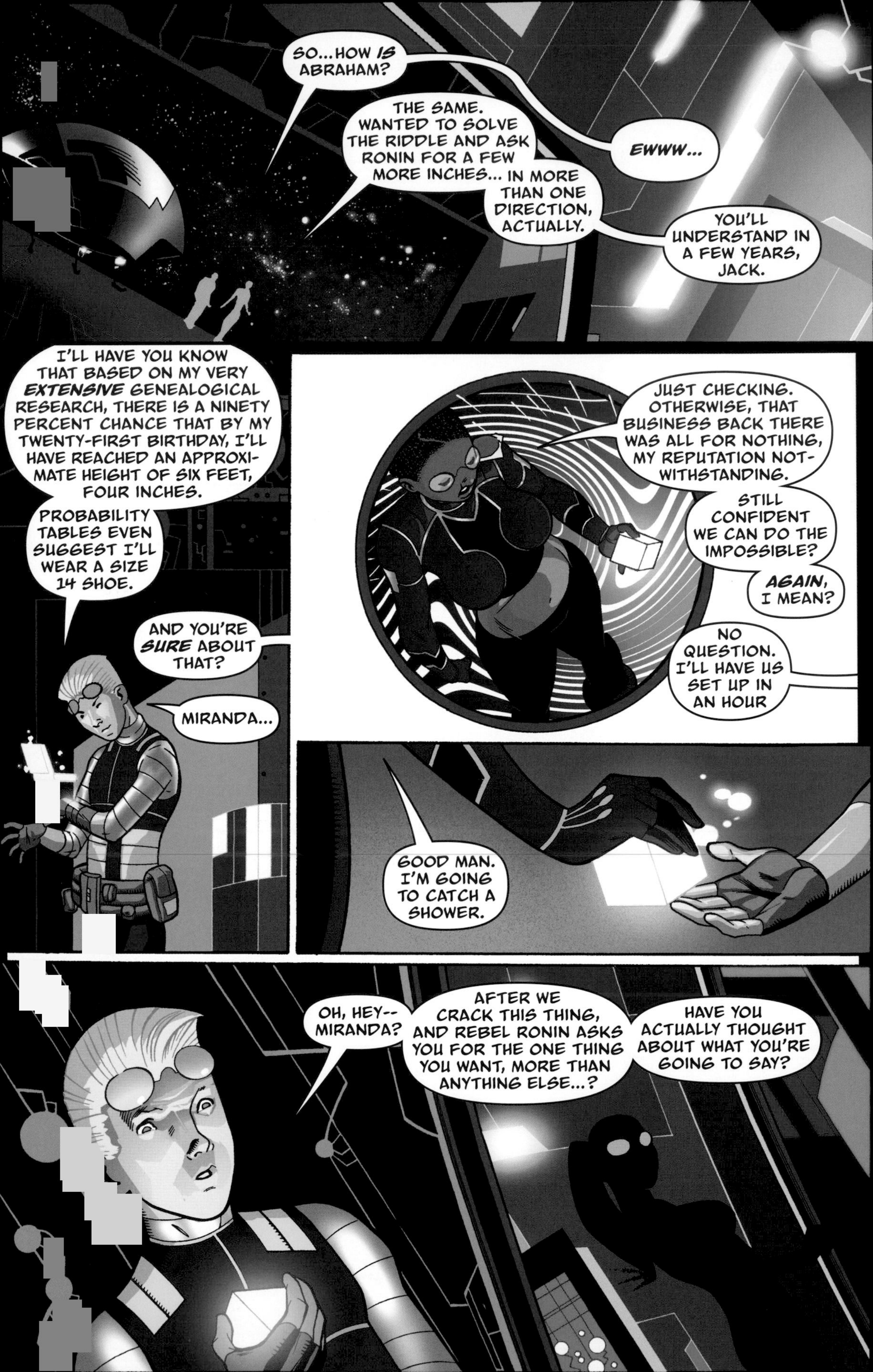
SO... HOW IS ABRAHAM?
THE SAME. WANTED TO SOLVE THE RIDDLE AND ASK RONIN FOR A FEW MORE INCHES... IN MORE THAN ONE DIRECTION, ACTUALLY.
EWWW...
YOU'LL UNDERSTAND IN A FEW YEARS, JACK.
I'LL HAVE YOU KNOW THAT BASED ON MY VERY EXTENSIVE GENEALOGICAL RESEARCH, THERE IS A NINETY PERCENT CHANCE THAT BY MY TWENTY-FIRST BIRTHDAY, I'LL HAVE REACHED AN APPROXIMATE HEIGHT OF SIX FEET, FOUR INCHES.
PROBABILITY TABLES EVEN SUGGEST I'LL WEAR A SIZE 14 SHOE.
AND YOU'RE SURE ABOUT THAT?
MIRANDA...
JUST CHECKING. OTHERWISE, THAT BUSINESS BACK THERE WAS ALL FOR NOTHING, MY REPUTATION NOT-WITHSTANDING.
STILL CONFIDENT WE CAN DO THE IMPOSSIBLE?
AGAIN, I MEAN?
NO QUESTION. I'LL HAVE US SET UP IN AN HOUR
GOOD MAN. I'M GOING TO CATCH A SHOWER.
OH, HEY-- MIRANDA?
AFTER WE CRACK THIS THING, AND REBEL RONIN ASKS YOU FOR THE ONE THING YOU WANT, MORE THAN ANYTHING ELSE...?
HAVE YOU ACTUALLY THOUGHT ABOUT WHAT YOU'RE GOING TO SAY?

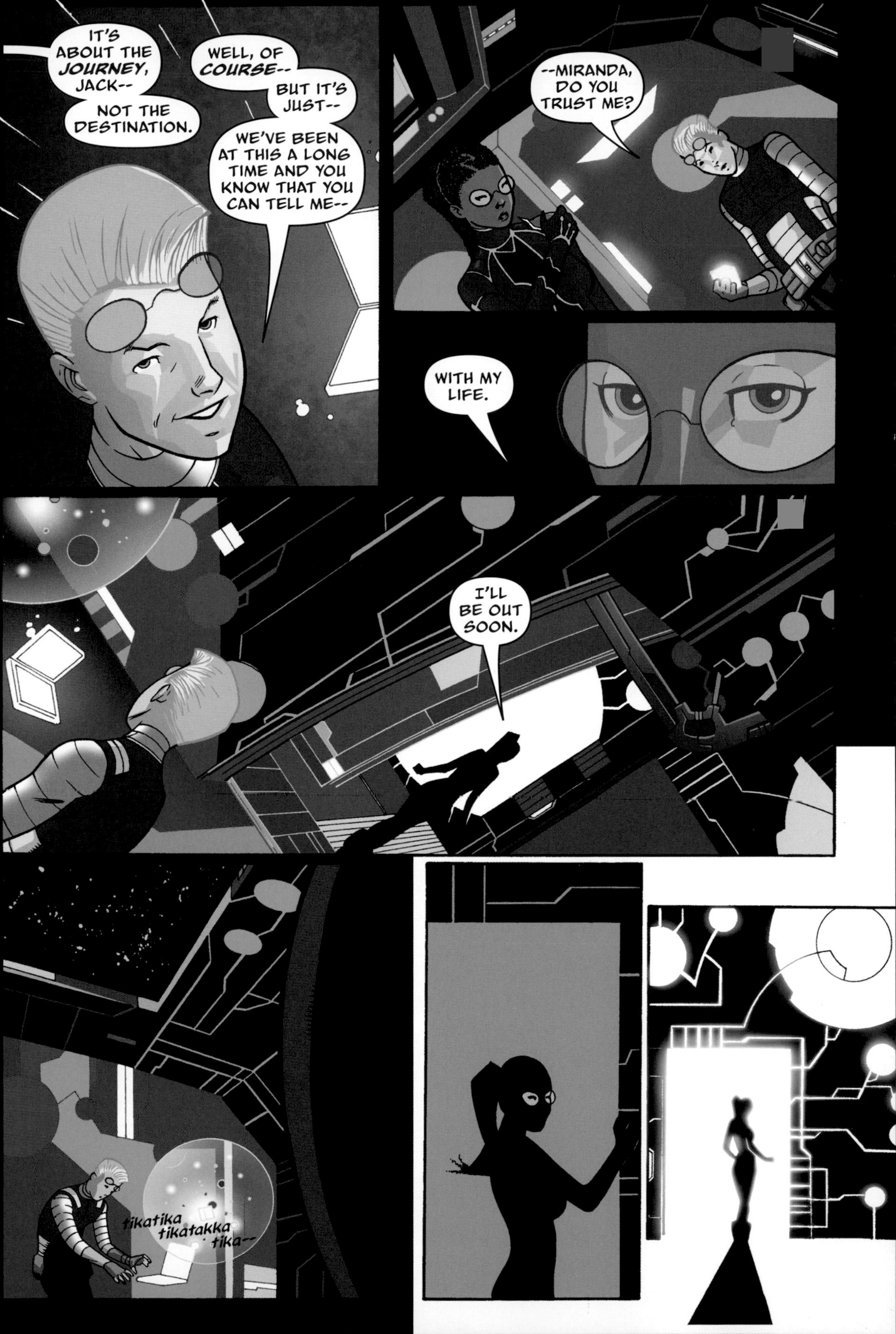
IT'S ABOUT THE *JOURNEY*, JACK--
NOT THE DESTINATION.
WELL, OF *COURSE*--
BUT IT'S JUST--
WE'VE BEEN AT THIS A LONG TIME AND YOU KNOW THAT YOU CAN TELL ME--
--MIRANDA, DO YOU TRUST ME?
WITH MY LIFE.
I'LL BE OUT SOON.
tikatika tikatakka tika--

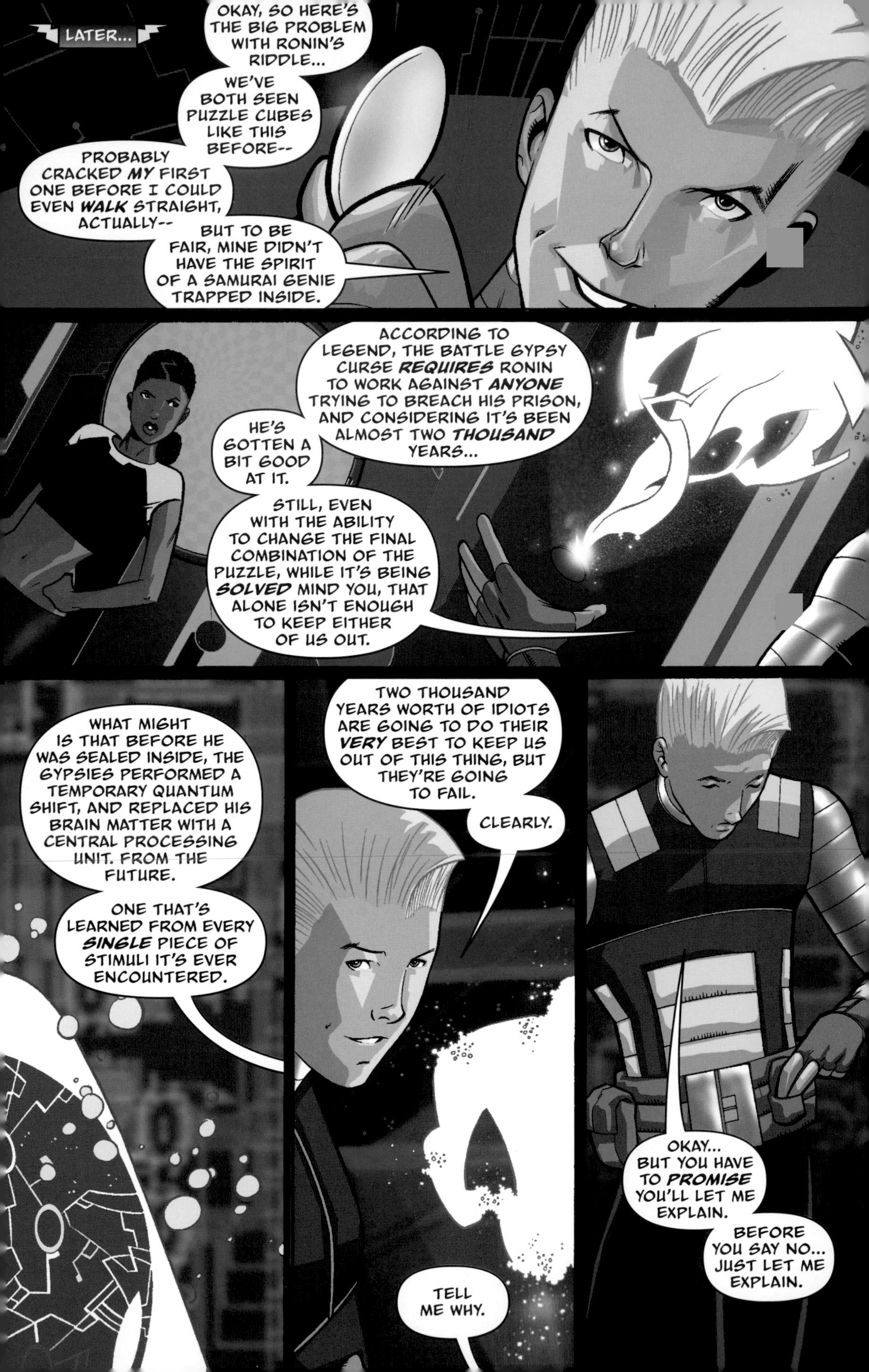
LATER...
OKAY, SO HERE'S THE BIG PROBLEM WITH RONIN'S RIDDLE...
WE'VE BOTH SEEN PUZZLE CUBES LIKE THIS BEFORE--
PROBABLY CRACKED MY FIRST ONE BEFORE I COULD EVEN WALK STRAIGHT, ACTUALLY--
BUT TO BE FAIR, MINE DIDN'T HAVE THE SPIRIT OF A SAMURAI GENIE TRAPPED INSIDE.
ACCORDING TO LEGEND, THE BATTLE GYPSY CURSE REQUIRES RONIN TO WORK AGAINST ANYONE TRYING TO BREACH HIS PRISON, AND CONSIDERING IT'S BEEN ALMOST TWO THOUSAND YEARS...
HE'S GOTTEN A BIT GOOD AT IT.
STILL, EVEN WITH THE ABILITY TO CHANGE THE FINAL COMBINATION OF THE PUZZLE, WHILE IT'S BEING SOLVED MIND YOU, THAT ALONE ISN'T ENOUGH TO KEEP EITHER OF US OUT.
WHAT MIGHT IS THAT BEFORE HE WAS SEALED INSIDE, THE GYPSIES PERFORMED A TEMPORARY QUANTUM SHIFT, AND REPLACED HIS BRAIN MATTER WITH A CENTRAL PROCESSING UNIT. FROM THE FUTURE.
ONE THAT'S LEARNED FROM EVERY SINGLE PIECE OF STIMULI IT'S EVER ENCOUNTERED.
TWO THOUSAND YEARS WORTH OF IDIOTS ARE GOING TO DO THEIR VERY BEST TO KEEP US OUT OF THIS THING, BUT THEY'RE GOING TO FAIL.
CLEARLY.
TELL ME WHY.
OKAY... BUT YOU HAVE TO PROMISE YOU'LL LET ME EXPLAIN.
BEFORE YOU SAY NO... JUST LET ME EXPLAIN.

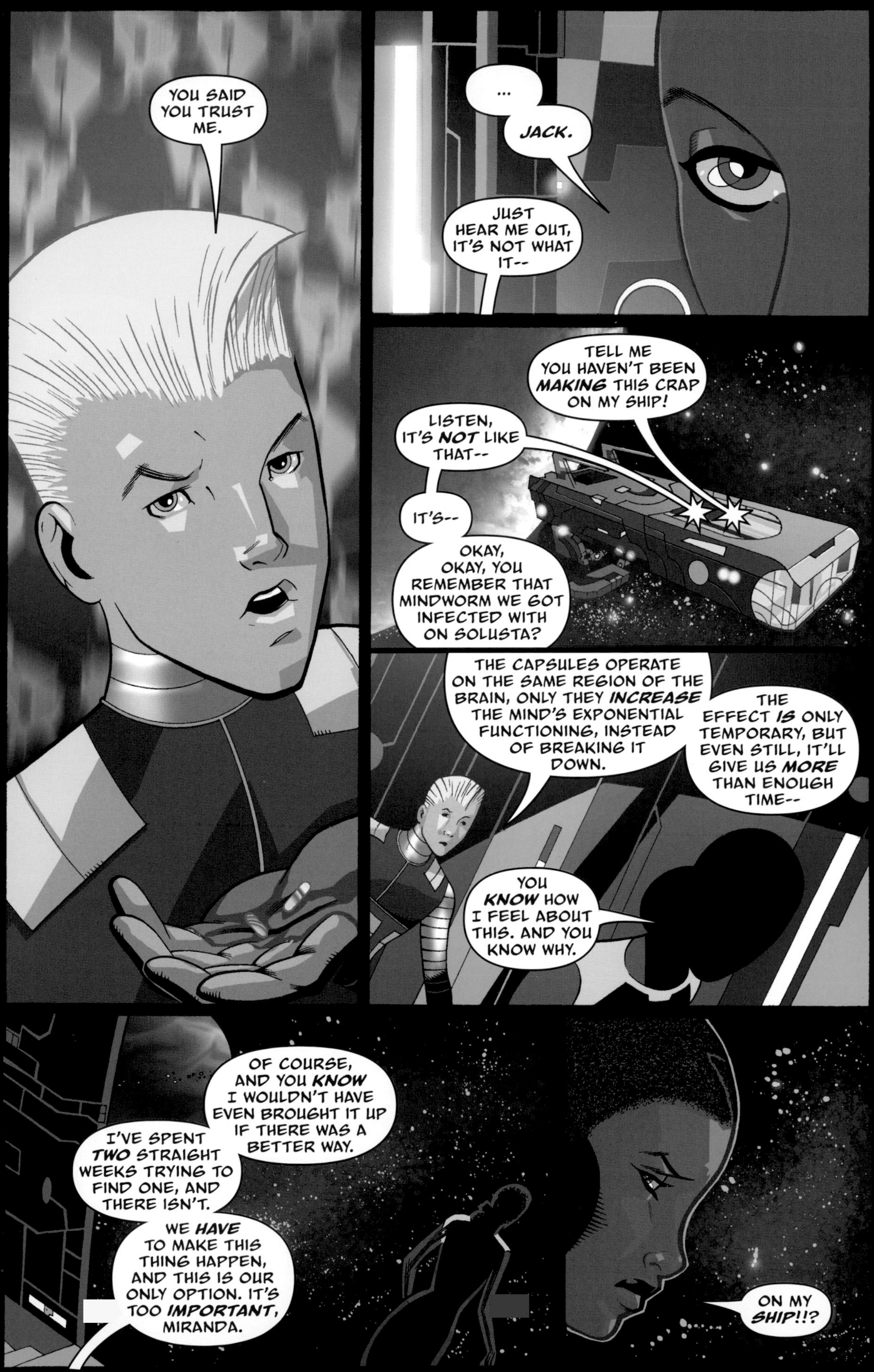
YOU SAID YOU TRUST ME.
...
JACK.
JUST HEAR ME OUT, IT'S NOT WHAT IT--
TELL ME YOU HAVEN'T BEEN MAKING THIS CRAP ON MY SHIP!
LISTEN, IT'S NOT LIKE THAT--
IT'S--
OKAY, OKAY, YOU REMEMBER THAT MINDWORM WE GOT INFECTED WITH ON SOLUSTA?
THE CAPSULES OPERATE ON THE SAME REGION OF THE BRAIN, ONLY THEY INCREASE THE MIND'S EXPONENTIAL FUNCTIONING, INSTEAD OF BREAKING IT DOWN.
THE EFFECT IS ONLY TEMPORARY, BUT EVEN STILL, IT'LL GIVE US MORE THAN ENOUGH TIME--
YOU KNOW HOW I FEEL ABOUT THIS. AND YOU KNOW WHY.
OF COURSE, AND YOU KNOW I WOULDN'T HAVE EVEN BROUGHT IT UP IF THERE WAS A BETTER WAY.
I'VE SPENT TWO STRAIGHT WEEKS TRYING TO FIND ONE, AND THERE ISN'T.
WE HAVE TO MAKE THIS THING HAPPEN, AND THIS IS OUR ONLY OPTION. IT'S TOO IMPORTANT, MIRANDA.
ON MY SHIP!!?

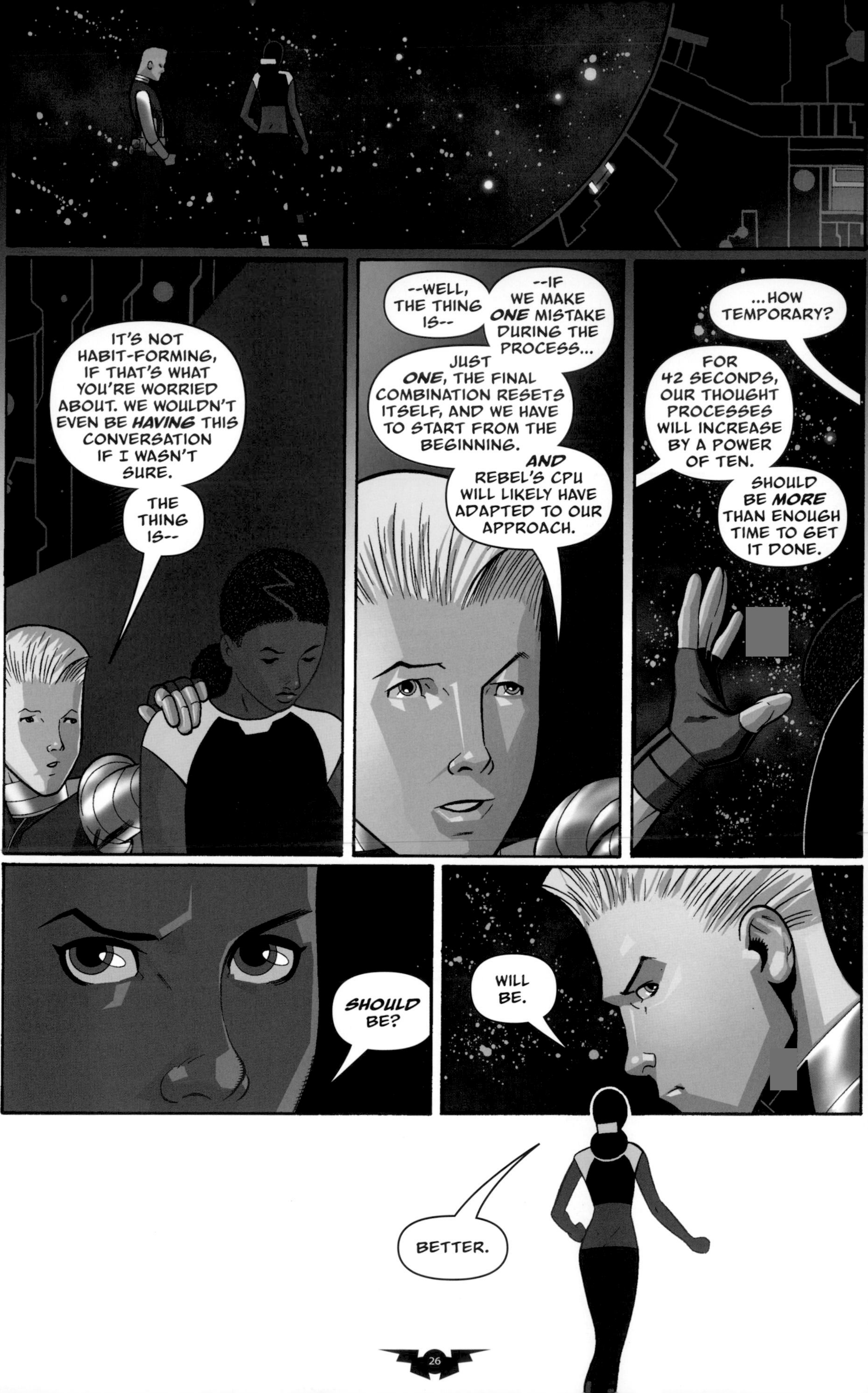
IT'S NOT HABIT-FORMING, IF THAT'S WHAT YOU'RE WORRIED ABOUT. WE WOULDN'T EVEN BE HAVING THIS CONVERSATION IF I WASN'T SURE.
THE THING IS--
--WELL, THE THING IS--
--IF WE MAKE ONE MISTAKE DURING THE PROCESS...
JUST ONE, THE FINAL COMBINATION RESETS ITSELF, AND WE HAVE TO START FROM THE BEGINNING.
AND REBEL'S CPU WILL LIKELY HAVE ADAPTED TO OUR APPROACH.
...HOW TEMPORARY?
FOR 42 SECONDS, OUR THOUGHT PROCESSES WILL INCREASE BY A POWER OF TEN.
SHOULD BE MORE THAN ENOUGH TIME TO GET IT DONE.
SHOULD BE?
WILL BE.
BETTER.

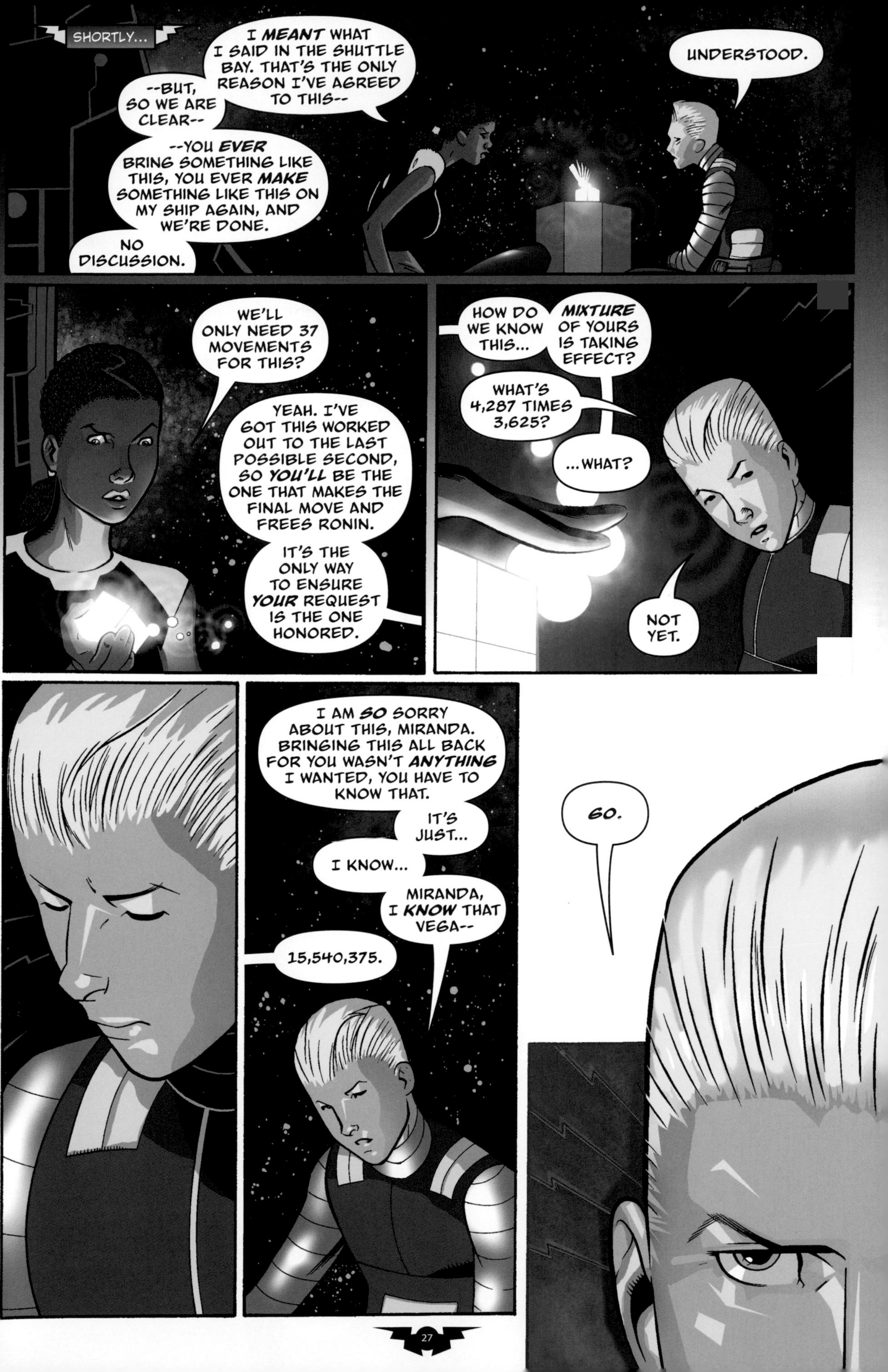
SHORTLY...
I MEANT WHAT I SAID IN THE SHUTTLE BAY. THAT'S THE ONLY REASON I'VE AGREED TO THIS--
--BUT, SO WE ARE CLEAR--
--YOU EVER BRING SOMETHING LIKE THIS, YOU EVER MAKE SOMETHING LIKE THIS ON MY SHIP AGAIN, AND WE'RE DONE.
NO DISCUSSION.
UNDERSTOOD.
WE'LL ONLY NEED 37 MOVEMENTS FOR THIS?
YEAH. I'VE GOT THIS WORKED OUT TO THE LAST POSSIBLE SECOND, SO YOU'LL BE THE ONE THAT MAKES THE FINAL MOVE AND FREES RONIN.
IT'S THE ONLY WAY TO ENSURE YOUR REQUEST IS THE ONE HONORED.
HOW DO WE KNOW THIS...
MIXTURE OF YOURS IS TAKING EFFECT?
WHAT'S 4,287 TIMES 3,625?
...WHAT?
NOT YET.
I AM SO SORRY ABOUT THIS, MIRANDA. BRINGING THIS ALL BACK FOR YOU WASN'T ANYTHING I WANTED, YOU HAVE TO KNOW THAT.
IT'S JUST...
I KNOW...
MIRANDA, I KNOW THAT VEGA--
15,540,375.
GO.

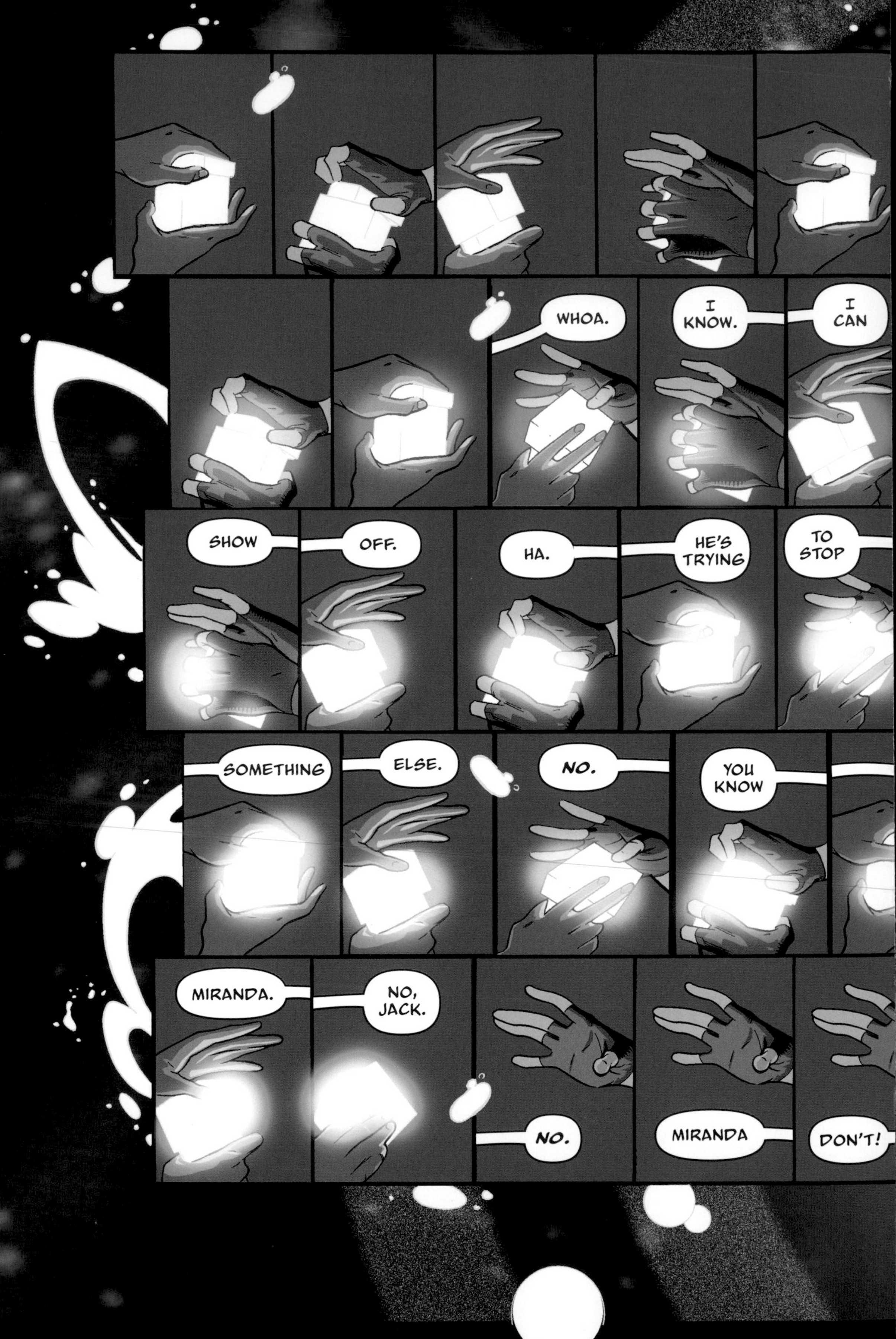
WHOA.
I KNOW.
I CAN
SHOW
OFF.
HA.
HE'S TRYING
TO STOP
SOMETHING
ELSE.
NO.
YOU KNOW
MIRANDA.
NO, JACK.
NO.
MIRANDA
DON'T!

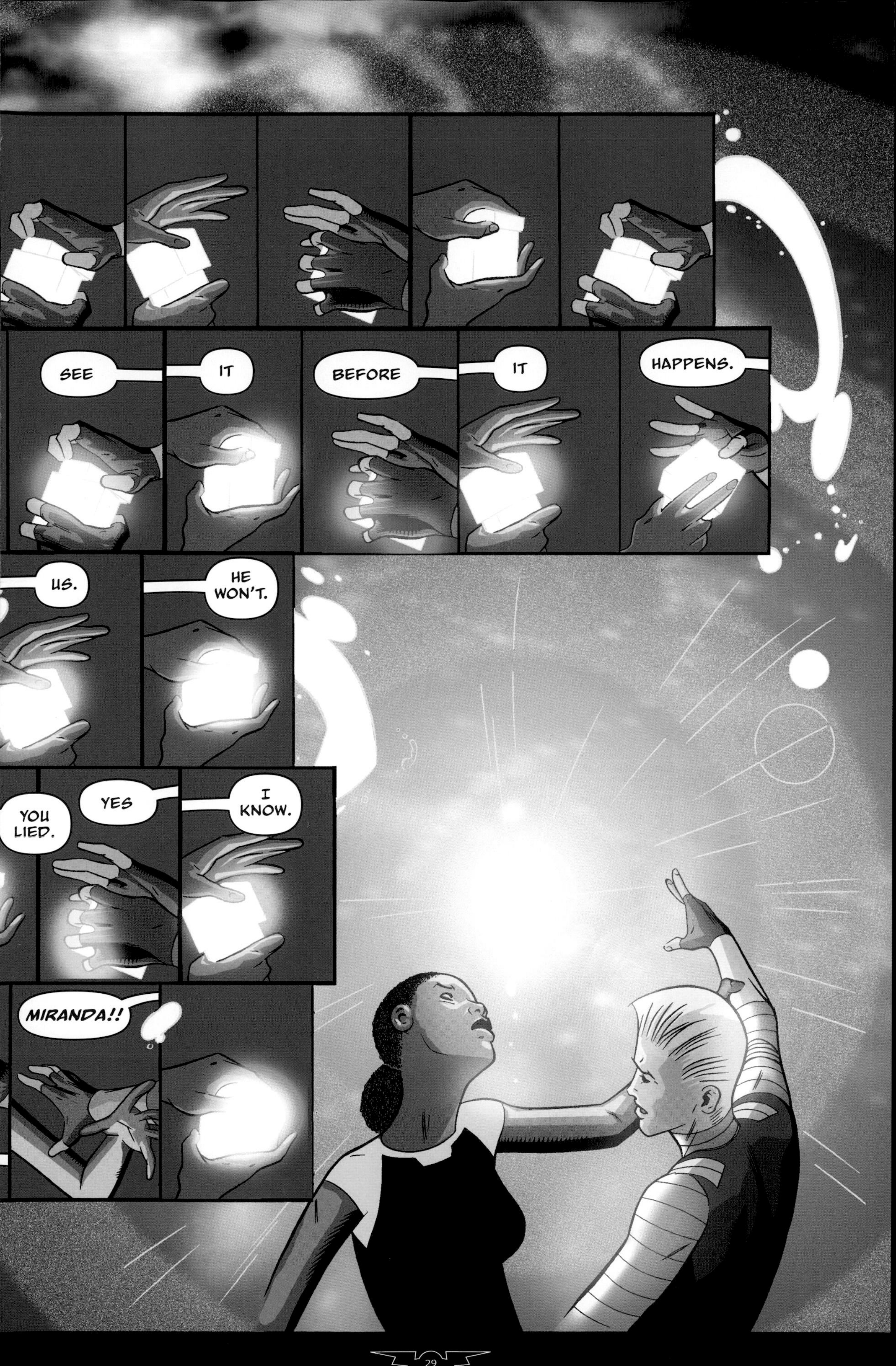
SEE
IT
BEFORE
IT
HAPPENS.
US.
HE WON'T.
YOU LIED.
YES
I KNOW.
MIRANDA!!

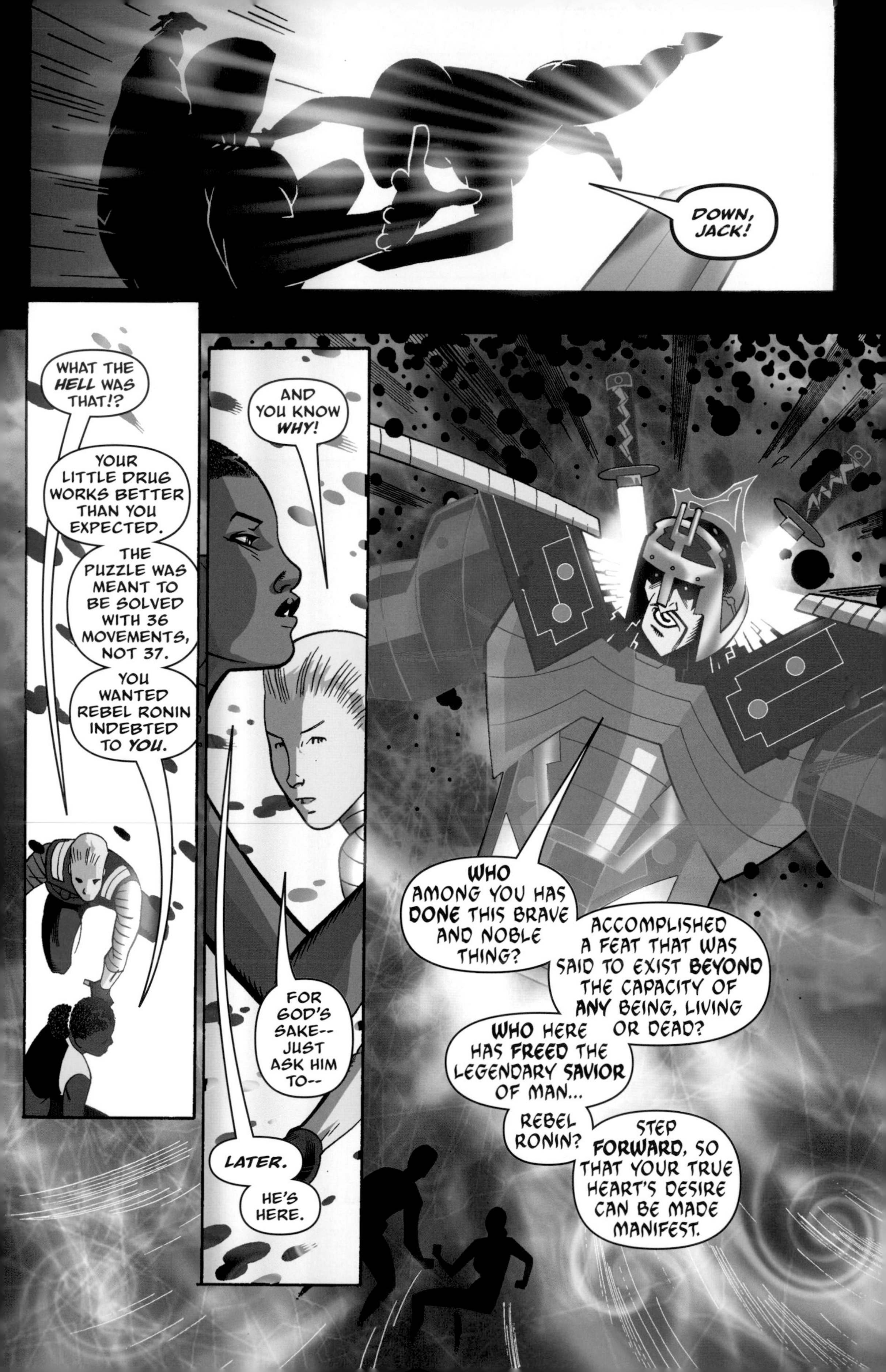
DOWN, JACK!
WHAT THE HELL WAS THAT!?
YOUR LITTLE DRUG WORKS BETTER THAN YOU EXPECTED.
THE PUZZLE WAS MEANT TO BE SOLVED WITH 36 MOVEMENTS, NOT 37.
YOU WANTED REBEL RONIN INDEBTED TO YOU.
AND YOU KNOW WHY!
FOR GOD'S SAKE-- JUST ASK HIM TO--
LATER.
HE'S HERE.
WHO AMONG YOU HAS DONE THIS BRAVE AND NOBLE THING?
ACCOMPLISHED A FEAT THAT WAS SAID TO EXIST BEYOND THE CAPACITY OF ANY BEING, LIVING OR DEAD?
WHO HERE HAS FREED THE LEGENDARY SAVIOR OF MAN...
REBEL RONIN?
STEP FORWARD, SO THAT YOUR TRUE HEART'S DESIRE CAN BE MADE MANIFEST.

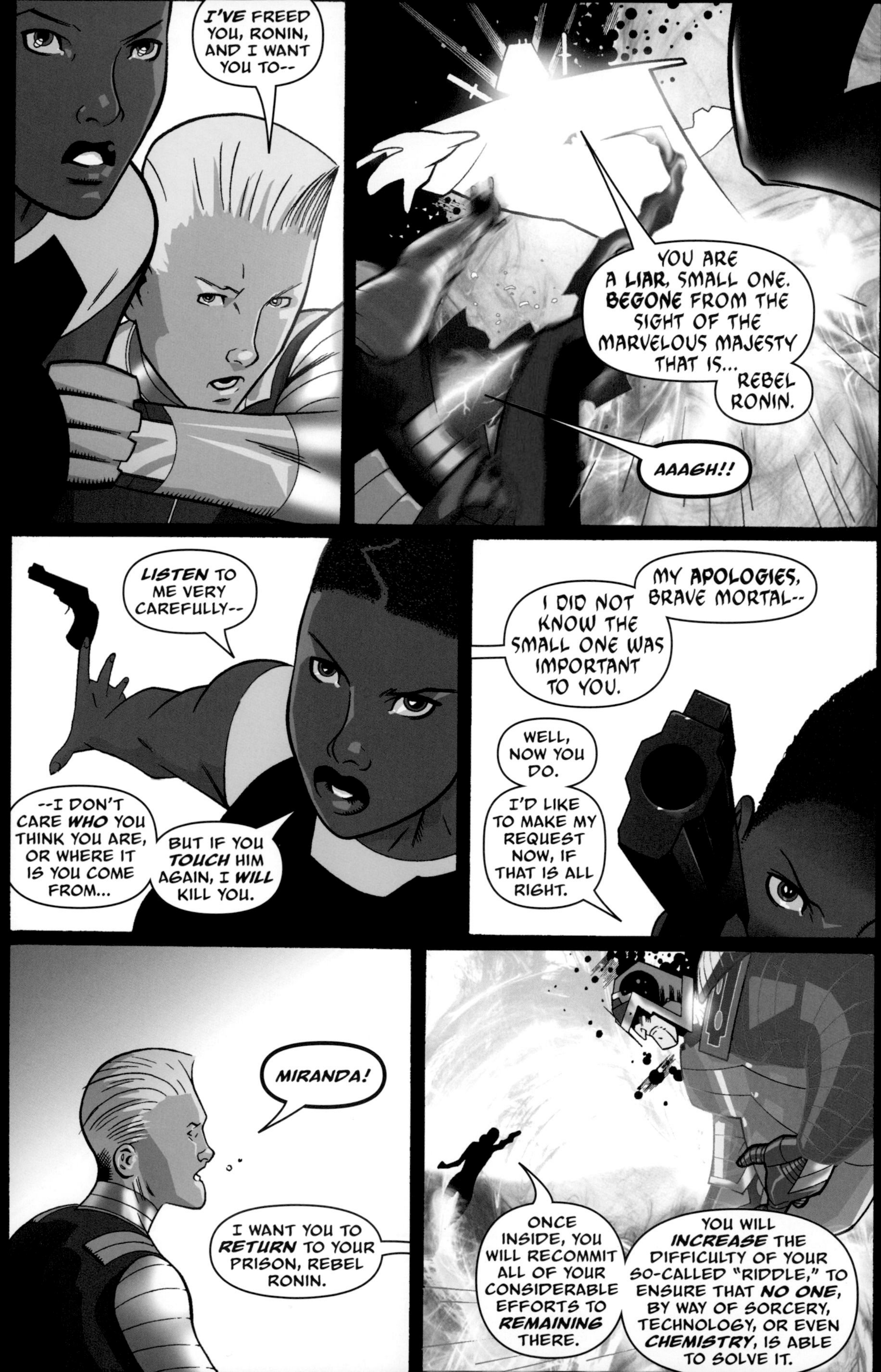
I'VE FREED YOU, RONIN, AND I WANT YOU TO--
YOU ARE A LIAR, SMALL ONE. BEGONE FROM THE SIGHT OF THE MARVELOUS MAJESTY THAT IS... REBEL RONIN.
AAAGH!!
LISTEN TO ME VERY CAREFULLY--
--I DON'T CARE WHO YOU THINK YOU ARE, OR WHERE IT IS YOU COME FROM...
BUT IF YOU TOUCH HIM AGAIN, I WILL KILL YOU.
MY APOLOGIES, BRAVE MORTAL--
I DID NOT KNOW THE SMALL ONE WAS IMPORTANT TO YOU.
WELL, NOW YOU DO.
I'D LIKE TO MAKE MY REQUEST NOW, IF THAT IS ALL RIGHT.
MIRANDA!
I WANT YOU TO RETURN TO YOUR PRISON, REBEL RONIN.
ONCE INSIDE, YOU WILL RECOMMIT ALL OF YOUR CONSIDERABLE EFFORTS TO REMAINING THERE.
YOU WILL INCREASE THE DIFFICULTY OF YOUR SO-CALLED "RIDDLE," TO ENSURE THAT NO ONE, BY WAY OF SORCERY, TECHNOLOGY, OR EVEN CHEMISTRY, IS ABLE TO SOLVE IT.

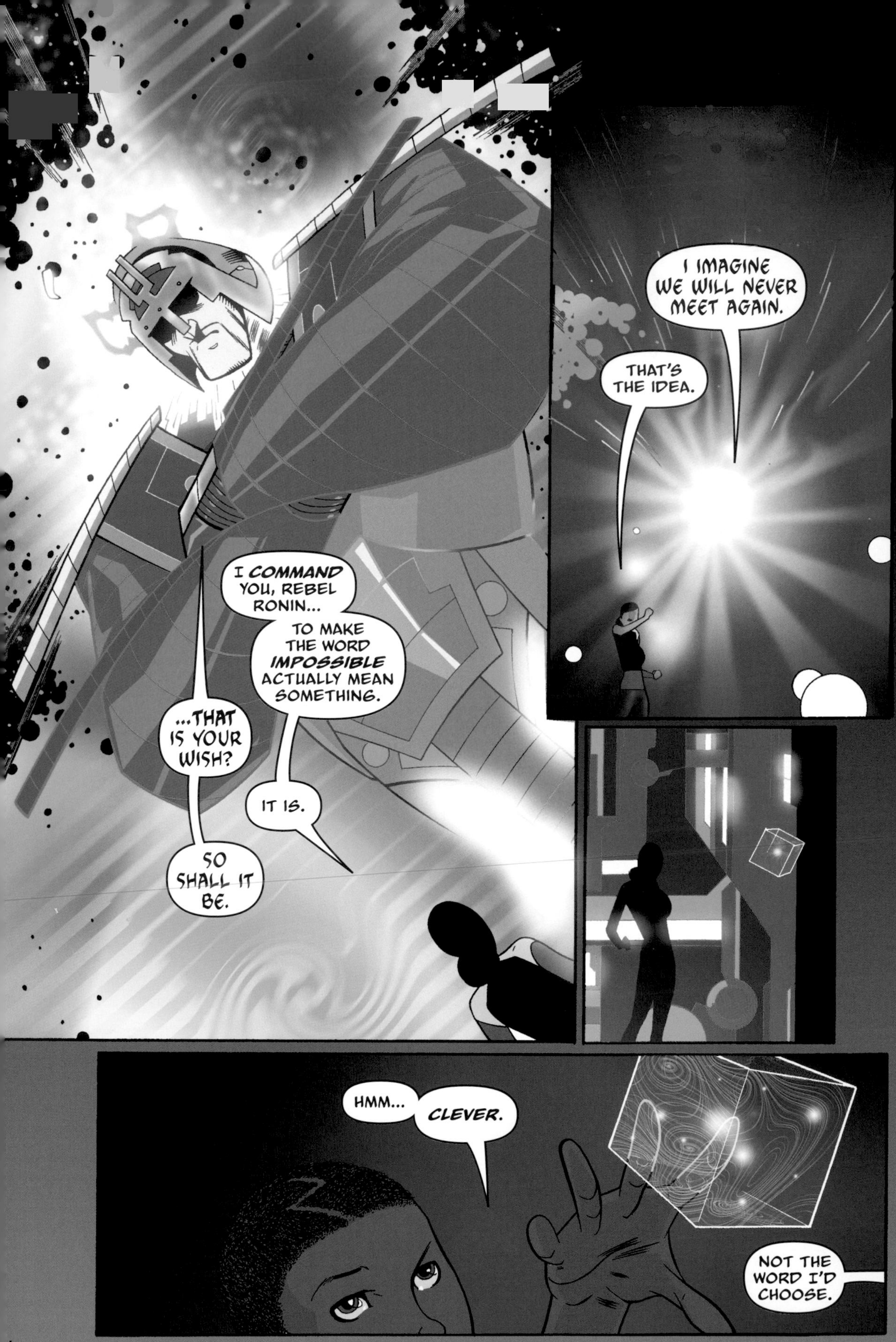

I COMMAND YOU, REBEL RONIN...
TO MAKE THE WORD IMPOSSIBLE ACTUALLY MEAN SOMETHING.
...THAT IS YOUR WISH?
IT IS.
SO SHALL IT BE.
I IMAGINE WE WILL NEVER MEET AGAIN.
THAT'S THE IDEA.
HMM...
CLEVER.
NOT THE WORD I'D CHOOSE.

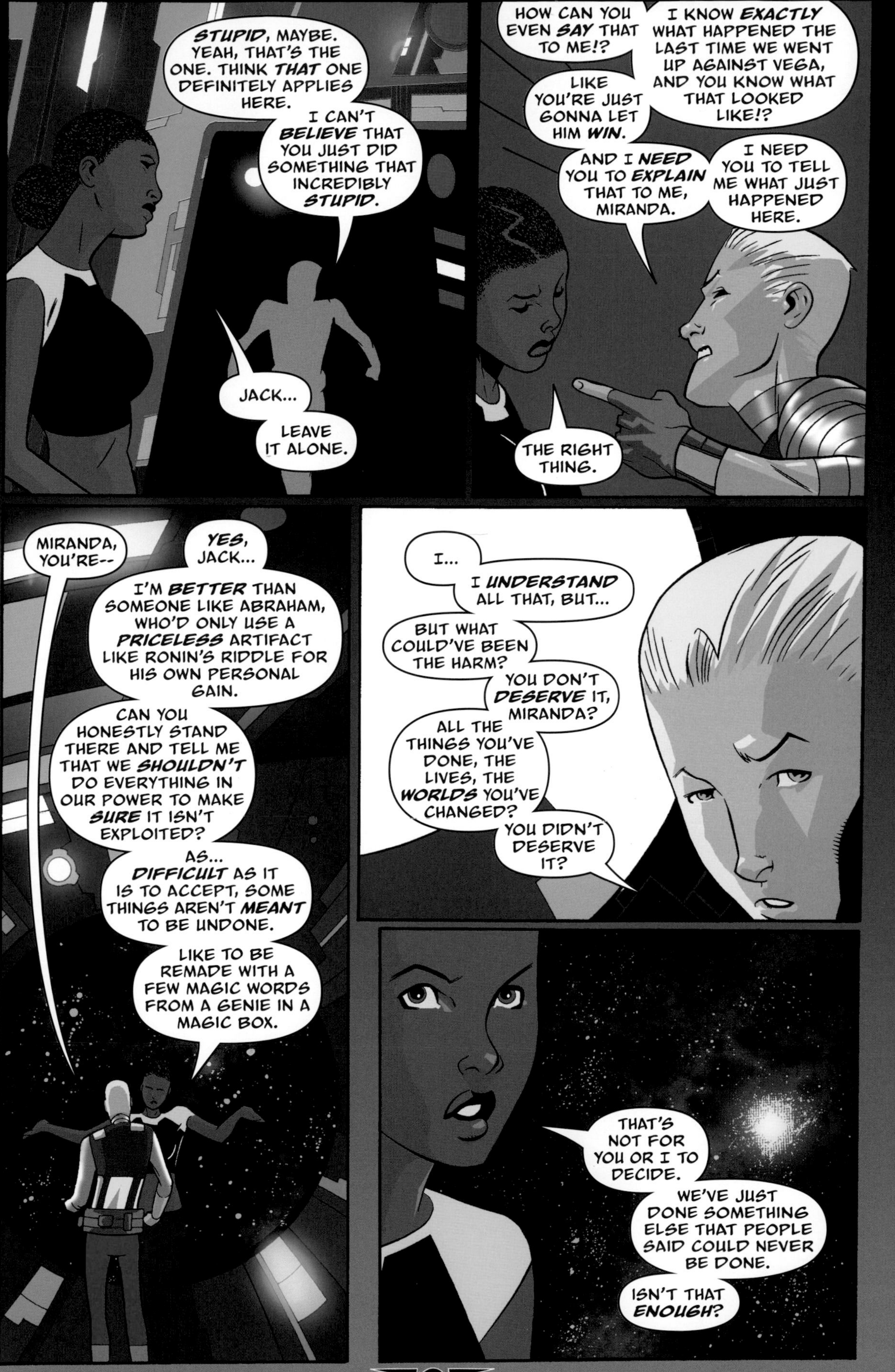
STUPID, MAYBE. YEAH, THAT'S THE ONE. THINK THAT ONE DEFINITELY APPLIES HERE.
I CAN'T BELIEVE THAT YOU JUST DID SOMETHING THAT INCREDIBLY STUPID.
JACK...
LEAVE IT ALONE.
HOW CAN YOU EVEN SAY THAT TO ME!?
LIKE YOU'RE JUST GONNA LET HIM WIN.
I KNOW EXACTLY WHAT HAPPENED THE LAST TIME WE WENT UP AGAINST VEGA, AND YOU KNOW WHAT THAT LOOKED LIKE!?
AND I NEED YOU TO EXPLAIN THAT TO ME, MIRANDA.
I NEED YOU TO TELL ME WHAT JUST HAPPENED HERE.
THE RIGHT THING.
MIRANDA, YOU'RE--
YES, JACK...
I'M BETTER THAN SOMEONE LIKE ABRAHAM, WHO'D ONLY USE A PRICELESS ARTIFACT LIKE RONIN'S RIDDLE FOR HIS OWN PERSONAL GAIN.
CAN YOU HONESTLY STAND THERE AND TELL ME THAT WE SHOULDN'T DO EVERYTHING IN OUR POWER TO MAKE SURE IT ISN'T EXPLOITED?
AS... DIFFICULT AS IT IS TO ACCEPT, SOME THINGS AREN'T MEANT TO BE UNDONE.
LIKE TO BE REMADE WITH A FEW MAGIC WORDS FROM A GENIE IN A MAGIC BOX.
I...
I UNDERSTAND ALL THAT, BUT...
BUT WHAT COULD'VE BEEN THE HARM?
YOU DON'T DESERVE IT, MIRANDA?
ALL THE THINGS YOU'VE DONE, THE LIVES, THE WORLDS YOU'VE CHANGED?
YOU DIDN'T DESERVE IT?
THAT'S NOT FOR YOU OR I TO DECIDE.
WE'VE JUST DONE SOMETHING ELSE THAT PEOPLE SAID COULD NEVER BE DONE.
ISN'T THAT ENOUGH?

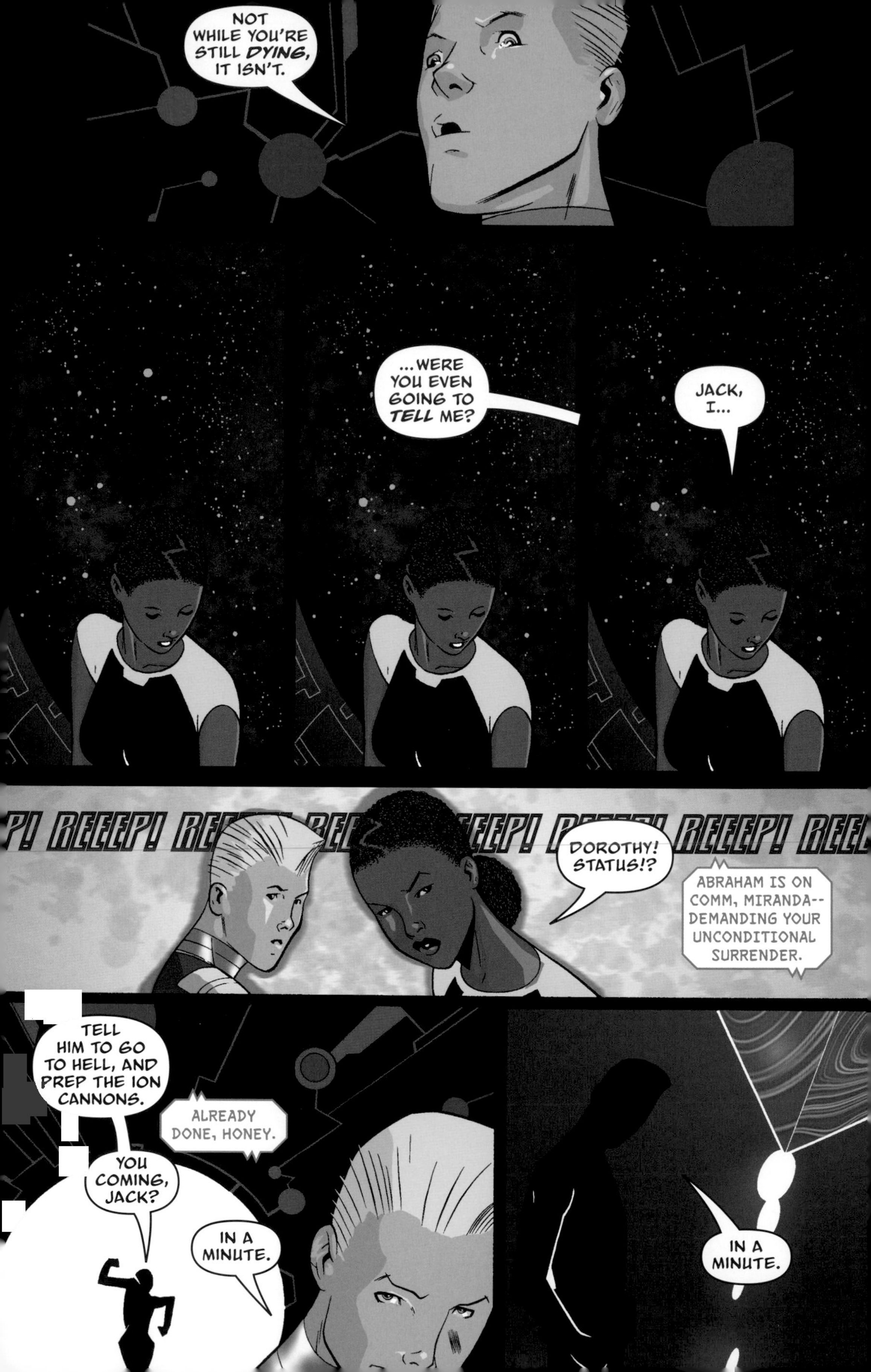
NOT WHILE YOU'RE STILL DYING, IT ISN'T.
...WERE YOU EVEN GOING TO TELL ME?
JACK, I...
REEEP! REEEP! REEEP!
DOROTHY! STATUS!?
ABRAHAM IS ON COMM, MIRANDA-- DEMANDING YOUR UNCONDITIONAL SURRENDER.
TELL HIM TO GO TO HELL, AND PREP THE ION CANNONS.
ALREADY DONE, HONEY.
YOU COMING, JACK?
IN A MINUTE.
IN A MINUTE.

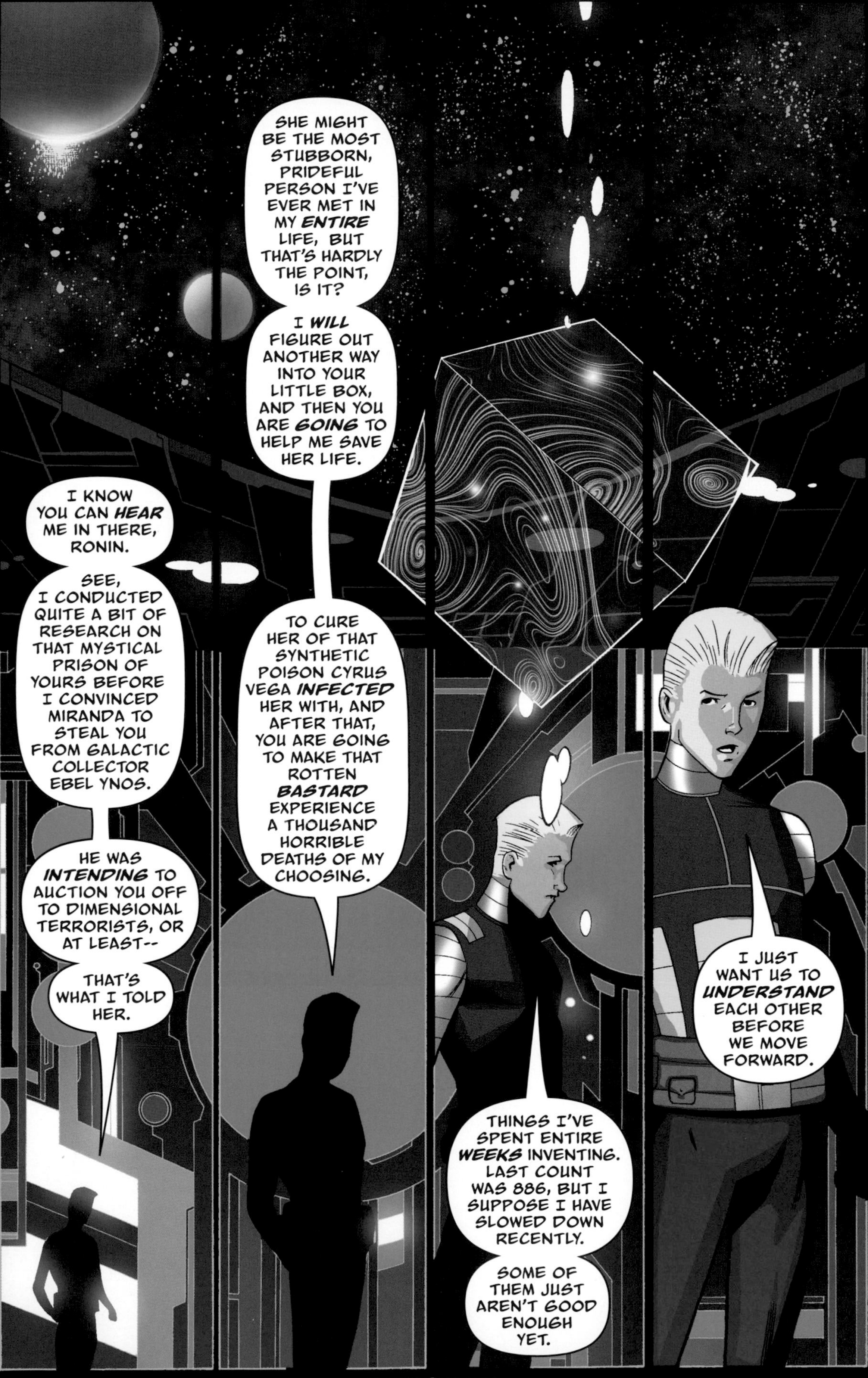
SHE MIGHT BE THE MOST STUBBORN, PRIDEFUL PERSON I'VE EVER MET IN MY ENTIRE LIFE, BUT THAT'S HARDLY THE POINT, IS IT?
I WILL FIGURE OUT ANOTHER WAY INTO YOUR LITTLE BOX, AND THEN YOU ARE GOING TO HELP ME SAVE HER LIFE.
I KNOW YOU CAN HEAR ME IN THERE, RONIN.
SEE, I CONDUCTED QUITE A BIT OF RESEARCH ON THAT MYSTICAL PRISON OF YOURS BEFORE I CONVINCED MIRANDA TO STEAL YOU FROM GALACTIC COLLECTOR EBEL YNOS.
HE WAS INTENDING TO AUCTION YOU OFF TO DIMENSIONAL TERRORISTS, OR AT LEAST--
THAT'S WHAT I TOLD HER.
TO CURE HER OF THAT SYNTHETIC POISON CYRUS VEGA INFECTED HER WITH, AND AFTER THAT, YOU ARE GOING TO MAKE THAT ROTTEN BASTARD EXPERIENCE A THOUSAND HORRIBLE DEATHS OF MY CHOOSING.
THINGS I'VE SPENT ENTIRE WEEKS INVENTING. LAST COUNT WAS 886, BUT I SUPPOSE I HAVE SLOWED DOWN RECENTLY.
SOME OF THEM JUST AREN'T GOOD ENOUGH YET.
I JUST WANT US TO UNDERSTAND EACH OTHER BEFORE WE MOVE FORWARD.

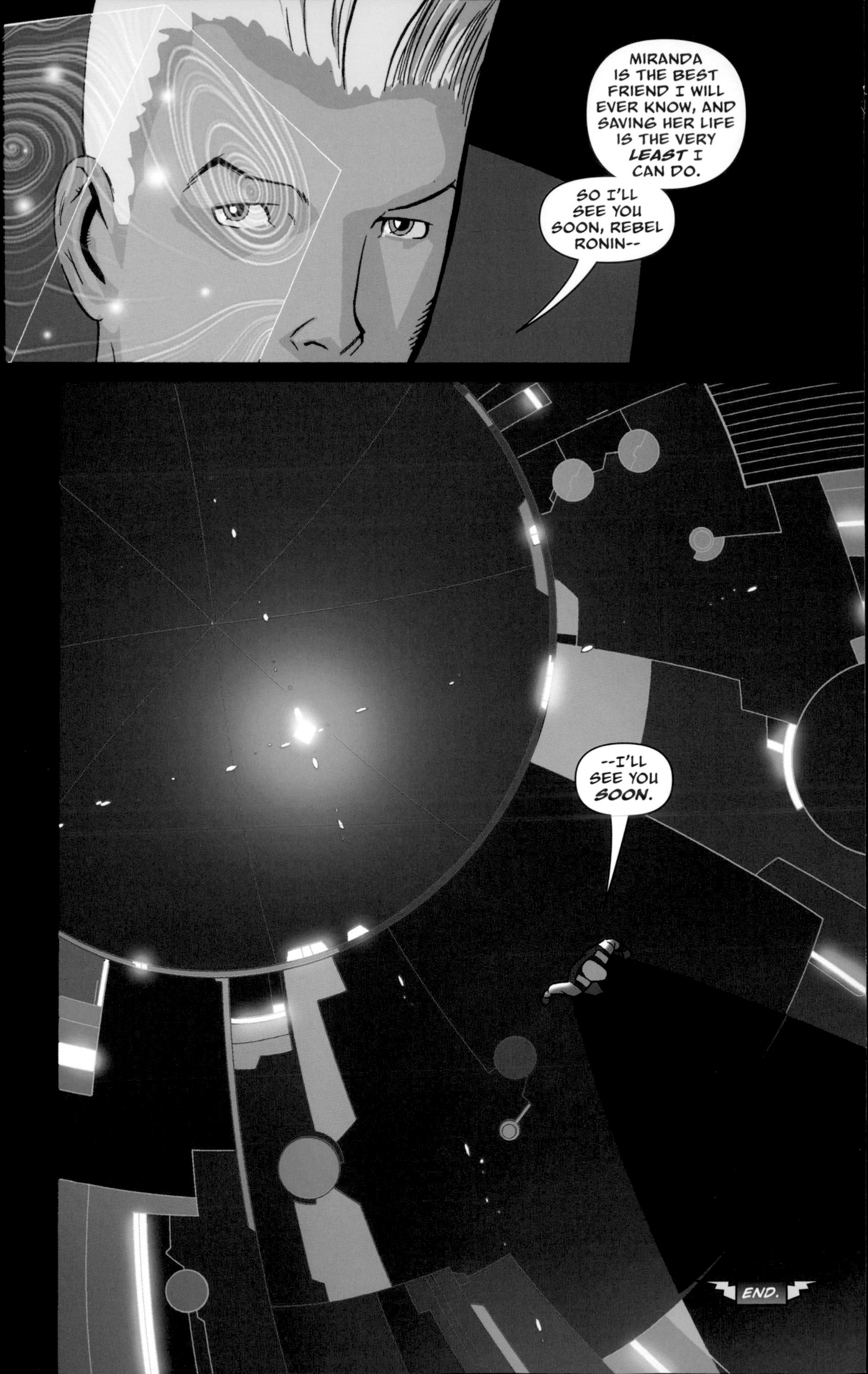
MIRANDA IS THE BEST FRIEND I WILL EVER KNOW, AND SAVING HER LIFE IS THE VERY LEAST I CAN DO.
SO I'LL SEE YOU SOON, REBEL RONIN--
--I'LL SEE YOU SOON.
END.

THE GLASS PLANET IS EXPERIENCING A FULL SCALE EXTINCTION LEVEL EVENT!

A WORLD THAT HAS LONG STOOD AS A GLEAMING TESTAMENT TO PROGRESS AND PROSPERITY ONLY HAS HOURS TO LIVE. FOR WEEKS A DESPERATE PLAN HAS BEEN IN MOTION TO SAVE BILLIONS--- ONE DEVELOPED AND EXECUTED BY MIRANDA MERCURY AND JACK WARNING.

THEY ARE NOW ONSITE TO ENSURE THAT EVERYTHING THAT HAPPENS NEXT DOES SO ACCORDING TO THIS BOLD PLAN.

EPISODE 296

MIRANDA MERCURY

AND THE DOOMED GLASS PLANET!

WRITER
BRANDON THOMAS

PENCILER
LEE FERGUSON

INKER
MARC DEERING

LETTERER
MATTY RYAN

COLORIST
FELIX SERRANO

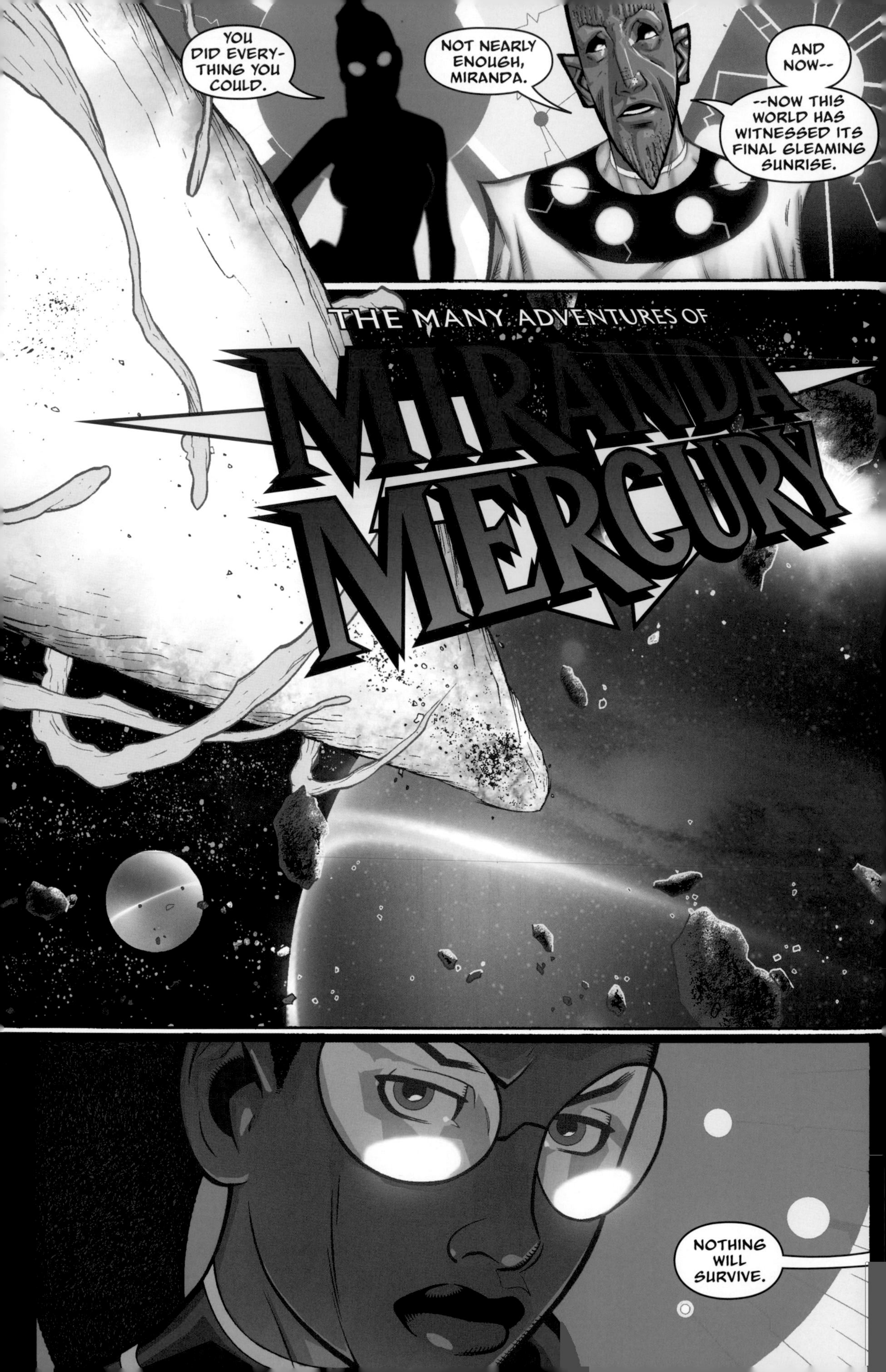
YOU DID EVERY-THING YOU COULD.
NOT NEARLY ENOUGH, MIRANDA.
AND NOW--
--NOW THIS WORLD HAS WITNESSED ITS FINAL GLEAMING SUNRISE.
THE MANY ADVENTURES OF
MIRANDA MERCURY
NOTHING WILL SURVIVE.

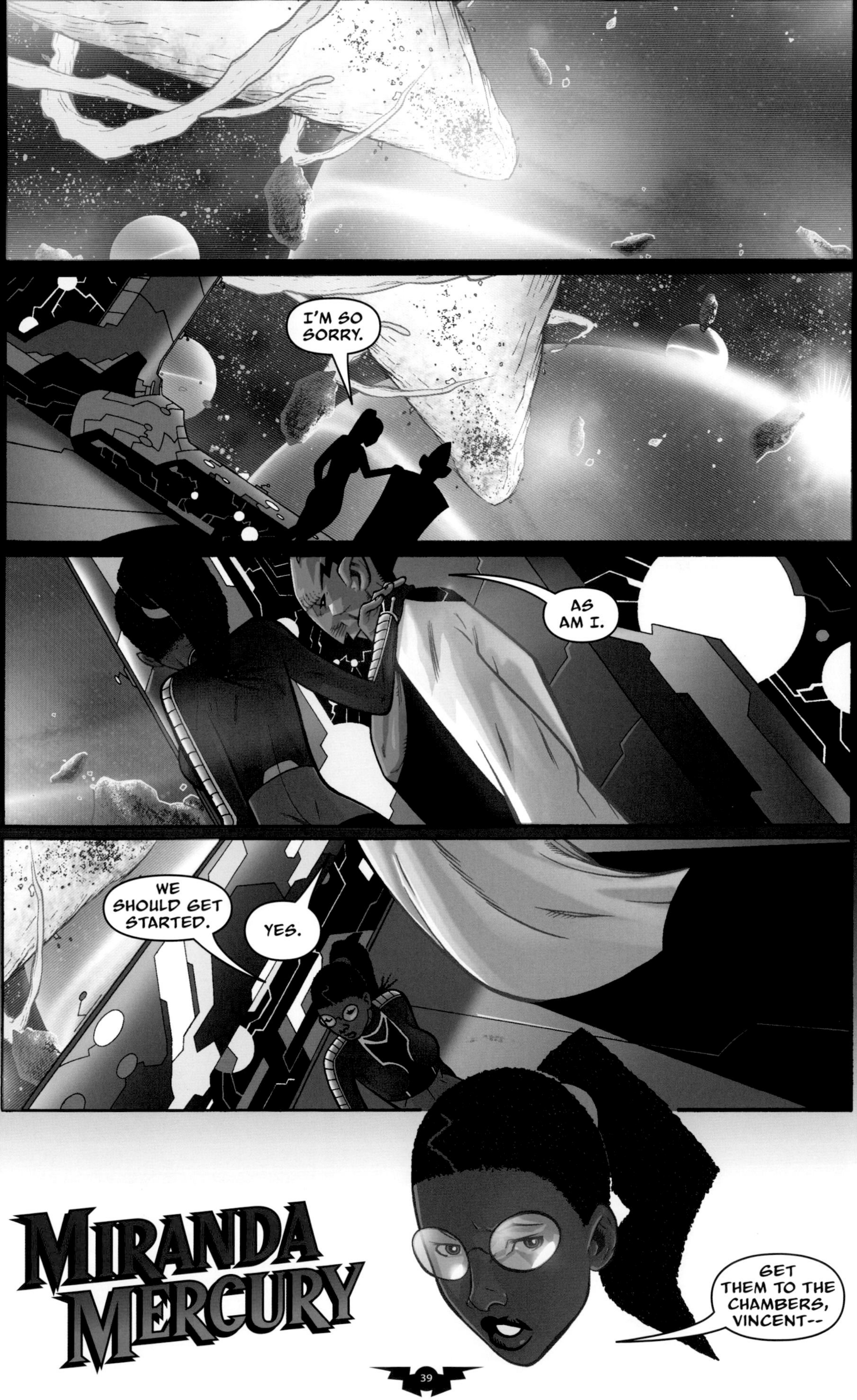
I'M SO SORRY.
AS AM I.
WE SHOULD GET STARTED.
YES.
MIRANDA MERCURY
GET THEM TO THE CHAMBERS, VINCENT--

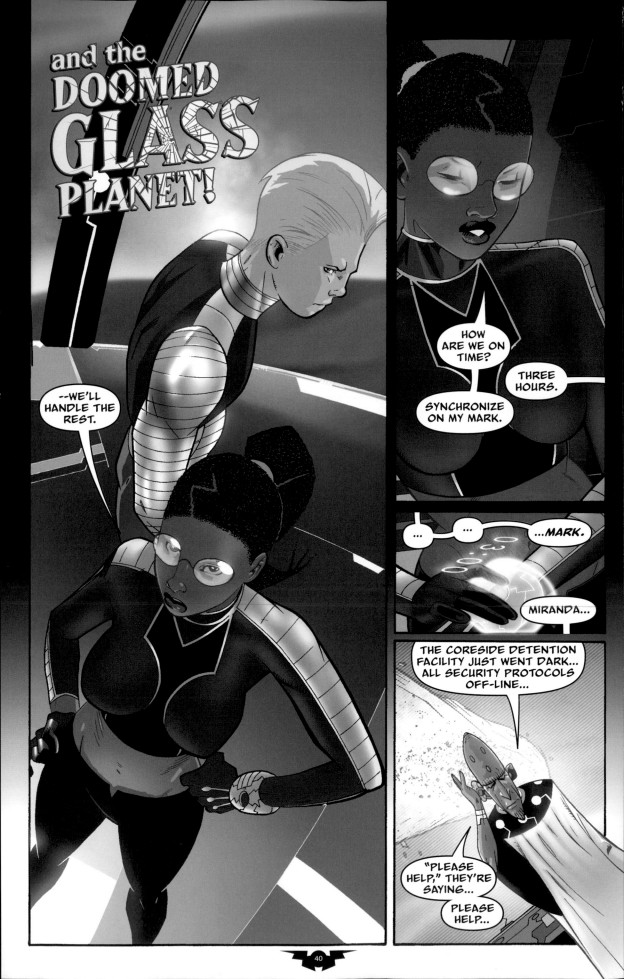

and the
DOOMED
GLASS
PLANET!

--WE'LL HANDLE THE REST.

HOW ARE WE ON TIME?

THREE HOURS.

SYNCHRONIZE ON MY MARK.

... ...MARK.

MIRANDA...

THE CORESIDE DETENTION FACILITY JUST WENT DARK... ALL SECURITY PROTOCOLS OFF-LINE...

"PLEASE HELP," THEY'RE SAYING...

PLEASE HELP...

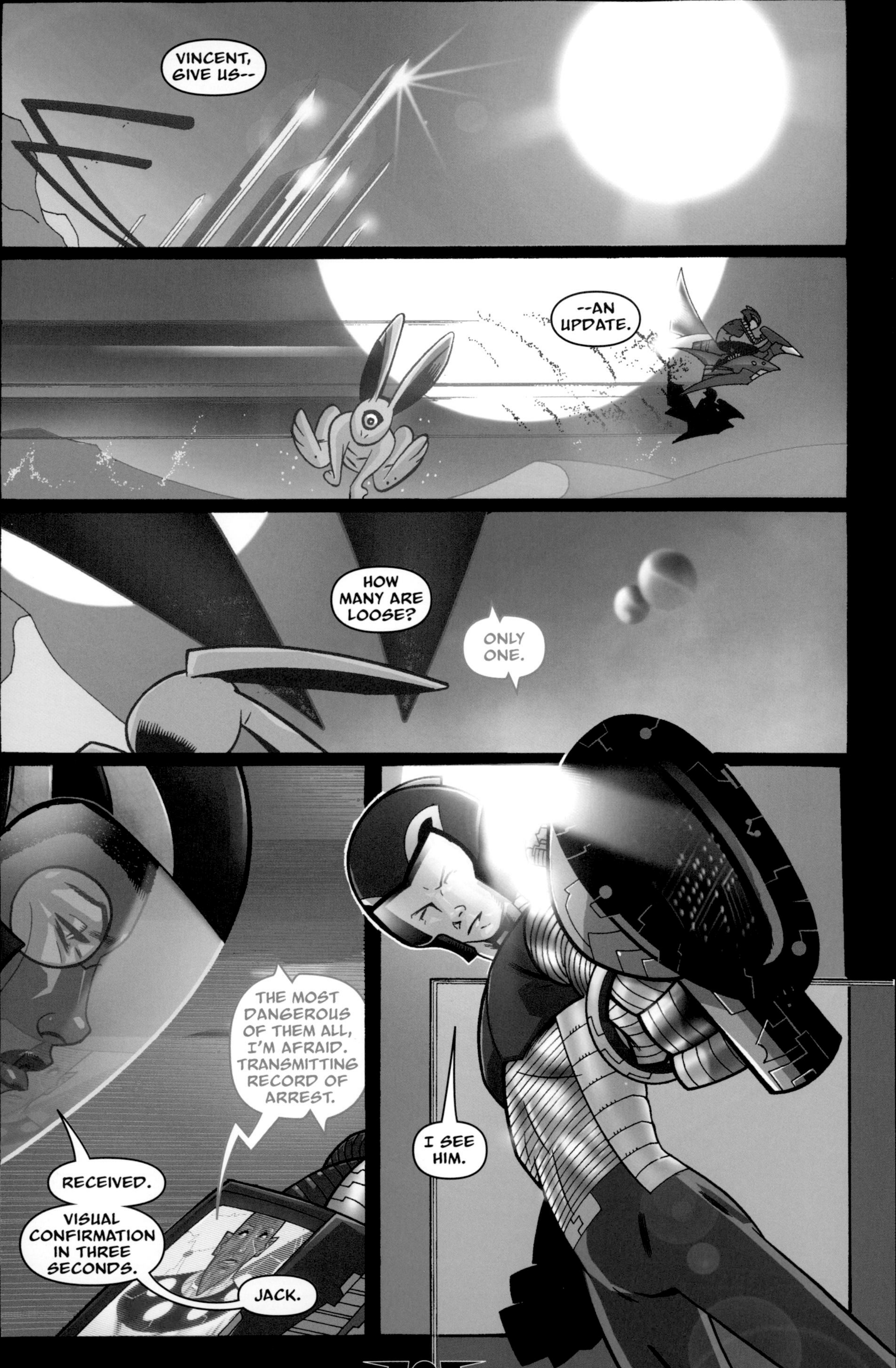
VINCENT, GIVE US--
--AN UPDATE.
HOW MANY ARE LOOSE?
ONLY ONE.
THE MOST DANGEROUS OF THEM ALL, I'M AFRAID. TRANSMITTING RECORD OF ARREST.
RECEIVED.
VISUAL CONFIRMATION IN THREE SECONDS.
JACK.
I SEE HIM.

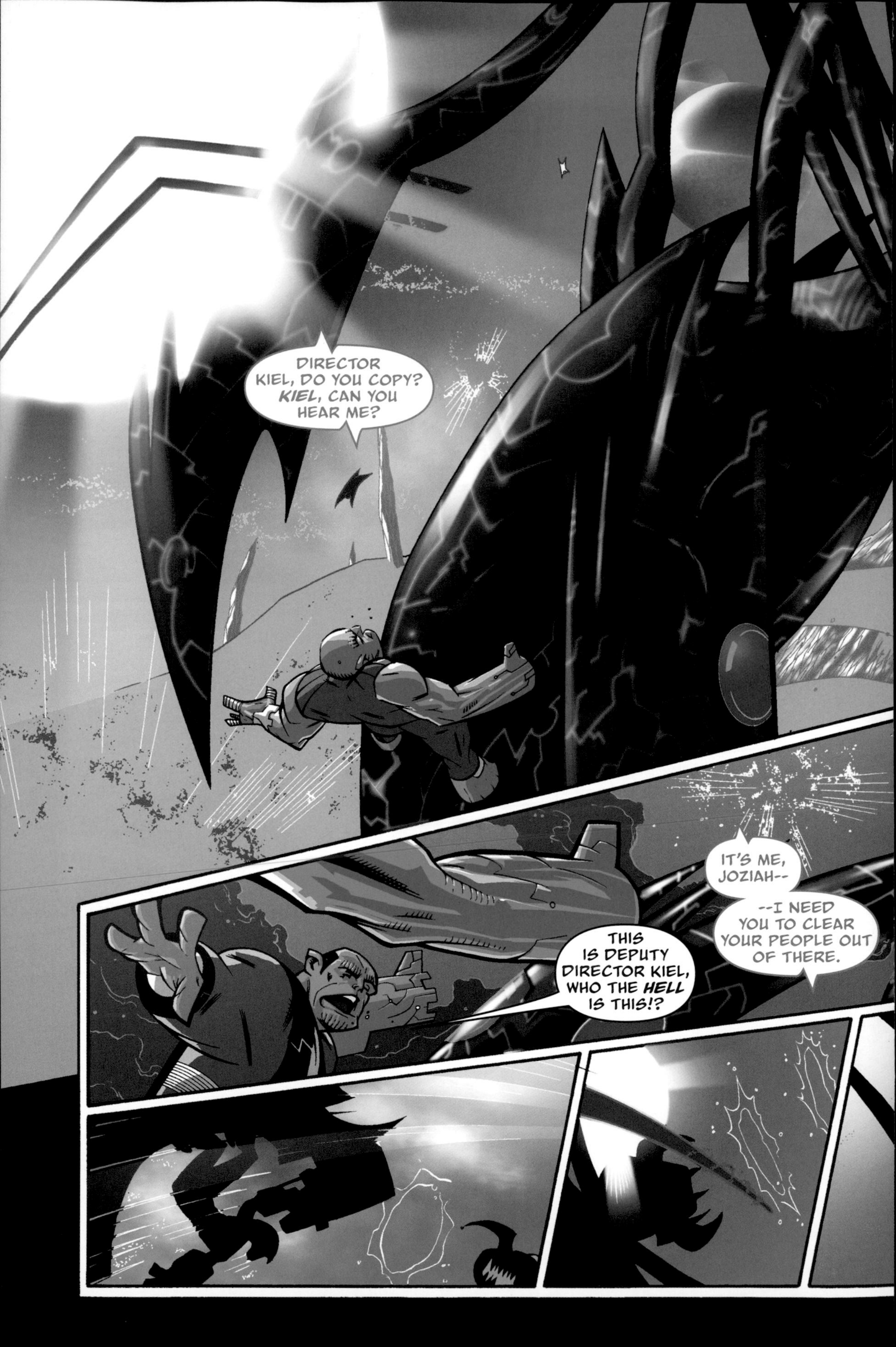
DIRECTOR KIEL, DO YOU COPY? KIEL, CAN YOU HEAR ME?
IT'S ME, JOZIAH--
--I NEED YOU TO CLEAR YOUR PEOPLE OUT OF THERE.
THIS IS DEPUTY DIRECTOR KIEL, WHO THE HELL IS THIS!?

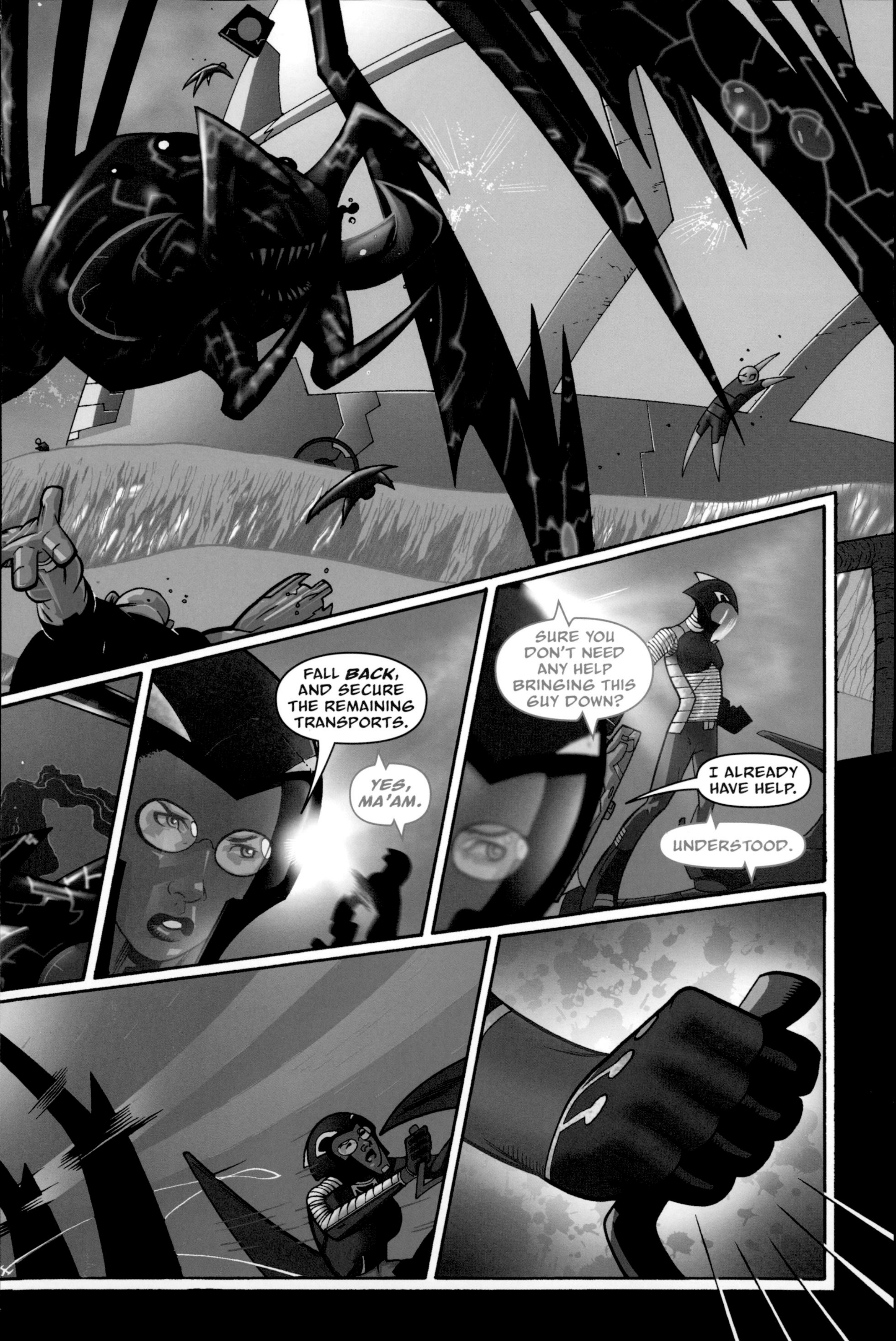
FALL BACK, AND SECURE THE REMAINING TRANSPORTS.
YES, MA'AM.
SURE YOU DON'T NEED ANY HELP BRINGING THIS GUY DOWN?
I ALREADY HAVE HELP.
UNDERSTOOD.

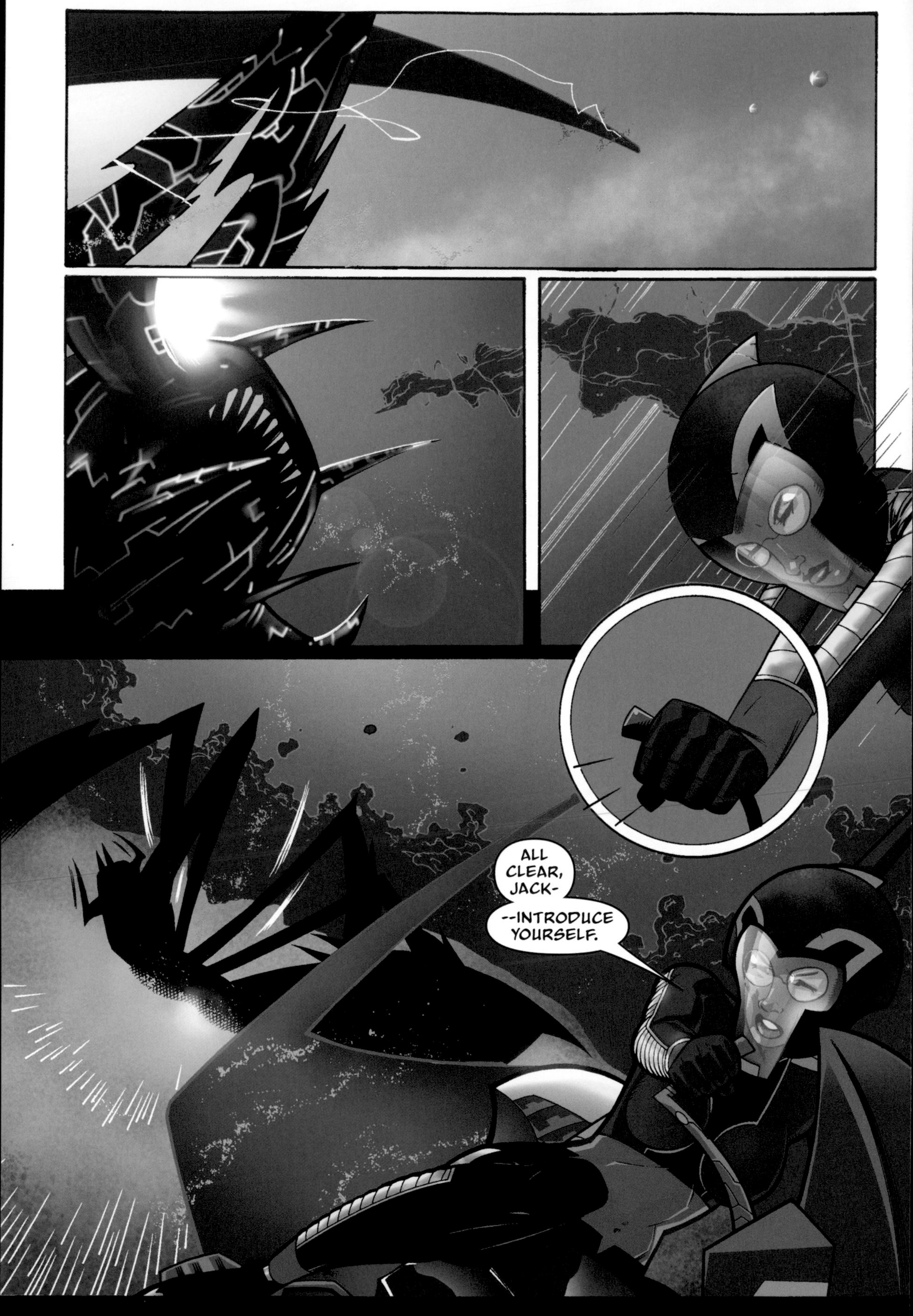
ALL CLEAR, JACK-
--INTRODUCE YOURSELF.

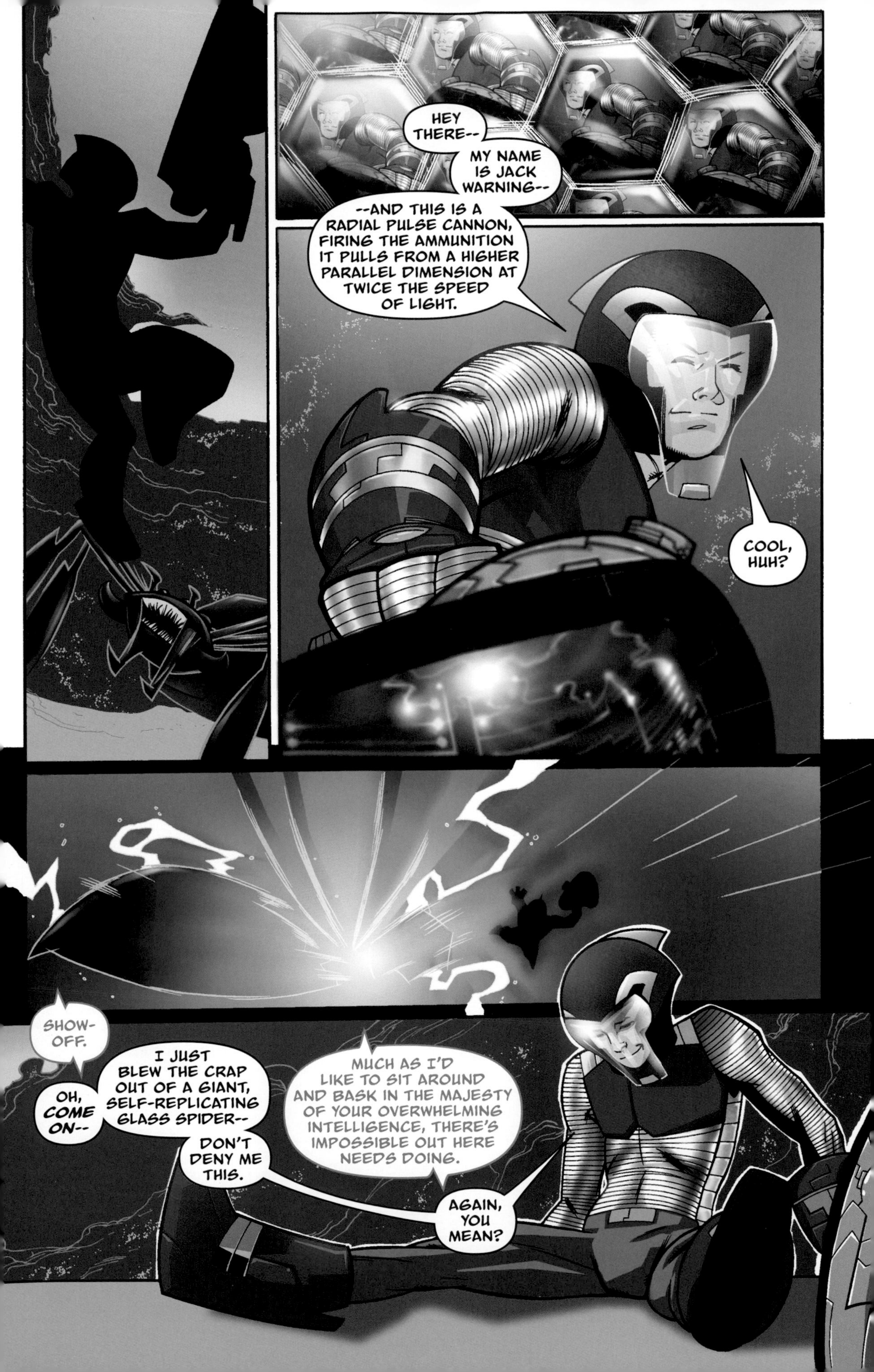
HEY THERE--
MY NAME IS JACK WARNING--
--AND THIS IS A RADIAL PULSE CANNON, FIRING THE AMMUNITION IT PULLS FROM A HIGHER PARALLEL DIMENSION AT TWICE THE SPEED OF LIGHT.
COOL, HUH?
SHOW-OFF.
OH, COME ON--
I JUST BLEW THE CRAP OUT OF A GIANT, SELF-REPLICATING GLASS SPIDER--
DON'T DENY ME THIS.
MUCH AS I'D LIKE TO SIT AROUND AND BASK IN THE MAJESTY OF YOUR OVERWHELMING INTELLIGENCE, THERE'S IMPOSSIBLE OUT HERE NEEDS DOING.
AGAIN, YOU MEAN?

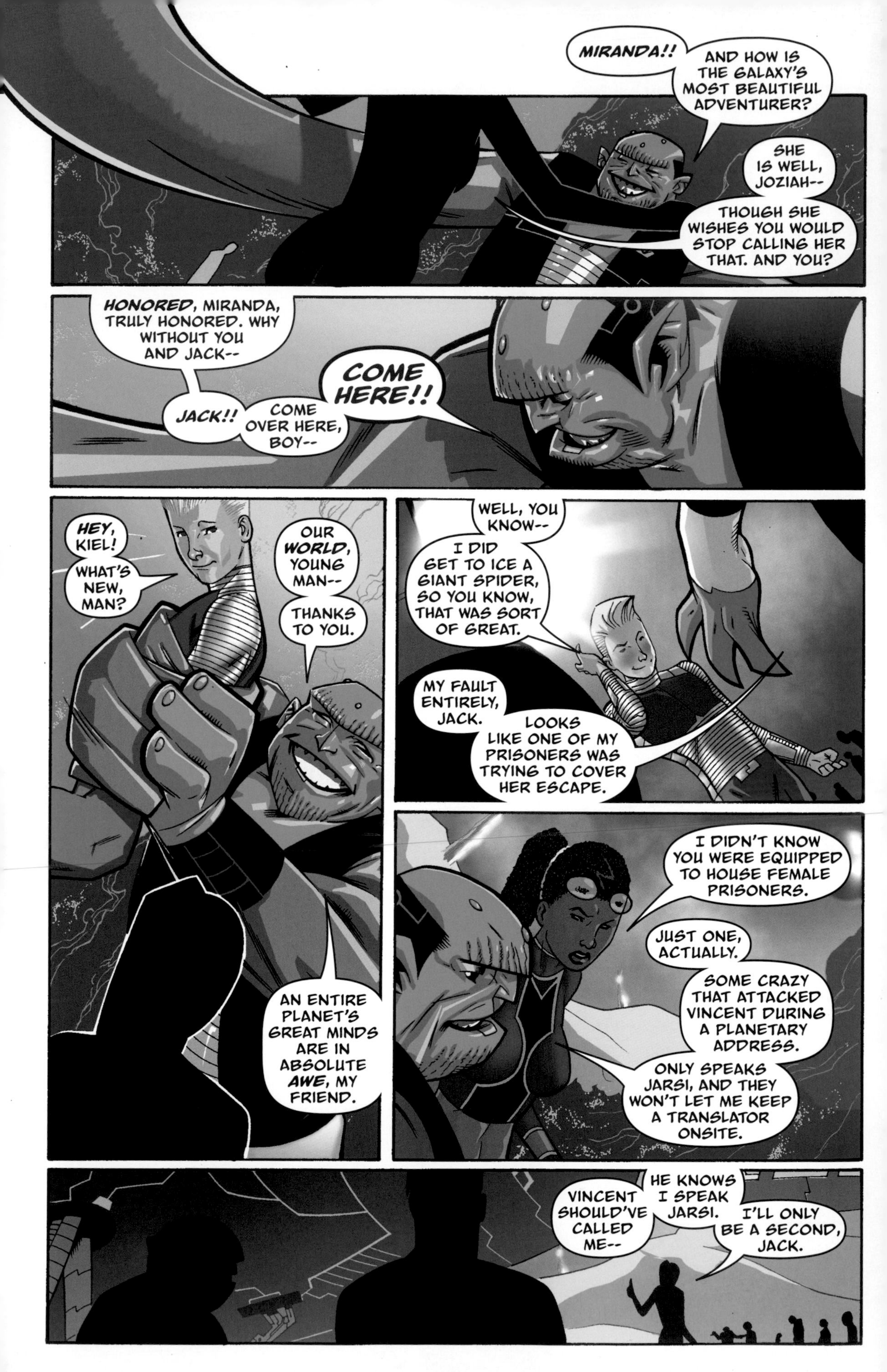
MIRANDA!!
AND HOW IS THE GALAXY'S MOST BEAUTIFUL ADVENTURER?
SHE IS WELL, JOZIAH--
THOUGH SHE WISHES YOU WOULD STOP CALLING HER THAT. AND YOU?
HONORED, MIRANDA, TRULY HONORED. WHY WITHOUT YOU AND JACK--
JACK!!
COME OVER HERE, BOY--
COME HERE!!
HEY, KIEL!
WHAT'S NEW, MAN?
OUR WORLD, YOUNG MAN--
THANKS TO YOU.
AN ENTIRE PLANET'S GREAT MINDS ARE IN ABSOLUTE AWE, MY FRIEND.
WELL, YOU KNOW--
I DID GET TO ICE A GIANT SPIDER, SO YOU KNOW, THAT WAS SORT OF GREAT.
MY FAULT ENTIRELY, JACK.
LOOKS LIKE ONE OF MY PRISONERS WAS TRYING TO COVER HER ESCAPE.
I DIDN'T KNOW YOU WERE EQUIPPED TO HOUSE FEMALE PRISONERS.
JUST ONE, ACTUALLY.
SOME CRAZY THAT ATTACKED VINCENT DURING A PLANETARY ADDRESS.
ONLY SPEAKS JARSI, AND THEY WON'T LET ME KEEP A TRANSLATOR ONSITE.
VINCENT SHOULD'VE CALLED ME--
HE KNOWS I SPEAK JARSI.
I'LL ONLY BE A SECOND, JACK.

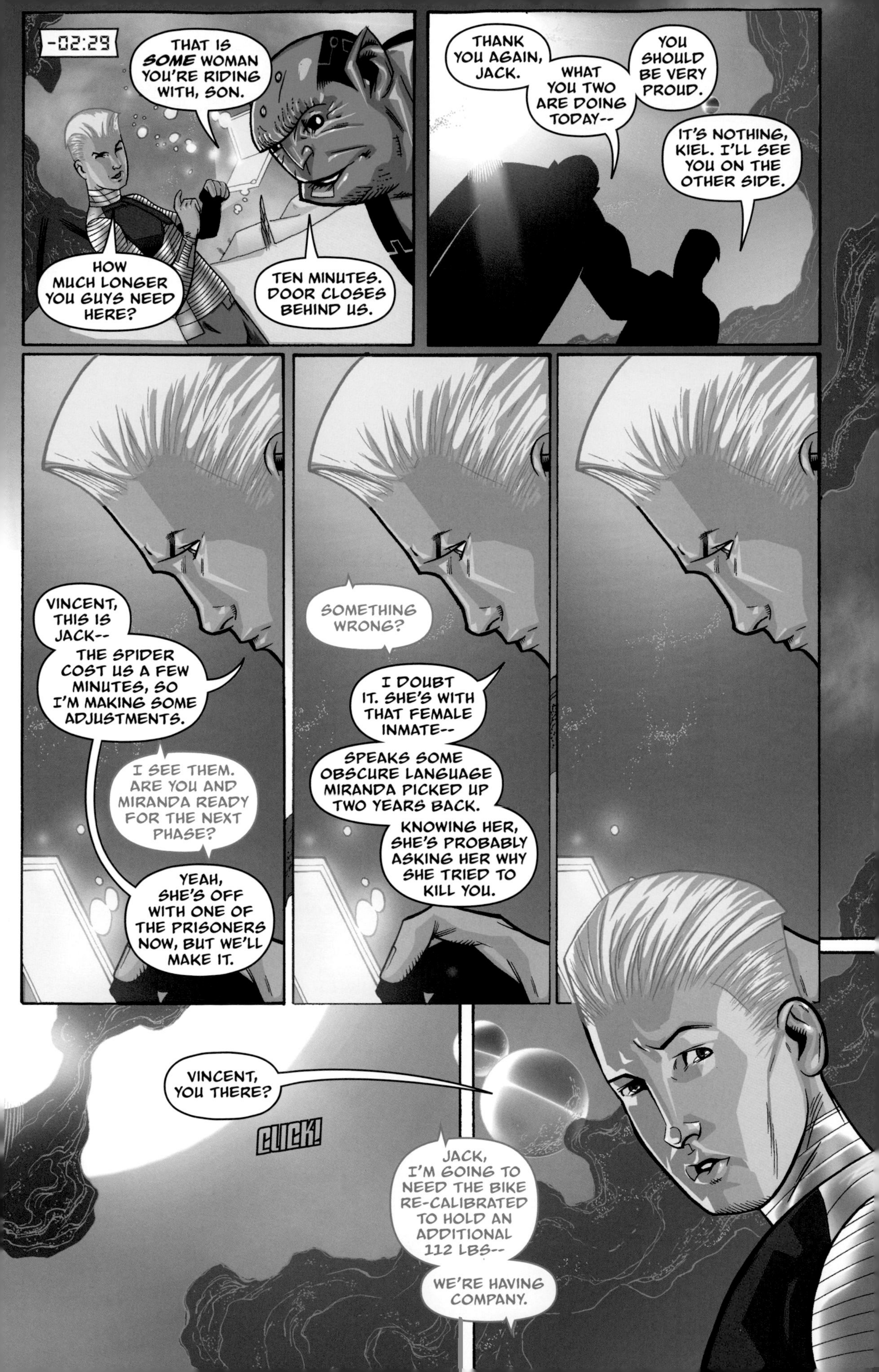
-02:29
THAT IS SOME WOMAN YOU'RE RIDING WITH, SON.
HOW MUCH LONGER YOU GUYS NEED HERE?
TEN MINUTES. DOOR CLOSES BEHIND US.
THANK YOU AGAIN, JACK.
WHAT YOU TWO ARE DOING TODAY--
YOU SHOULD BE VERY PROUD.
IT'S NOTHING, KIEL. I'LL SEE YOU ON THE OTHER SIDE.
VINCENT, THIS IS JACK--
THE SPIDER COST US A FEW MINUTES, SO I'M MAKING SOME ADJUSTMENTS.
I SEE THEM. ARE YOU AND MIRANDA READY FOR THE NEXT PHASE?
YEAH, SHE'S OFF WITH ONE OF THE PRISONERS NOW, BUT WE'LL MAKE IT.
SOMETHING WRONG?
I DOUBT IT. SHE'S WITH THAT FEMALE INMATE--
SPEAKS SOME OBSCURE LANGUAGE MIRANDA PICKED UP TWO YEARS BACK.
KNOWING HER, SHE'S PROBABLY ASKING HER WHY SHE TRIED TO KILL YOU.
VINCENT, YOU THERE?
CLICK!
JACK, I'M GOING TO NEED THE BIKE RE-CALIBRATED TO HOLD AN ADDITIONAL 112 LBS--
WE'RE HAVING COMPANY.

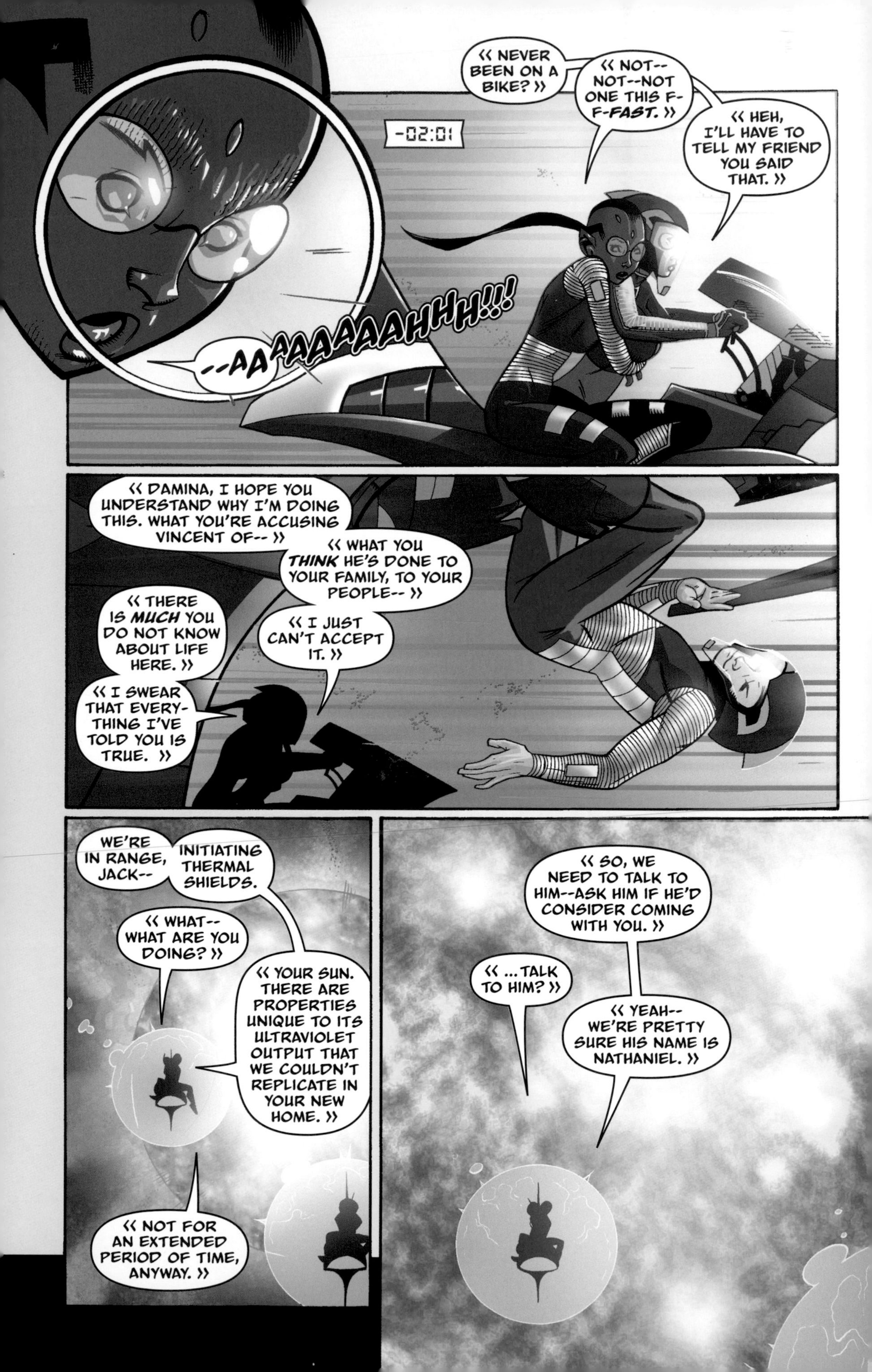

«NEVER BEEN ON A BIKE?»
«NOT--NOT--NOT ONE THIS F-F-FAST.»
«HEH, I'LL HAVE TO TELL MY FRIEND YOU SAID THAT.»
-02:01
--AAAAAAAAAHHH!!!
«DAMINA, I HOPE YOU UNDERSTAND WHY I'M DOING THIS. WHAT YOU'RE ACCUSING VINCENT OF--»
«WHAT YOU THINK HE'S DONE TO YOUR FAMILY, TO YOUR PEOPLE--»
«I JUST CAN'T ACCEPT IT.»
«THERE IS MUCH YOU DO NOT KNOW ABOUT LIFE HERE.»
«I SWEAR THAT EVERYTHING I'VE TOLD YOU IS TRUE.»
WE'RE IN RANGE, JACK--
INITIATING THERMAL SHIELDS.
«WHAT--WHAT ARE YOU DOING?»
«YOUR SUN. THERE ARE PROPERTIES UNIQUE TO ITS ULTRAVIOLET OUTPUT THAT WE COULDN'T REPLICATE IN YOUR NEW HOME.»
«NOT FOR AN EXTENDED PERIOD OF TIME, ANYWAY.»
«SO, WE NEED TO TALK TO HIM--ASK HIM IF HE'D CONSIDER COMING WITH YOU.»
«...TALK TO HIM?»
«YEAH--WE'RE PRETTY SURE HIS NAME IS NATHANIEL.»

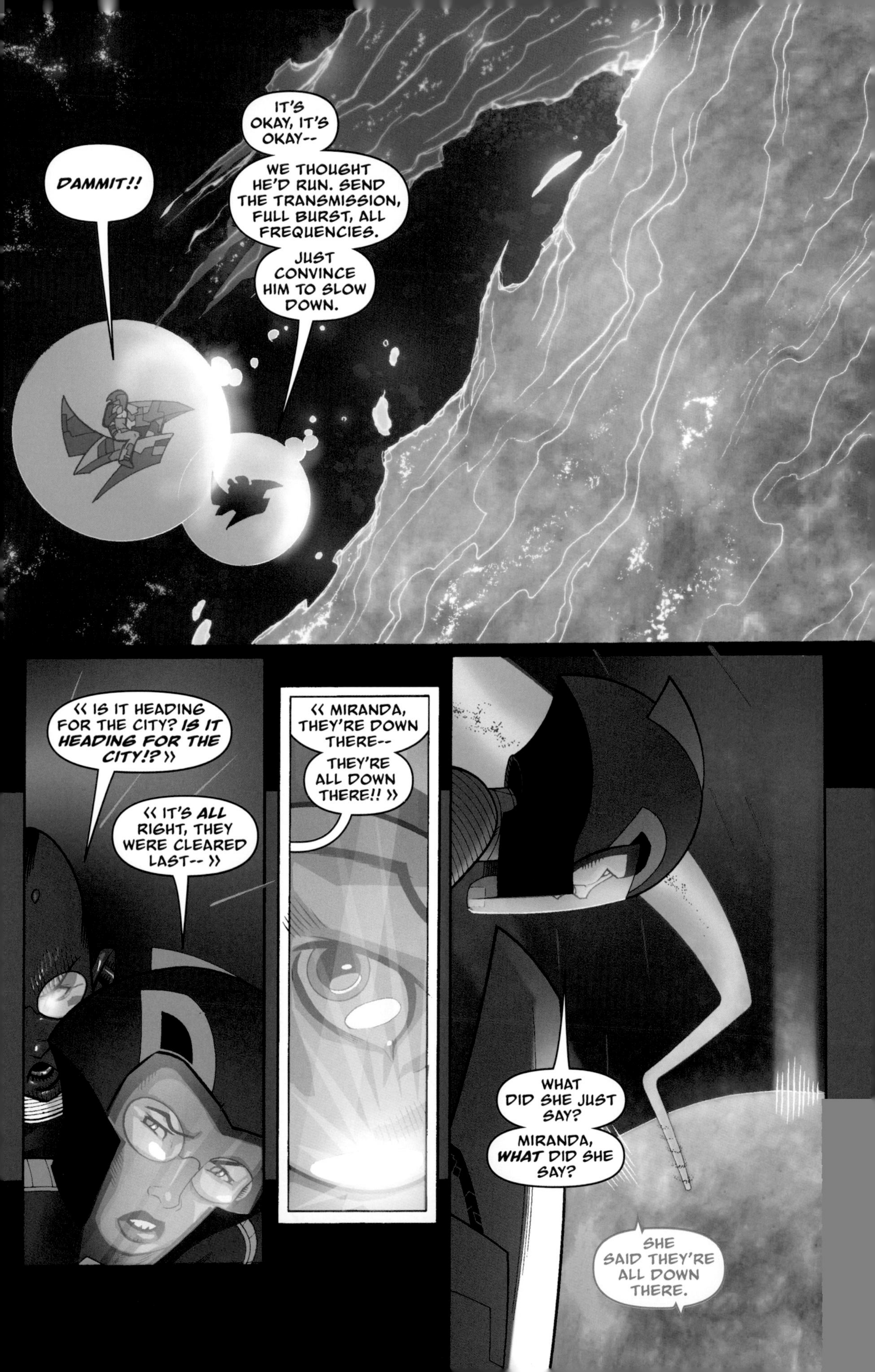
DAMMIT!!
IT'S OKAY, IT'S OKAY--
WE THOUGHT HE'D RUN. SEND THE TRANSMISSION, FULL BURST, ALL FREQUENCIES.
JUST CONVINCE HIM TO SLOW DOWN.
« IS IT HEADING FOR THE CITY? IS IT HEADING FOR THE CITY!? »
« IT'S ALL RIGHT, THEY WERE CLEARED LAST-- »
« MIRANDA, THEY'RE DOWN THERE--
THEY'RE ALL DOWN THERE!! »
WHAT DID SHE JUST SAY?
MIRANDA, WHAT DID SHE SAY?
SHE SAID THEY'RE ALL DOWN THERE.

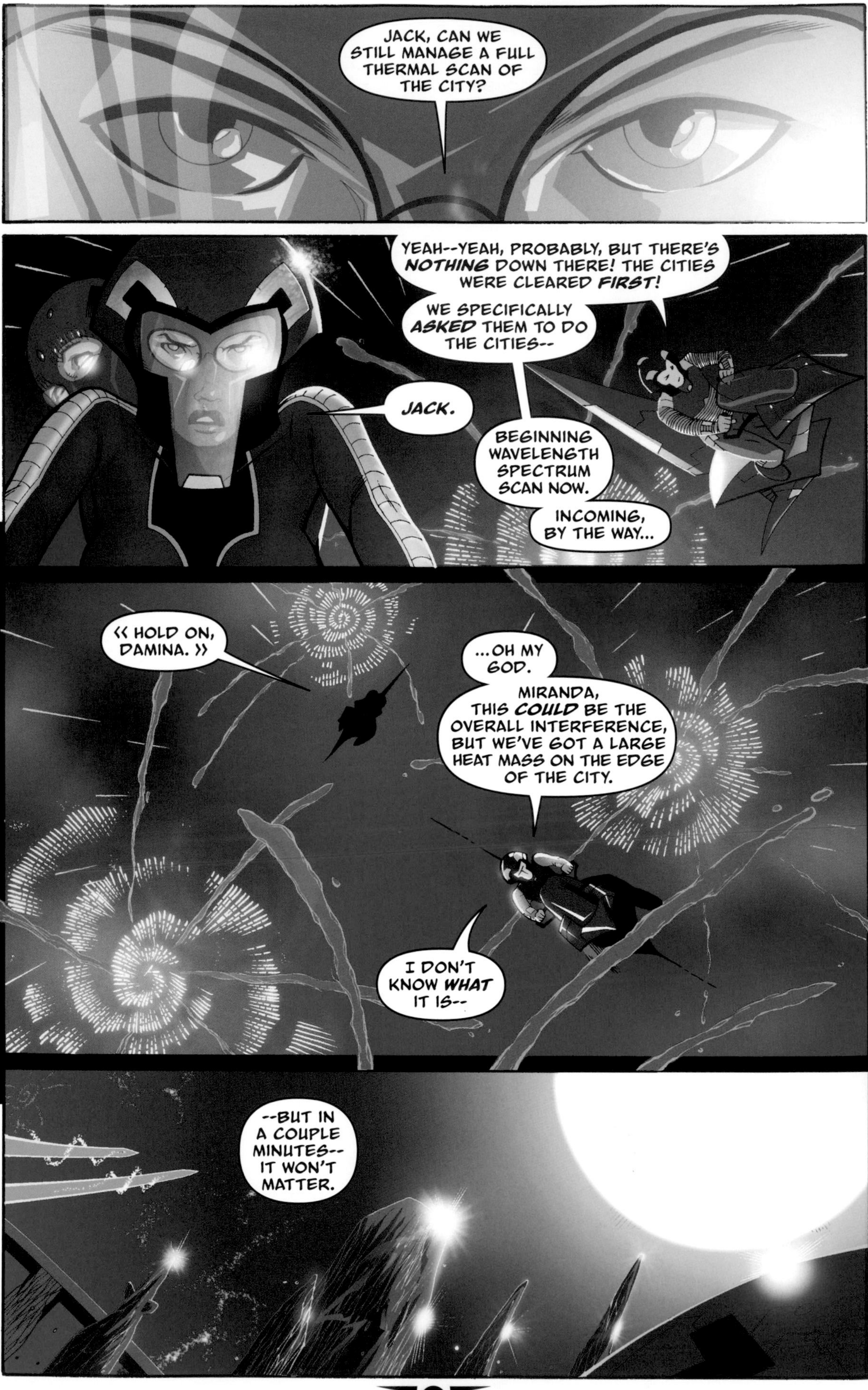
JACK, CAN WE STILL MANAGE A FULL THERMAL SCAN OF THE CITY?
YEAH--YEAH, PROBABLY, BUT THERE'S NOTHING DOWN THERE! THE CITIES WERE CLEARED FIRST!
WE SPECIFICALLY ASKED THEM TO DO THE CITIES--
JACK.
BEGINNING WAVELENGTH SPECTRUM SCAN NOW.
INCOMING, BY THE WAY...
‹‹ HOLD ON, DAMINA. ››
...OH MY GOD.
MIRANDA, THIS COULD BE THE OVERALL INTERFERENCE, BUT WE'VE GOT A LARGE HEAT MASS ON THE EDGE OF THE CITY.
I DON'T KNOW WHAT IT IS--
--BUT IN A COUPLE MINUTES-- IT WON'T MATTER.

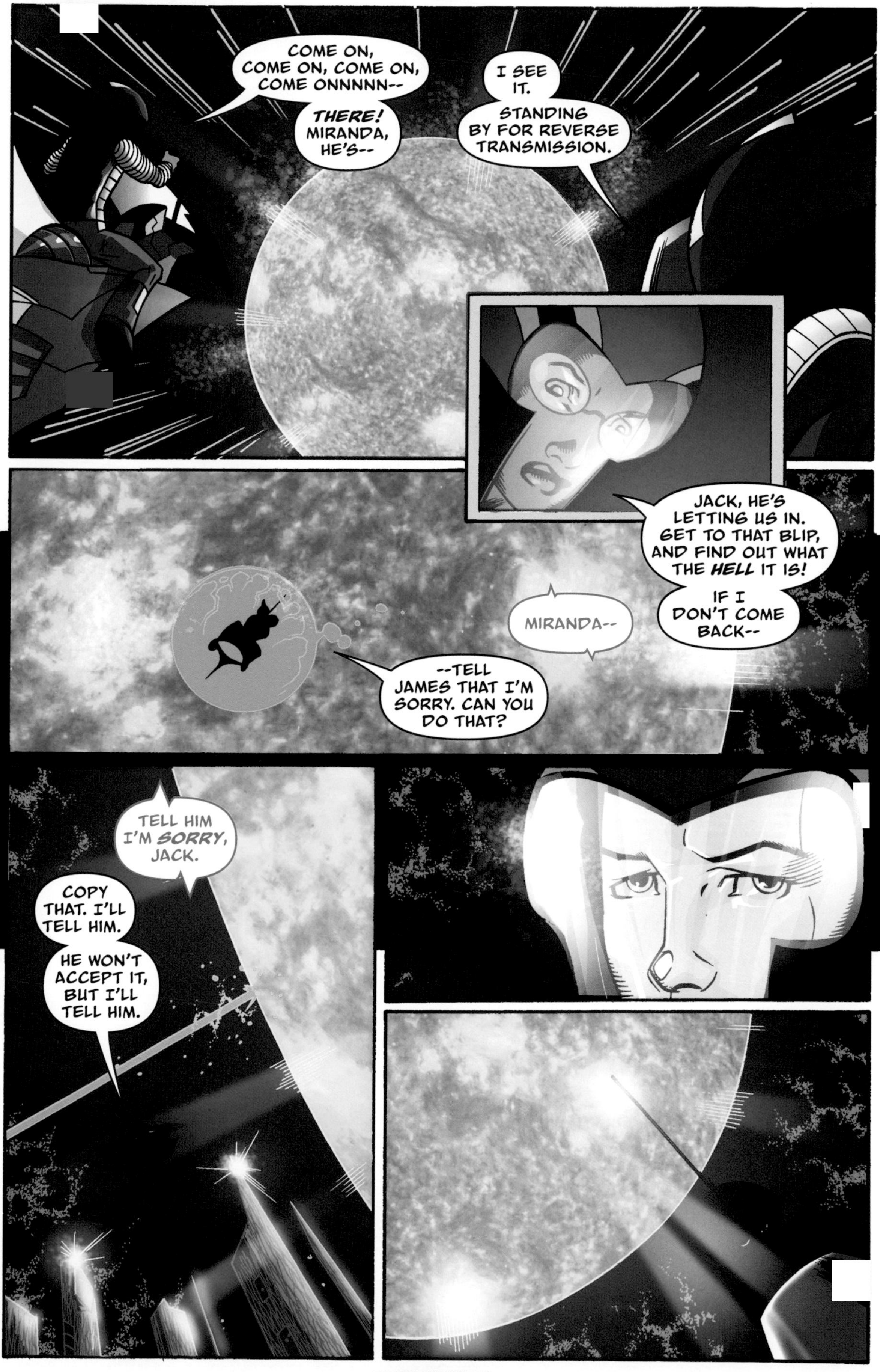
COME ON, COME ON, COME ON, COME ONNNNN--
THERE! MIRANDA, HE'S--
I SEE IT.
STANDING BY FOR REVERSE TRANSMISSION.
JACK, HE'S LETTING US IN. GET TO THAT BLIP, AND FIND OUT WHAT THE HELL IT IS!
IF I DON'T COME BACK--
MIRANDA--
--TELL JAMES THAT I'M SORRY. CAN YOU DO THAT?
TELL HIM I'M SORRY, JACK.
COPY THAT. I'LL TELL HIM.
HE WON'T ACCEPT IT, BUT I'LL TELL HIM.

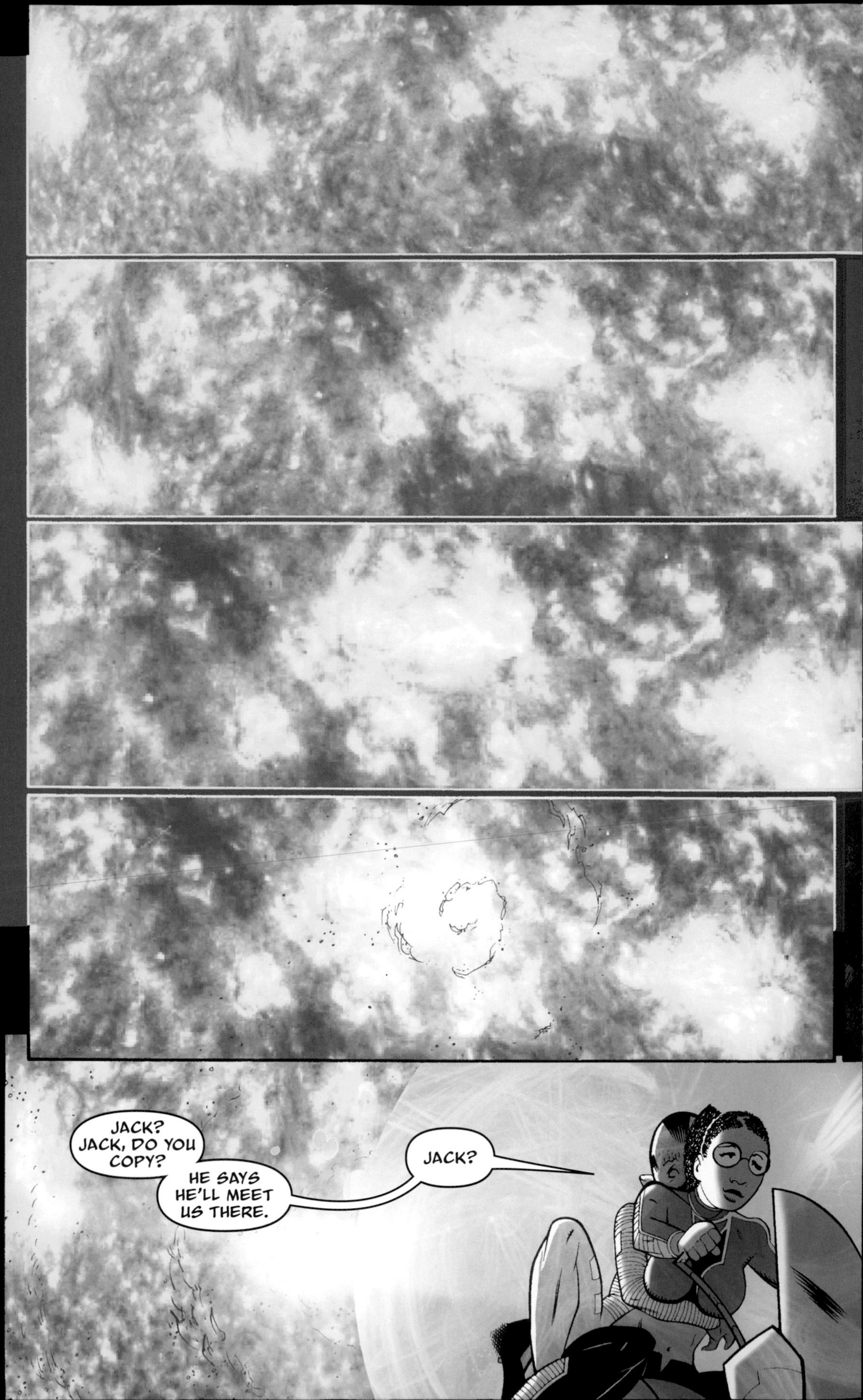
JACK? JACK, DO YOU COPY?
HE SAYS HE'LL MEET US THERE.
JACK?

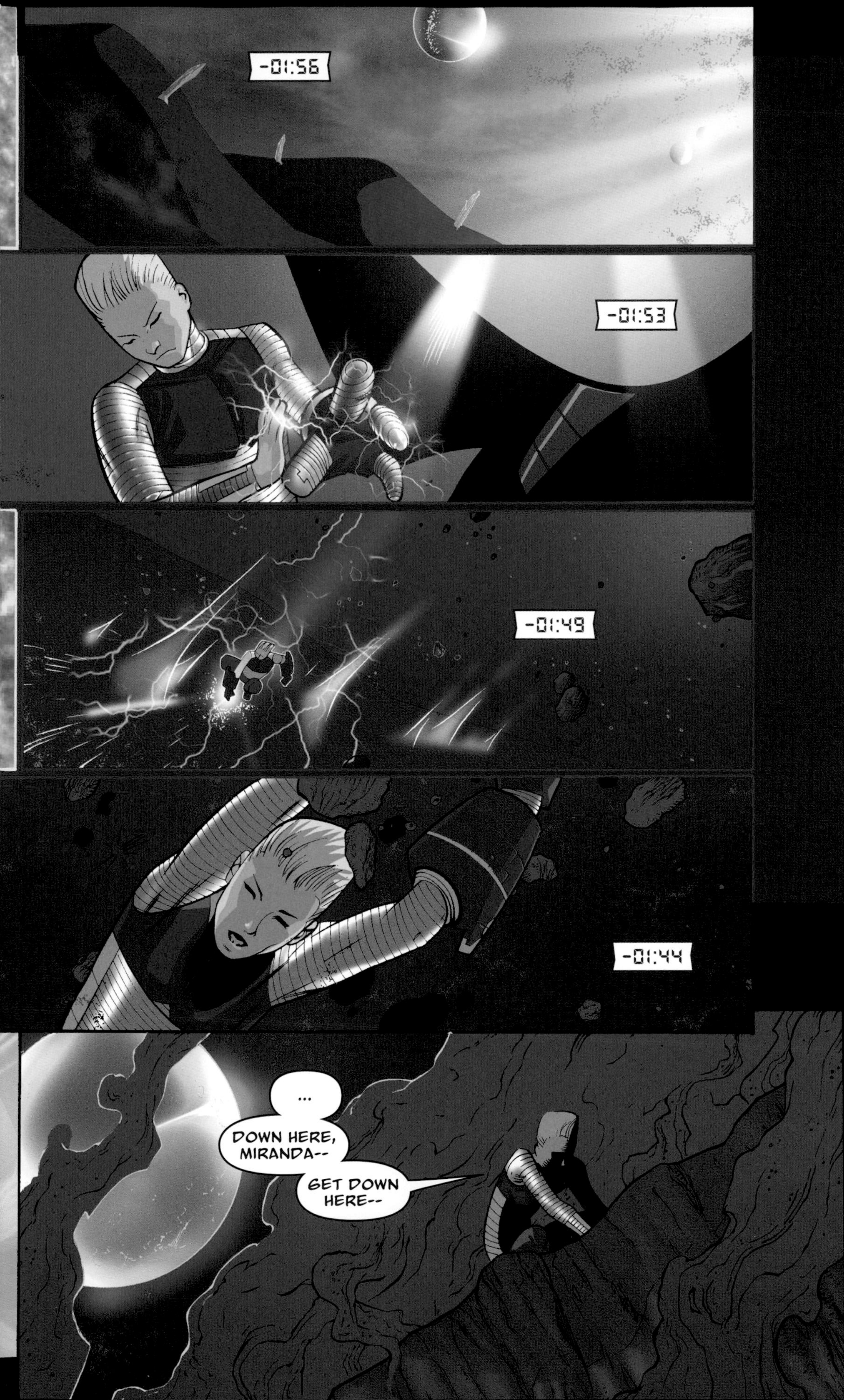
-01:56
-01:53
-01:49
-01:44
...
DOWN HERE, MIRANDA--
GET DOWN HERE--

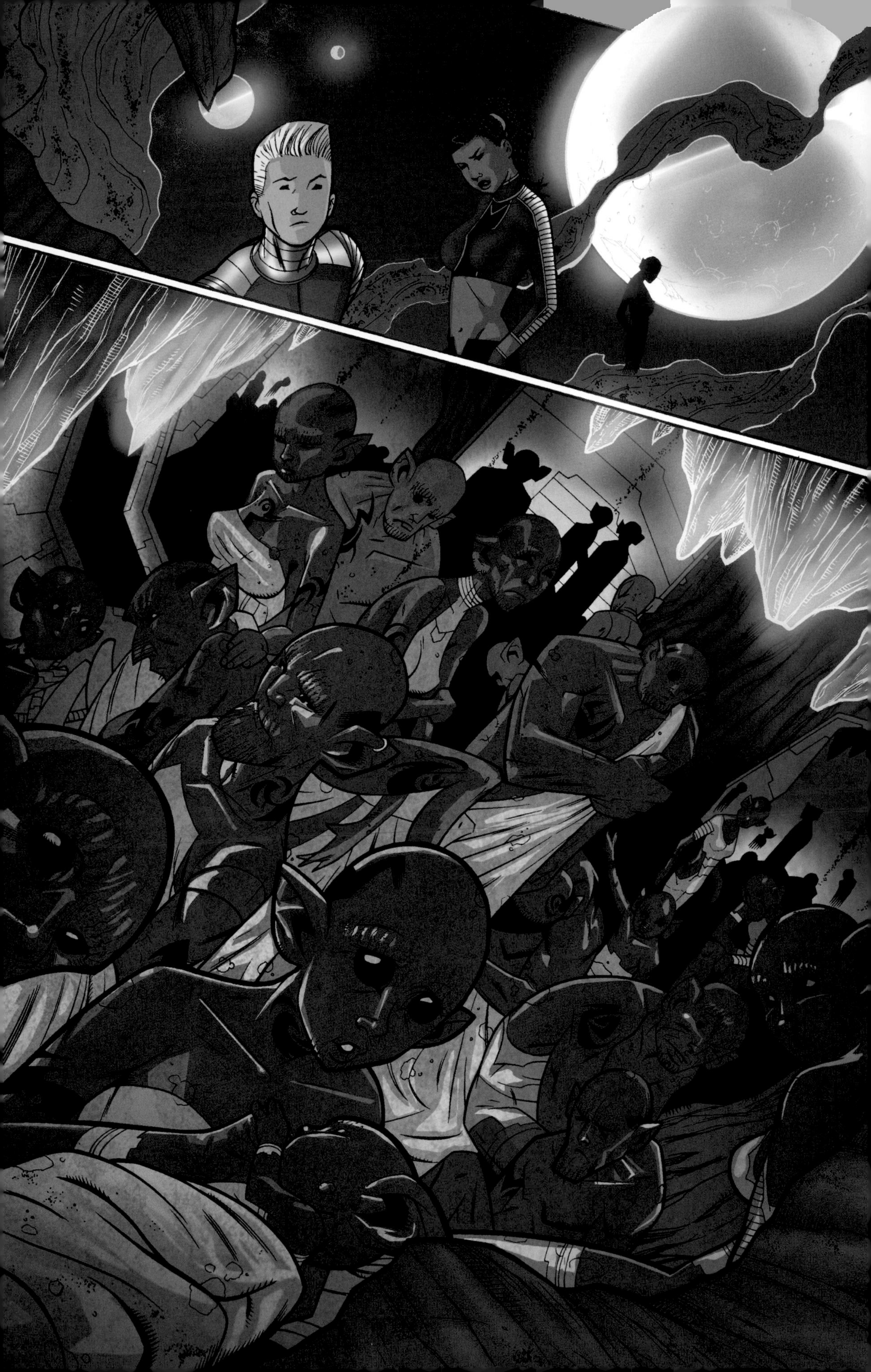

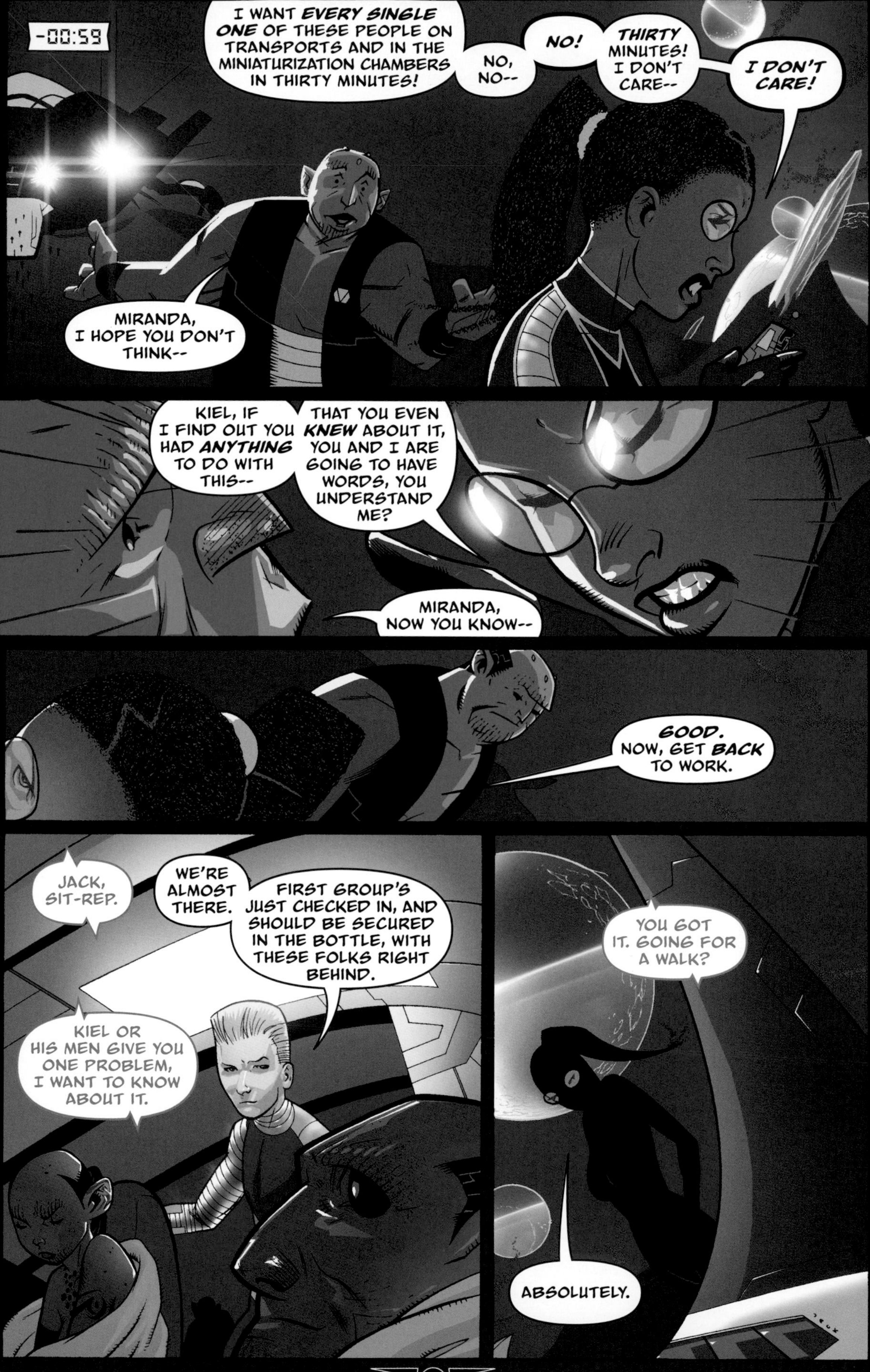
-00:59
I WANT EVERY SINGLE ONE OF THESE PEOPLE ON TRANSPORTS AND IN THE MINIATURIZATION CHAMBERS IN THIRTY MINUTES!
NO, NO--
NO!
THIRTY MINUTES! I DON'T CARE--
I DON'T CARE!
MIRANDA, I HOPE YOU DON'T THINK--
KIEL, IF I FIND OUT YOU HAD ANYTHING TO DO WITH THIS--
THAT YOU EVEN KNEW ABOUT IT, YOU AND I ARE GOING TO HAVE WORDS, YOU UNDERSTAND ME?
MIRANDA, NOW YOU KNOW--
GOOD. NOW, GET BACK TO WORK.
JACK, SIT-REP.
WE'RE ALMOST THERE.
FIRST GROUP'S JUST CHECKED IN, AND SHOULD BE SECURED IN THE BOTTLE, WITH THESE FOLKS RIGHT BEHIND.
KIEL OR HIS MEN GIVE YOU ONE PROBLEM, I WANT TO KNOW ABOUT IT.
YOU GOT IT. GOING FOR A WALK?
ABSOLUTELY.

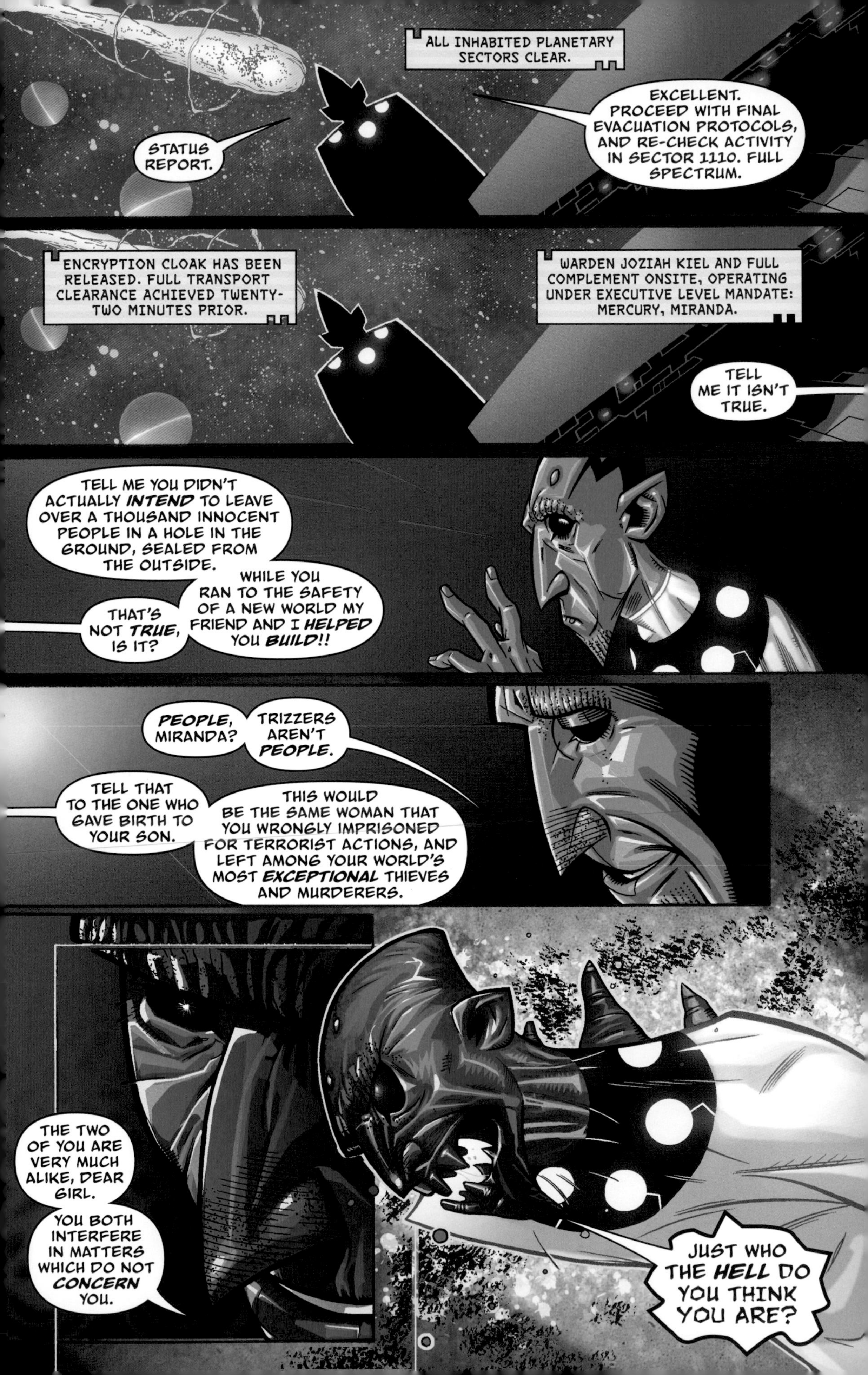
ALL INHABITED PLANETARY SECTORS CLEAR.
STATUS REPORT.
EXCELLENT. PROCEED WITH FINAL EVACUATION PROTOCOLS, AND RE-CHECK ACTIVITY IN SECTOR 1110. FULL SPECTRUM.
ENCRYPTION CLOAK HAS BEEN RELEASED. FULL TRANSPORT CLEARANCE ACHIEVED TWENTY-TWO MINUTES PRIOR.
WARDEN JOZIAH KIEL AND FULL COMPLEMENT ONSITE, OPERATING UNDER EXECUTIVE LEVEL MANDATE: MERCURY, MIRANDA.
TELL ME IT ISN'T TRUE.
TELL ME YOU DIDN'T ACTUALLY *INTEND* TO LEAVE OVER A THOUSAND INNOCENT PEOPLE IN A HOLE IN THE GROUND, SEALED FROM THE OUTSIDE.
THAT'S NOT *TRUE*, IS IT?
WHILE YOU RAN TO THE SAFETY OF A NEW WORLD MY FRIEND AND I *HELPED* YOU *BUILD*!!
PEOPLE, MIRANDA?
TRIZZERS AREN'T *PEOPLE*.
TELL THAT TO THE ONE WHO GAVE BIRTH TO YOUR SON.
THIS WOULD BE THE SAME WOMAN THAT YOU WRONGLY IMPRISONED FOR TERRORIST ACTIONS, AND LEFT AMONG YOUR WORLD'S MOST *EXCEPTIONAL* THIEVES AND MURDERERS.
THE TWO OF YOU ARE VERY MUCH ALIKE, DEAR GIRL.
YOU BOTH INTERFERE IN MATTERS WHICH DO NOT *CONCERN* YOU.
JUST WHO THE *HELL* DO YOU THINK YOU ARE?

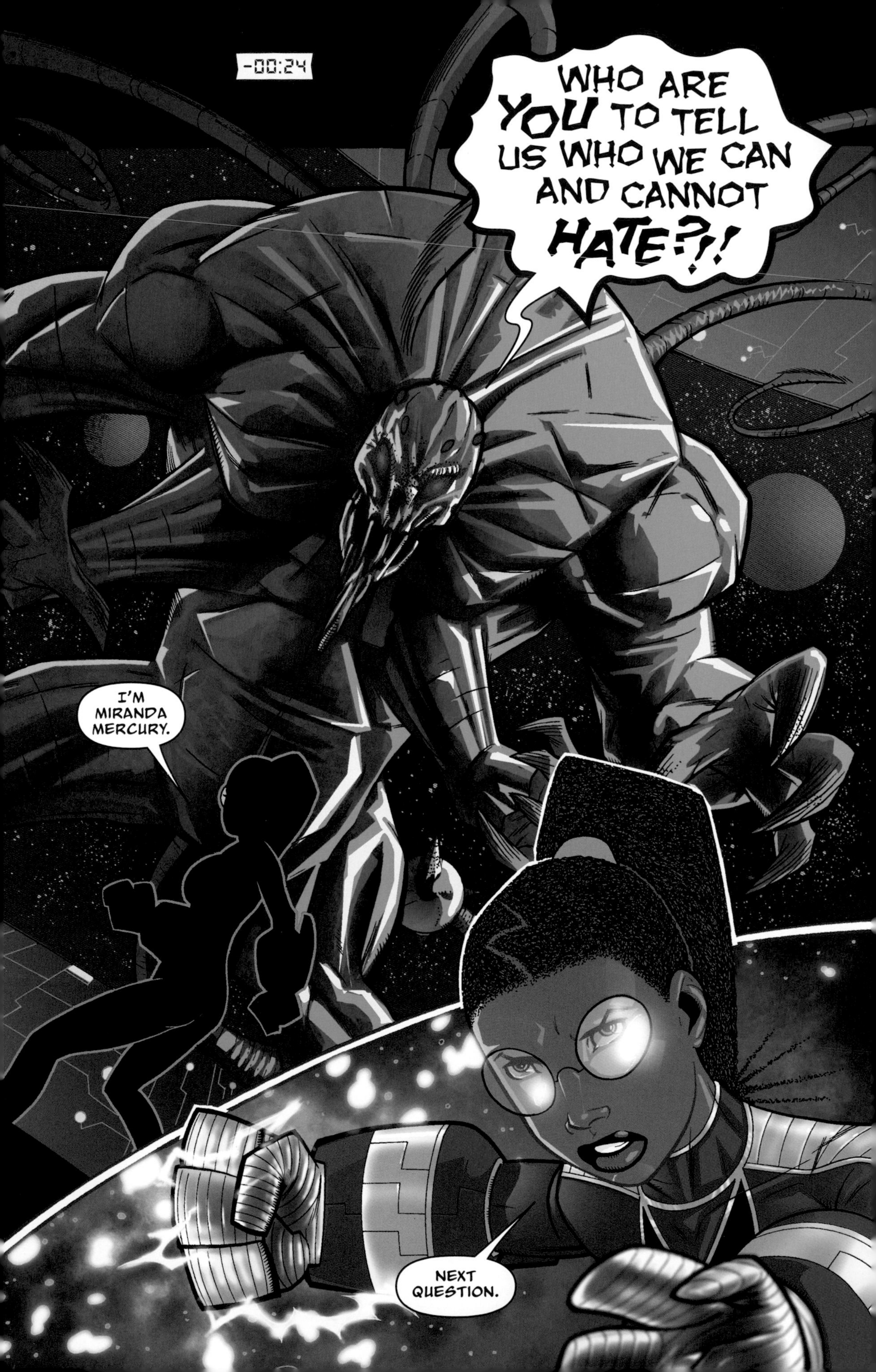
-00:24
WHO ARE YOU TO TELL US WHO WE CAN AND CANNOT HATE?!
I'M MIRANDA MERCURY.
NEXT QUESTION.

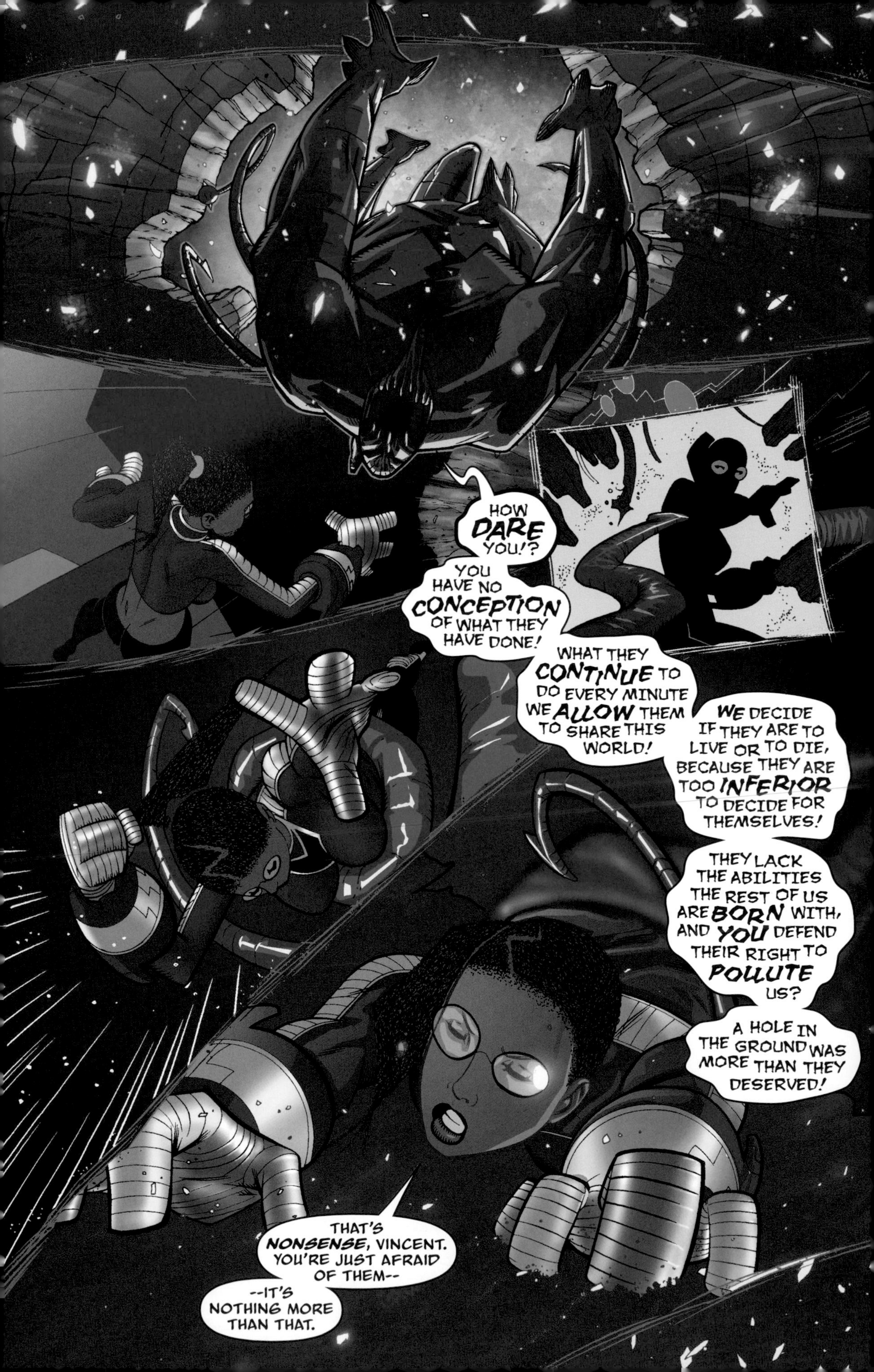
HOW DARE YOU!?
YOU HAVE NO CONCEPTION OF WHAT THEY HAVE DONE!
WHAT THEY CONTINUE TO DO EVERY MINUTE WE ALLOW THEM TO SHARE THIS WORLD!
WE DECIDE IF THEY ARE TO LIVE OR TO DIE, BECAUSE THEY ARE TOO INFERIOR TO DECIDE FOR THEMSELVES!
THEY LACK THE ABILITIES THE REST OF US ARE BORN WITH, AND YOU DEFEND THEIR RIGHT TO POLLUTE US?
A HOLE IN THE GROUND WAS MORE THAN THEY DESERVED!
THAT'S NONSENSE, VINCENT. YOU'RE JUST AFRAID OF THEM--
--IT'S NOTHING MORE THAN THAT.

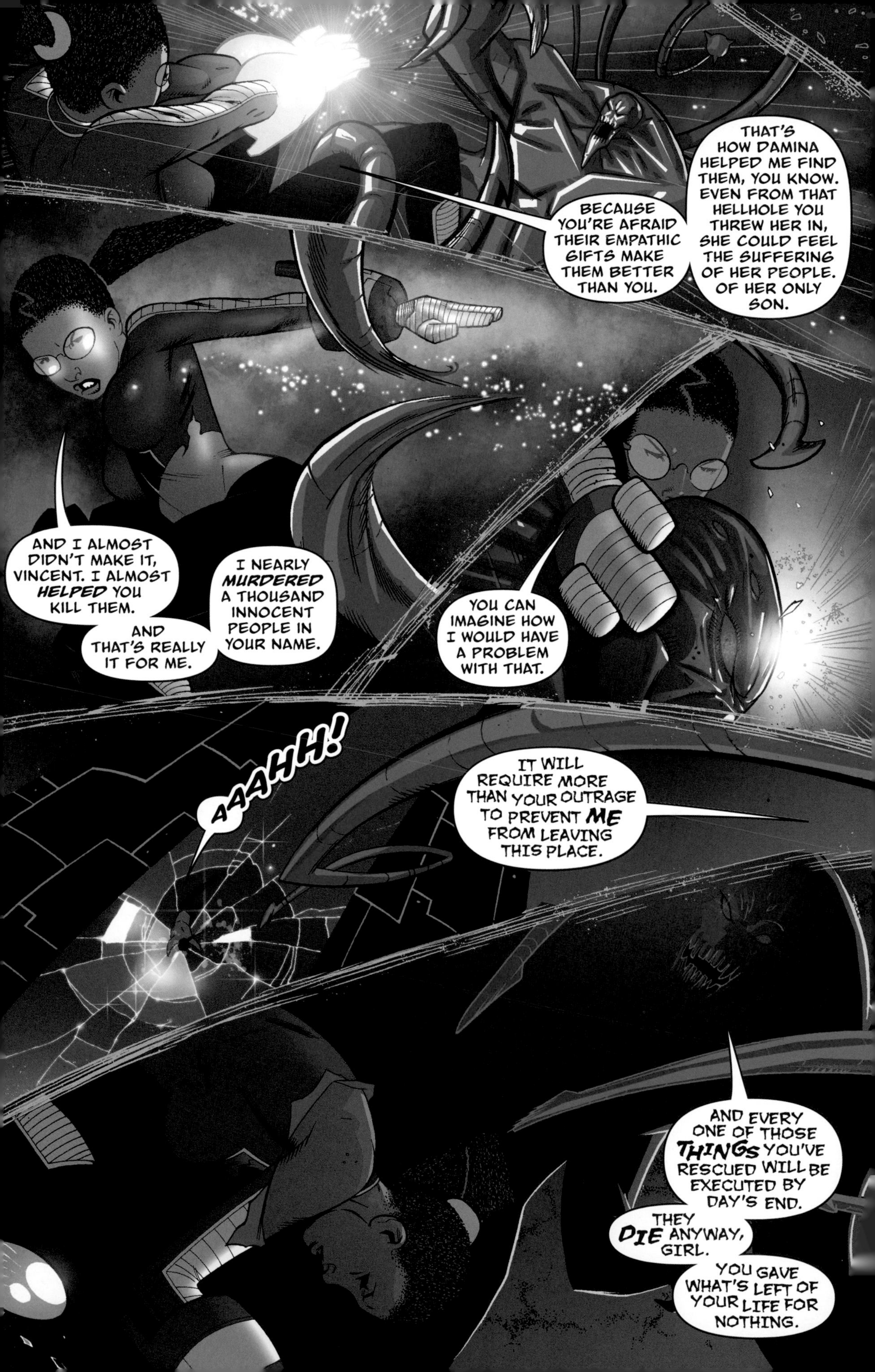
BECAUSE YOU'RE AFRAID THEIR EMPATHIC GIFTS MAKE THEM BETTER THAN YOU.
THAT'S HOW DAMINA HELPED ME FIND THEM, YOU KNOW. EVEN FROM THAT HELLHOLE YOU THREW HER IN, SHE COULD FEEL THE SUFFERING OF HER PEOPLE. OF HER ONLY SON.
AND I ALMOST DIDN'T MAKE IT, VINCENT. I ALMOST HELPED YOU KILL THEM.
AND THAT'S REALLY IT FOR ME.
I NEARLY MURDERED A THOUSAND INNOCENT PEOPLE IN YOUR NAME.
YOU CAN IMAGINE HOW I WOULD HAVE A PROBLEM WITH THAT.
AAAHH!
IT WILL REQUIRE MORE THAN YOUR OUTRAGE TO PREVENT ME FROM LEAVING THIS PLACE.
AND EVERY ONE OF THOSE THINGS YOU'VE RESCUED WILL BE EXECUTED BY DAY'S END.
THEY DIE ANYWAY, GIRL.
YOU GAVE WHAT'S LEFT OF YOUR LIFE FOR NOTHING.

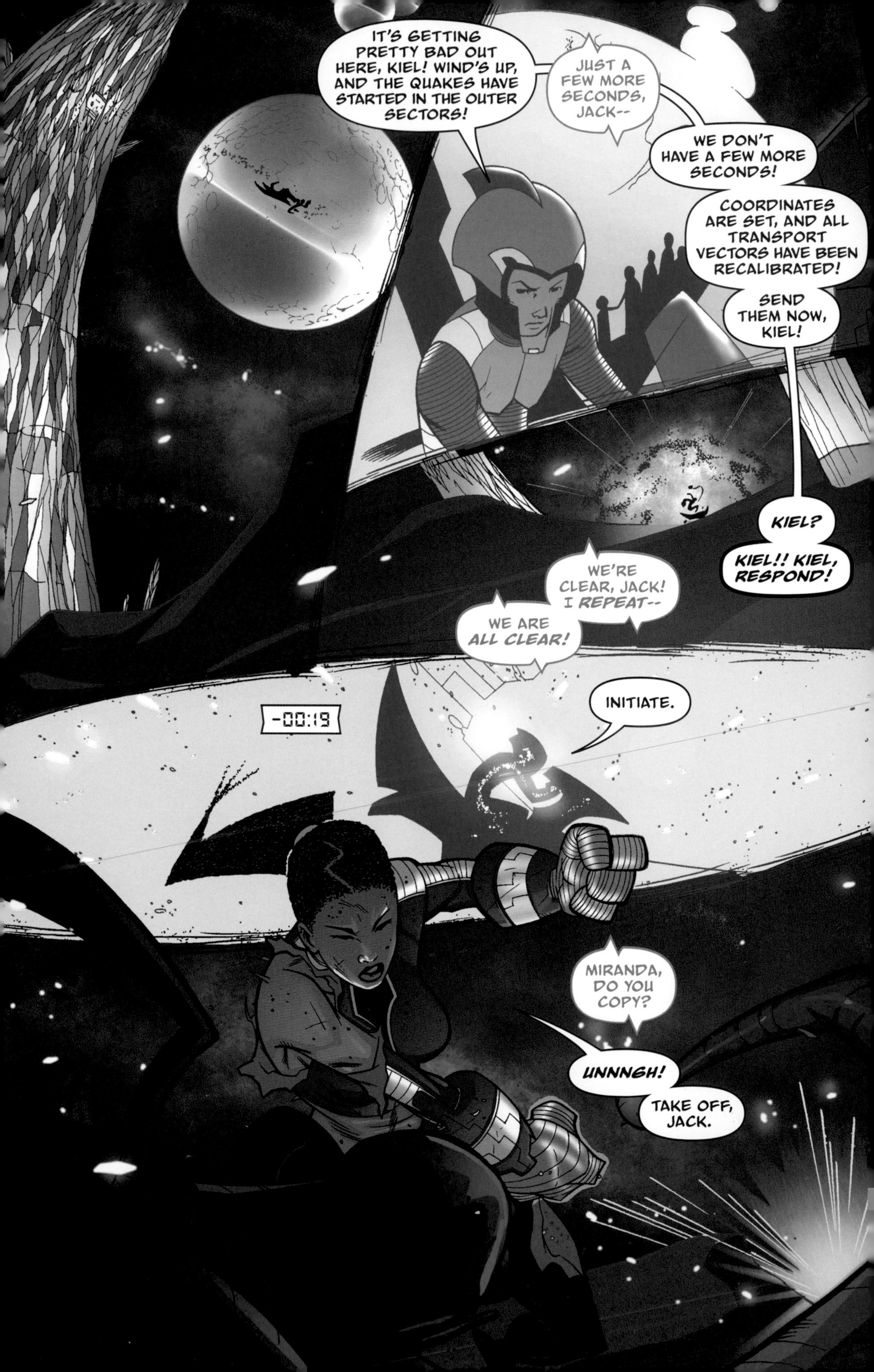
IT'S GETTING PRETTY BAD OUT HERE, KIEL! WIND'S UP, AND THE QUAKES HAVE STARTED IN THE OUTER SECTORS!
JUST A FEW MORE SECONDS, JACK--
WE DON'T HAVE A FEW MORE SECONDS!
COORDINATES ARE SET, AND ALL TRANSPORT VECTORS HAVE BEEN RECALIBRATED!
SEND THEM NOW, KIEL!
KIEL?
KIEL!! KIEL, RESPOND!
WE'RE CLEAR, JACK! I REPEAT--
WE ARE ALL CLEAR!
-00:19
INITIATE.
MIRANDA, DO YOU COPY?
UNNNGH!
TAKE OFF, JACK.

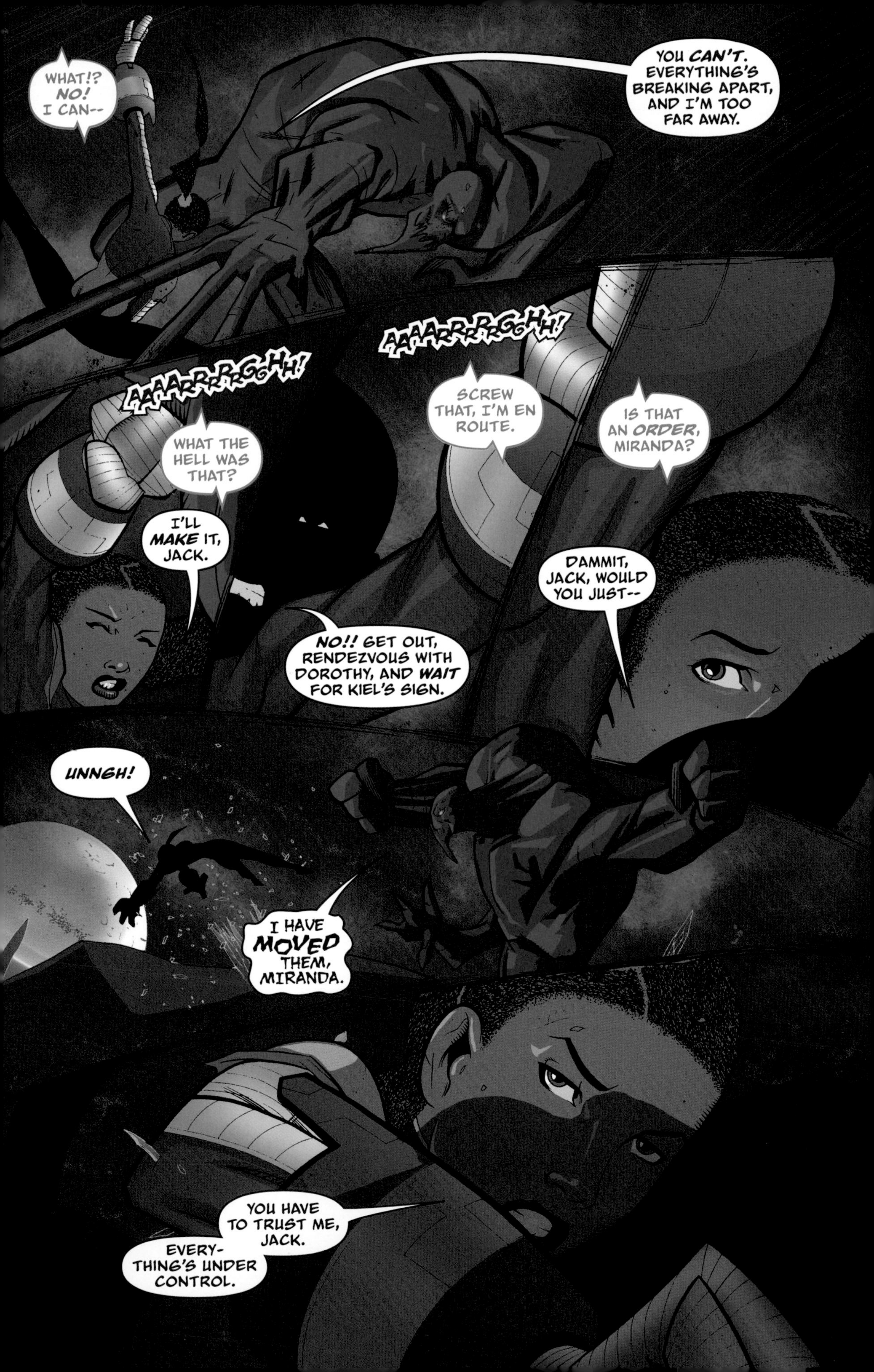
WHAT!? NO! I CAN--
YOU CAN'T. EVERYTHING'S BREAKING APART, AND I'M TOO FAR AWAY.
AAAARRRRRGGHH!
WHAT THE HELL WAS THAT?
I'LL MAKE IT, JACK.
AAAARRRRRGGHH!
SCREW THAT, I'M EN ROUTE.
NO!! GET OUT, RENDEZVOUS WITH DOROTHY, AND WAIT FOR KIEL'S SIGN.
IS THAT AN ORDER, MIRANDA?
DAMMIT, JACK, WOULD YOU JUST--
UNNGH!
I HAVE MOVED THEM, MIRANDA.
YOU HAVE TO TRUST ME, JACK.
EVERY-THING'S UNDER CONTROL.

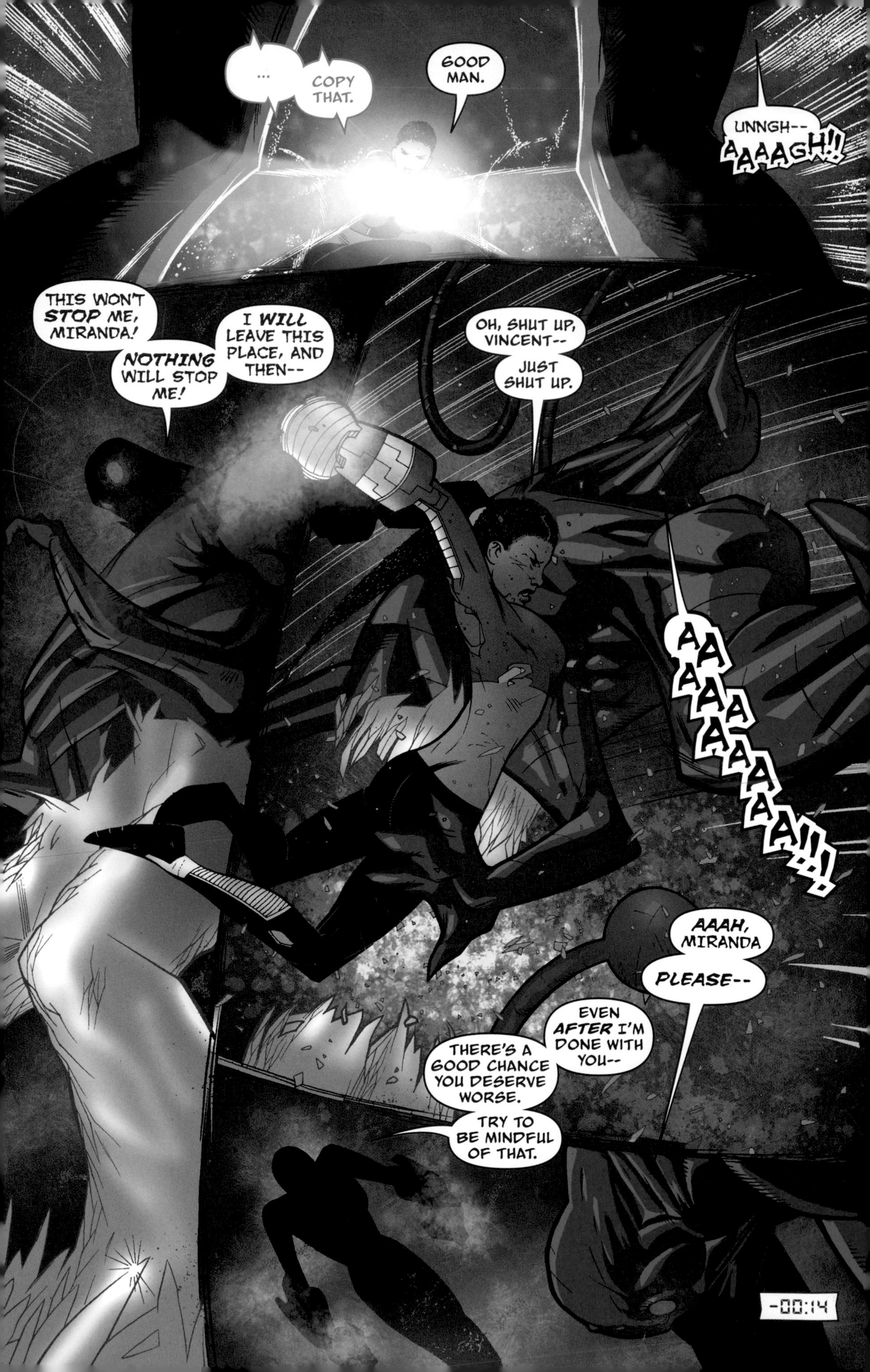
...
COPY THAT.
GOOD MAN.
UNNGH--AAAAGH!!
THIS WON'T STOP ME, MIRANDA!
NOTHING WILL STOP ME!
I WILL LEAVE THIS PLACE, AND THEN--
OH, SHUT UP, VINCENT--
JUST SHUT UP.
AAAAAAAAAA!!!
AAAH, MIRANDA
PLEASE--
EVEN AFTER I'M DONE WITH YOU--
THERE'S A GOOD CHANCE YOU DESERVE WORSE.
TRY TO BE MINDFUL OF THAT.
-00:14

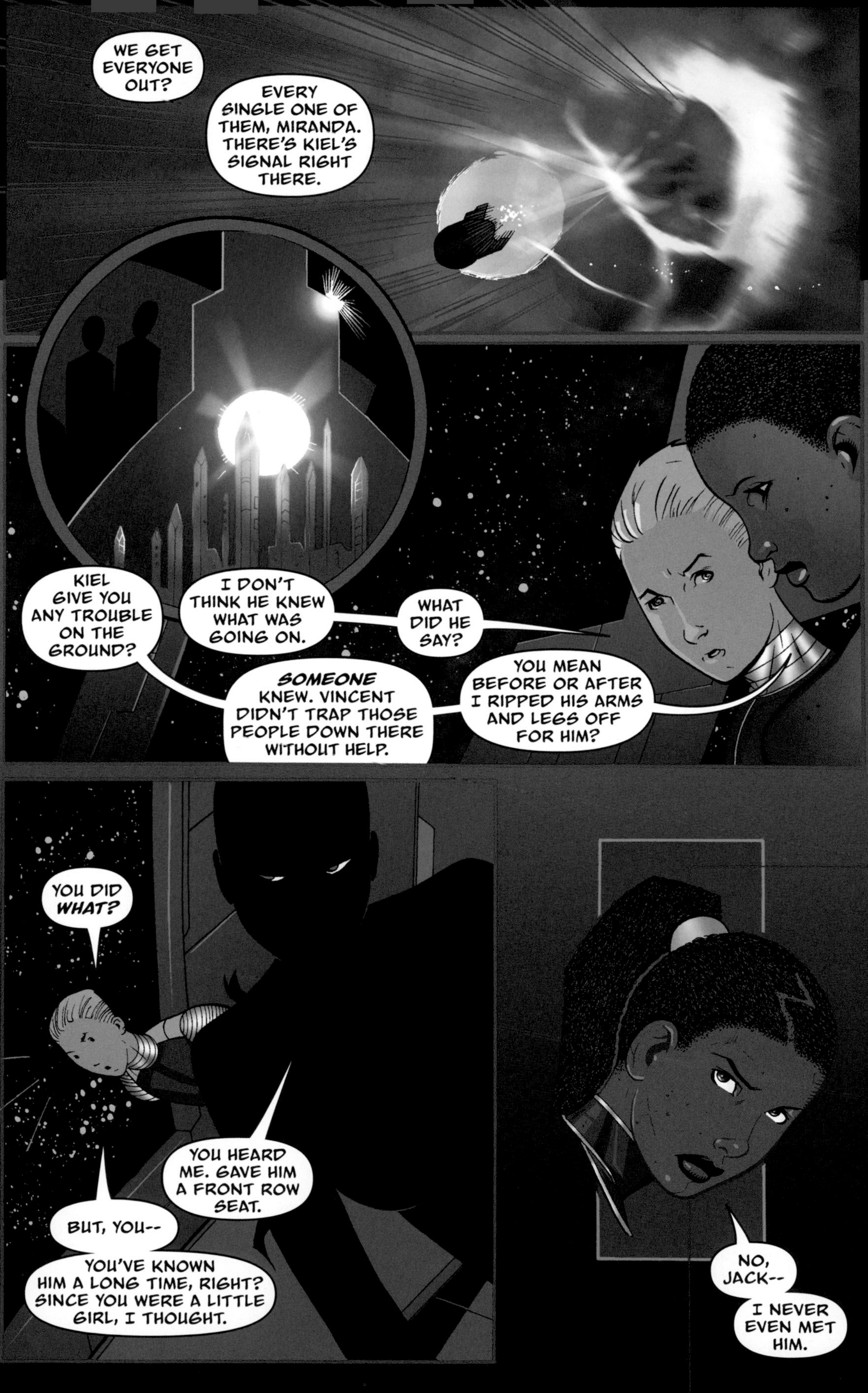
WE GET EVERYONE OUT?
EVERY SINGLE ONE OF THEM, MIRANDA. THERE'S KIEL'S SIGNAL RIGHT THERE.
KIEL GIVE YOU ANY TROUBLE ON THE GROUND?
I DON'T THINK HE KNEW WHAT WAS GOING ON.
WHAT DID HE SAY?
SOMEONE KNEW. VINCENT DIDN'T TRAP THOSE PEOPLE DOWN THERE WITHOUT HELP.
YOU MEAN BEFORE OR AFTER I RIPPED HIS ARMS AND LEGS OFF FOR HIM?
YOU DID *WHAT?*
YOU HEARD ME. GAVE HIM A FRONT ROW SEAT.
BUT, YOU--
YOU'VE KNOWN HIM A LONG TIME, RIGHT? SINCE YOU WERE A LITTLE GIRL, I THOUGHT.
NO, JACK--
I NEVER EVEN MET HIM.

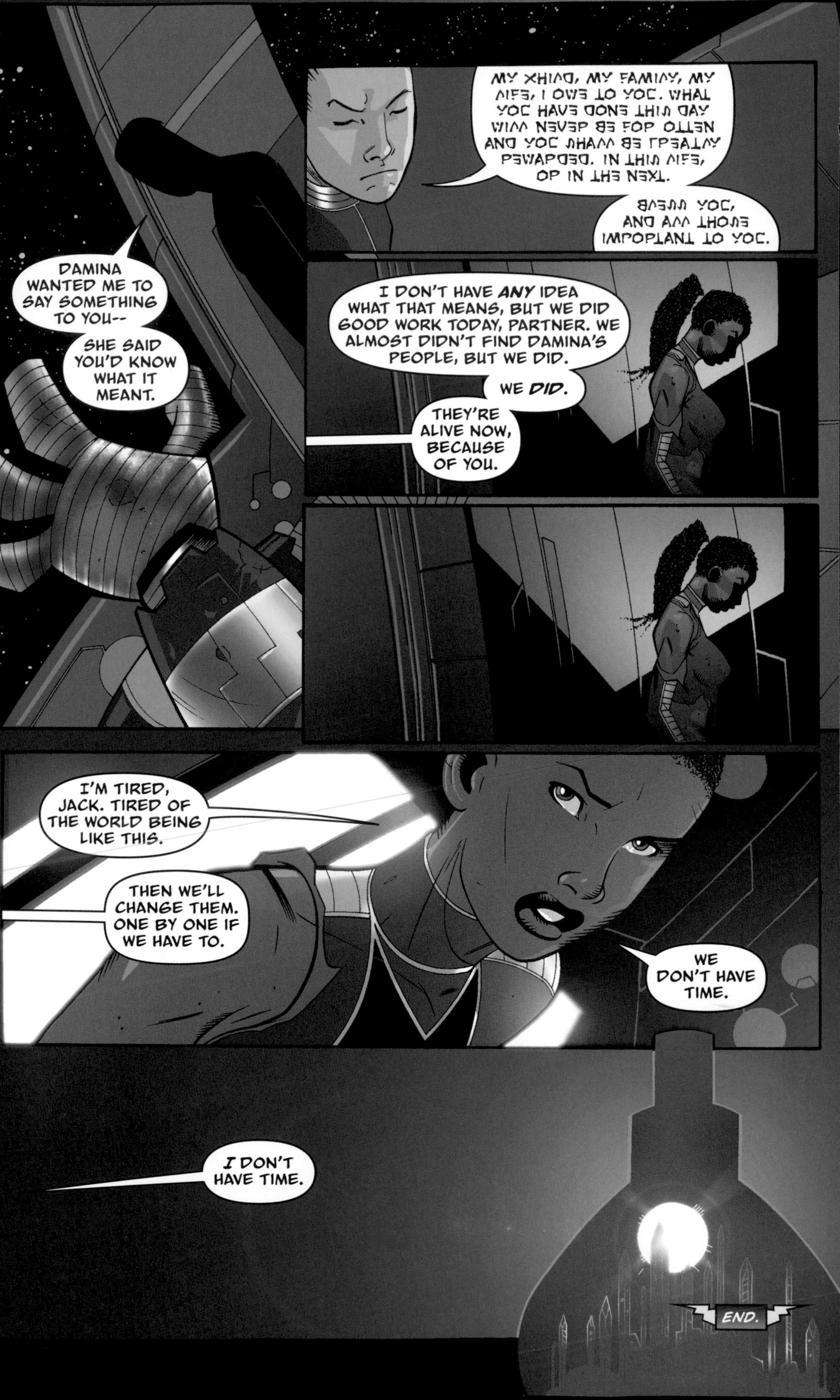

MY XHIAD, MY FAMIAY, MY AIFE, I OWE TO YOC. WHAT YOC HAVE DONE THIS DAY WIAA NEVEP BE FOP OTTEN AND YOC SHAAA BE PEATAY PEWAPDED. IN THIS AIFE, OP IN THE NEXT.
BAESS YOC, AND AAA THOSE IMPOPTANT TO YOC.
DAMINA WANTED ME TO SAY SOMETHING TO YOU--
SHE SAID YOU'D KNOW WHAT IT MEANT.
I DON'T HAVE ANY IDEA WHAT THAT MEANS, BUT WE DID GOOD WORK TODAY, PARTNER. WE ALMOST DIDN'T FIND DAMINA'S PEOPLE, BUT WE DID.
WE DID.
THEY'RE ALIVE NOW, BECAUSE OF YOU.
I'M TIRED, JACK. TIRED OF THE WORLD BEING LIKE THIS.
THEN WE'LL CHANGE THEM. ONE BY ONE IF WE HAVE TO.
WE DON'T HAVE TIME.
I DON'T HAVE TIME.
END.

AN AGE-OLD ALLIANCE BETWEEN MAN AND DINOSAUR IS UNDER ATTACK!

THOUGH THE TWO SPECIES HAVE LIVED IN HARMONY ON THE PLANET PALEO FOR EONS A WAVE OF XENOPHOBIA IS SPREADING THROUGHOUT THE POPULACE. SUICIDE BOMBINGS AND POLITICAL UNREST HAVE BECOME THE NORM AND PEOPLE ARE AFRAID TO LEAVE THEIR HOMES. YET THE QUESTIONS REMAIN---

WHY IS IT HAPPENING HERE?

WHY IS IT HAPPENING NOW?

EPISODE 297

MIRANDA MERCURY
AND THE RAIDERS OF ___ TIME!

BRANDON THOMAS

LEE FERGUSON

MARC DEERING

MATTY RYAN

JORDAN BOYD

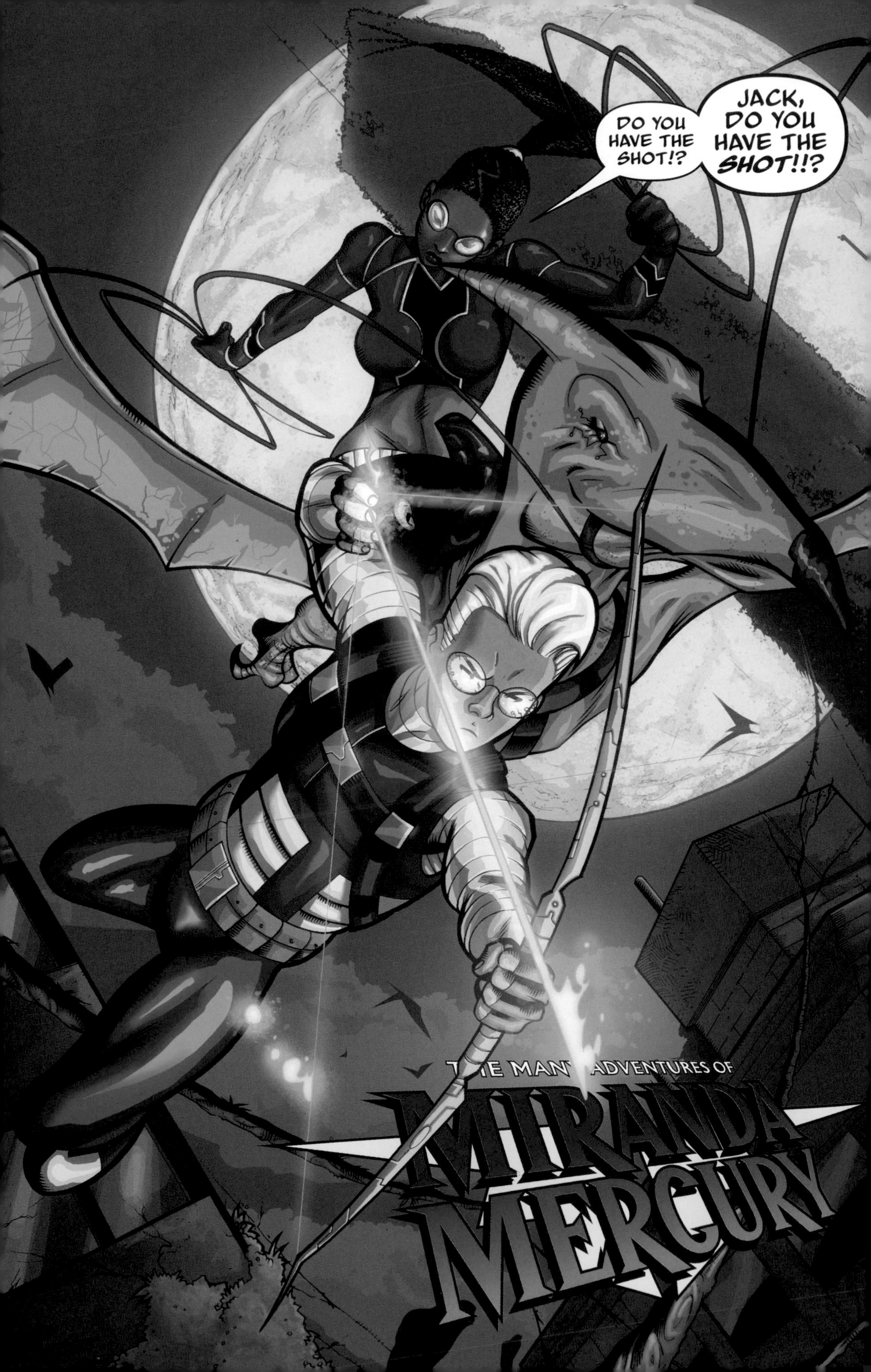
DO YOU HAVE THE SHOT!?
JACK, DO YOU HAVE THE SHOT!!?
THE MANY ADVENTURES OF
MIRANDA MERCURY

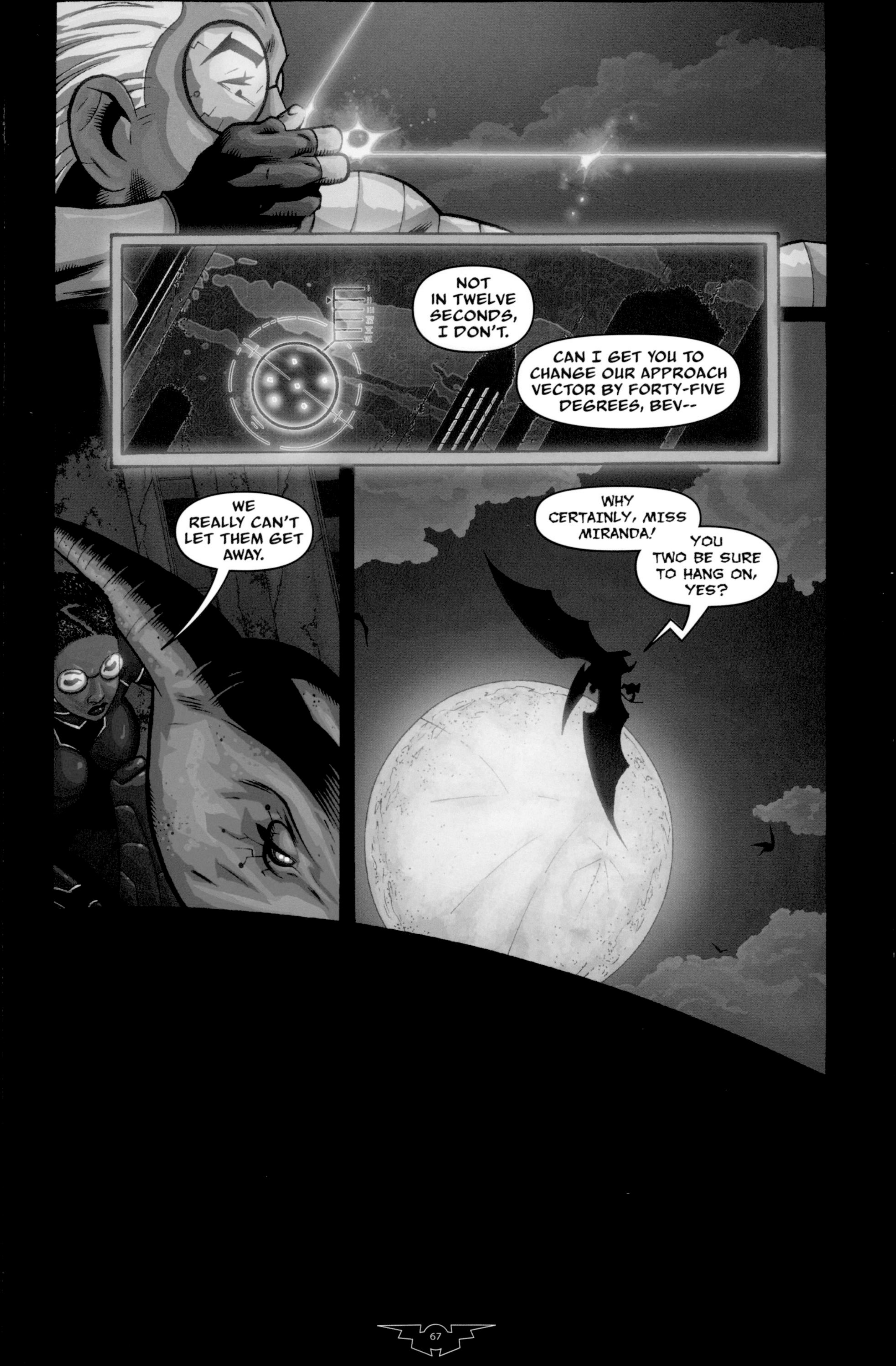
NOT IN TWELVE SECONDS, I DON'T.
CAN I GET YOU TO CHANGE OUR APPROACH VECTOR BY FORTY-FIVE DEGREES, BEV--
WE REALLY CAN'T LET THEM GET AWAY.
WHY CERTAINLY, MISS MIRANDA!
YOU TWO BE SURE TO HANG ON, YES?

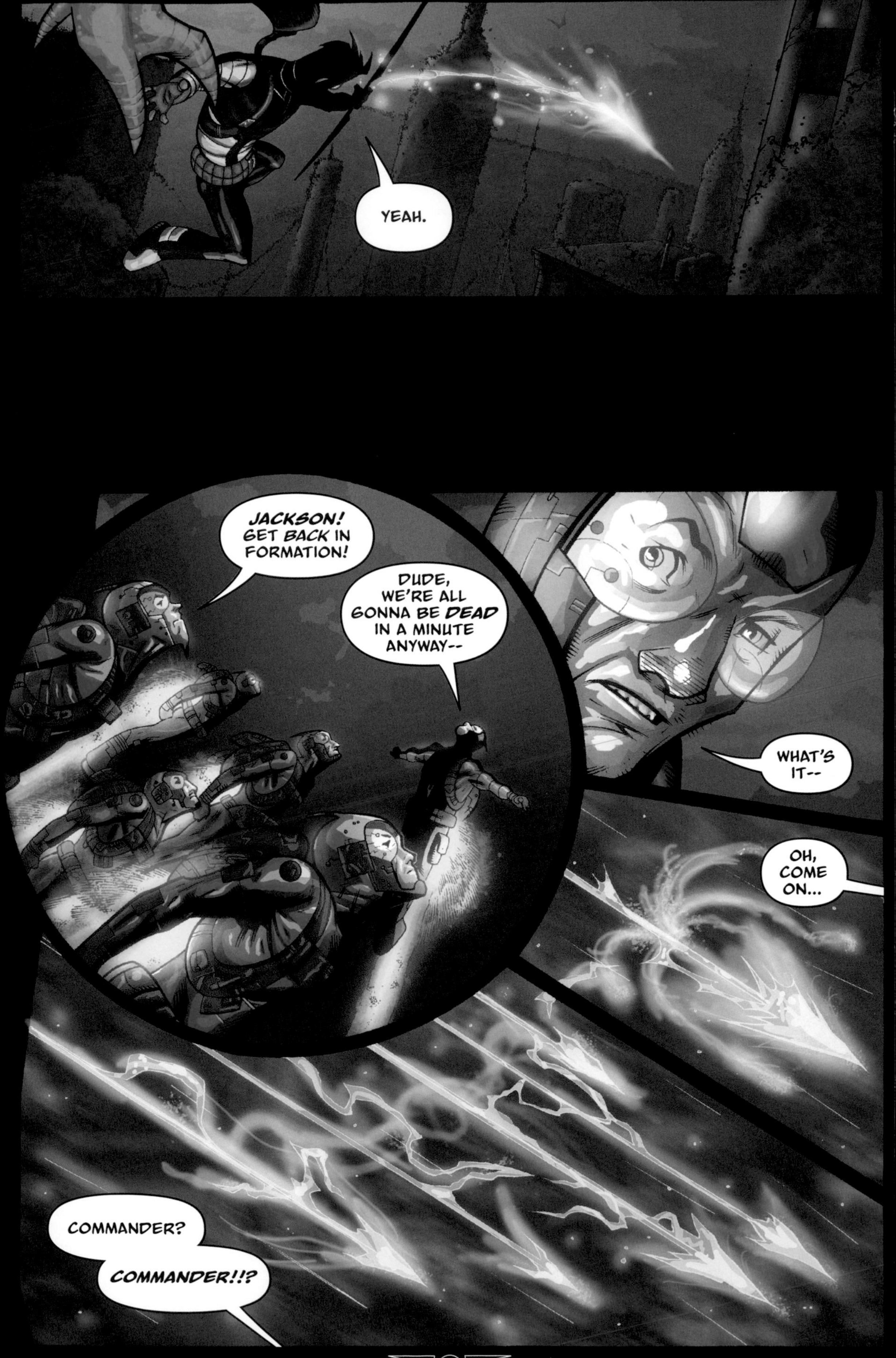

YEAH.
JACKSON! GET BACK IN FORMATION!
DUDE, WE'RE ALL GONNA BE DEAD IN A MINUTE ANYWAY--
WHAT'S IT--
OH, COME ON...
COMMANDER?
COMMANDER!!?

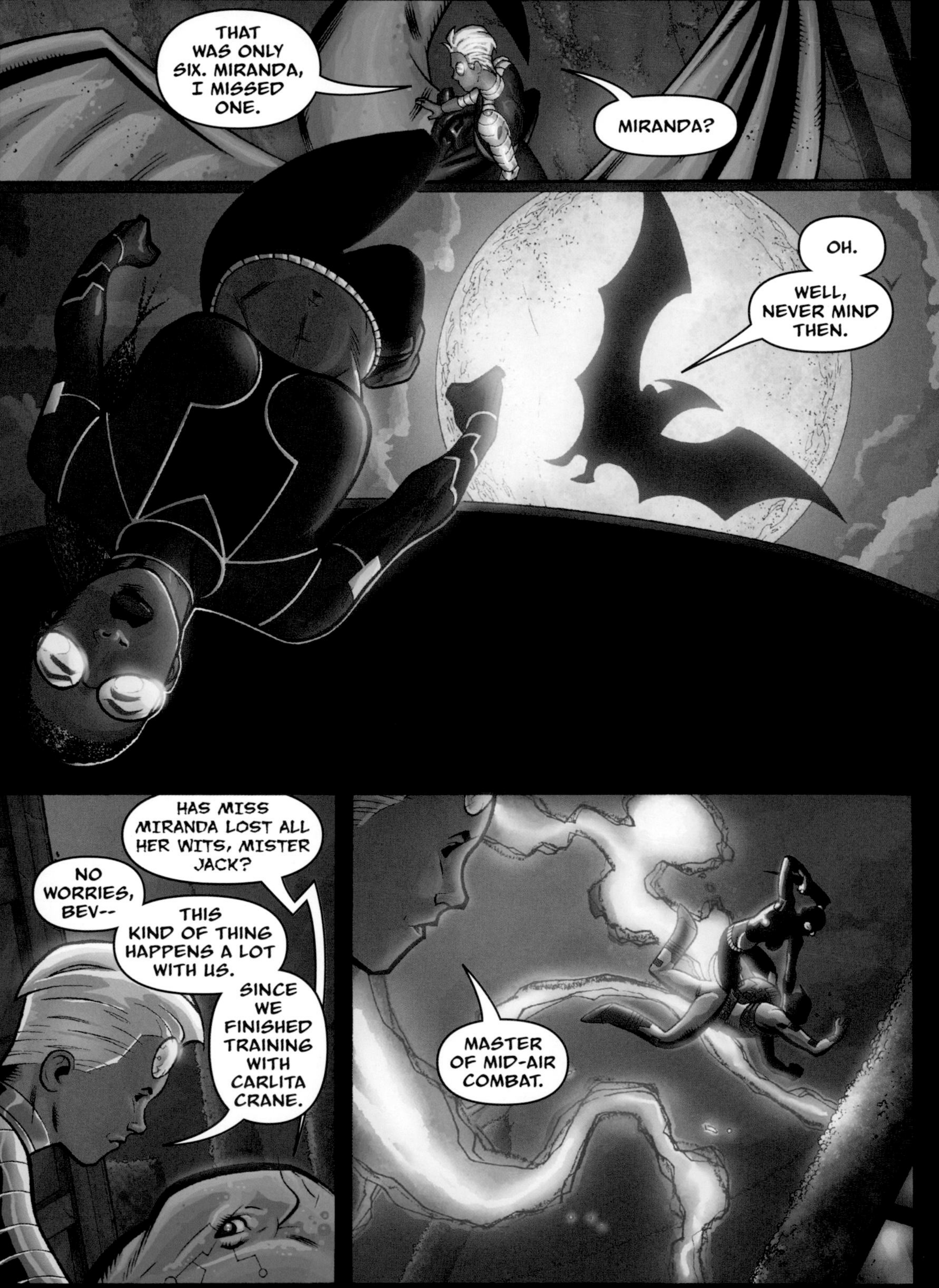
THAT WAS ONLY SIX. MIRANDA, I MISSED ONE.
MIRANDA?
OH.
WELL, NEVER MIND THEN.
HAS MISS MIRANDA LOST ALL HER WITS, MISTER JACK?
NO WORRIES, BEV--
THIS KIND OF THING HAPPENS A LOT WITH US.
SINCE WE FINISHED TRAINING WITH CARLITA CRANE.
MASTER OF MID-AIR COMBAT.

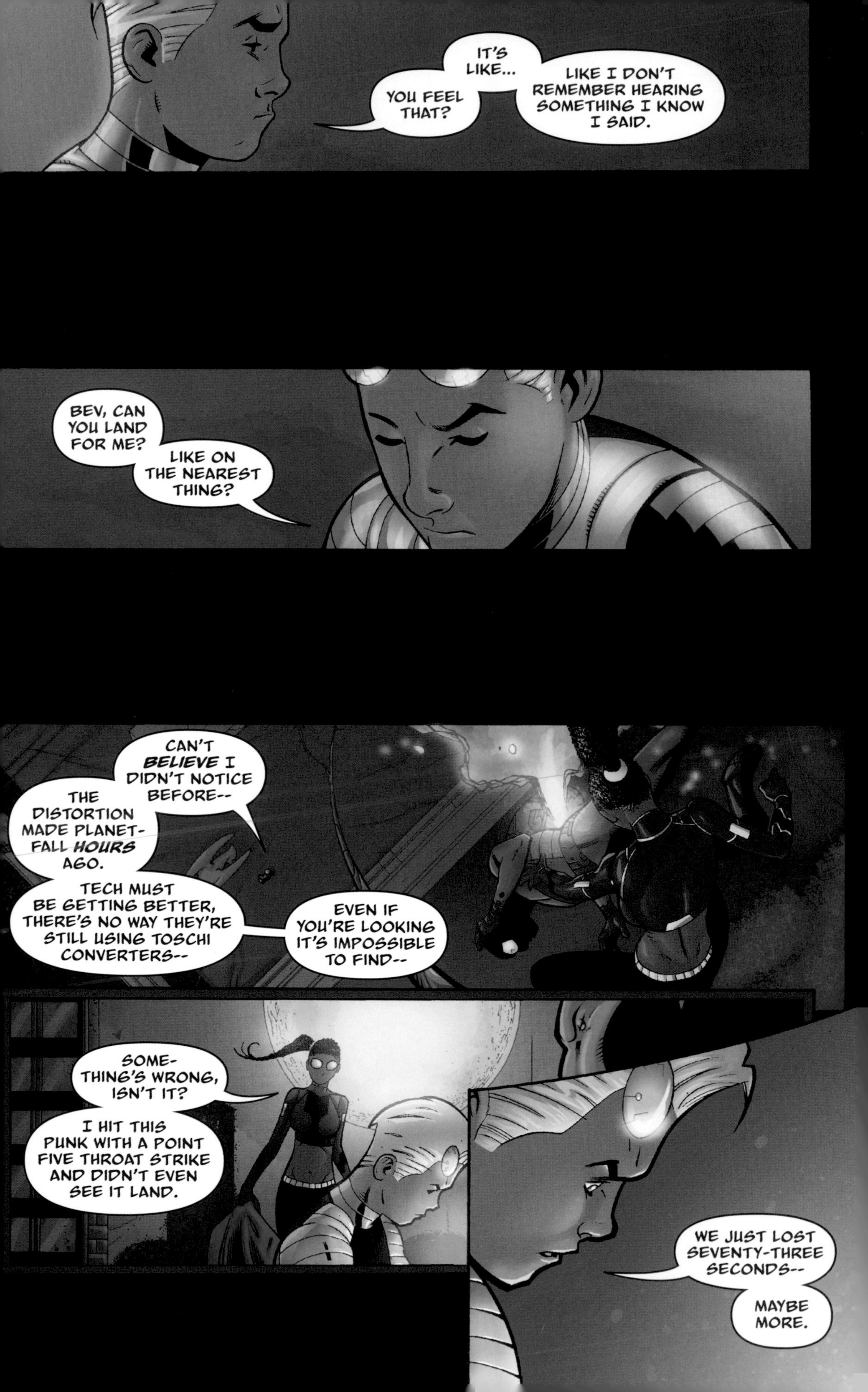
YOU FEEL THAT?
IT'S LIKE...
LIKE I DON'T REMEMBER HEARING SOMETHING I KNOW I SAID.
BEV, CAN YOU LAND FOR ME?
LIKE ON THE NEAREST THING?
CAN'T *BELIEVE* I DIDN'T NOTICE BEFORE--
THE DISTORTION MADE PLANET-FALL *HOURS* AGO.
TECH MUST BE GETTING BETTER, THERE'S NO WAY THEY'RE STILL USING TOSCHI CONVERTERS--
EVEN IF YOU'RE LOOKING IT'S IMPOSSIBLE TO FIND--
SOME-THING'S WRONG, ISN'T IT?
I HIT THIS PUNK WITH A POINT FIVE THROAT STRIKE AND DIDN'T EVEN SEE IT LAND.
WE JUST LOST SEVENTY-THREE SECONDS--
MAYBE MORE.

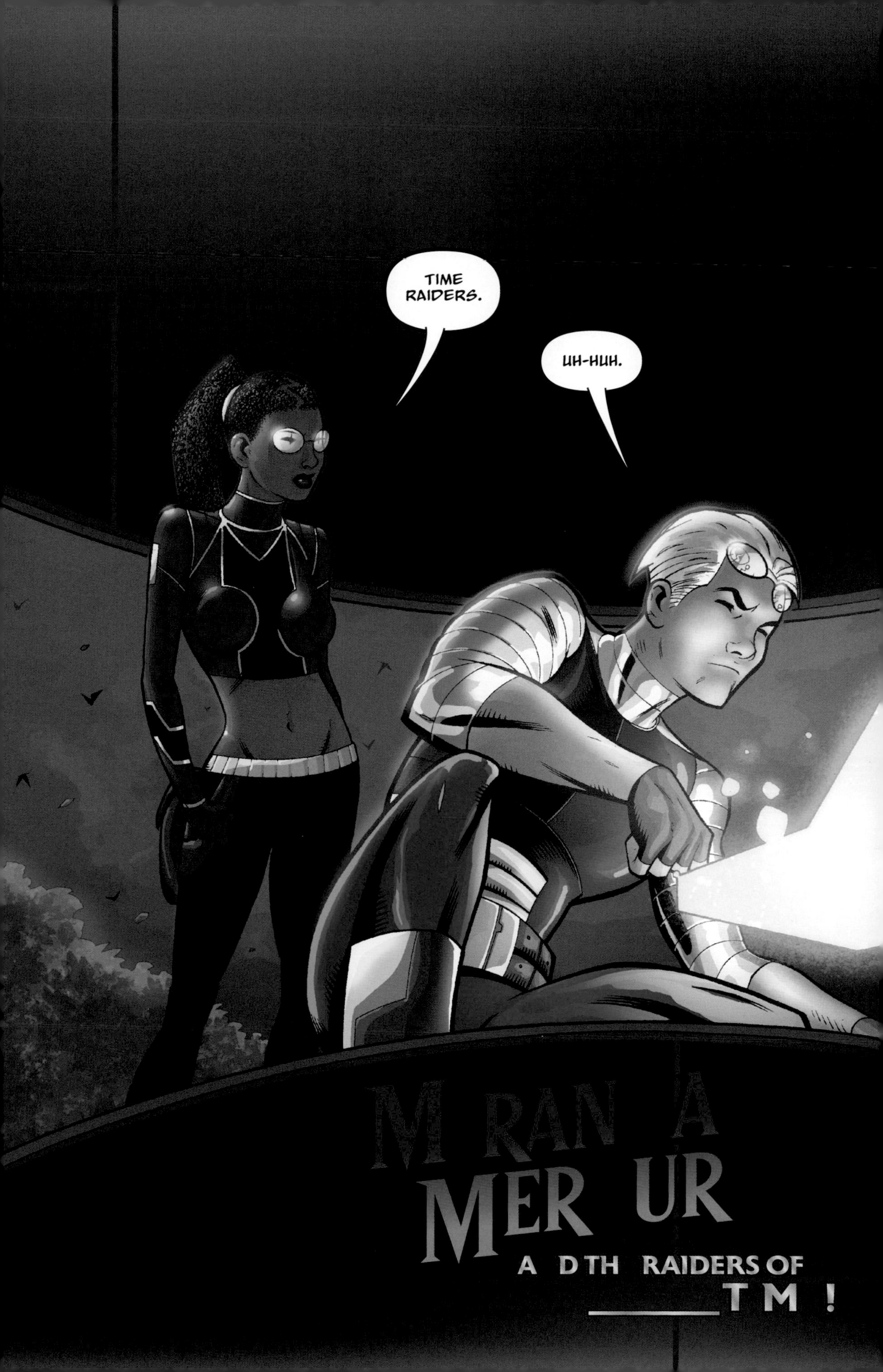
TIME RAIDERS.
UH-HUH.
M RAN A
MER UR
A DTH RAIDERS OF
T M !

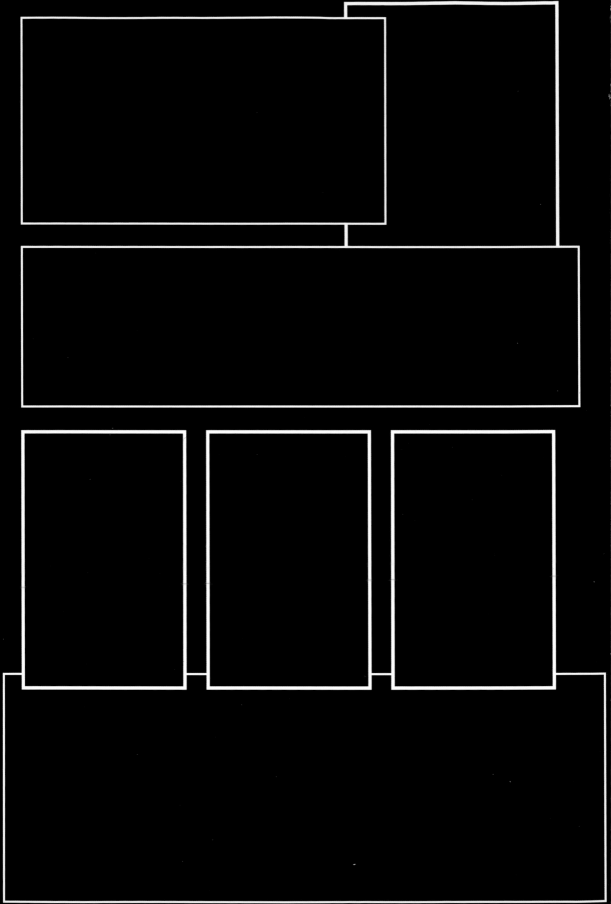

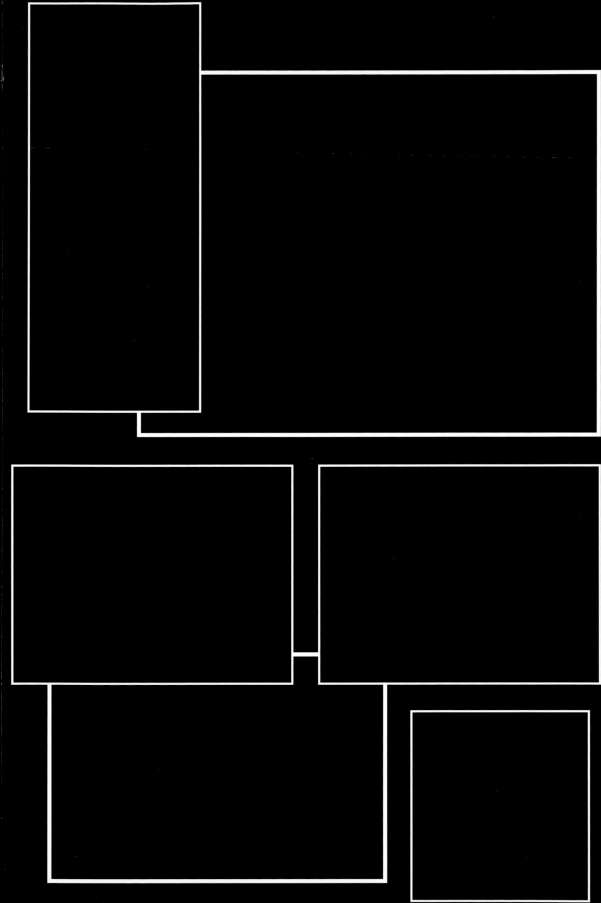

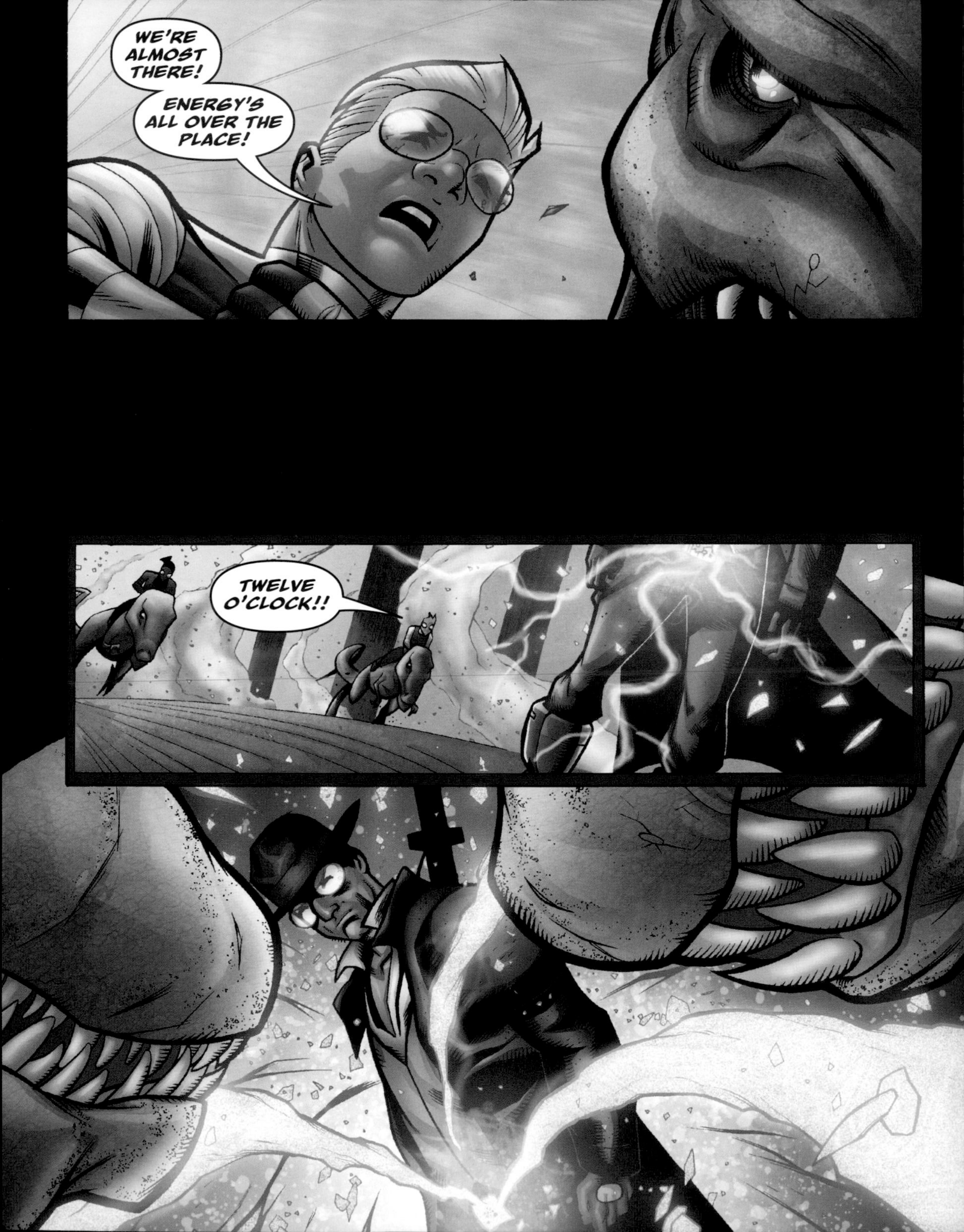
WE'RE ALMOST THERE!
ENERGY'S ALL OVER THE PLACE!
TWELVE O'CLOCK!!

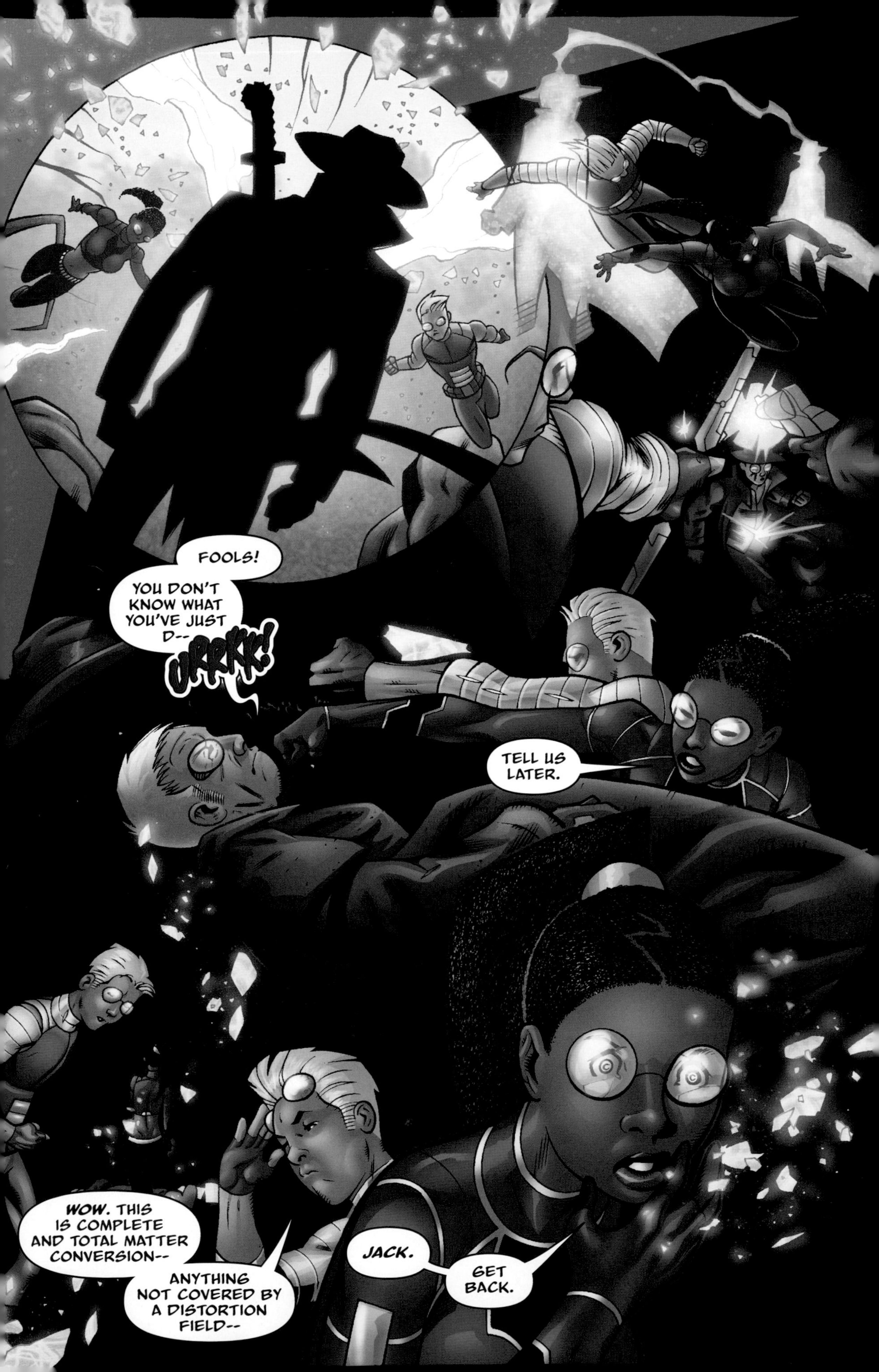
FOOLS!
YOU DON'T KNOW WHAT YOU'VE JUST D--
URRKK!
TELL US LATER.
WOW. THIS IS COMPLETE AND TOTAL MATTER CONVERSION--
ANYTHING NOT COVERED BY A DISTORTION FIELD--
JACK.
GET BACK.

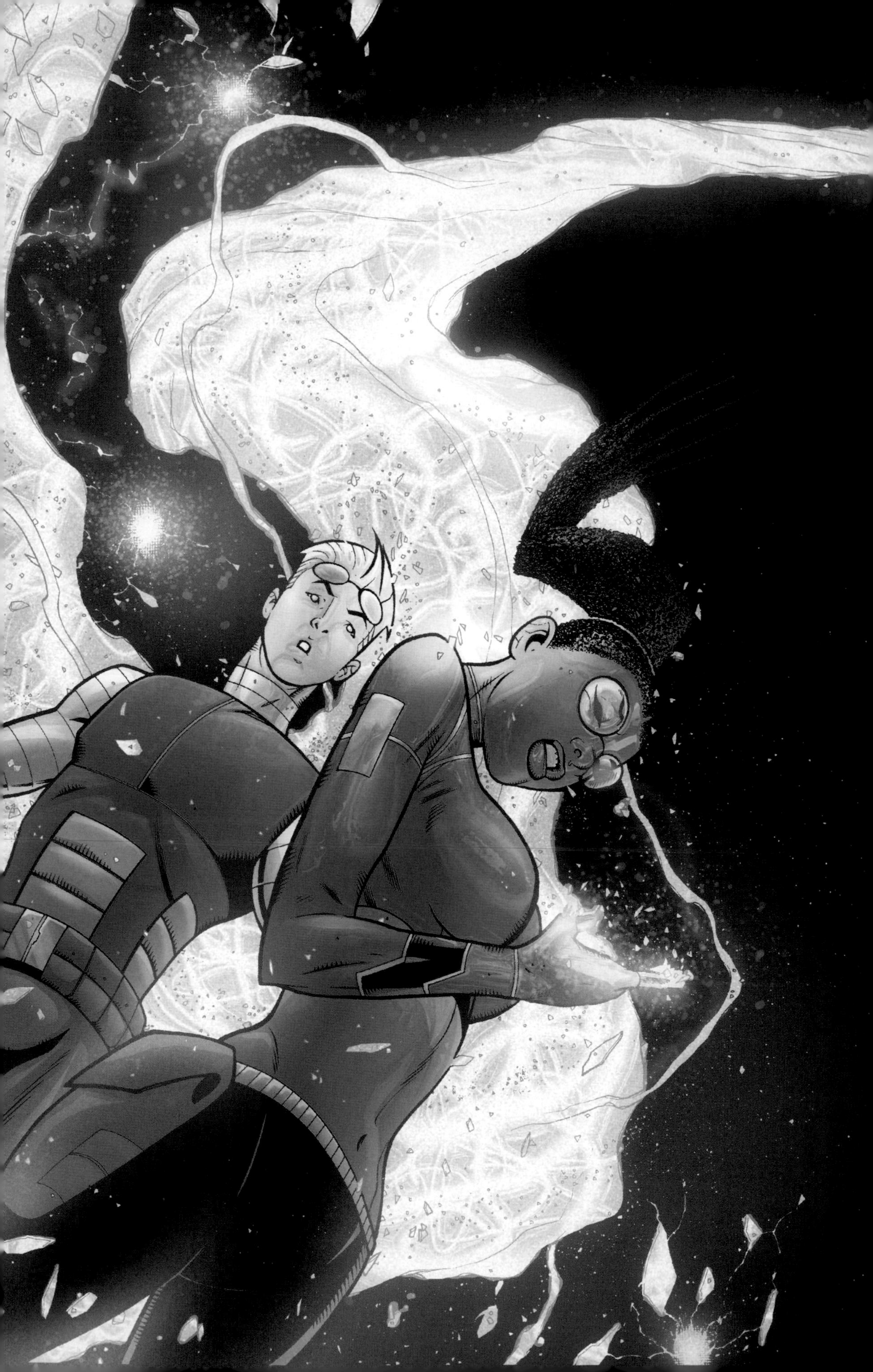

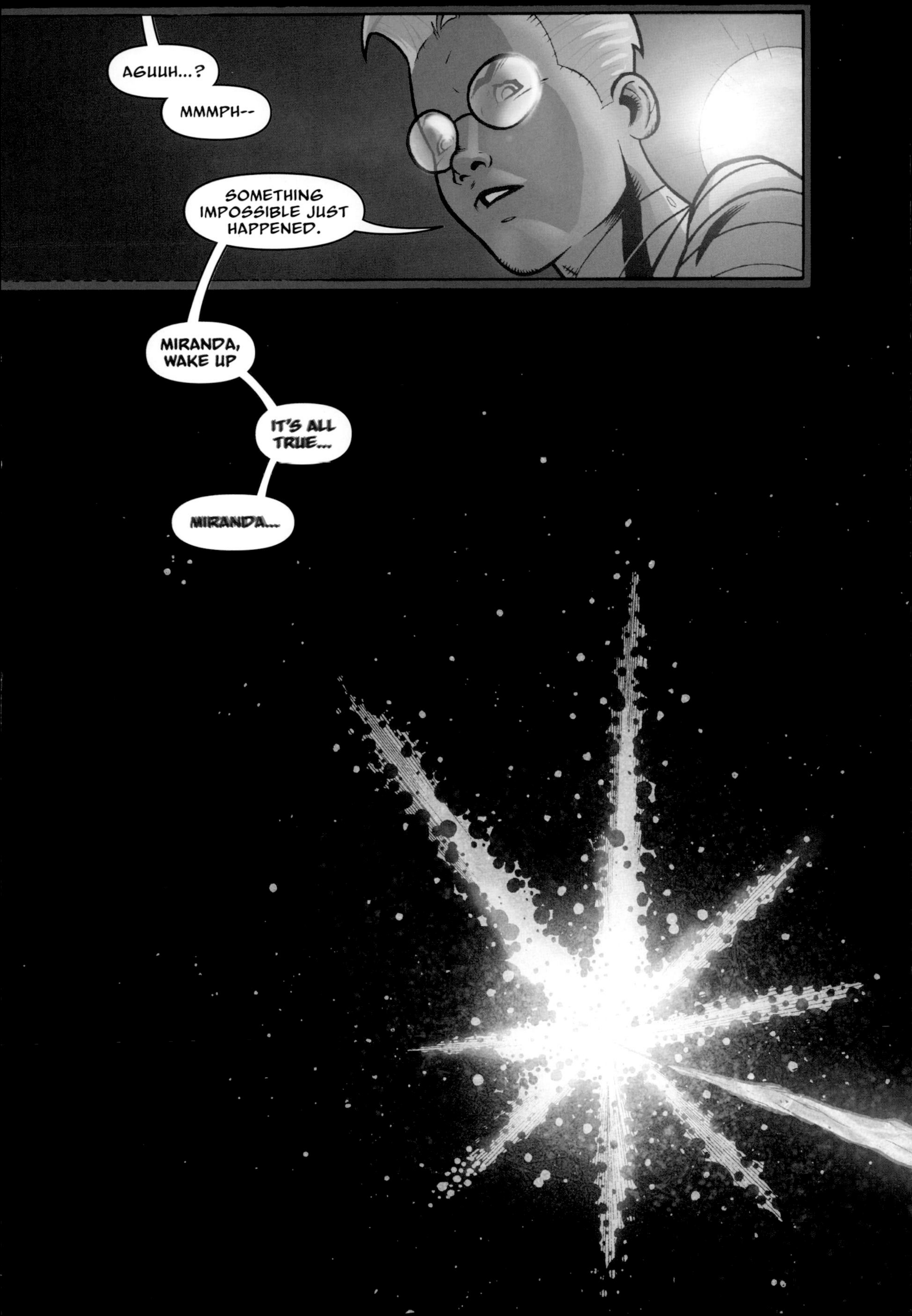
AGUUH...?
MMMPH--
SOMETHING IMPOSSIBLE JUST HAPPENED.
MIRANDA, WAKE UP
IT'S ALL TRUE...
MIRANDA...

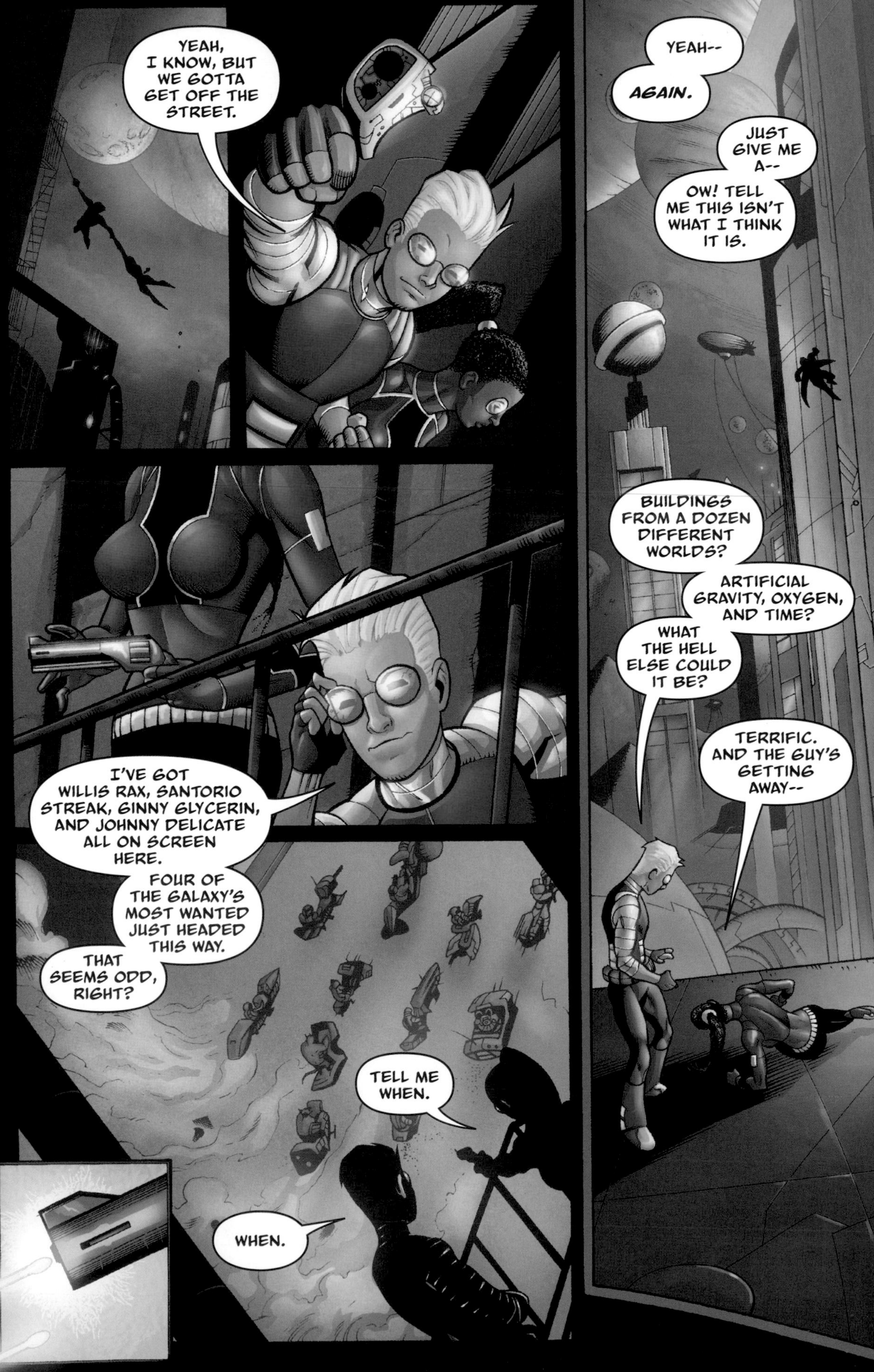
YEAH, I KNOW, BUT WE GOTTA GET OFF THE STREET.
I'VE GOT WILLIS RAX, SANTORIO STREAK, GINNY GLYCERIN, AND JOHNNY DELICATE ALL ON SCREEN HERE.
FOUR OF THE GALAXY'S MOST WANTED JUST HEADED THIS WAY.
THAT SEEMS ODD, RIGHT?
TELL ME WHEN.
WHEN.
YEAH--
AGAIN.
JUST GIVE ME A--
OW! TELL ME THIS ISN'T WHAT I THINK IT IS.
BUILDINGS FROM A DOZEN DIFFERENT WORLDS?
ARTIFICIAL GRAVITY, OXYGEN, AND TIME?
WHAT THE HELL ELSE COULD IT BE?
TERRIFIC. AND THE GUY'S GETTING AWAY--

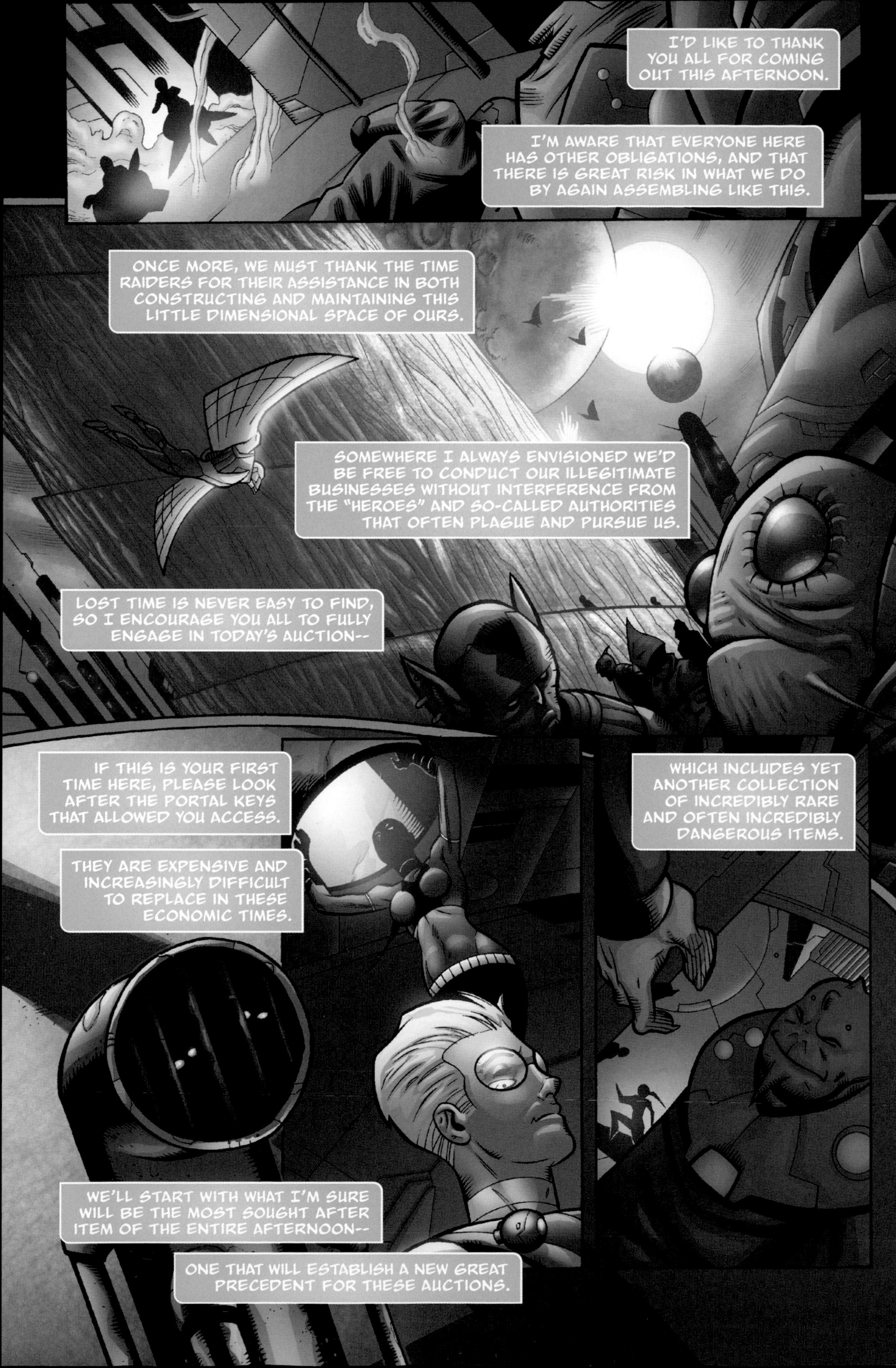
I'D LIKE TO THANK YOU ALL FOR COMING OUT THIS AFTERNOON.
I'M AWARE THAT EVERYONE HERE HAS OTHER OBLIGATIONS, AND THAT THERE IS GREAT RISK IN WHAT WE DO BY AGAIN ASSEMBLING LIKE THIS.
ONCE MORE, WE MUST THANK THE TIME RAIDERS FOR THEIR ASSISTANCE IN BOTH CONSTRUCTING AND MAINTAINING THIS LITTLE DIMENSIONAL SPACE OF OURS.
SOMEWHERE I ALWAYS ENVISIONED WE'D BE FREE TO CONDUCT OUR ILLEGITIMATE BUSINESSES WITHOUT INTERFERENCE FROM THE "HEROES" AND SO-CALLED AUTHORITIES THAT OFTEN PLAGUE AND PURSUE US.
LOST TIME IS NEVER EASY TO FIND, SO I ENCOURAGE YOU ALL TO FULLY ENGAGE IN TODAY'S AUCTION--
IF THIS IS YOUR FIRST TIME HERE, PLEASE LOOK AFTER THE PORTAL KEYS THAT ALLOWED YOU ACCESS.
THEY ARE EXPENSIVE AND INCREASINGLY DIFFICULT TO REPLACE IN THESE ECONOMIC TIMES.
WHICH INCLUDES YET ANOTHER COLLECTION OF INCREDIBLY RARE AND OFTEN INCREDIBLY DANGEROUS ITEMS.
WE'LL START WITH WHAT I'M SURE WILL BE THE MOST SOUGHT AFTER ITEM OF THE ENTIRE AFTERNOON--
ONE THAT WILL ESTABLISH A NEW GREAT PRECEDENT FOR THESE AUCTIONS.

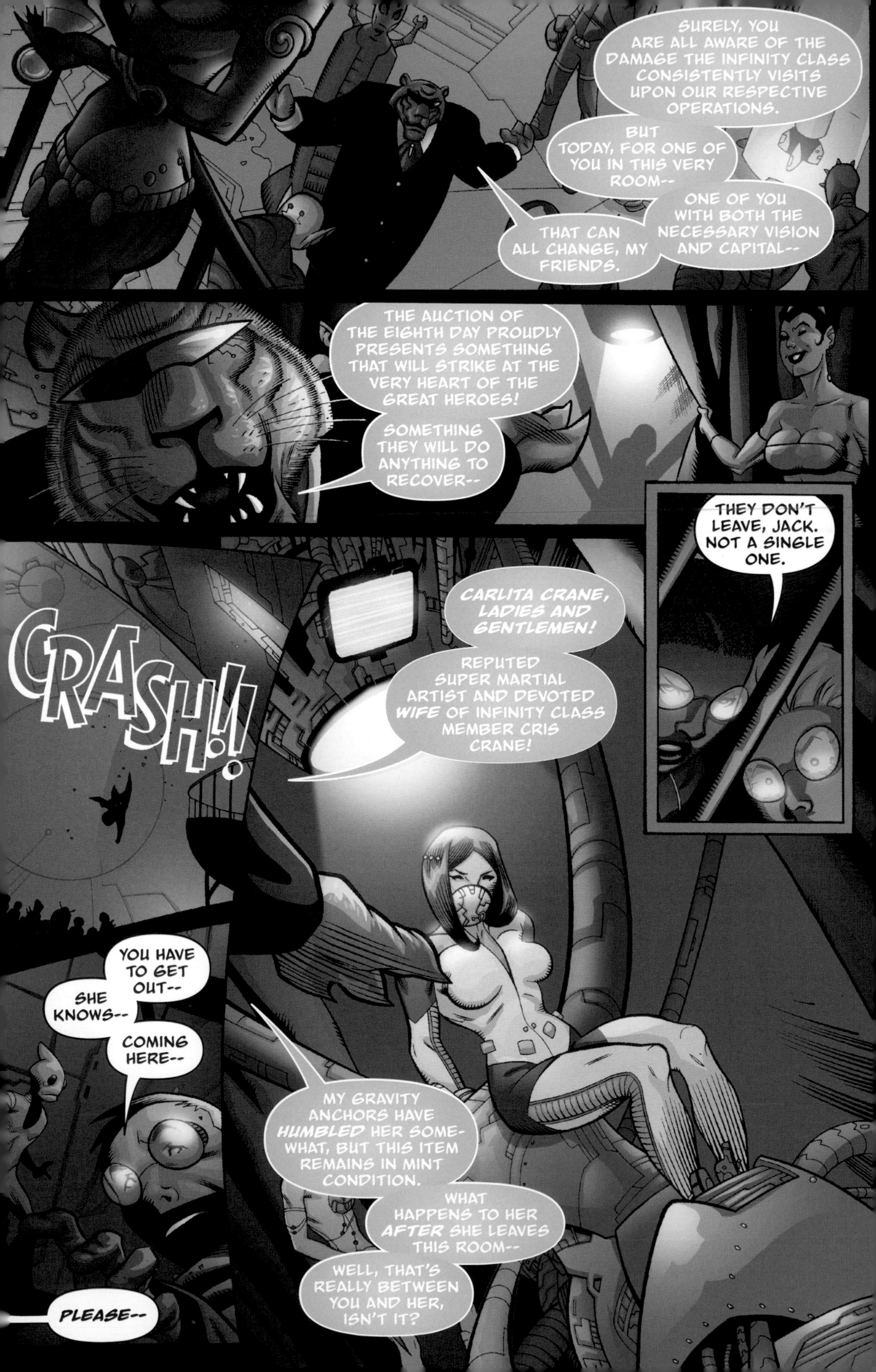
SURELY, YOU ARE ALL AWARE OF THE DAMAGE THE INFINITY CLASS CONSISTENTLY VISITS UPON OUR RESPECTIVE OPERATIONS.
BUT TODAY, FOR ONE OF YOU IN THIS VERY ROOM--
ONE OF YOU WITH BOTH THE NECESSARY VISION AND CAPITAL--
THAT CAN ALL CHANGE, MY FRIENDS.
THE AUCTION OF THE EIGHTH DAY PROUDLY PRESENTS SOMETHING THAT WILL STRIKE AT THE VERY HEART OF THE GREAT HEROES!
SOMETHING THEY WILL DO ANYTHING TO RECOVER--
THEY DON'T LEAVE, JACK. NOT A SINGLE ONE.
CARLITA CRANE, LADIES AND GENTLEMEN!
REPUTED SUPER MARTIAL ARTIST AND DEVOTED WIFE OF INFINITY CLASS MEMBER CRIS CRANE!
CRASH!!
YOU HAVE TO GET OUT--
SHE KNOWS--
COMING HERE--
PLEASE--
MY GRAVITY ANCHORS HAVE HUMBLED HER SOME-WHAT, BUT THIS ITEM REMAINS IN MINT CONDITION.
WHAT HAPPENS TO HER AFTER SHE LEAVES THIS ROOM--
WELL, THAT'S REALLY BETWEEN YOU AND HER, ISN'T IT?

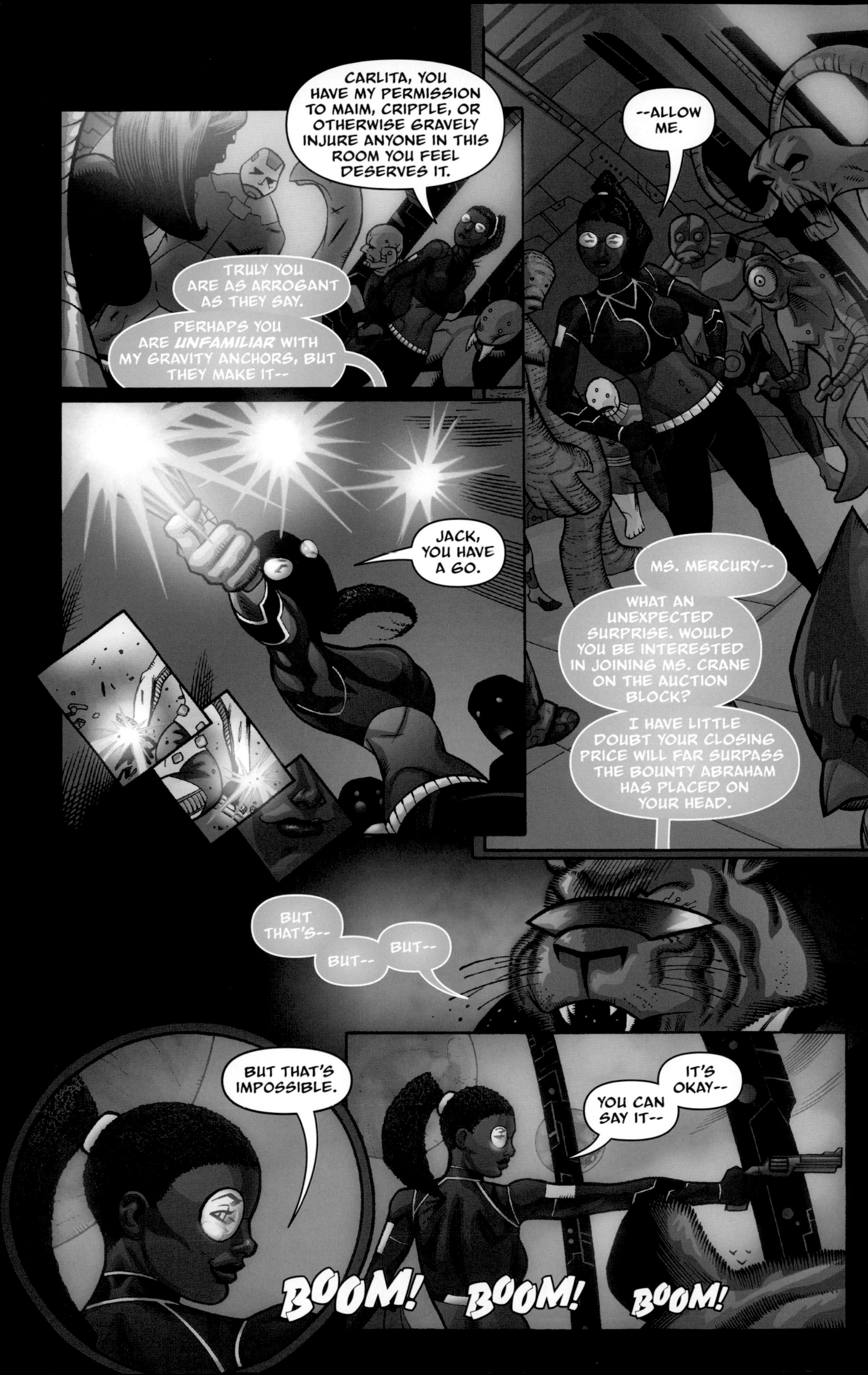
CARLITA, YOU HAVE MY PERMISSION TO MAIM, CRIPPLE, OR OTHERWISE GRAVELY INJURE ANYONE IN THIS ROOM YOU FEEL DESERVES IT.
TRULY YOU ARE AS ARROGANT AS THEY SAY.
PERHAPS YOU ARE UNFAMILIAR WITH MY GRAVITY ANCHORS, BUT THEY MAKE IT--
--ALLOW ME.
JACK, YOU HAVE A GO.
MS. MERCURY--
WHAT AN UNEXPECTED SURPRISE. WOULD YOU BE INTERESTED IN JOINING MS. CRANE ON THE AUCTION BLOCK?
I HAVE LITTLE DOUBT YOUR CLOSING PRICE WILL FAR SURPASS THE BOUNTY ABRAHAM HAS PLACED ON YOUR HEAD.
BUT THAT'S--
BUT--
BUT--
BUT THAT'S IMPOSSIBLE.
IT'S OKAY--
YOU CAN SAY IT--
BOOM!
BOOM!
BOOM!

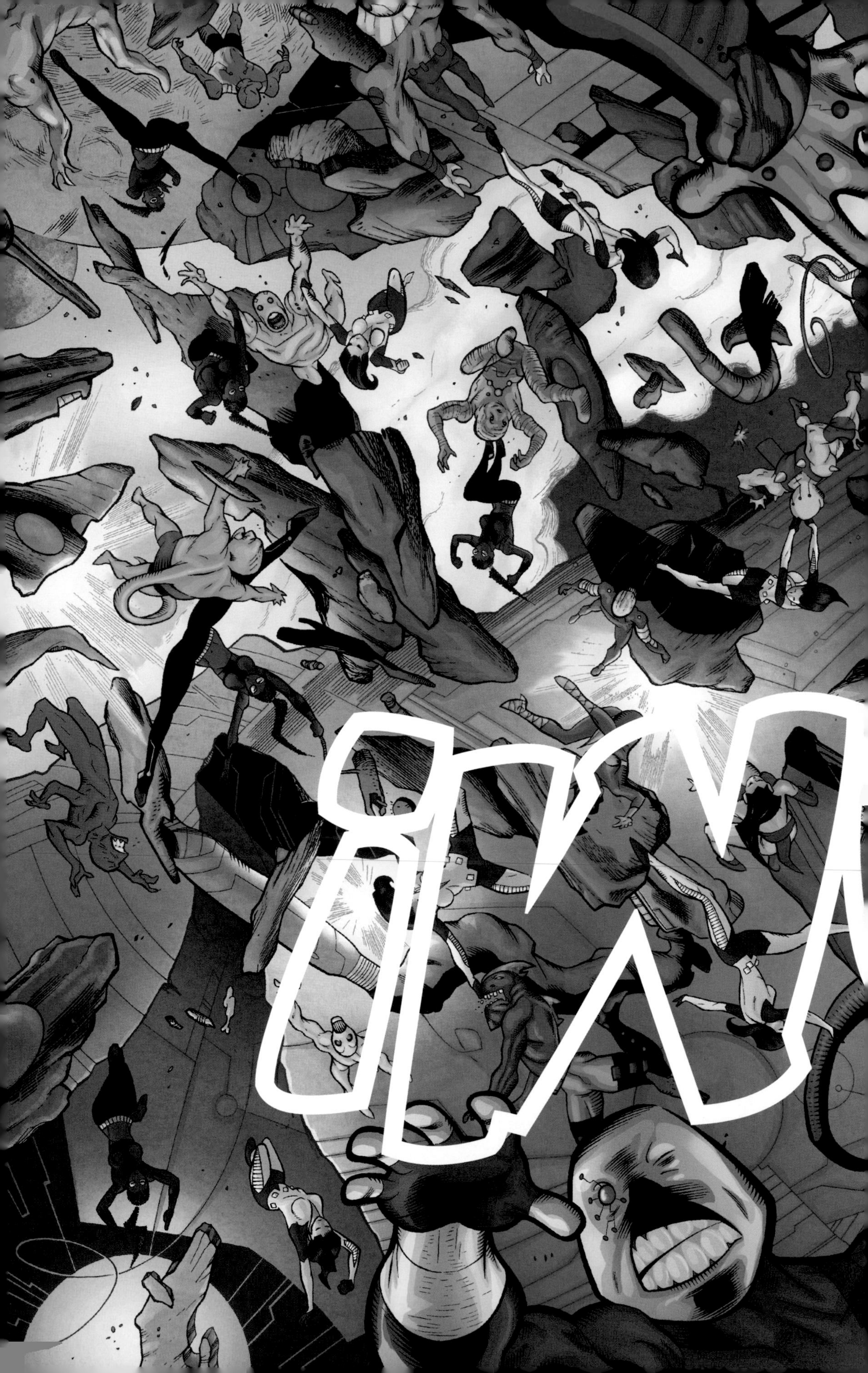

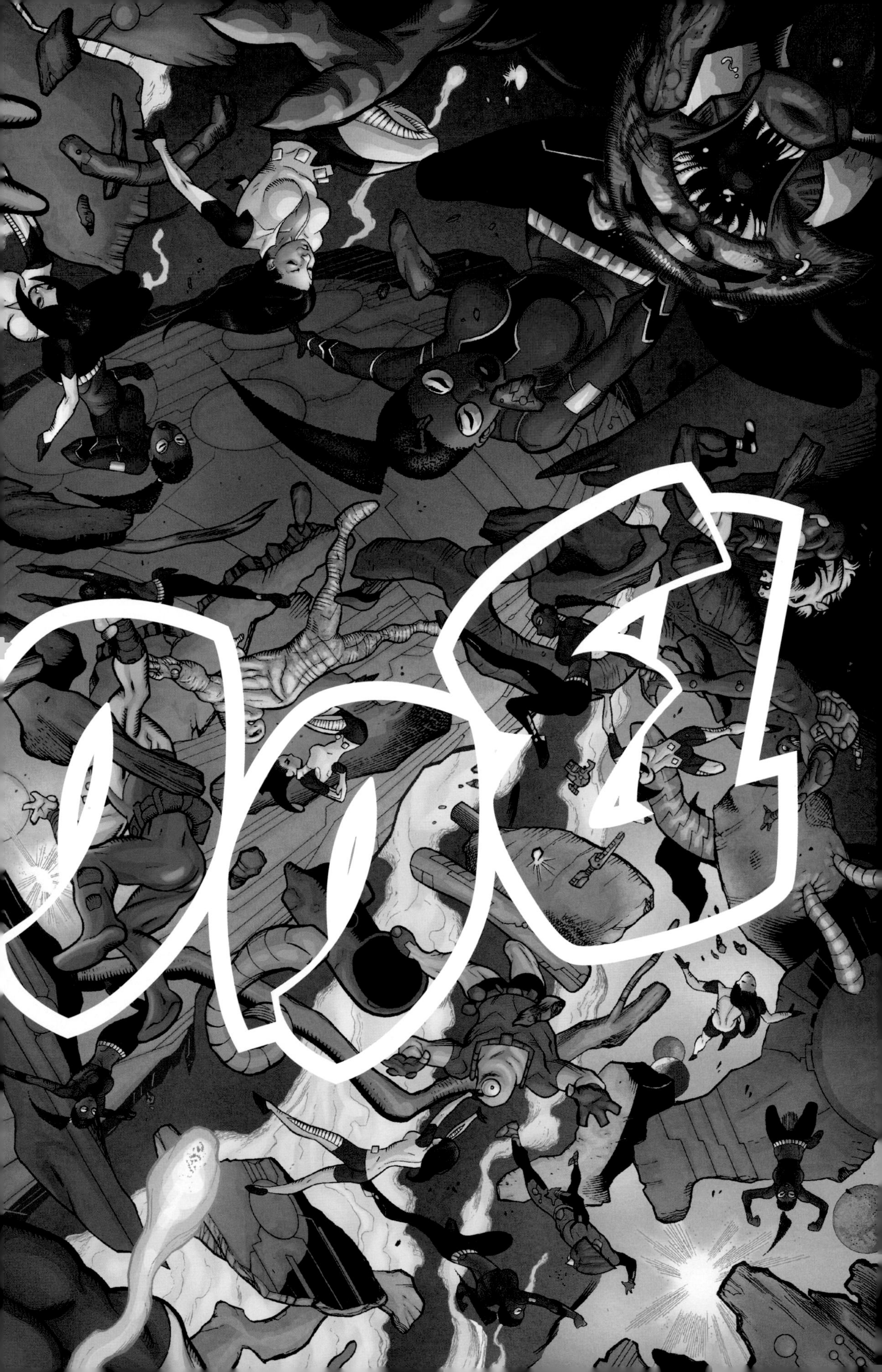

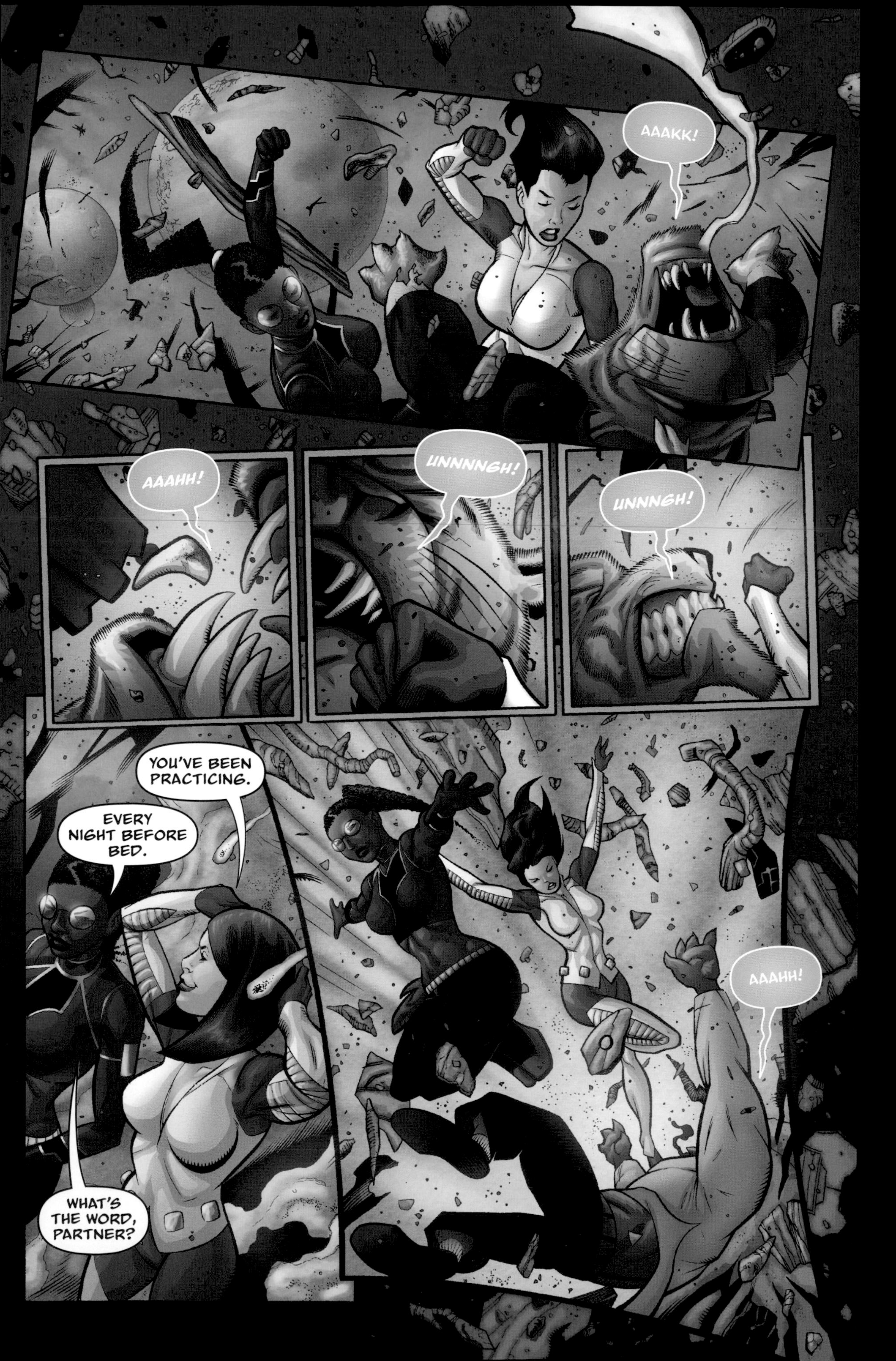
AAAKK!
AAAHH!
UNNNNGH!
UNNNGH!
YOU'VE BEEN PRACTICING.
EVERY NIGHT BEFORE BED.
WHAT'S THE WORD, PARTNER?
AAAHH!

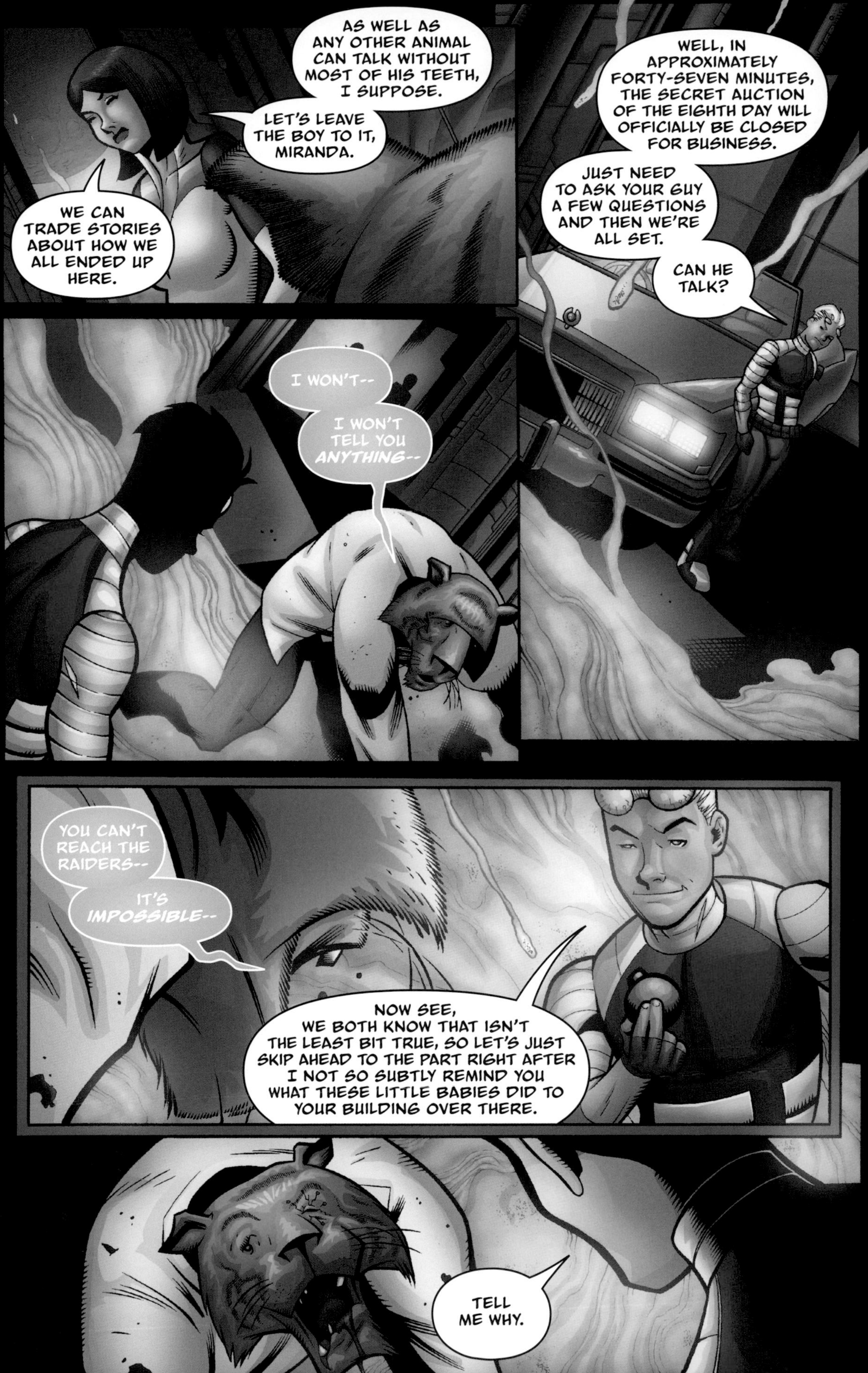
WELL, IN APPROXIMATELY FORTY-SEVEN MINUTES, THE SECRET AUCTION OF THE EIGHTH DAY WILL OFFICIALLY BE CLOSED FOR BUSINESS.
JUST NEED TO ASK YOUR GUY A FEW QUESTIONS AND THEN WE'RE ALL SET.
CAN HE TALK?
AS WELL AS ANY OTHER ANIMAL CAN TALK WITHOUT MOST OF HIS TEETH, I SUPPOSE.
LET'S LEAVE THE BOY TO IT, MIRANDA.
WE CAN TRADE STORIES ABOUT HOW WE ALL ENDED UP HERE.
I WON'T--
I WON'T TELL YOU *ANYTHING*--
YOU CAN'T REACH THE RAIDERS--
IT'S *IMPOSSIBLE*--
NOW SEE, WE BOTH KNOW THAT ISN'T THE LEAST BIT TRUE, SO LET'S JUST SKIP AHEAD TO THE PART RIGHT AFTER I NOT SO SUBTLY REMIND YOU WHAT THESE LITTLE BABIES DID TO YOUR BUILDING OVER THERE.
TELL ME WHY.

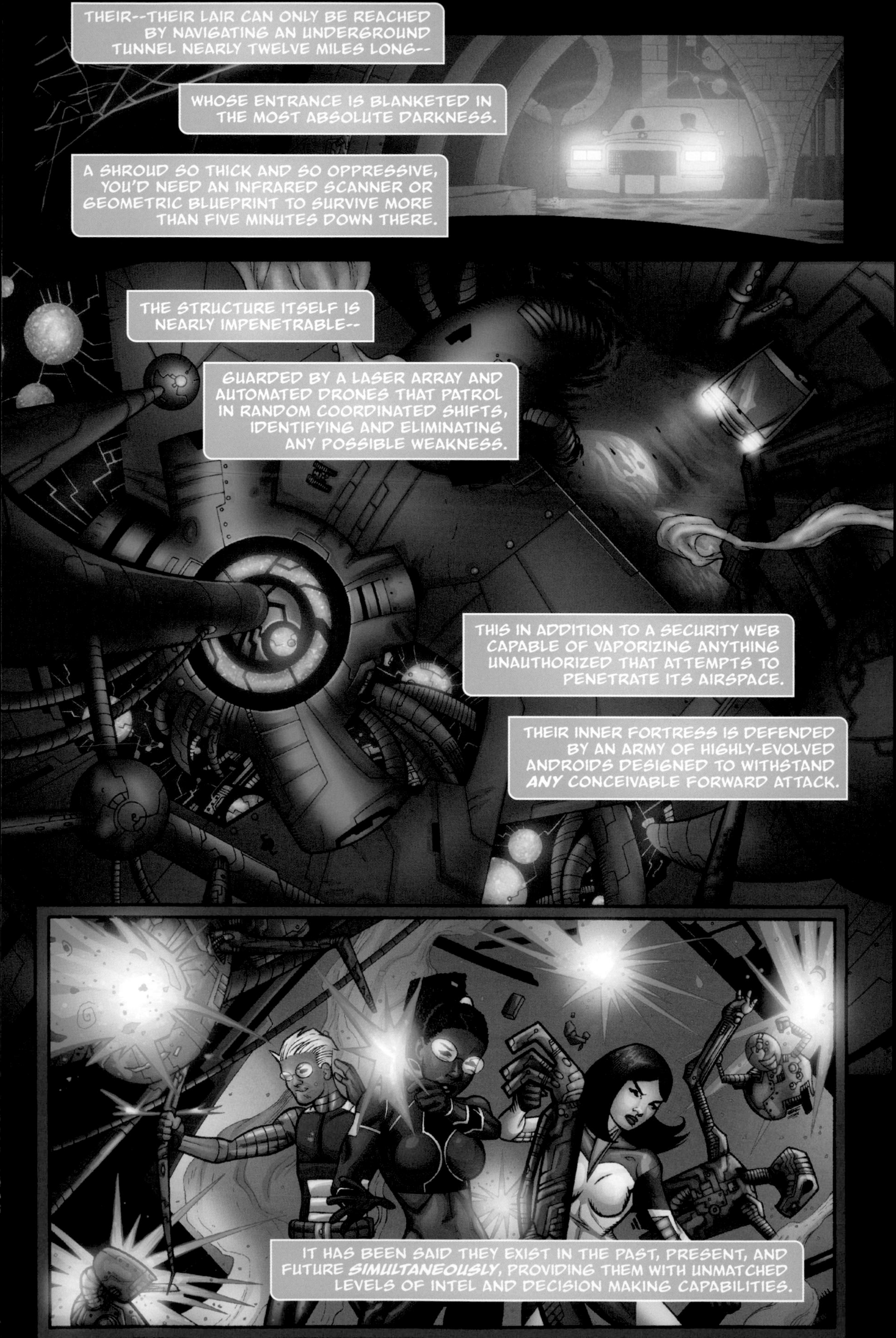
THEIR--THEIR LAIR CAN ONLY BE REACHED BY NAVIGATING AN UNDERGROUND TUNNEL NEARLY TWELVE MILES LONG--
WHOSE ENTRANCE IS BLANKETED IN THE MOST ABSOLUTE DARKNESS.
A SHROUD SO THICK AND SO OPPRESSIVE, YOU'D NEED AN INFRARED SCANNER OR GEOMETRIC BLUEPRINT TO SURVIVE MORE THAN FIVE MINUTES DOWN THERE.
THE STRUCTURE ITSELF IS NEARLY IMPENETRABLE--
GUARDED BY A LASER ARRAY AND AUTOMATED DRONES THAT PATROL IN RANDOM COORDINATED SHIFTS, IDENTIFYING AND ELIMINATING ANY POSSIBLE WEAKNESS.
THIS IN ADDITION TO A SECURITY WEB CAPABLE OF VAPORIZING ANYTHING UNAUTHORIZED THAT ATTEMPTS TO PENETRATE ITS AIRSPACE.
THEIR INNER FORTRESS IS DEFENDED BY AN ARMY OF HIGHLY-EVOLVED ANDROIDS DESIGNED TO WITHSTAND *ANY* CONCEIVABLE FORWARD ATTACK.
IT HAS BEEN SAID THEY EXIST IN THE PAST, PRESENT, AND FUTURE *SIMULTANEOUSLY*, PROVIDING THEM WITH UNMATCHED LEVELS OF INTEL AND DECISION MAKING CAPABILITIES.

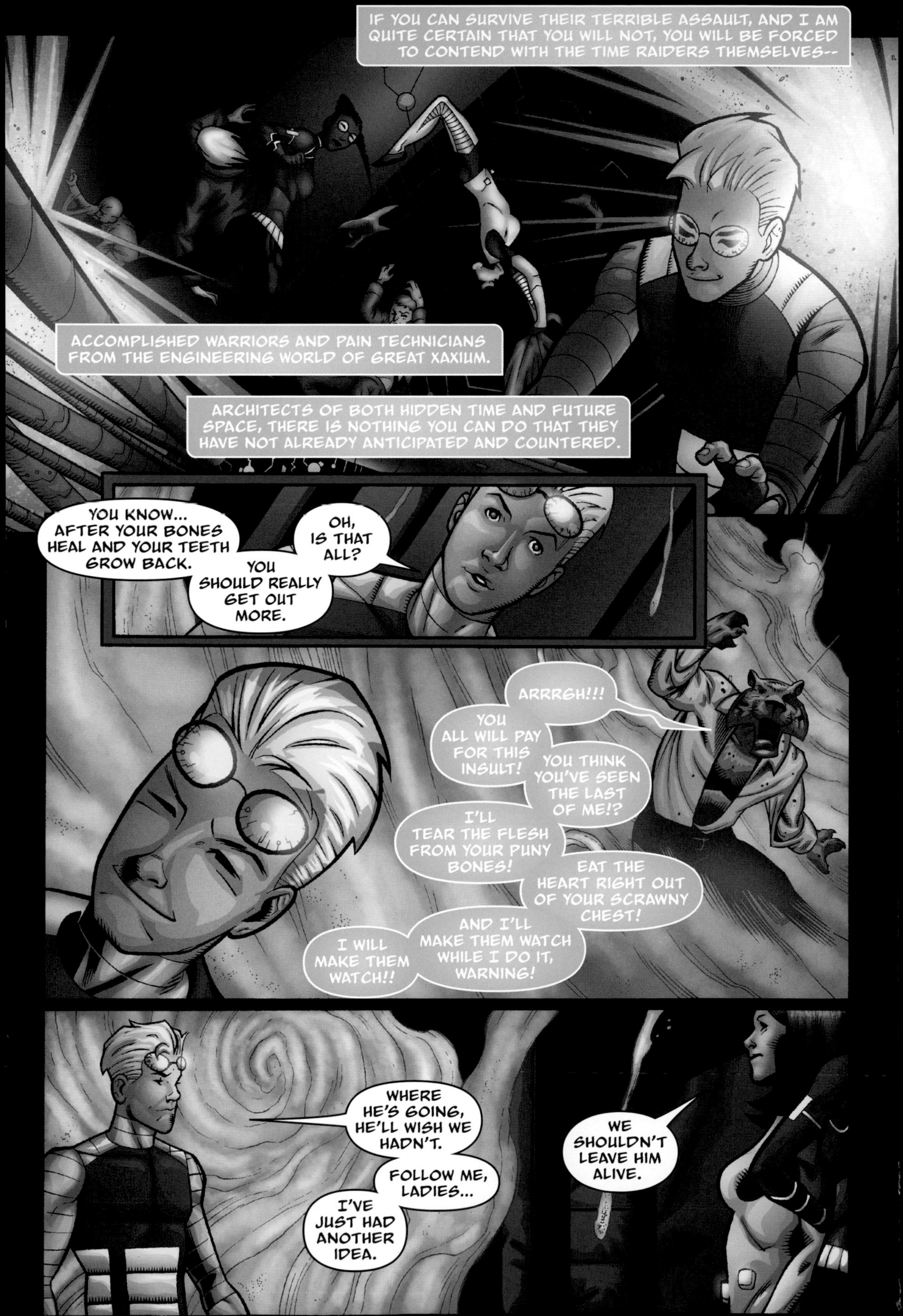
IF YOU CAN SURVIVE THEIR TERRIBLE ASSAULT, AND I AM QUITE CERTAIN THAT YOU WILL NOT, YOU WILL BE FORCED TO CONTEND WITH THE TIME RAIDERS THEMSELVES--
ACCOMPLISHED WARRIORS AND PAIN TECHNICIANS FROM THE ENGINEERING WORLD OF GREAT XAXIUM.
ARCHITECTS OF BOTH HIDDEN TIME AND FUTURE SPACE, THERE IS NOTHING YOU CAN DO THAT THEY HAVE NOT ALREADY ANTICIPATED AND COUNTERED.
OH, IS THAT ALL?
YOU KNOW... AFTER YOUR BONES HEAL AND YOUR TEETH GROW BACK.
YOU SHOULD REALLY GET OUT MORE.
ARRRGH!!!
YOU ALL WILL PAY FOR THIS INSULT!
YOU THINK YOU'VE SEEN THE LAST OF ME!?
I'LL TEAR THE FLESH FROM YOUR PUNY BONES!
EAT THE HEART RIGHT OUT OF YOUR SCRAWNY CHEST!
AND I'LL MAKE THEM WATCH WHILE I DO IT, WARNING!
I WILL MAKE THEM WATCH!!
WE SHOULDN'T LEAVE HIM ALIVE.
WHERE HE'S GOING, HE'LL WISH WE HADN'T.
FOLLOW ME, LADIES...
I'VE JUST HAD ANOTHER IDEA.

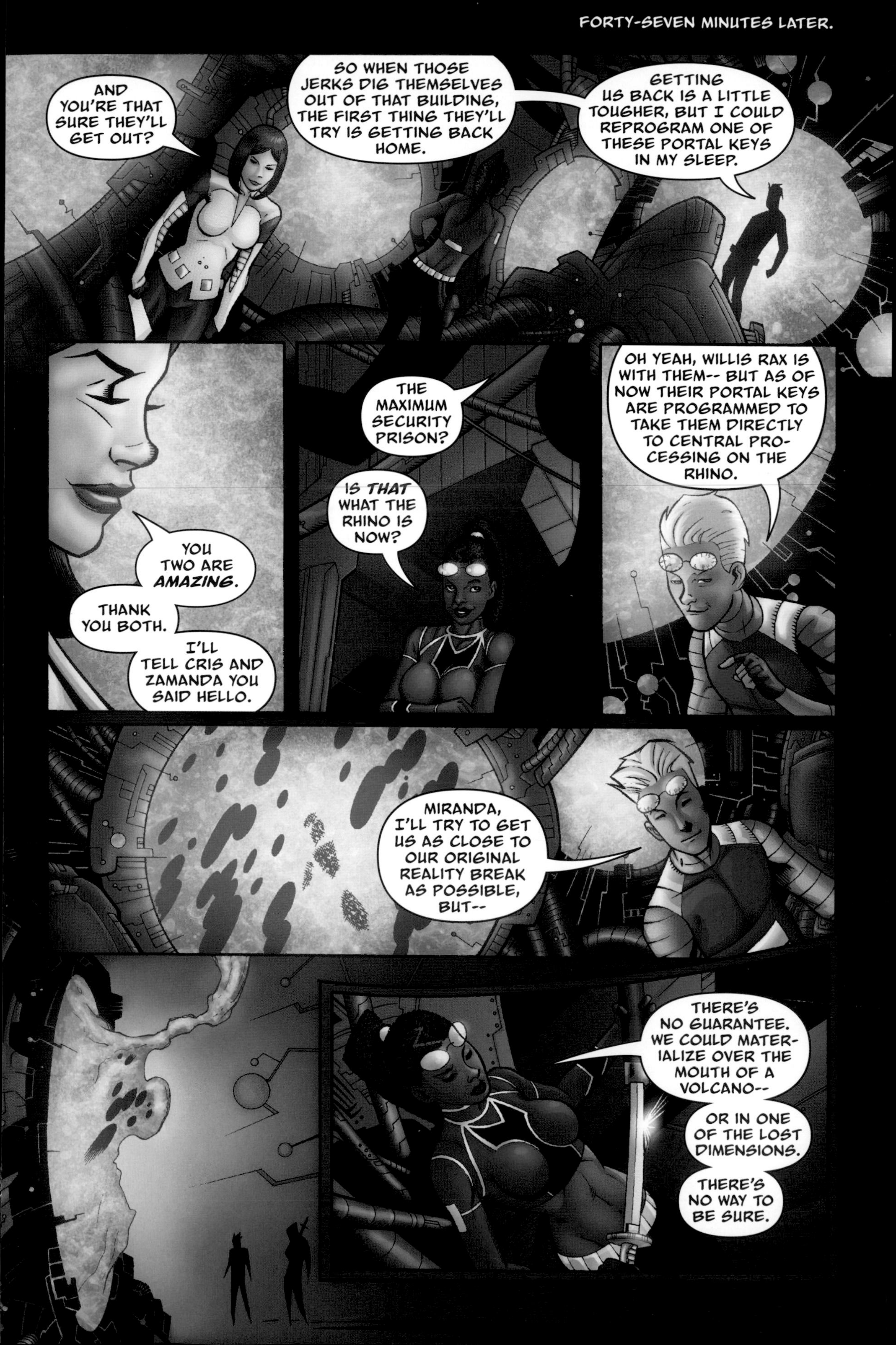
FORTY-SEVEN MINUTES LATER.
AND YOU'RE THAT SURE THEY'LL GET OUT?
SO WHEN THOSE JERKS DIG THEMSELVES OUT OF THAT BUILDING, THE FIRST THING THEY'LL TRY IS GETTING BACK HOME.
GETTING US BACK IS A LITTLE TOUGHER, BUT I COULD REPROGRAM ONE OF THESE PORTAL KEYS IN MY SLEEP.
YOU TWO ARE *AMAZING*.
THANK YOU BOTH.
I'LL TELL CRIS AND ZAMANDA YOU SAID HELLO.
THE MAXIMUM SECURITY PRISON?
IS *THAT* WHAT THE RHINO IS NOW?
OH YEAH, WILLIS RAX IS WITH THEM-- BUT AS OF NOW THEIR PORTAL KEYS ARE PROGRAMMED TO TAKE THEM DIRECTLY TO CENTRAL PRO-CESSING ON THE RHINO.
MIRANDA, I'LL TRY TO GET US AS CLOSE TO OUR ORIGINAL REALITY BREAK AS POSSIBLE, BUT--
THERE'S NO GUARANTEE. WE COULD MATER-IALIZE OVER THE MOUTH OF A VOLCANO--
OR IN ONE OF THE LOST DIMENSIONS.
THERE'S NO WAY TO BE SURE.

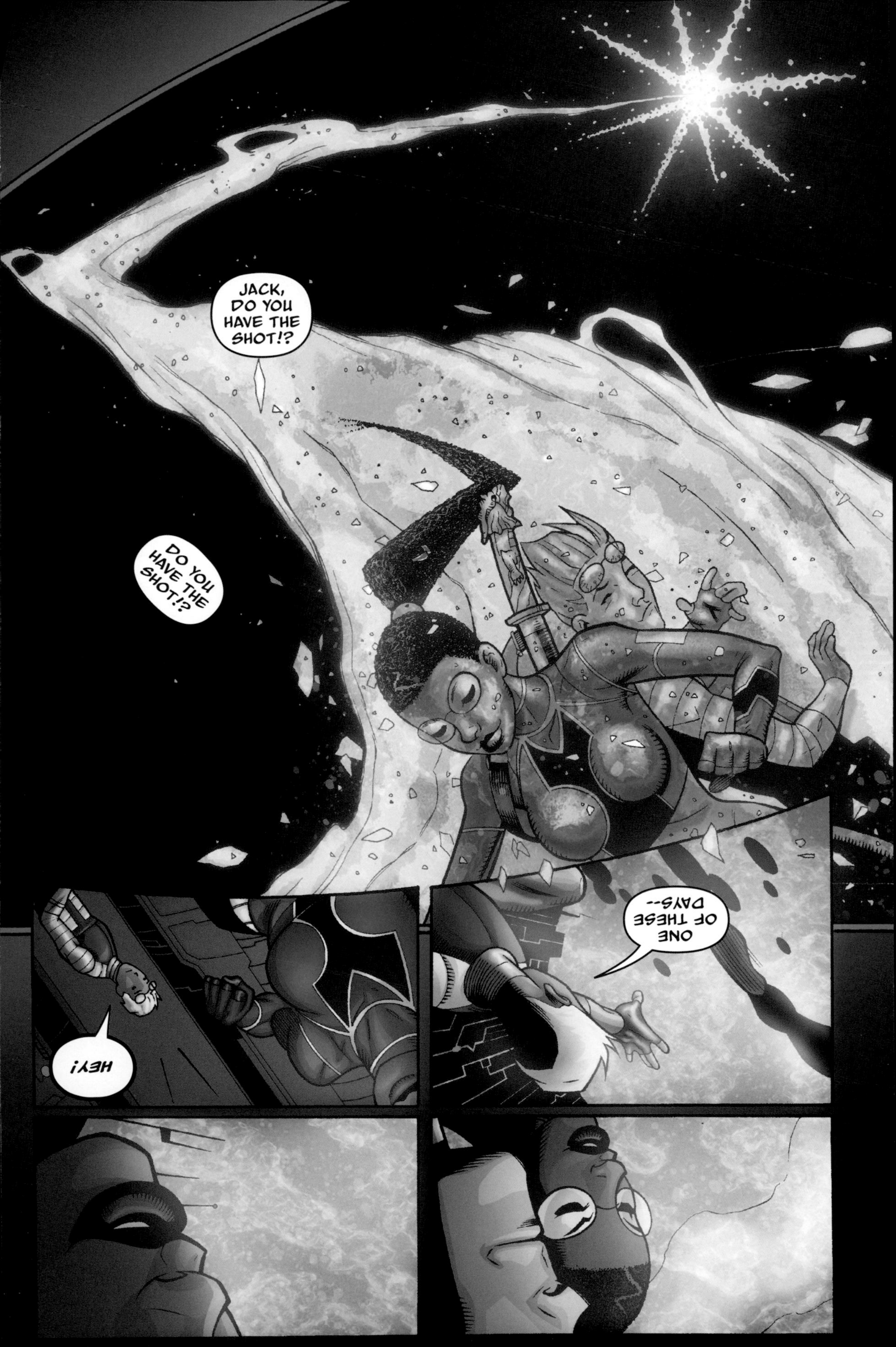
JACK, DO YOU HAVE THE SHOT!?
DO YOU HAVE THE SHOT!?
HEY!
ONE OF THESE DAYS--

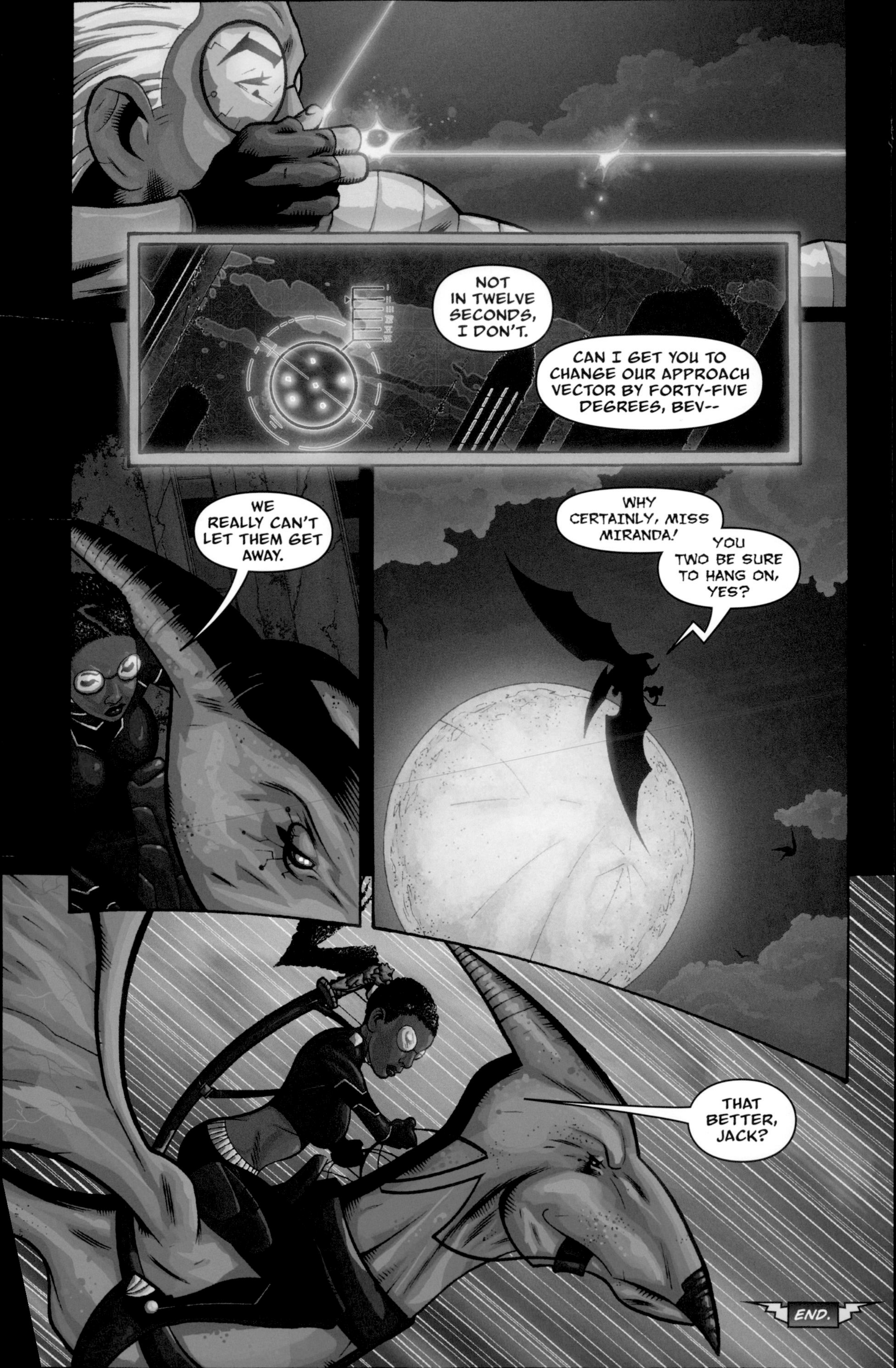
NOT IN TWELVE SECONDS, I DON'T.
CAN I GET YOU TO CHANGE OUR APPROACH VECTOR BY FORTY-FIVE DEGREES, BEV--
WE REALLY CAN'T LET THEM GET AWAY.
WHY CERTAINLY, MISS MIRANDA!
YOU TWO BE SURE TO HANG ON, YES?
THAT BETTER, JACK?
END.

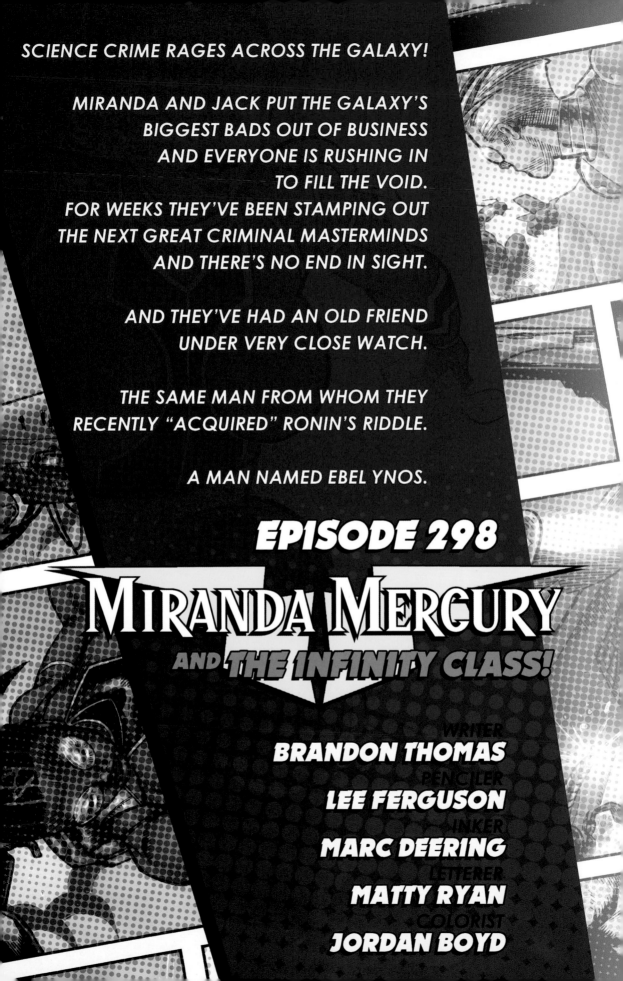

SCIENCE CRIME RAGES ACROSS THE GALAXY!

MIRANDA AND JACK PUT THE GALAXY'S
BIGGEST BADS OUT OF BUSINESS
AND EVERYONE IS RUSHING IN
TO FILL THE VOID.
FOR WEEKS THEY'VE BEEN STAMPING OUT
THE NEXT GREAT CRIMINAL MASTERMINDS
AND THERE'S NO END IN SIGHT.

AND THEY'VE HAD AN OLD FRIEND
UNDER VERY CLOSE WATCH.

THE SAME MAN FROM WHOM THEY
RECENTLY "ACQUIRED" RONIN'S RIDDLE.

A MAN NAMED EBEL YNOS.

EPISODE 298

MIRANDA MERCURY
AND THE INFINITY CLASS!

WRITER
BRANDON THOMAS
PENCILER
LEE FERGUSON
INKER
MARC DEERING
LETTERER
MATTY RYAN
COLORIST
JORDAN BOYD

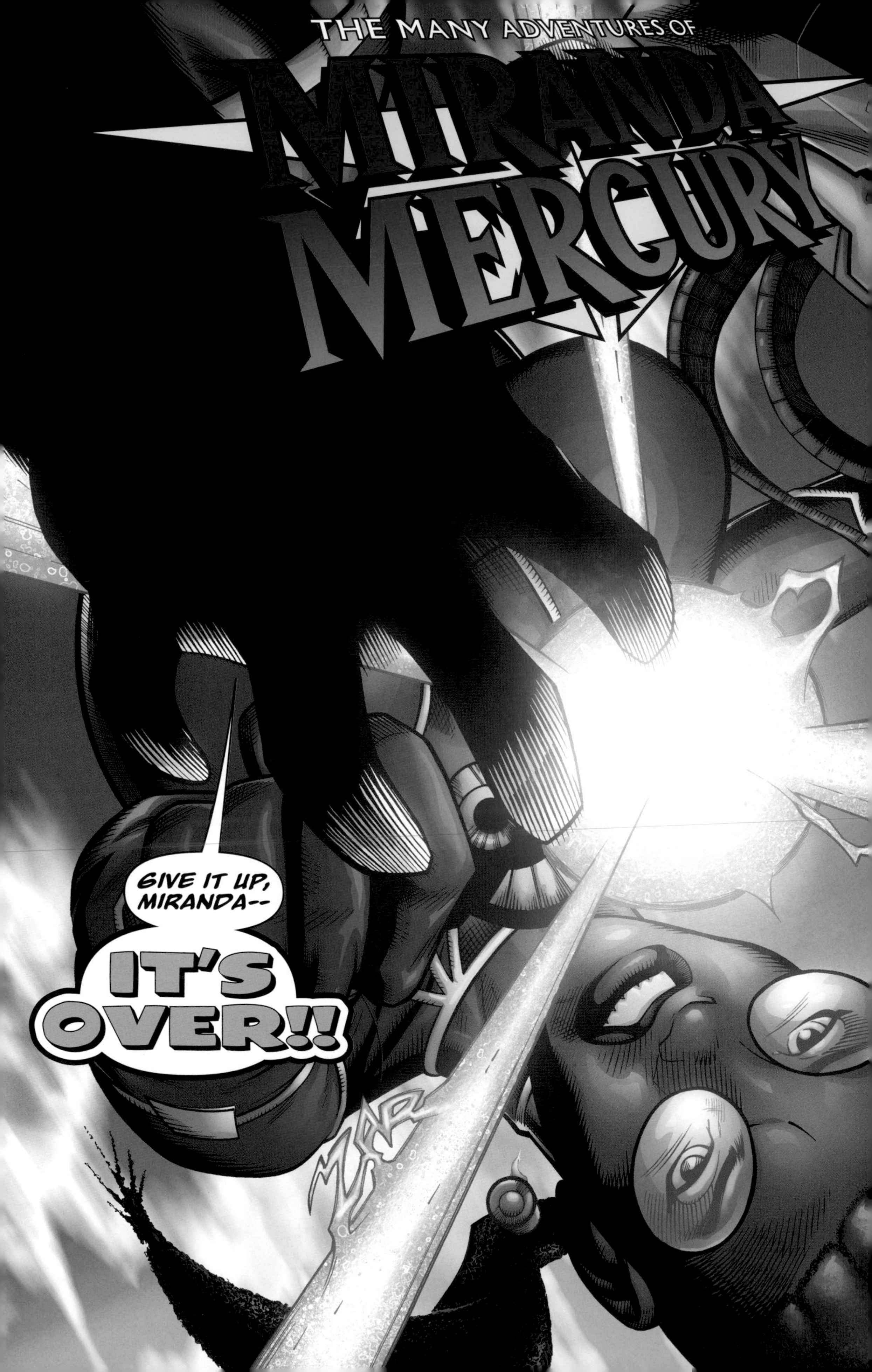
THE MANY ADVENTURES OF
MIRANDA MERCURY
GIVE IT UP, MIRANDA--
IT'S OVER!!
ZZAP

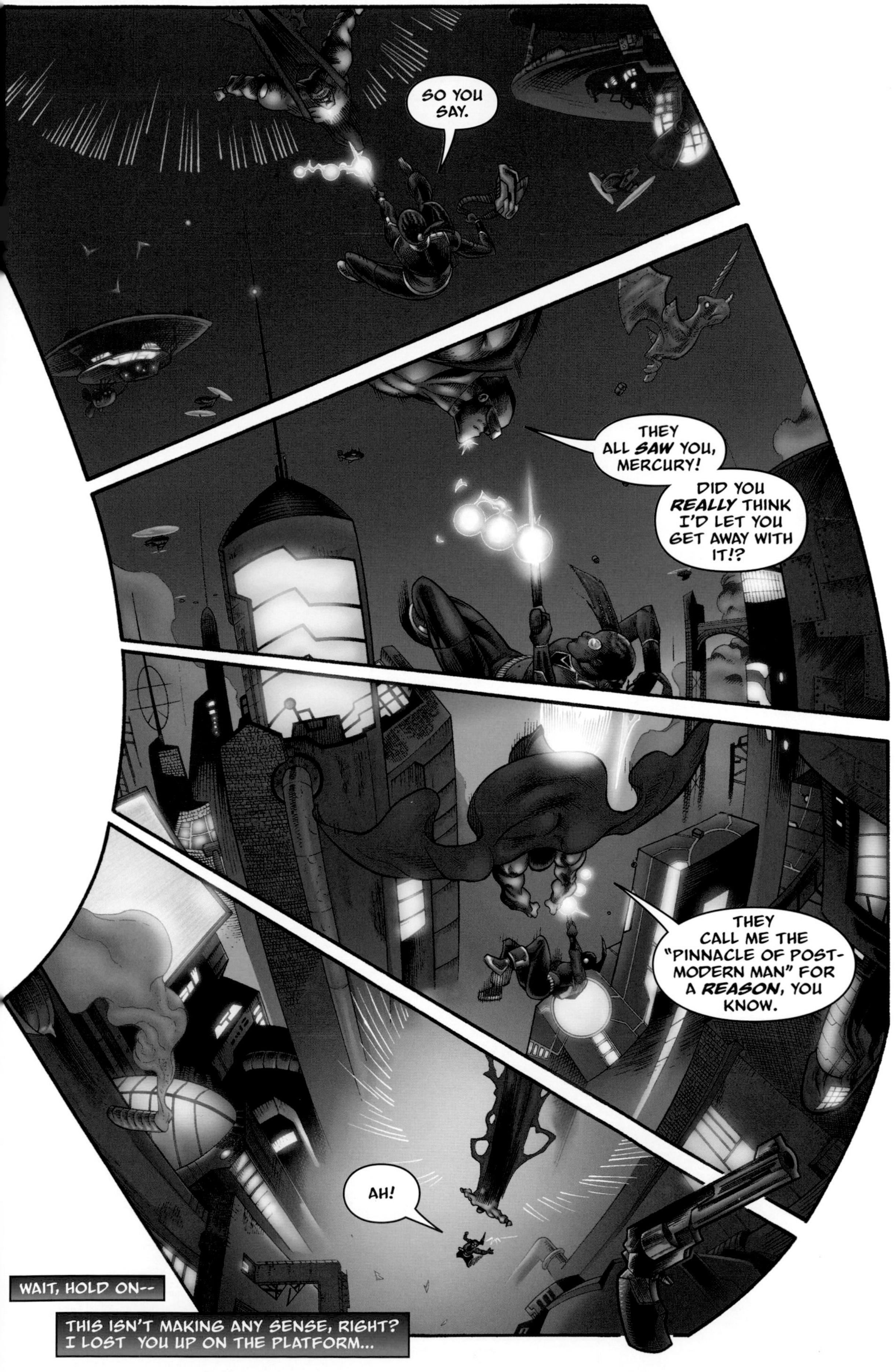
SO YOU SAY.
THEY ALL SAW YOU, MERCURY!
DID YOU REALLY THINK I'D LET YOU GET AWAY WITH IT!?
THEY CALL ME THE "PINNACLE OF POST-MODERN MAN" FOR A REASON, YOU KNOW.
AH!
WAIT, HOLD ON--
THIS ISN'T MAKING ANY SENSE, RIGHT? I LOST YOU UP ON THE PLATFORM...

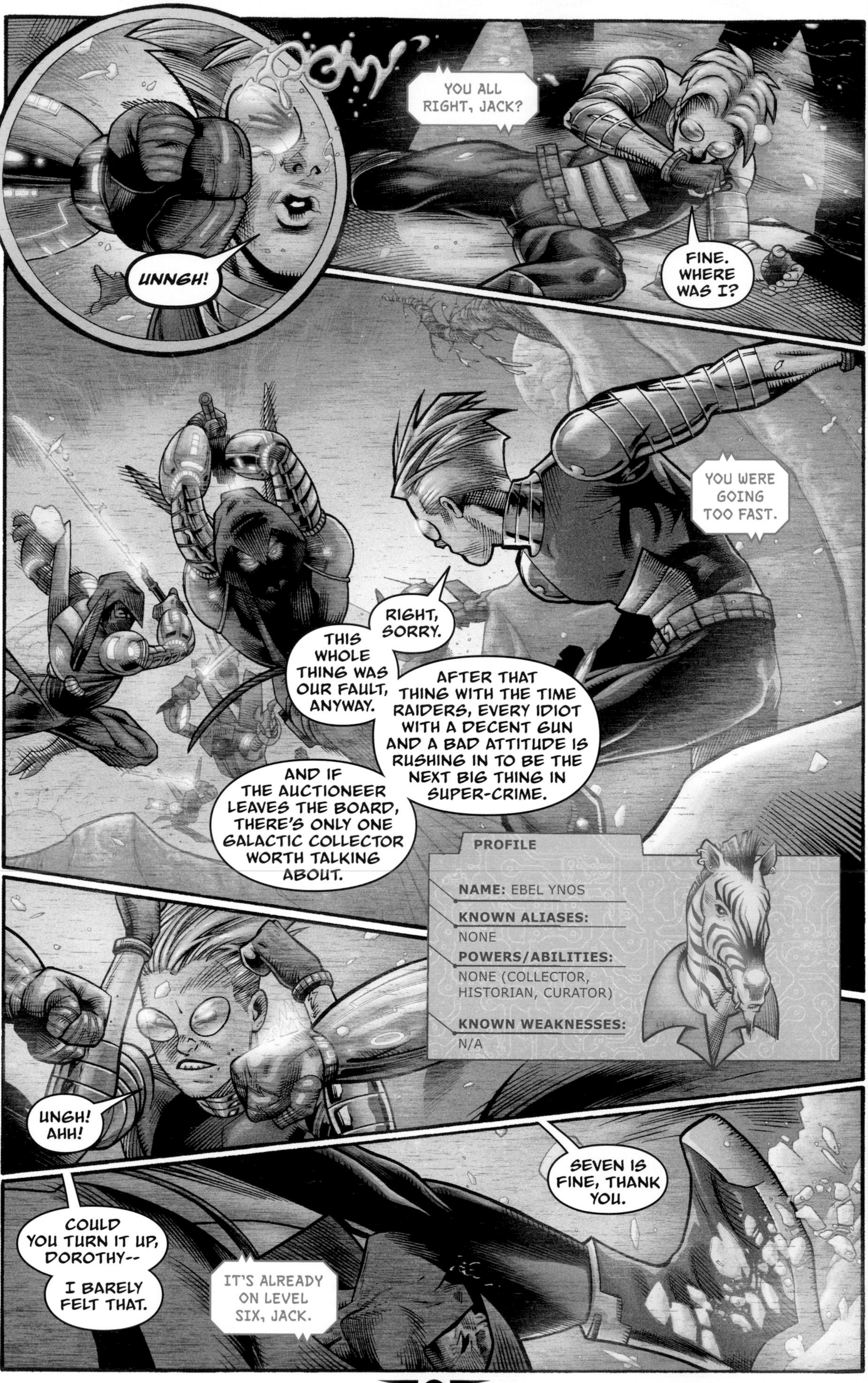

POCK!
YOU ALL RIGHT, JACK?
UNNGH!
FINE. WHERE WAS I?
YOU WERE GOING TOO FAST.
RIGHT, SORRY.
THIS WHOLE THING WAS OUR FAULT, ANYWAY.
AFTER THAT THING WITH THE TIME RAIDERS, EVERY IDIOT WITH A DECENT GUN AND A BAD ATTITUDE IS RUSHING IN TO BE THE NEXT BIG THING IN SUPER-CRIME.
AND IF THE AUCTIONEER LEAVES THE BOARD, THERE'S ONLY ONE GALACTIC COLLECTOR WORTH TALKING ABOUT.
PROFILE
NAME: EBEL YNOS
KNOWN ALIASES:
NONE
POWERS/ABILITIES:
NONE (COLLECTOR, HISTORIAN, CURATOR)
KNOWN WEAKNESSES:
N/A
UNGH! AHH!
SEVEN IS FINE, THANK YOU.
COULD YOU TURN IT UP, DOROTHY--
I BARELY FELT THAT.
IT'S ALREADY ON LEVEL SIX, JACK.

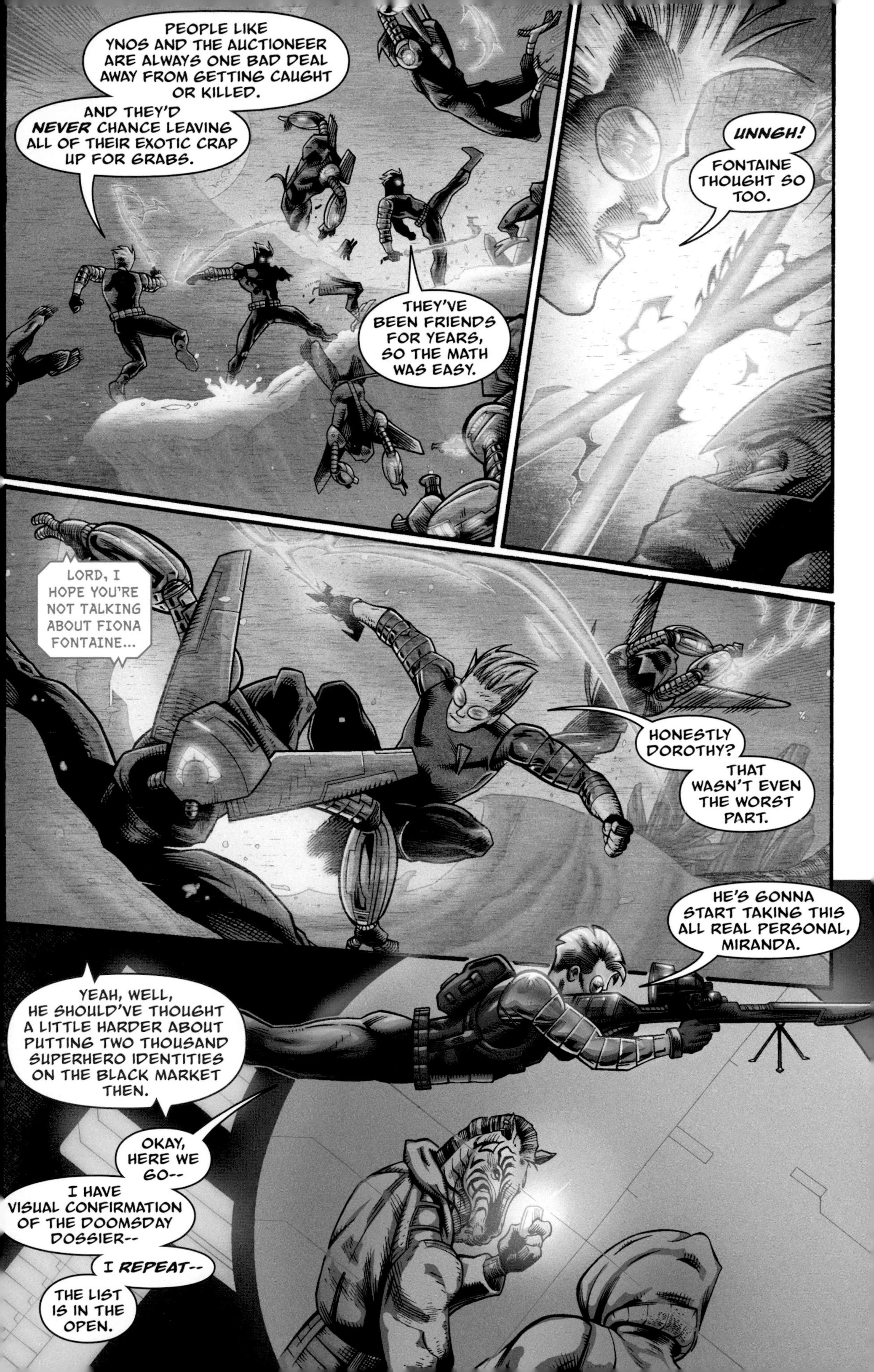
PEOPLE LIKE YNOS AND THE AUCTIONEER ARE ALWAYS ONE BAD DEAL AWAY FROM GETTING CAUGHT OR KILLED.
AND THEY'D *NEVER* CHANCE LEAVING ALL OF THEIR EXOTIC CRAP UP FOR GRABS.
THEY'VE BEEN FRIENDS FOR YEARS, SO THE MATH WAS EASY.
UNNGH!
FONTAINE THOUGHT SO TOO.
LORD, I HOPE YOU'RE NOT TALKING ABOUT FIONA FONTAINE...
HONESTLY DOROTHY?
THAT WASN'T EVEN THE WORST PART.
HE'S GONNA START TAKING THIS ALL REAL PERSONAL, MIRANDA.
YEAH, WELL, HE SHOULD'VE THOUGHT A LITTLE HARDER ABOUT PUTTING TWO THOUSAND SUPERHERO IDENTITIES ON THE BLACK MARKET THEN.
OKAY, HERE WE GO--
I HAVE VISUAL CONFIRMATION OF THE DOOMSDAY DOSSIER--
I *REPEAT*--
THE LIST IS IN THE OPEN.

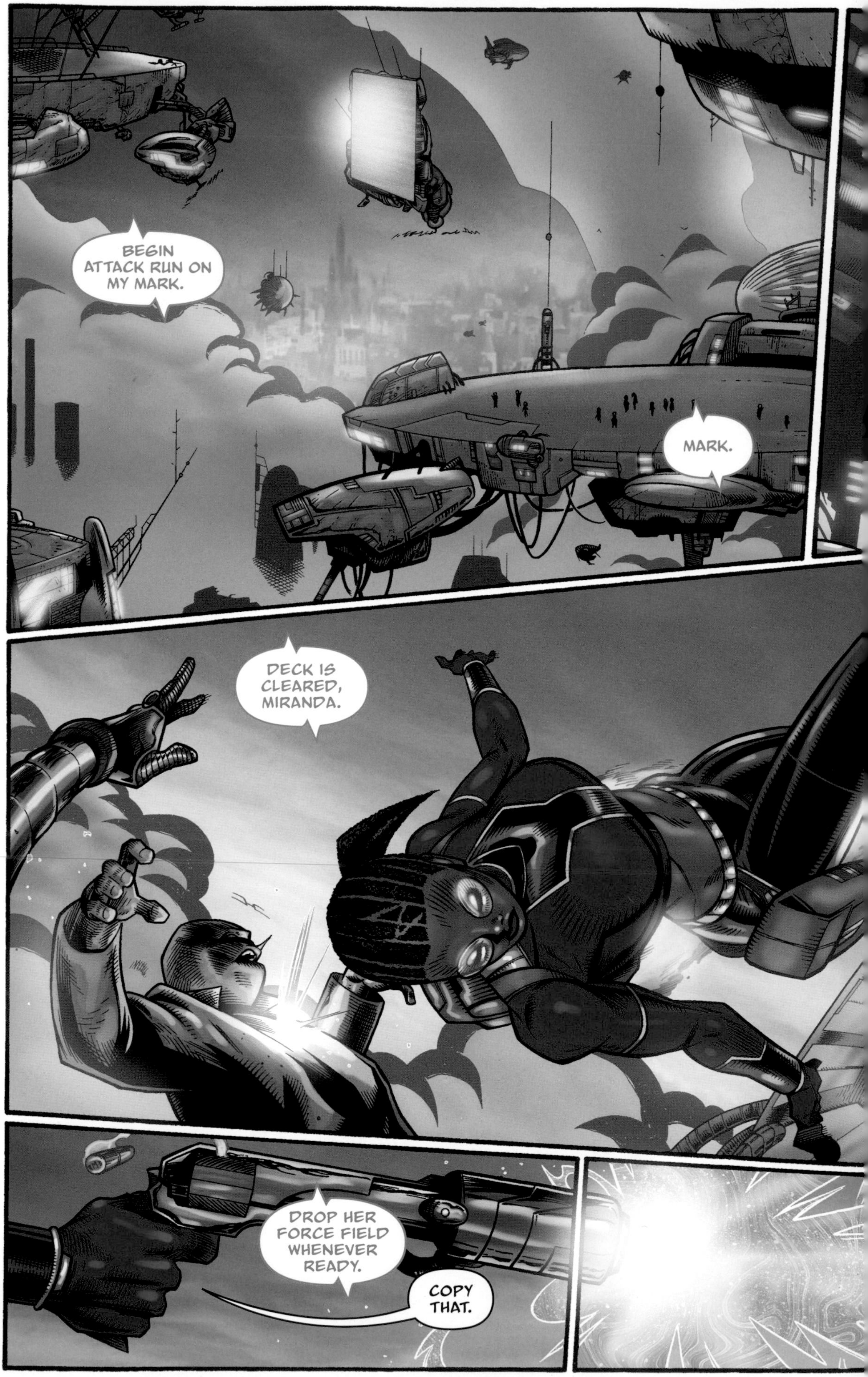
BEGIN ATTACK RUN ON MY MARK.
MARK.
DECK IS CLEARED, MIRANDA.
DROP HER FORCE FIELD WHENEVER READY.
COPY THAT.

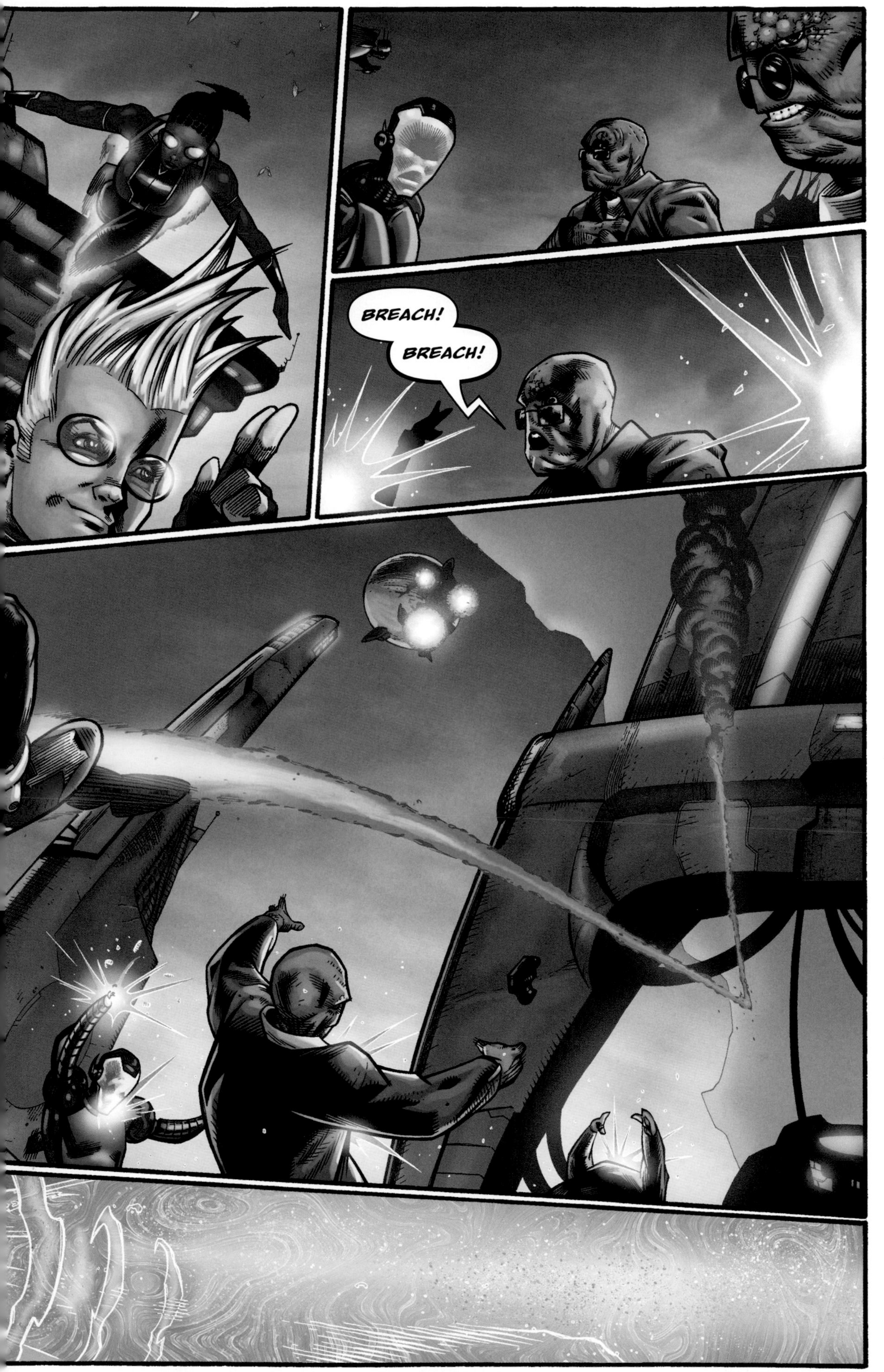
BREACH!
BREACH!

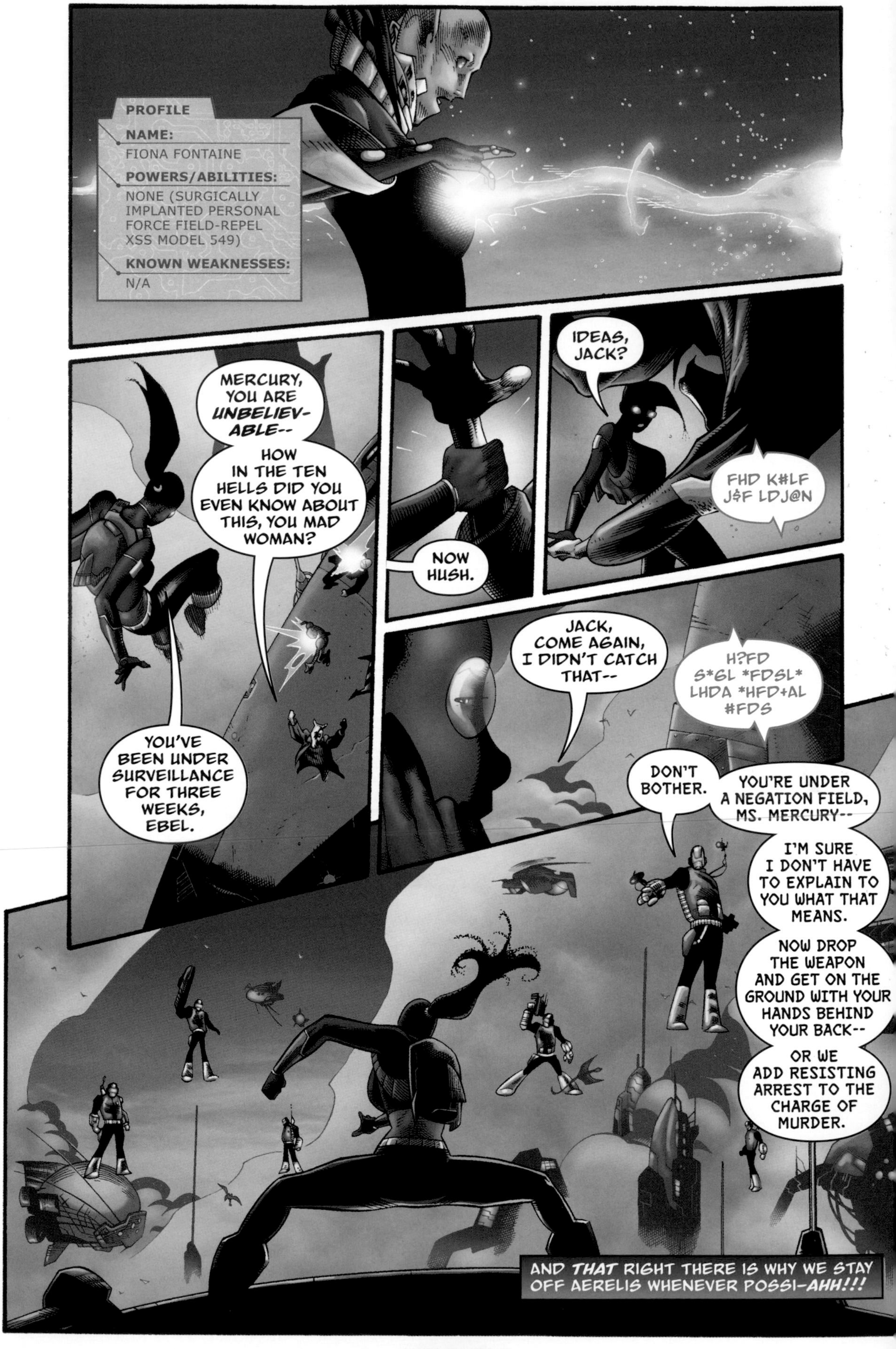
PROFILE
NAME:
FIONA FONTAINE
POWERS/ABILITIES:
NONE (SURGICALLY IMPLANTED PERSONAL FORCE FIELD-REPEL XSS MODEL 549)
KNOWN WEAKNESSES:
N/A
MERCURY, YOU ARE UNBELIEV-ABLE--
HOW IN THE TEN HELLS DID YOU EVEN KNOW ABOUT THIS, YOU MAD WOMAN?
YOU'VE BEEN UNDER SURVEILLANCE FOR THREE WEEKS, EBEL.
NOW HUSH.
IDEAS, JACK?
FHD K#LF J$F LDJ@N
JACK, COME AGAIN, I DIDN'T CATCH THAT--
H?FD S*GL *FDSL* LHDA *HFD+AL #FDS
DON'T BOTHER.
YOU'RE UNDER A NEGATION FIELD, MS. MERCURY--
I'M SURE I DON'T HAVE TO EXPLAIN TO YOU WHAT THAT MEANS.
NOW DROP THE WEAPON AND GET ON THE GROUND WITH YOUR HANDS BEHIND YOUR BACK--
OR WE ADD RESISTING ARREST TO THE CHARGE OF MURDER.
AND THAT RIGHT THERE IS WHY WE STAY OFF AERELIS WHENEVER POSSI-AHH!!!

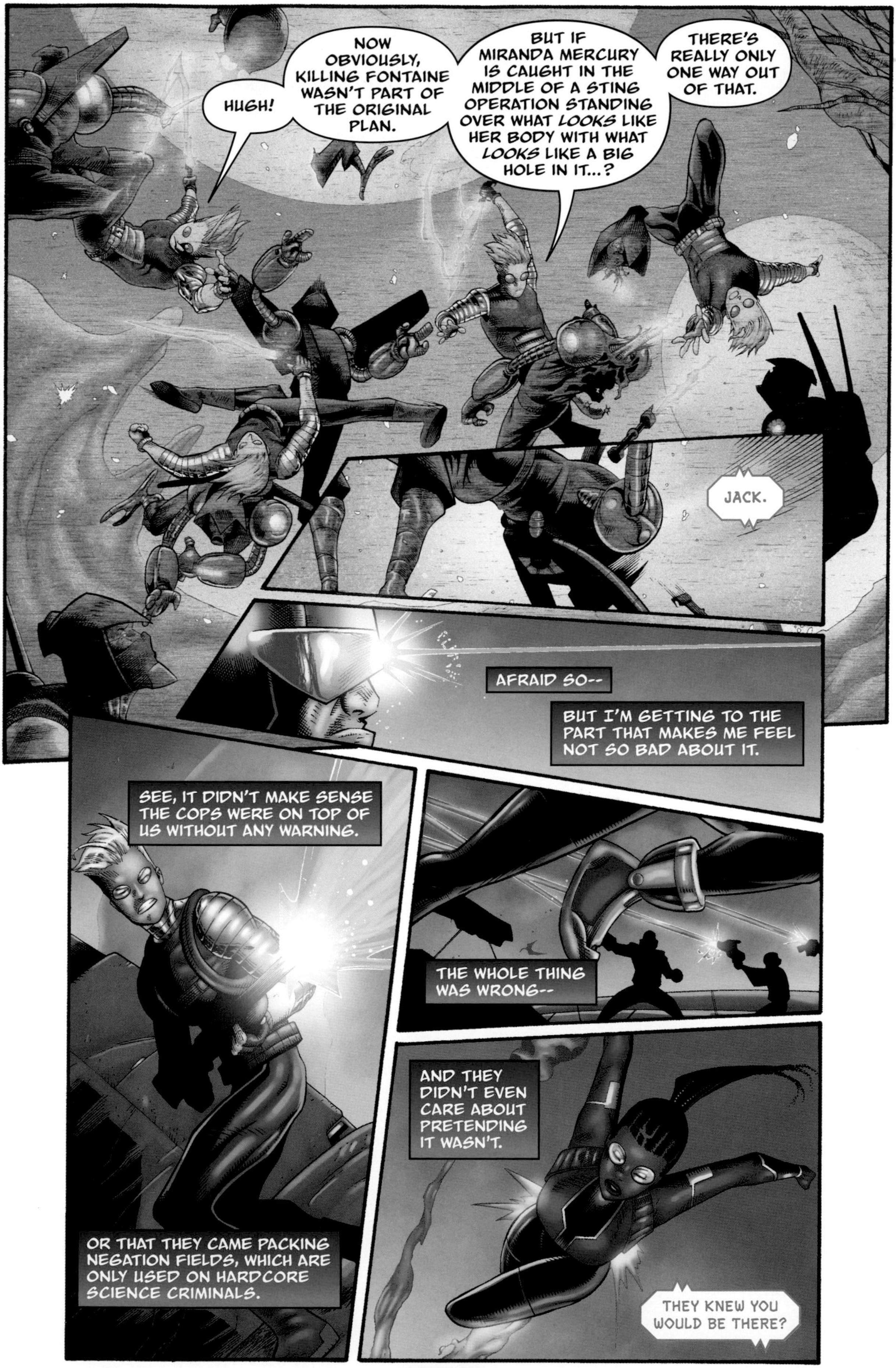
HUGH!
NOW OBVIOUSLY, KILLING FONTAINE WASN'T PART OF THE ORIGINAL PLAN.
BUT IF MIRANDA MERCURY IS CAUGHT IN THE MIDDLE OF A STING OPERATION STANDING OVER WHAT LOOKS LIKE HER BODY WITH WHAT LOOKS LIKE A BIG HOLE IN IT...?
THERE'S REALLY ONLY ONE WAY OUT OF THAT.
JACK.
AFRAID SO--
BUT I'M GETTING TO THE PART THAT MAKES ME FEEL NOT SO BAD ABOUT IT.
SEE, IT DIDN'T MAKE SENSE THE COPS WERE ON TOP OF US WITHOUT ANY WARNING.
OR THAT THEY CAME PACKING NEGATION FIELDS, WHICH ARE ONLY USED ON HARDCORE SCIENCE CRIMINALS.
THE WHOLE THING WAS WRONG--
AND THEY DIDN'T EVEN CARE ABOUT PRETENDING IT WASN'T.
THEY KNEW YOU WOULD BE THERE?

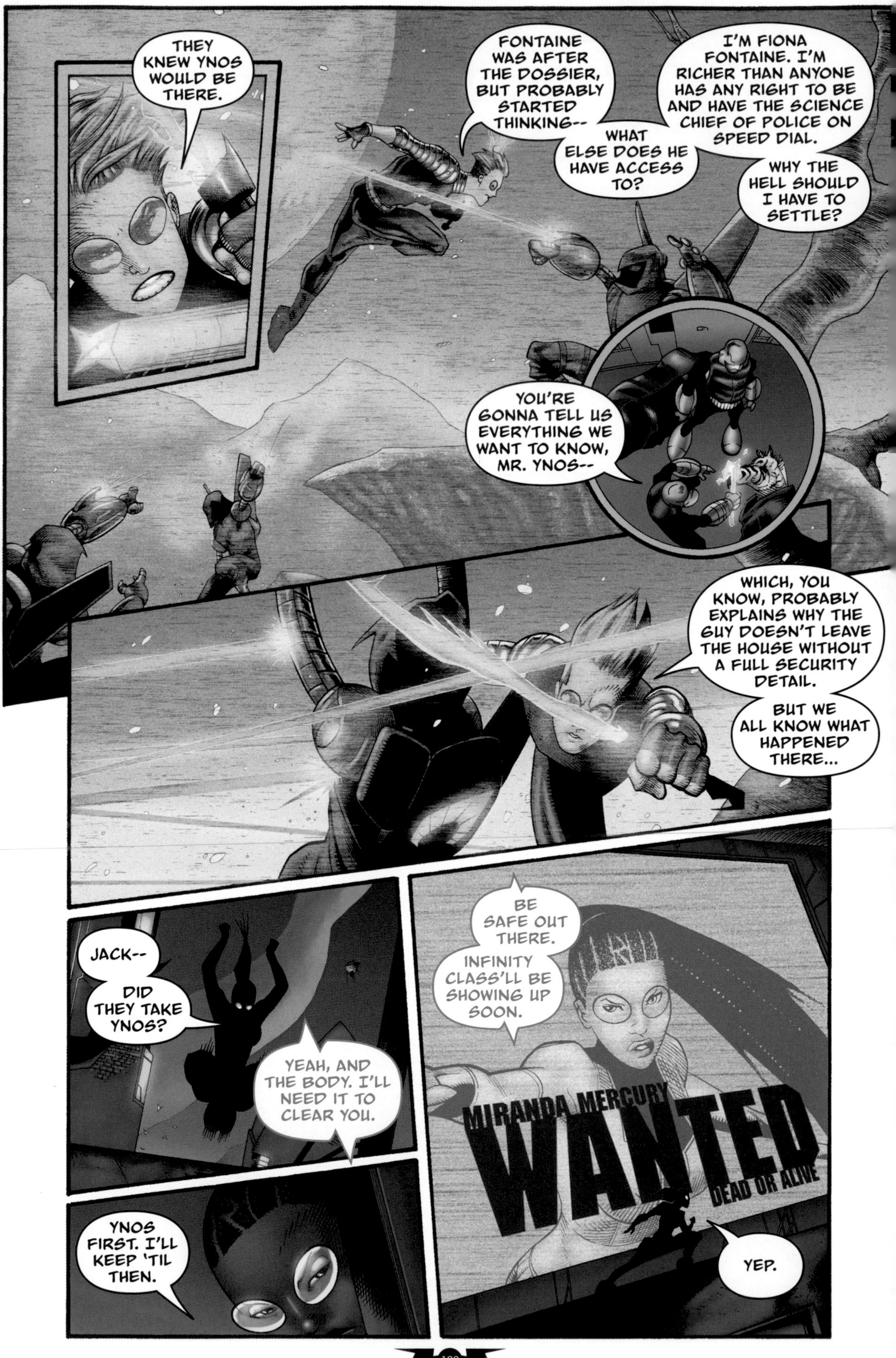
THEY KNEW YNOS WOULD BE THERE.
FONTAINE WAS AFTER THE DOSSIER, BUT PROBABLY STARTED THINKING--
WHAT ELSE DOES HE HAVE ACCESS TO?
I'M FIONA FONTAINE. I'M RICHER THAN ANYONE HAS ANY RIGHT TO BE AND HAVE THE SCIENCE CHIEF OF POLICE ON SPEED DIAL.
WHY THE HELL SHOULD I HAVE TO SETTLE?
YOU'RE GONNA TELL US EVERYTHING WE WANT TO KNOW, MR. YNOS--
WHICH, YOU KNOW, PROBABLY EXPLAINS WHY THE GUY DOESN'T LEAVE THE HOUSE WITHOUT A FULL SECURITY DETAIL.
BUT WE ALL KNOW WHAT HAPPENED THERE...
JACK--
DID THEY TAKE YNOS?
YEAH, AND THE BODY. I'LL NEED IT TO CLEAR YOU.
YNOS FIRST. I'LL KEEP 'TIL THEN.
BE SAFE OUT THERE.
INFINITY CLASS'LL BE SHOWING UP SOON.
MIRANDA MERCURY
WANTED
DEAD OR ALIVE
YEP.

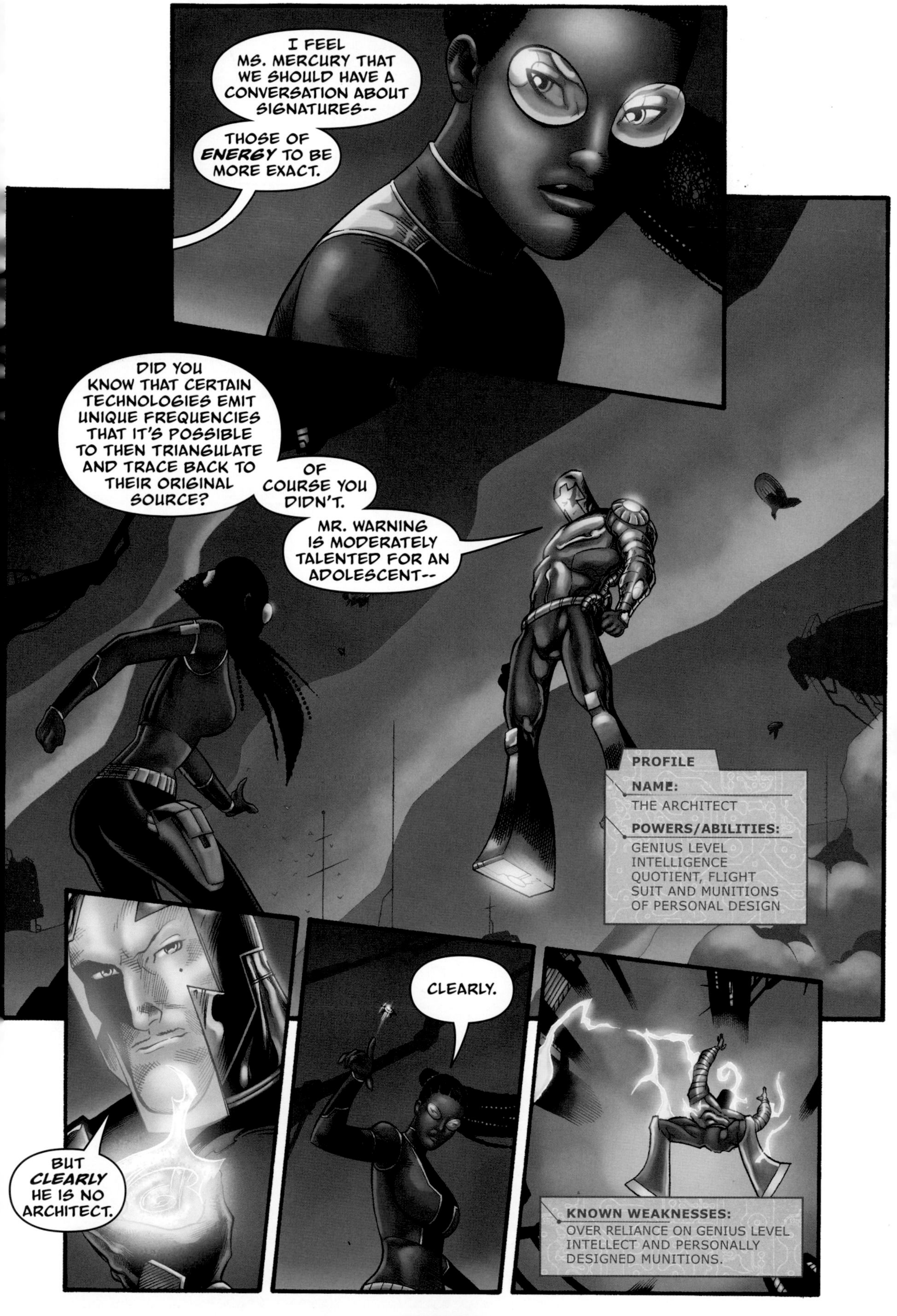

I FEEL MS. MERCURY THAT WE SHOULD HAVE A CONVERSATION ABOUT SIGNATURES--
THOSE OF ENERGY TO BE MORE EXACT.
DID YOU KNOW THAT CERTAIN TECHNOLOGIES EMIT UNIQUE FREQUENCIES THAT IT'S POSSIBLE TO THEN TRIANGULATE AND TRACE BACK TO THEIR ORIGINAL SOURCE?
OF COURSE YOU DIDN'T.
MR. WARNING IS MODERATELY TALENTED FOR AN ADOLESCENT--
PROFILE
NAME:
THE ARCHITECT
POWERS/ABILITIES:
GENIUS LEVEL INTELLIGENCE QUOTIENT, FLIGHT SUIT AND MUNITIONS OF PERSONAL DESIGN
BUT CLEARLY HE IS NO ARCHITECT.
CLEARLY.
KNOWN WEAKNESSES:
OVER RELIANCE ON GENIUS LEVEL INTELLECT AND PERSONALLY DESIGNED MUNITIONS.

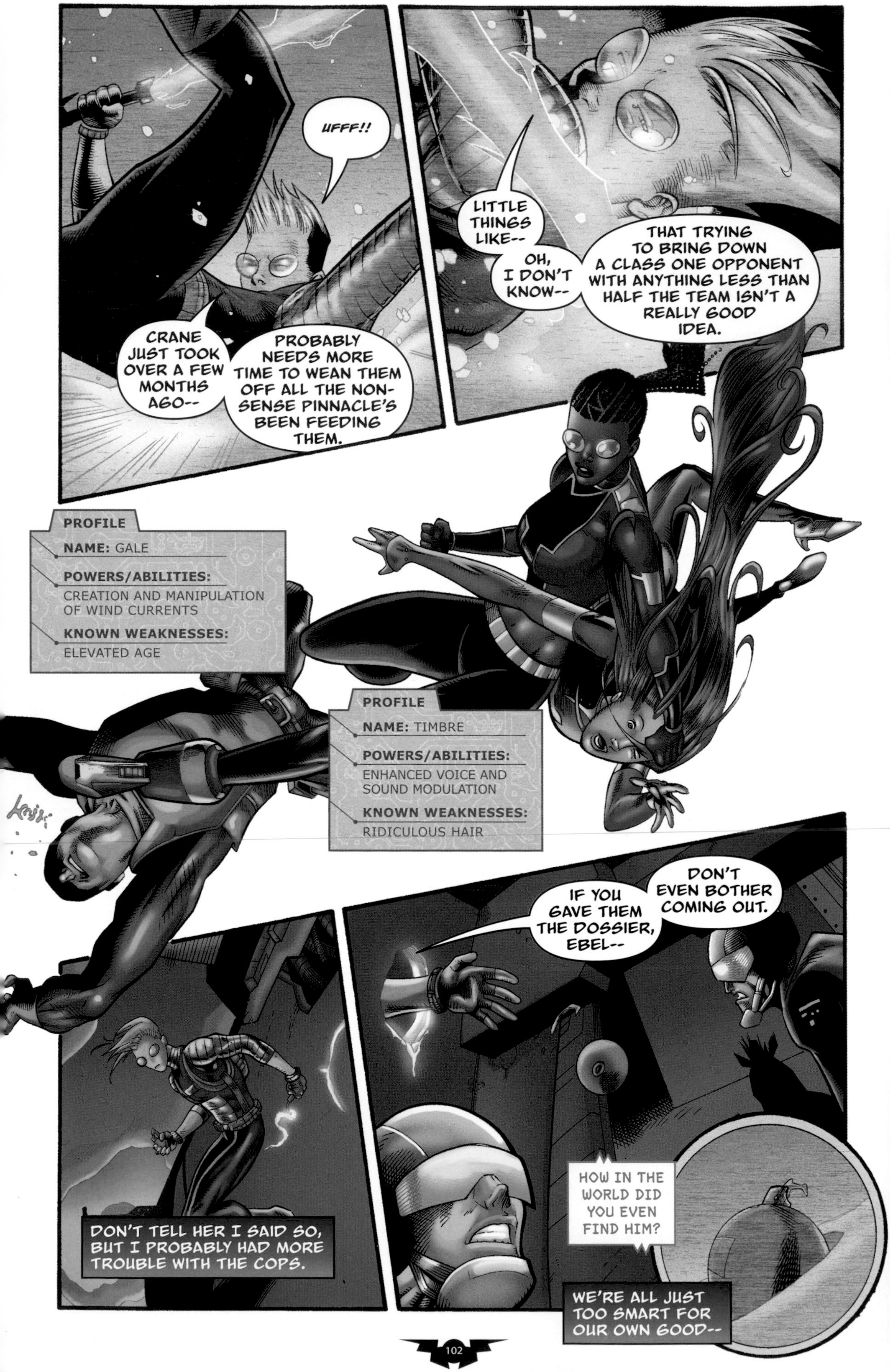
UFFF!!
LITTLE THINGS LIKE--
OH, I DON'T KNOW--
THAT TRYING TO BRING DOWN A CLASS ONE OPPONENT WITH ANYTHING LESS THAN HALF THE TEAM ISN'T A REALLY GOOD IDEA.
CRANE JUST TOOK OVER A FEW MONTHS AGO--
PROBABLY NEEDS MORE TIME TO WEAN THEM OFF ALL THE NON-SENSE PINNACLE'S BEEN FEEDING THEM.
PROFILE
NAME: GALE
POWERS/ABILITIES:
CREATION AND MANIPULATION OF WIND CURRENTS
KNOWN WEAKNESSES:
ELEVATED AGE
PROFILE
NAME: TIMBRE
POWERS/ABILITIES:
ENHANCED VOICE AND SOUND MODULATION
KNOWN WEAKNESSES:
RIDICULOUS HAIR
DON'T TELL HER I SAID SO, BUT I PROBABLY HAD MORE TROUBLE WITH THE COPS.
DON'T EVEN BOTHER COMING OUT.
IF YOU GAVE THEM THE DOSSIER, EBEL--
HOW IN THE WORLD DID YOU EVEN FIND HIM?
WE'RE ALL JUST TOO SMART FOR OUR OWN GOOD--

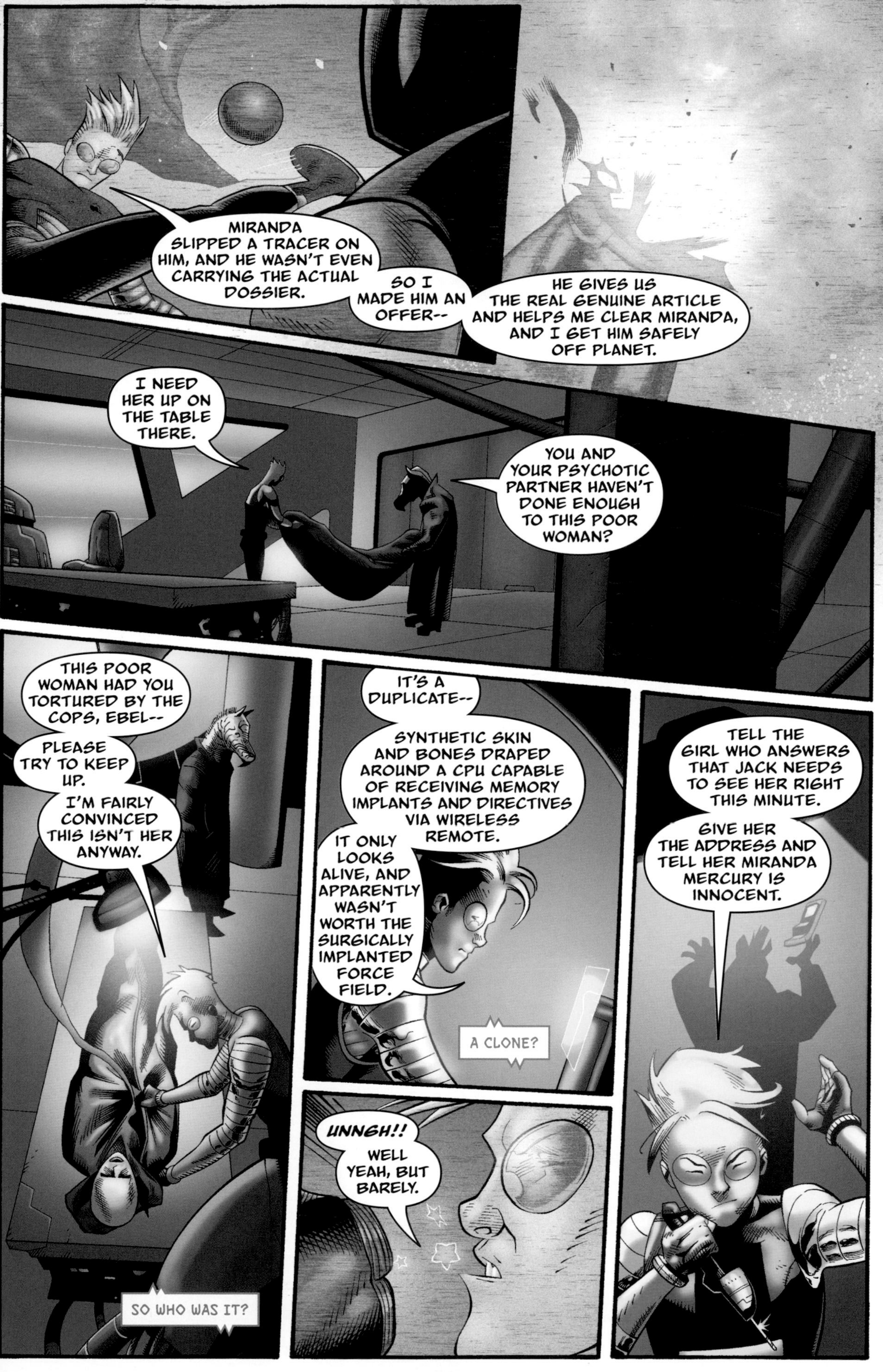
MIRANDA SLIPPED A TRACER ON HIM, AND HE WASN'T EVEN CARRYING THE ACTUAL DOSSIER.
SO I MADE HIM AN OFFER--
HE GIVES US THE REAL GENUINE ARTICLE AND HELPS ME CLEAR MIRANDA, AND I GET HIM SAFELY OFF PLANET.
I NEED HER UP ON THE TABLE THERE.
YOU AND YOUR PSYCHOTIC PARTNER HAVEN'T DONE ENOUGH TO THIS POOR WOMAN?
THIS POOR WOMAN HAD YOU TORTURED BY THE COPS, EBEL--
PLEASE TRY TO KEEP UP.
I'M FAIRLY CONVINCED THIS ISN'T HER ANYWAY.
SO WHO WAS IT?
IT'S A DUPLICATE--
SYNTHETIC SKIN AND BONES DRAPED AROUND A CPU CAPABLE OF RECEIVING MEMORY IMPLANTS AND DIRECTIVES VIA WIRELESS REMOTE.
IT ONLY LOOKS ALIVE, AND APPARENTLY WASN'T WORTH THE SURGICALLY IMPLANTED FORCE FIELD.
A CLONE?
UNNGH!!
WELL YEAH, BUT BARELY.
TELL THE GIRL WHO ANSWERS THAT JACK NEEDS TO SEE HER RIGHT THIS MINUTE.
GIVE HER THE ADDRESS AND TELL HER MIRANDA MERCURY IS INNOCENT.

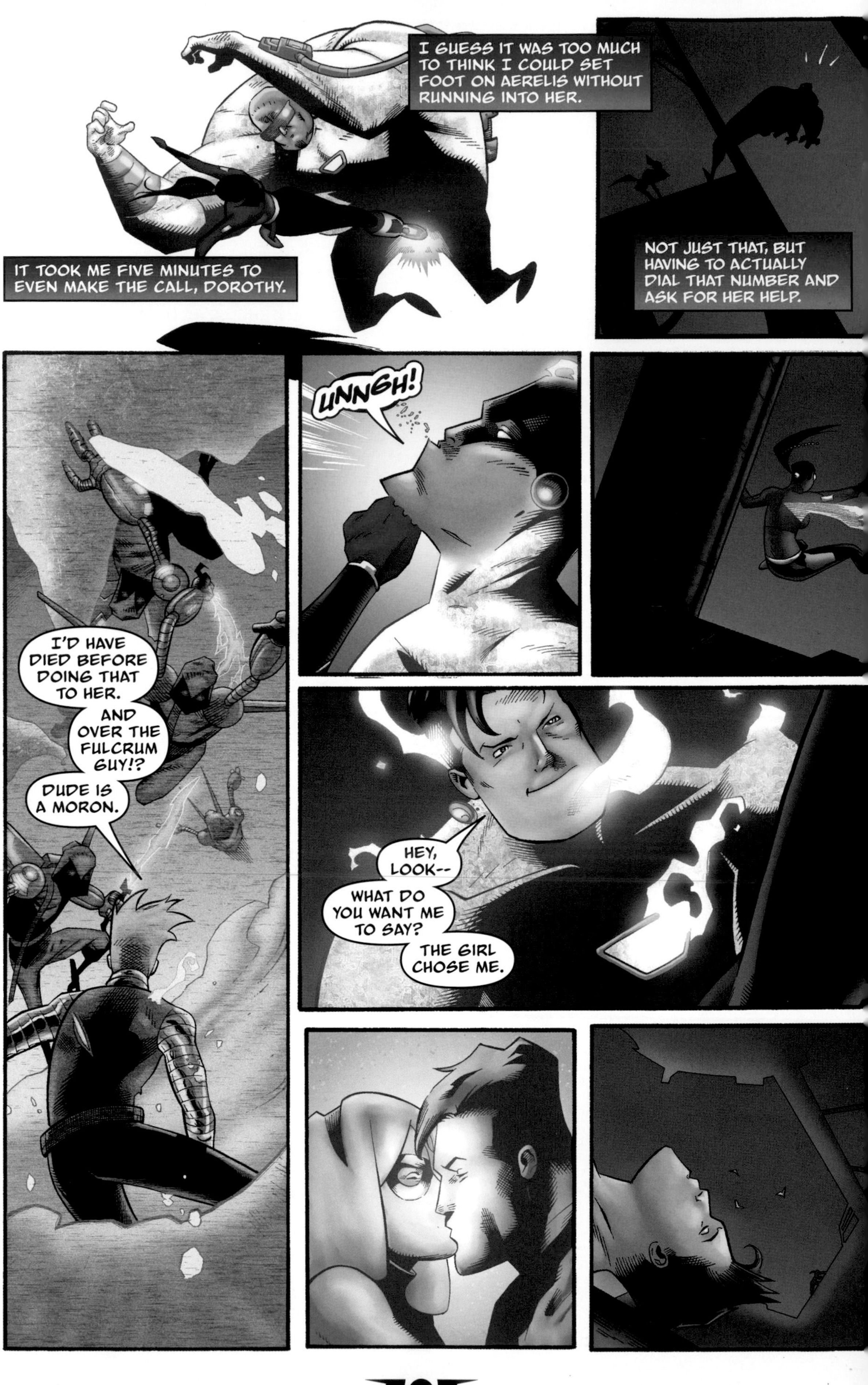
I GUESS IT WAS TOO MUCH TO THINK I COULD SET FOOT ON AERELIS WITHOUT RUNNING INTO HER.
IT TOOK ME FIVE MINUTES TO EVEN MAKE THE CALL, DOROTHY.
NOT JUST THAT, BUT HAVING TO ACTUALLY DIAL THAT NUMBER AND ASK FOR HER HELP.
I'D HAVE DIED BEFORE DOING THAT TO HER.
AND OVER THE FULCRUM GUY!?
DUDE IS A MORON.
UNNGH!
HEY, LOOK--
WHAT DO YOU WANT ME TO SAY?
THE GIRL CHOSE ME.

GAHH!

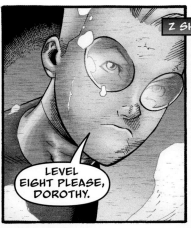

LEVEL EIGHT PLEASE, DOROTHY.

Z SHOULD'VE TOLD ME.

I DIDN'T HAVE TO FIND OUT LIKE THAT.

DON'T TELL Z I TOLD YOU THIS-- BUT YOU'RE GOOD.

SERIOUSLY.

IS THAT SUPPOSED TO BE FUNNY?

THE LITTLE MAN'LL GET OVER IT.

PROFILE

NAME:
FULCRUM

POWERS/ABILITIES:
ENHANCED SPEED, STRENGTH, AND AGILITY

KNOWN WEAKNESSES:
POWERS AND ABILITIES CAN ONLY MANIFEST AND BE MAINTAINED WHEN HOSTS ARE IN CLOSE PROXIMITY

JACK, HOW WE DOING?

ZAMANDA'S HAVING THE APB RESCINDED NOW.

I THINK WE'RE OKAY.

... INCOMING.

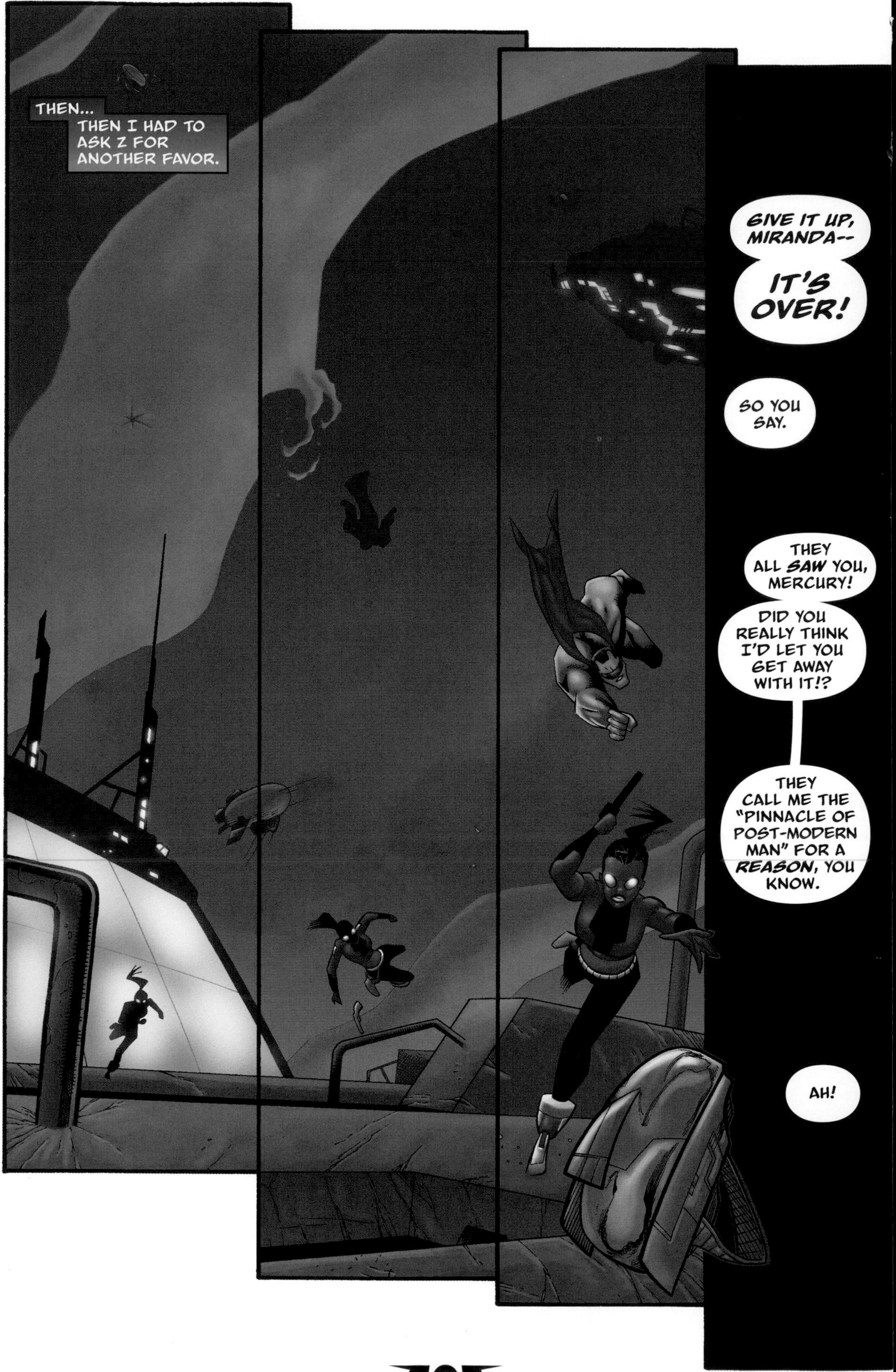
THEN...
THEN I HAD TO ASK Z FOR ANOTHER FAVOR.
GIVE IT UP, MIRANDA--
IT'S OVER!
SO YOU SAY.
THEY ALL SAW YOU, MERCURY!
DID YOU REALLY THINK I'D LET YOU GET AWAY WITH IT!?
THEY CALL ME THE "PINNACLE OF POST-MODERN MAN" FOR A REASON, YOU KNOW.
AH!

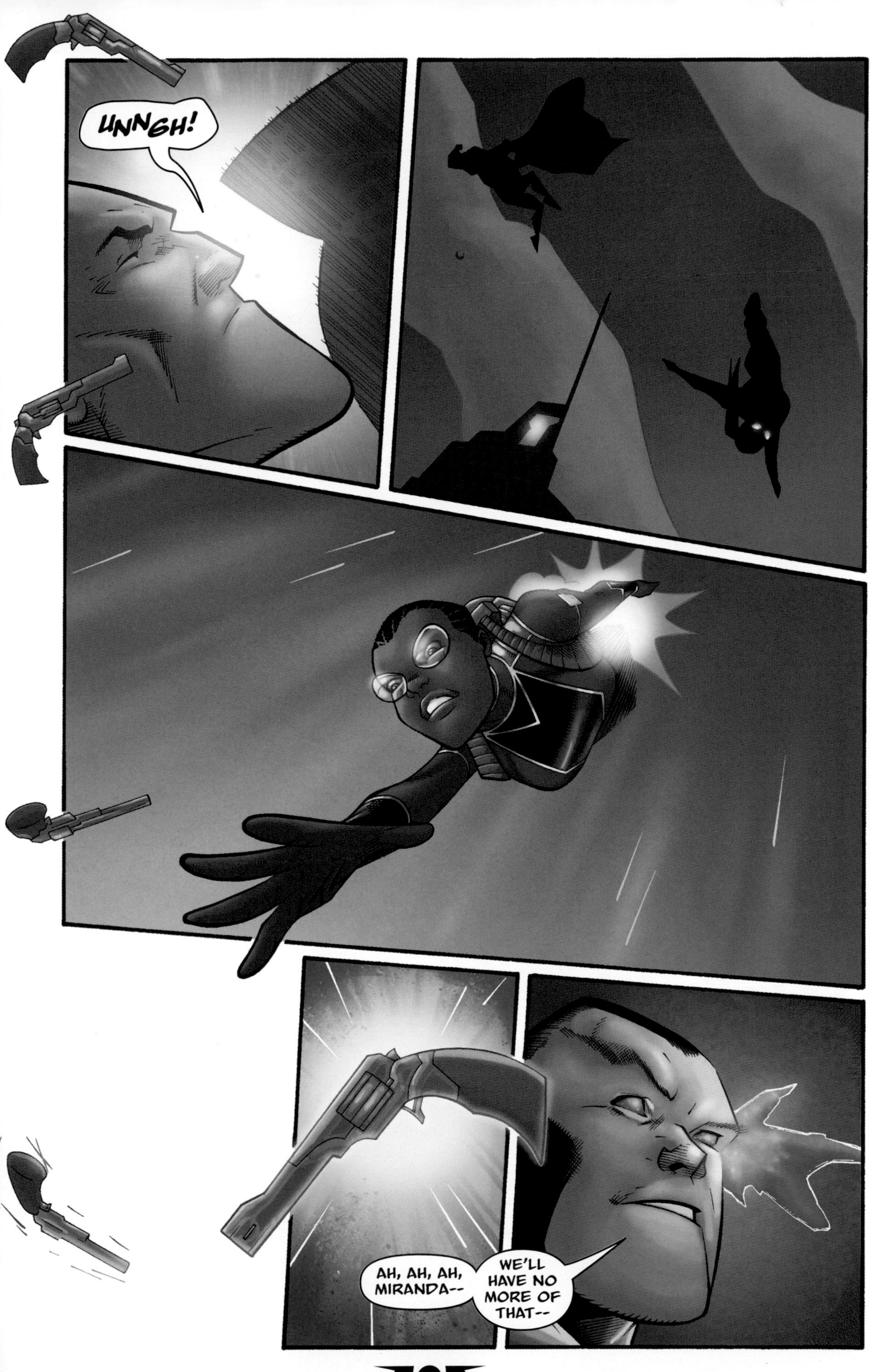
UNNGH!
AH, AH, AH, MIRANDA--
WE'LL HAVE NO MORE OF THAT--

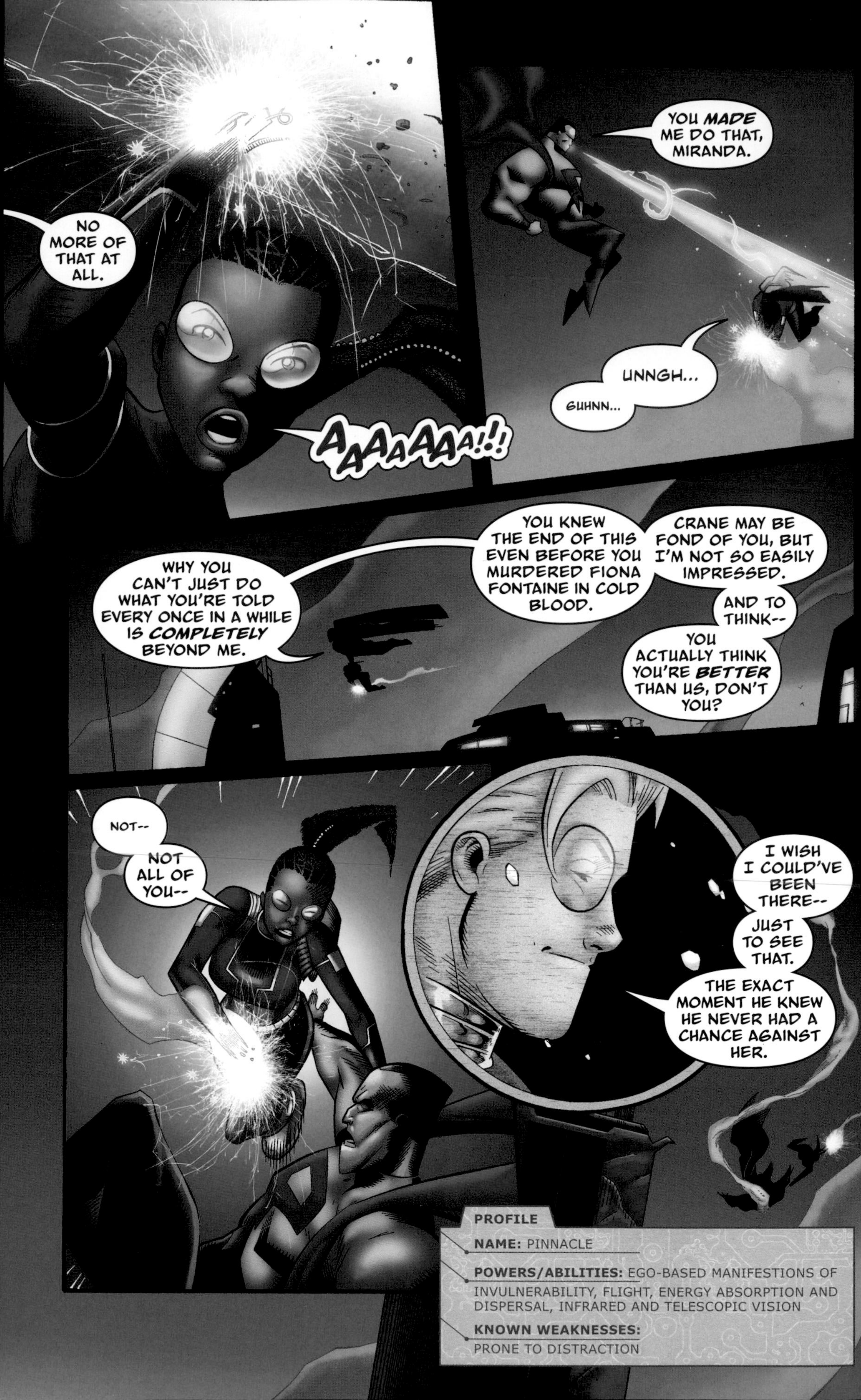
NO MORE OF THAT AT ALL.
AAAAAAA!!!
YOU MADE ME DO THAT, MIRANDA.
UNNGH...
GUHNN...
WHY YOU CAN'T JUST DO WHAT YOU'RE TOLD EVERY ONCE IN A WHILE IS COMPLETELY BEYOND ME.
YOU KNEW THE END OF THIS EVEN BEFORE YOU MURDERED FIONA FONTAINE IN COLD BLOOD.
CRANE MAY BE FOND OF YOU, BUT I'M NOT SO EASILY IMPRESSED.
AND TO THINK--
YOU ACTUALLY THINK YOU'RE BETTER THAN US, DON'T YOU?
NOT--
NOT ALL OF YOU--
I WISH I COULD'VE BEEN THERE--
JUST TO SEE THAT.
THE EXACT MOMENT HE KNEW HE NEVER HAD A CHANCE AGAINST HER.
PROFILE
NAME: PINNACLE
POWERS/ABILITIES: EGO-BASED MANIFESTIONS OF INVULNERABILITY, FLIGHT, ENERGY ABSORPTION AND DISPERSAL, INFRARED AND TELESCOPIC VISION
KNOWN WEAKNESSES: PRONE TO DISTRACTION

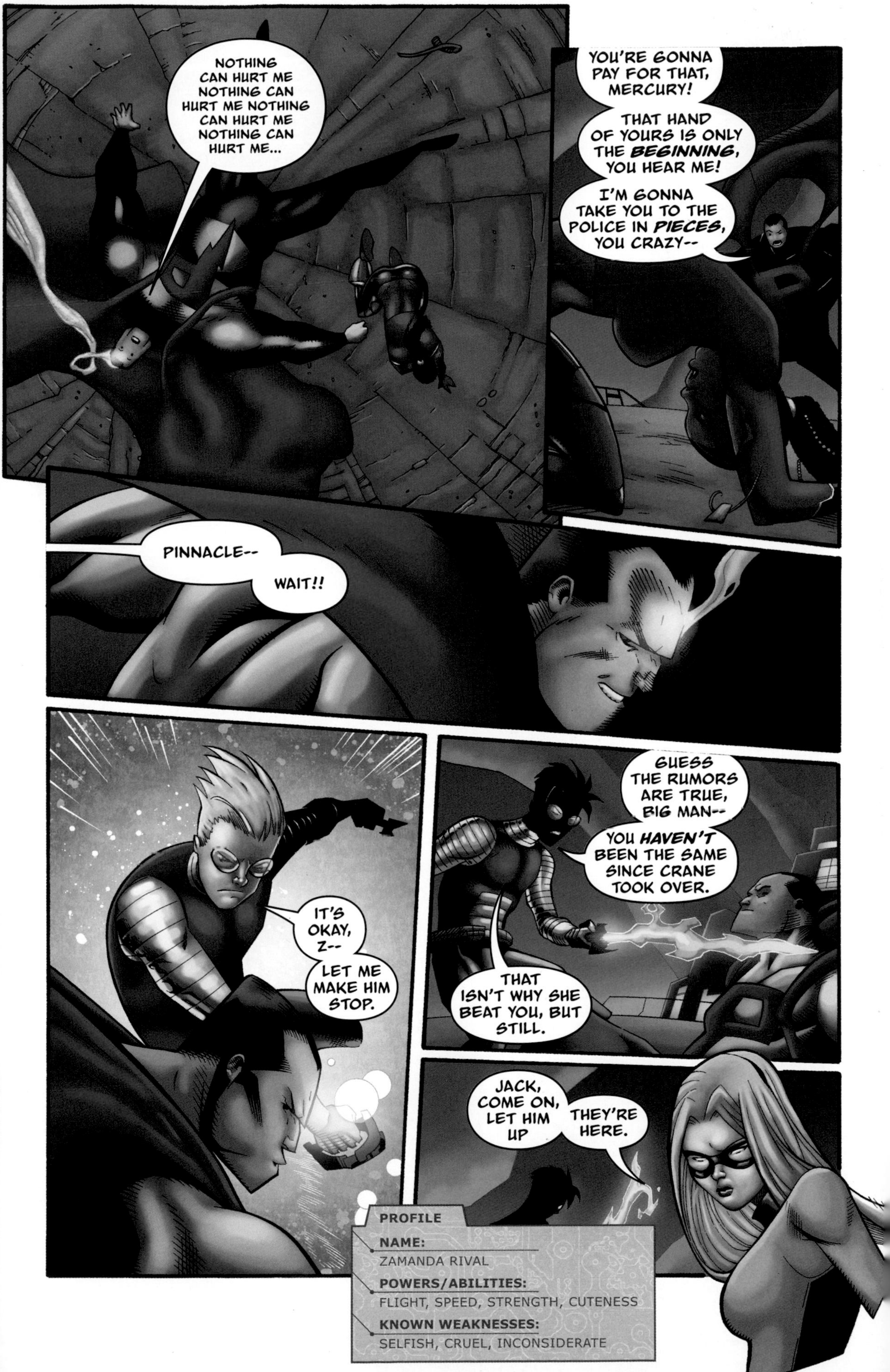
NOTHING CAN HURT ME NOTHING CAN HURT ME NOTHING CAN HURT ME NOTHING CAN HURT ME...
YOU'RE GONNA PAY FOR THAT, MERCURY!
THAT HAND OF YOURS IS ONLY THE *BEGINNING*, YOU HEAR ME!
I'M GONNA TAKE YOU TO THE POLICE IN *PIECES*, YOU CRAZY--
PINNACLE--
WAIT!!
IT'S OKAY, Z--
LET ME MAKE HIM STOP.
GUESS THE RUMORS ARE TRUE, BIG MAN--
YOU *HAVEN'T* BEEN THE SAME SINCE CRANE TOOK OVER.
THAT ISN'T WHY SHE BEAT YOU, BUT STILL.
JACK, COME ON, LET HIM UP
THEY'RE HERE.
PROFILE
NAME:
ZAMANDA RIVAL
POWERS/ABILITIES:
FLIGHT, SPEED, STRENGTH, CUTENESS
KNOWN WEAKNESSES:
SELFISH, CRUEL, INCONSIDERATE

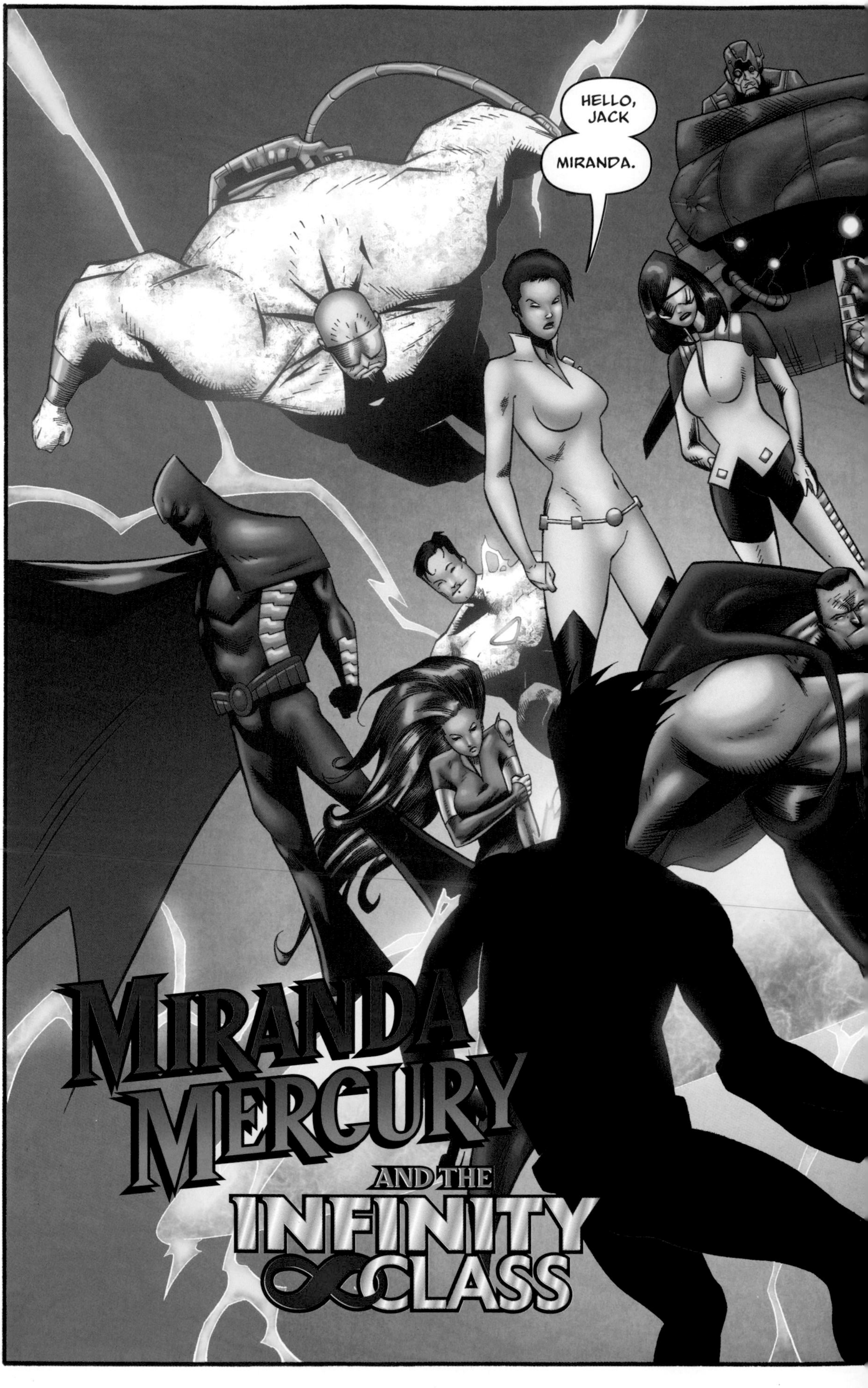
HELLO, JACK
MIRANDA.
MIRANDA MERCURY
AND THE
INFINITY CLASS

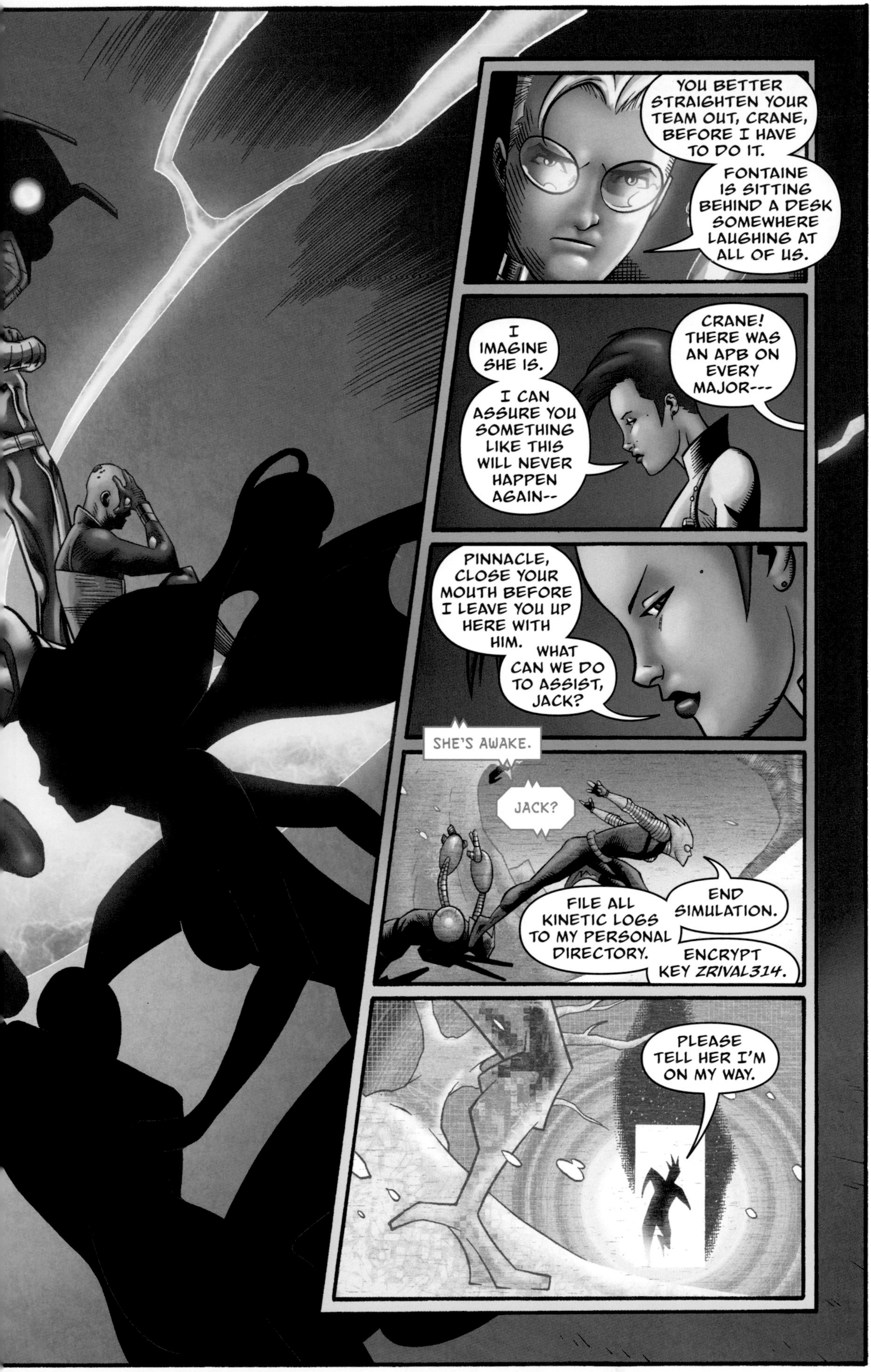

YOU BETTER STRAIGHTEN YOUR TEAM OUT, CRANE, BEFORE I HAVE TO DO IT.
FONTAINE IS SITTING BEHIND A DESK SOMEWHERE LAUGHING AT ALL OF US.
CRANE! THERE WAS AN APB ON EVERY MAJOR---
I IMAGINE SHE IS.
I CAN ASSURE YOU SOMETHING LIKE THIS WILL NEVER HAPPEN AGAIN--
PINNACLE, CLOSE YOUR MOUTH BEFORE I LEAVE YOU UP HERE WITH HIM.
WHAT CAN WE DO TO ASSIST, JACK?
SHE'S AWAKE.
JACK?
END SIMULATION.
FILE ALL KINETIC LOGS TO MY PERSONAL DIRECTORY.
ENCRYPT KEY ZRIVAL314.
PLEASE TELL HER I'M ON MY WAY.

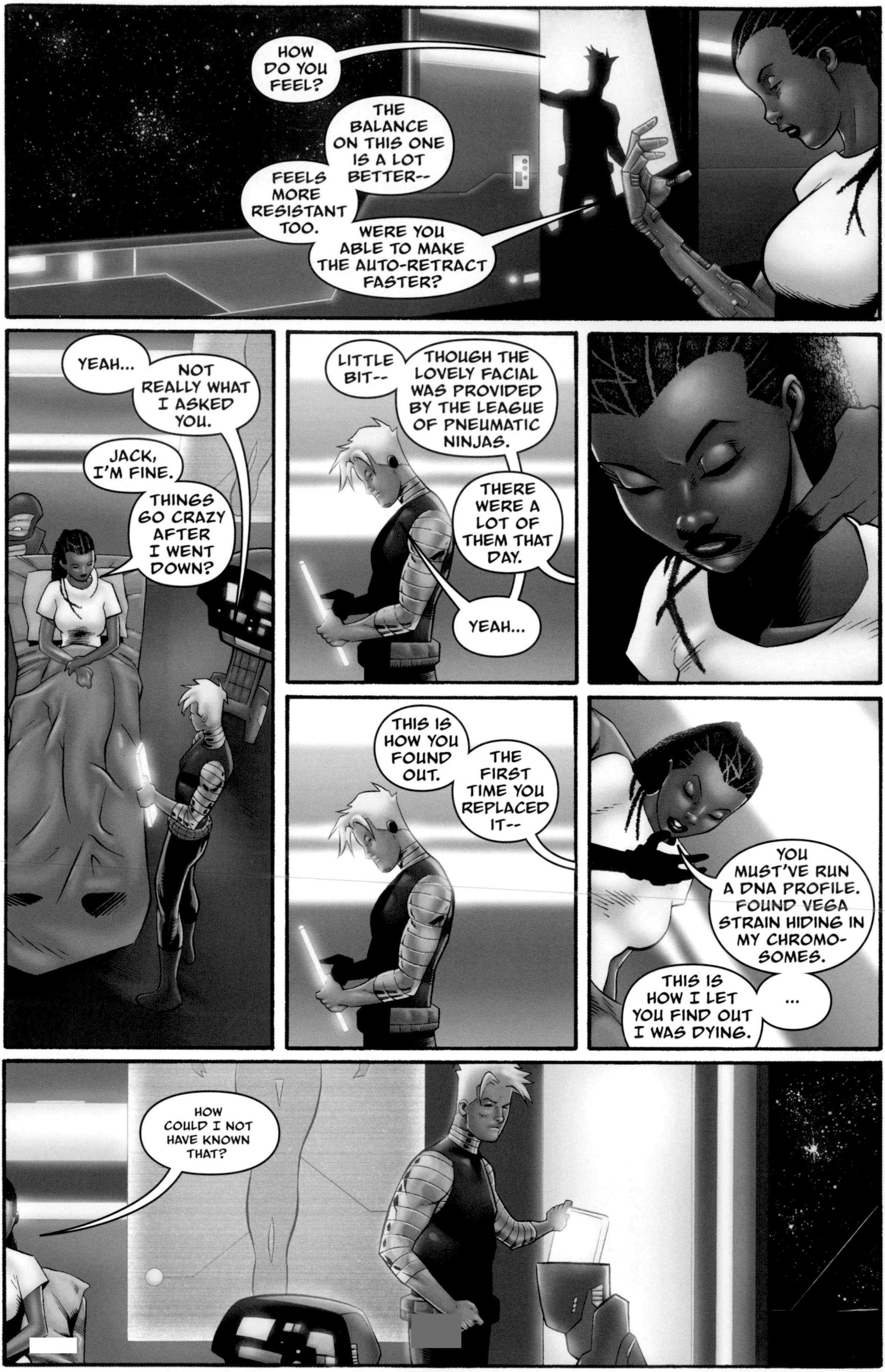
HOW DO YOU FEEL?
THE BALANCE ON THIS ONE IS A LOT BETTER--
FEELS MORE RESISTANT TOO.
WERE YOU ABLE TO MAKE THE AUTO-RETRACT FASTER?
YEAH...
NOT REALLY WHAT I ASKED YOU.
JACK, I'M FINE.
THINGS GO CRAZY AFTER I WENT DOWN?
LITTLE BIT--
THOUGH THE LOVELY FACIAL WAS PROVIDED BY THE LEAGUE OF PNEUMATIC NINJAS.
THERE WERE A LOT OF THEM THAT DAY.
YEAH...
THIS IS HOW YOU FOUND OUT.
THE FIRST TIME YOU REPLACED IT--
YOU MUST'VE RUN A DNA PROFILE. FOUND VEGA STRAIN HIDING IN MY CHROMO-SOMES.
THIS IS HOW I LET YOU FIND OUT I WAS DYING.
...
HOW COULD I NOT HAVE KNOWN THAT?

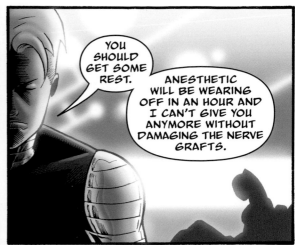

YOU SHOULD GET SOME REST.

ANESTHETIC WILL BE WEARING OFF IN AN HOUR AND I CAN'T GIVE YOU ANYMORE WITHOUT DAMAGING THE NERVE GRAFTS.

I'LL BE BACK LATER WITH FOOD.

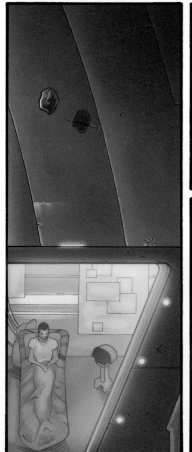

AND YOU'RE SURE ABOUT THIS, JACK?

THE VIRUS IS GETTING WORSE, AND SHE WON'T SLOW DOWN, DOROTHY.

THIS IS WHAT WE'RE DOING NOW.

I--I UNDERSTAND, SWEETIE, BUT THIS CAN'T BE WHAT SHE'D WANT FROM YOU.

I DON'T CARE.

AFTER EVERYTHING THAT HORRIBLE MAN HAS DONE TO HER--

I DON'T CARE!

SHE ALMOST *DIED* ON THE TABLE, DOROTHY!!

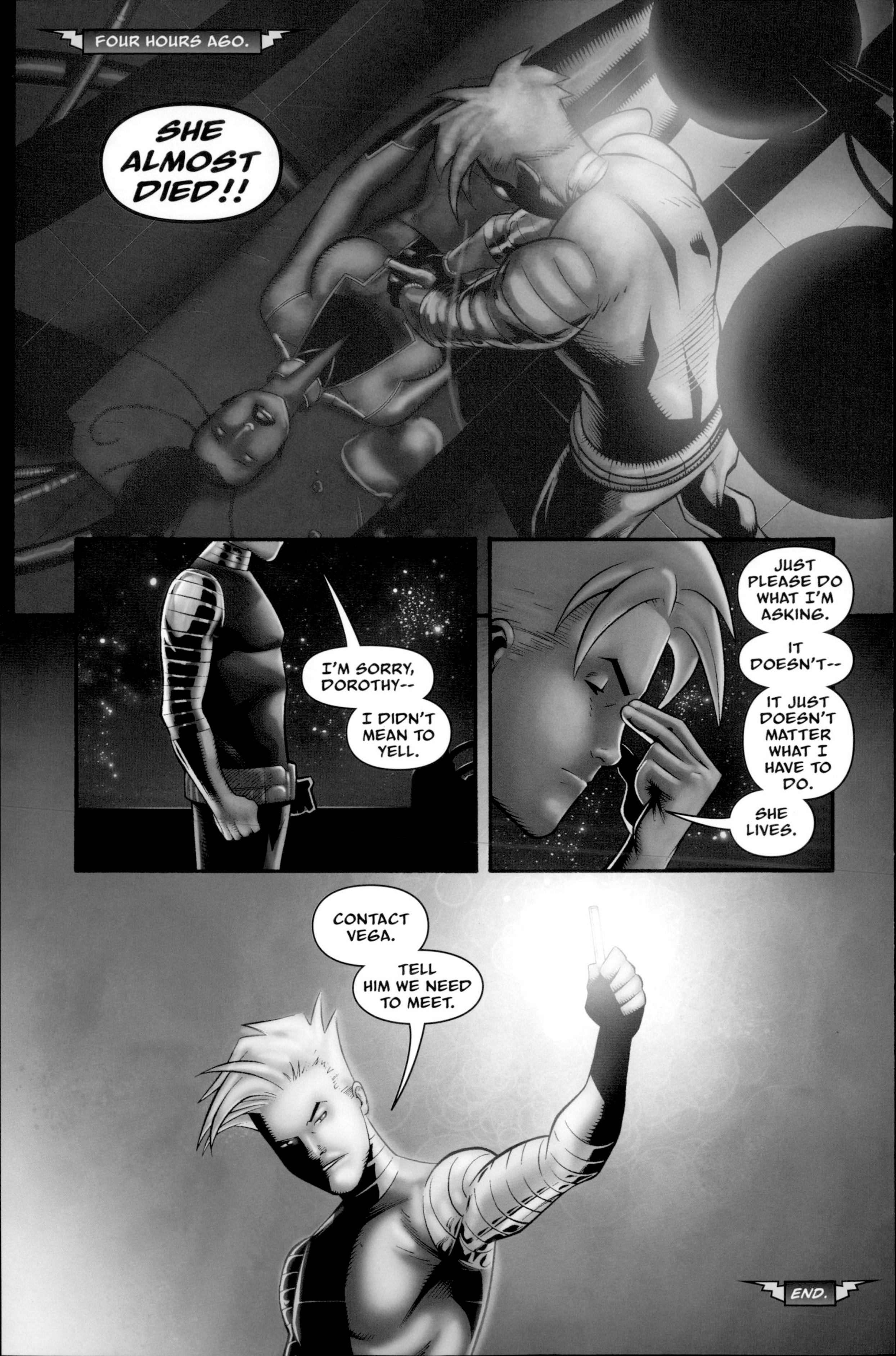
FOUR HOURS AGO.
SHE ALMOST DIED!!
I'M SORRY, DOROTHY--
I DIDN'T MEAN TO YELL.
JUST PLEASE DO WHAT I'M ASKING.
IT DOESN'T--
IT JUST DOESN'T MATTER WHAT I HAVE TO DO.
SHE LIVES.
CONTACT VEGA.
TELL HIM WE NEED TO MEET.
END.

IT WAS A TRAP!

MIRANDA AND JACK RECEIVED INTEL
THAT BROTHER SYNN WAS PLANNING TO SEIZE
A DIPLOMATIC ENVOY AND DEMAND RANSOM
FROM THE DELEGATION'S HOME PLANET.
WHAT THEY FOUND INSTEAD
WAS A SHUTTLE FILLED WITH BOUNTY HUNTERS,
READY AND WAITING FOR THEIR ARRIVAL.

SYNN'S CREW WANTS
SOMETHING FROM THEM.

AND THEY'VE BEEN TOLD TO DO
WHATEVER THEY HAVE TO
IN ORDER TO GET IT.

EPISODE 299

MIRANDA MERCURY
AND THE PERILS OF YOR!

WRITER
BRANDON THOMAS

PENCILER
LEE FERGUSON

INKER
MARC DEERING

LETTERER
MATTY RYAN

COLORIST
CRAIG CERMAK

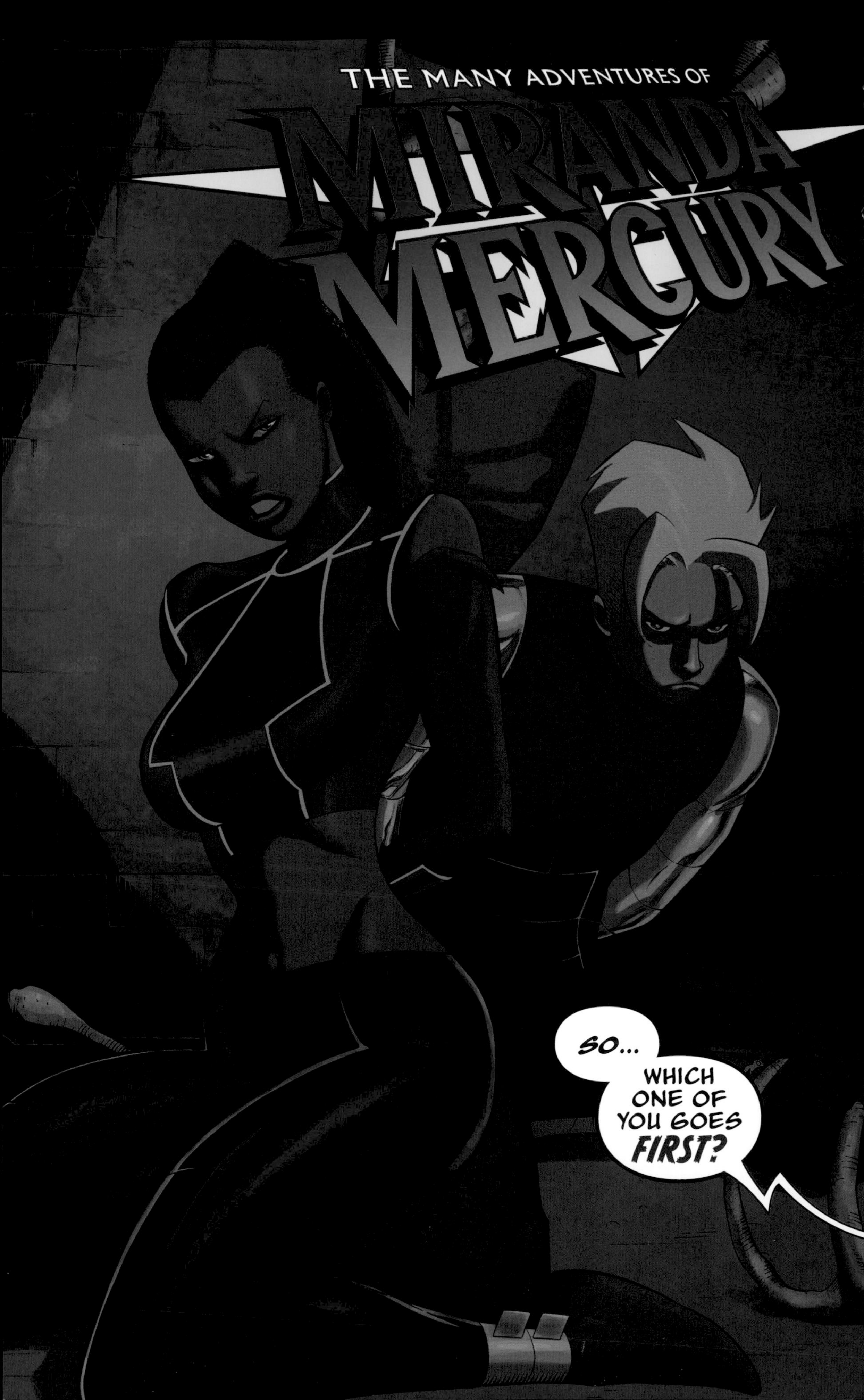
THE MANY ADVENTURES OF
MIRANDA MERCURY
SO...
WHICH ONE OF YOU GOES FIRST?

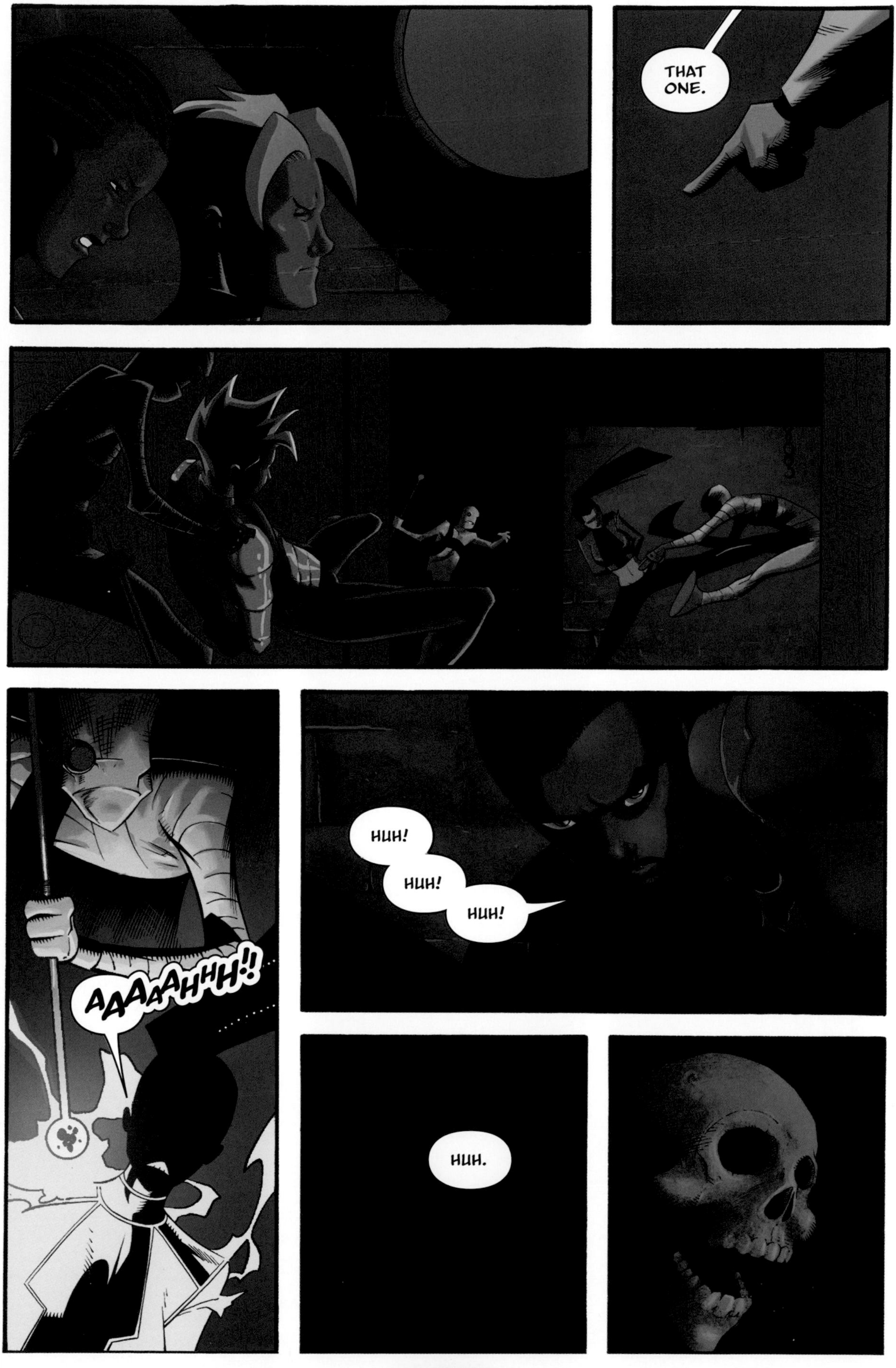
THAT ONE.
AAAAAHHH!!
HUH!
HUH!
HUH!
HUH.

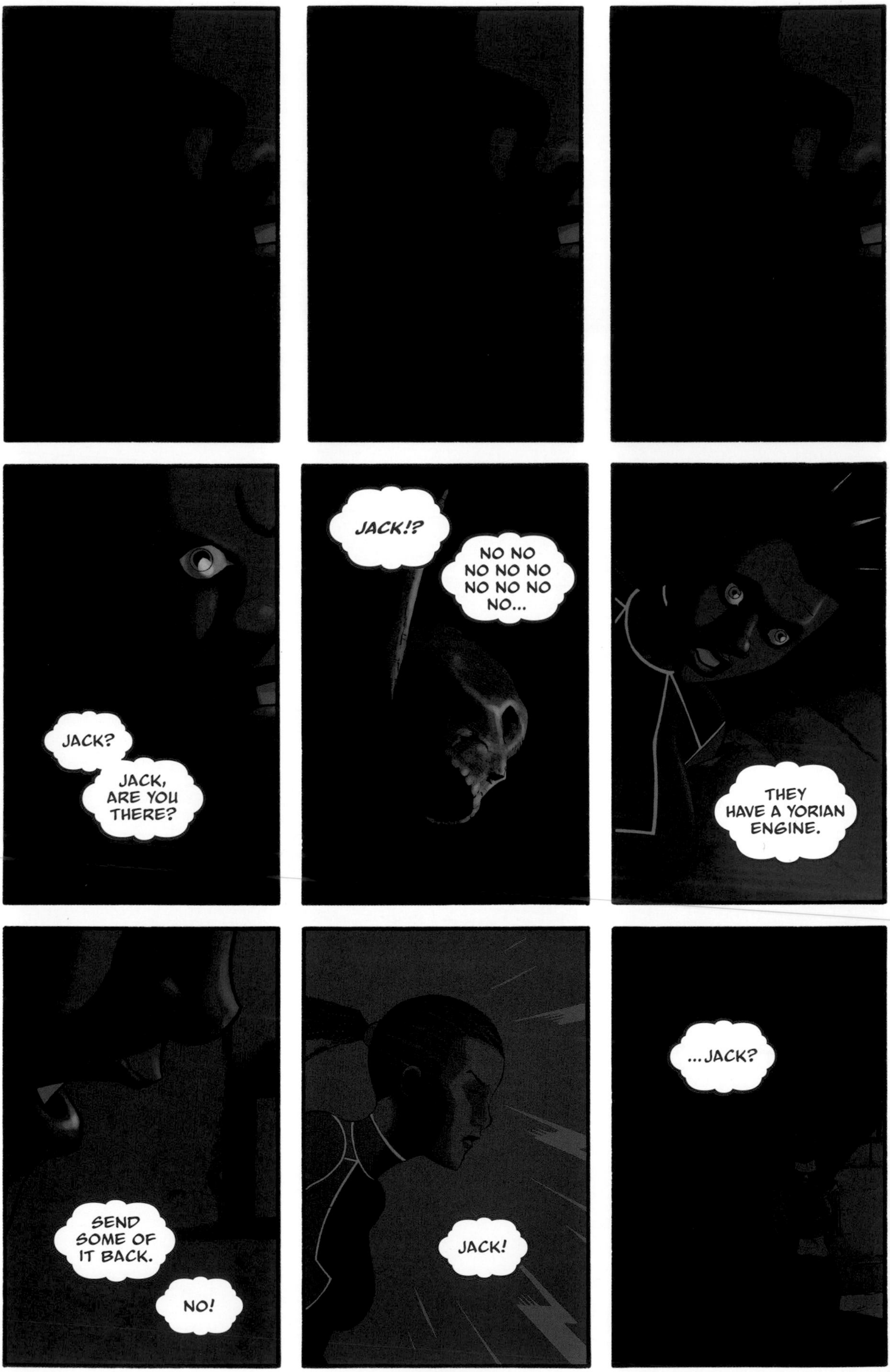
JACK?
JACK, ARE YOU THERE?
JACK!?
NO NO NO NO NO NO NO NO NO...
THEY HAVE A YORIAN ENGINE.
SEND SOME OF IT BACK.
NO!
JACK!
...JACK?

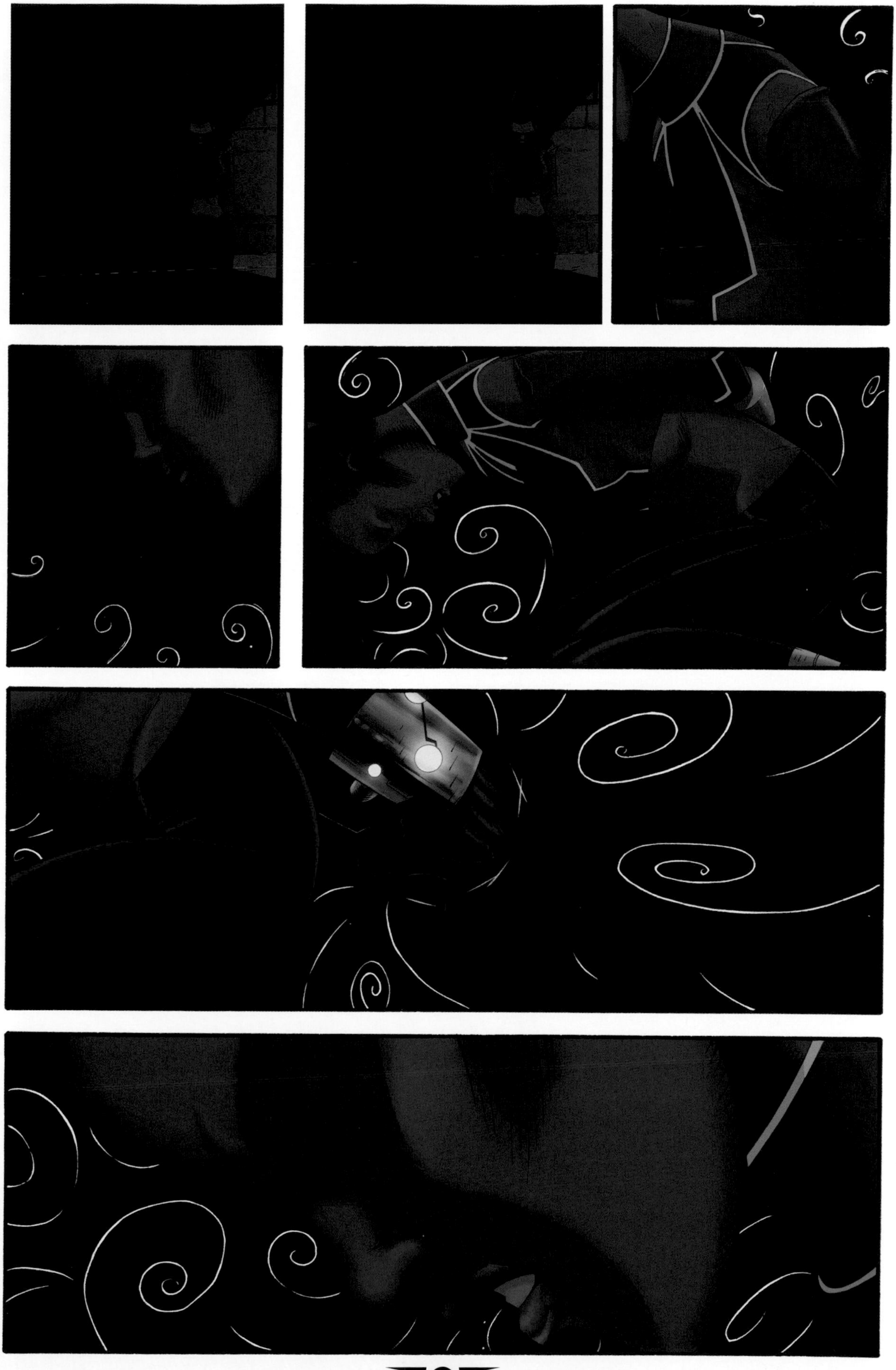

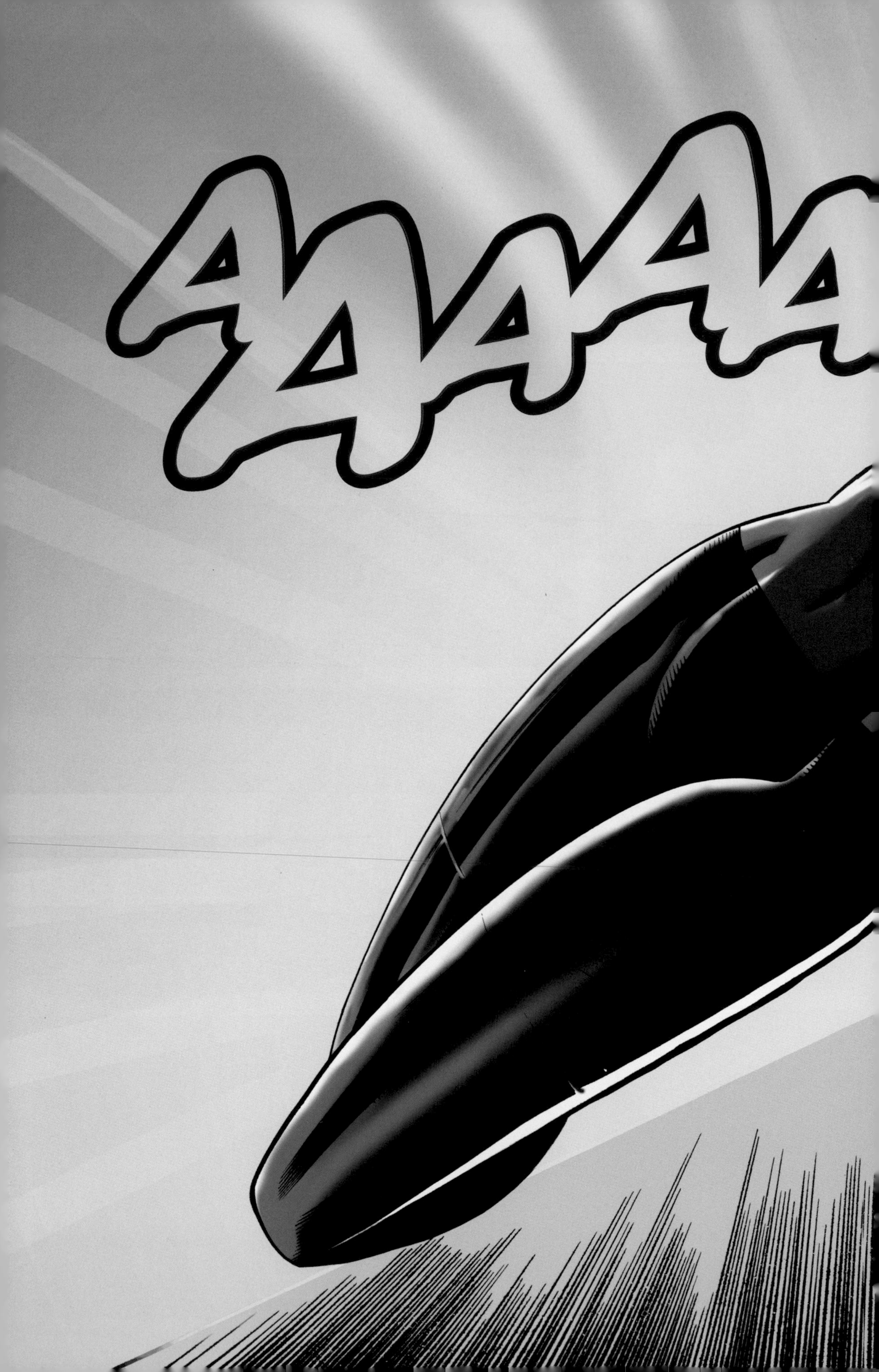
AAAA

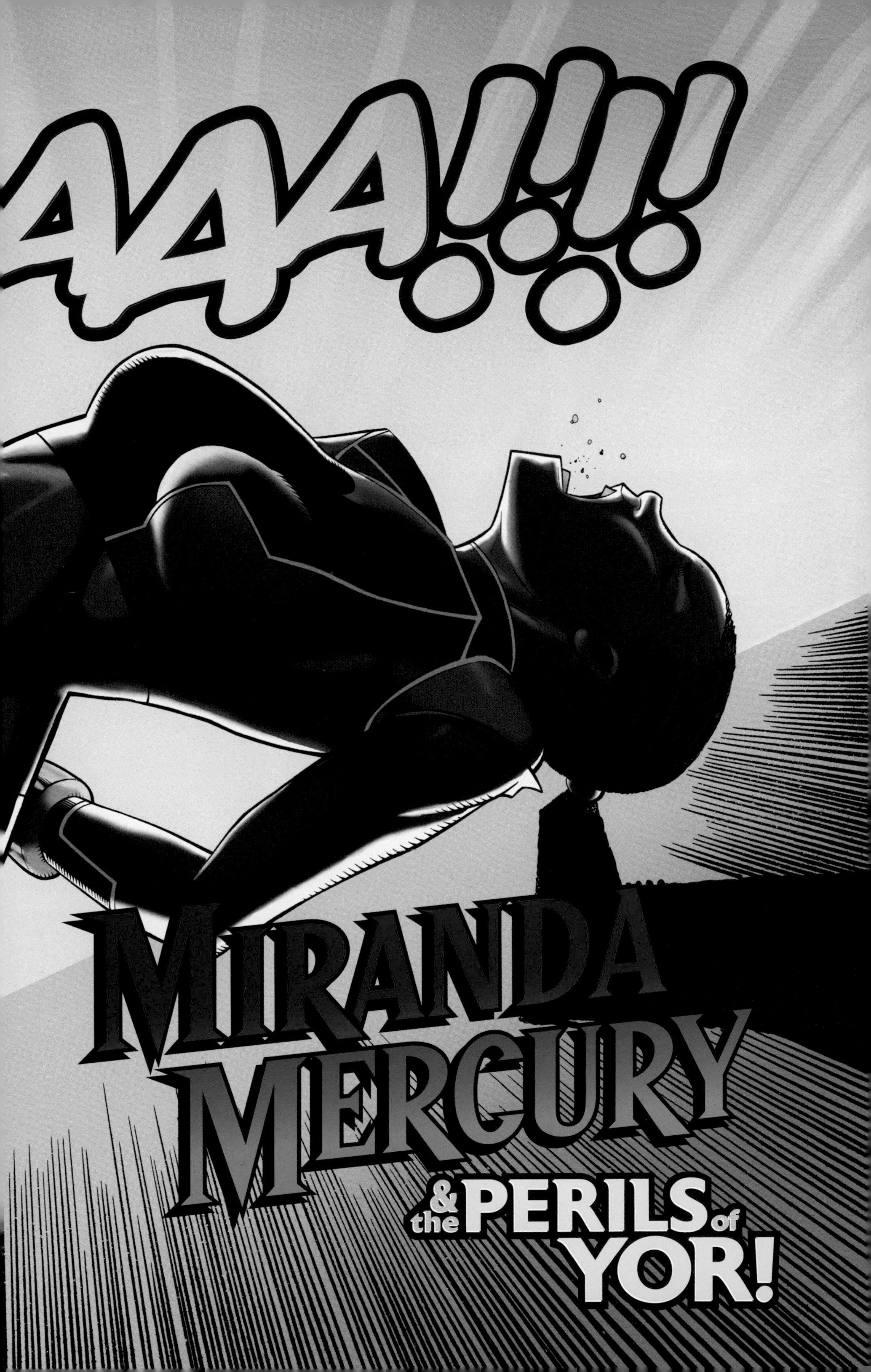
AAAI!!!
MIRANDA MERCURY
& the PERILS of YOR!

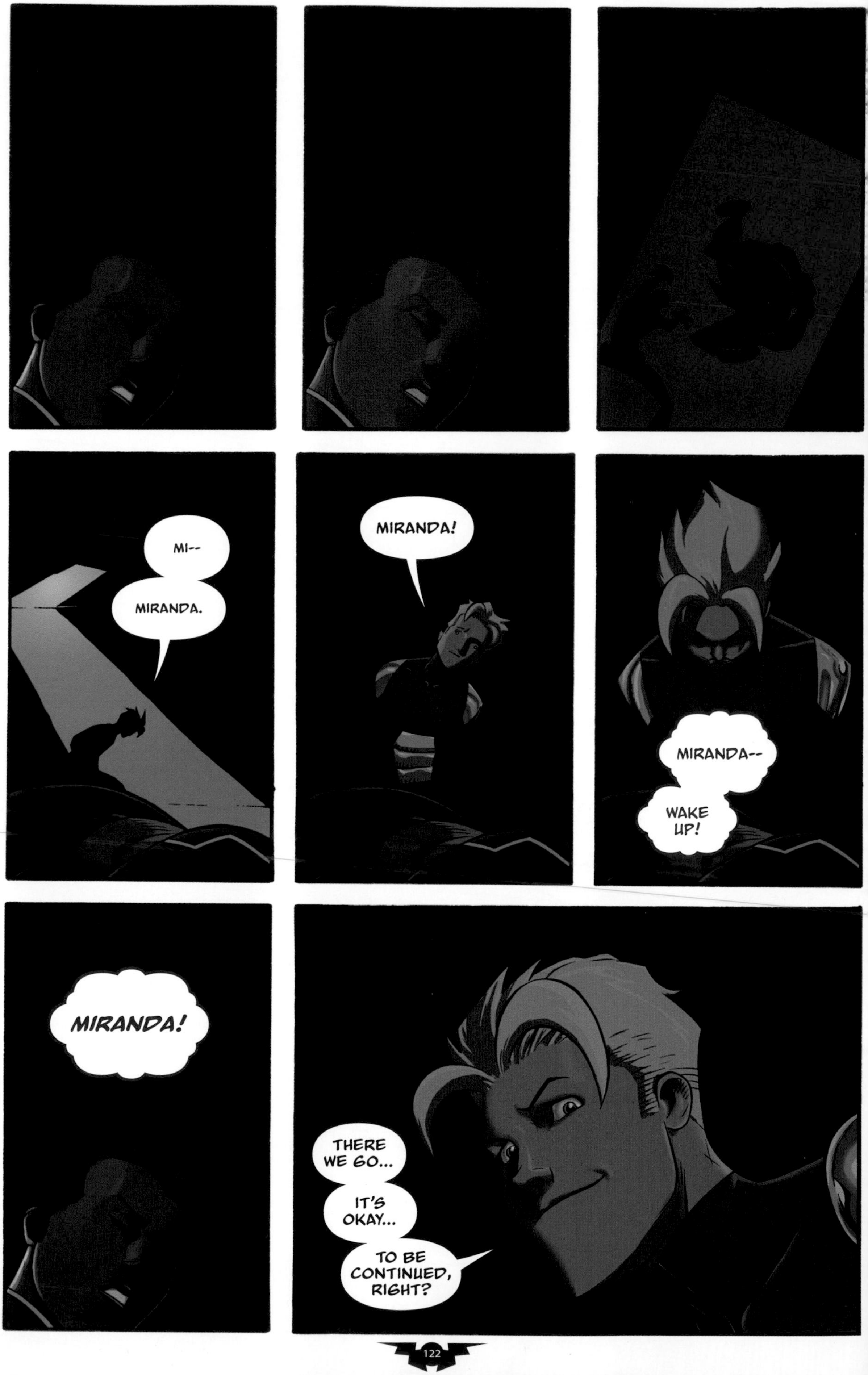
MI--
MIRANDA.
MIRANDA!
MIRANDA--
WAKE UP!
MIRANDA!
THERE WE GO...
IT'S OKAY...
TO BE CONTINUED, RIGHT?

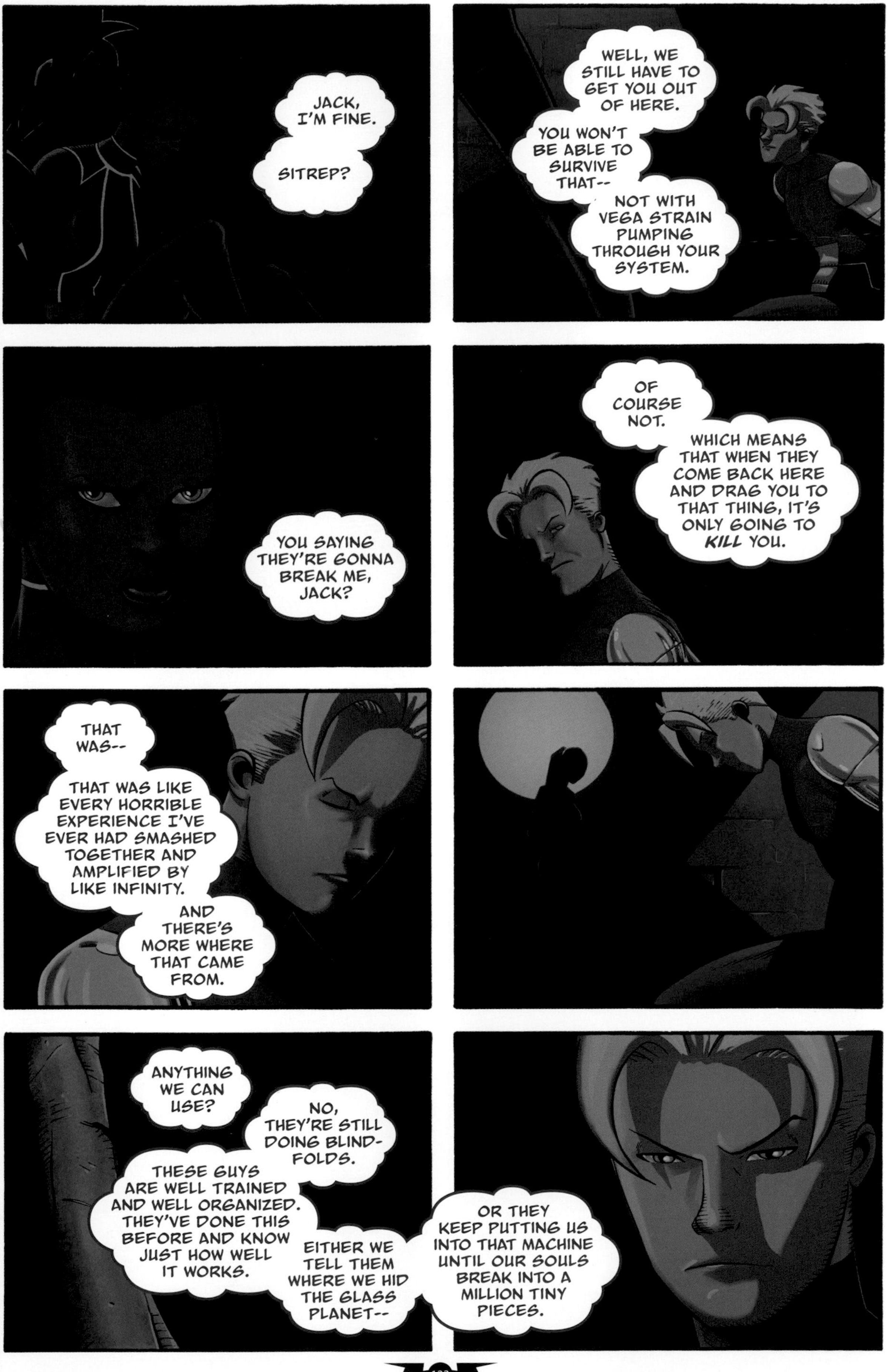
JACK, I'M FINE.
SITREP?
WELL, WE STILL HAVE TO GET YOU OUT OF HERE.
YOU WON'T BE ABLE TO SURVIVE THAT--
NOT WITH VEGA STRAIN PUMPING THROUGH YOUR SYSTEM.
YOU SAYING THEY'RE GONNA BREAK ME, JACK?
OF COURSE NOT.
WHICH MEANS THAT WHEN THEY COME BACK HERE AND DRAG YOU TO THAT THING, IT'S ONLY GOING TO KILL YOU.
THAT WAS--
THAT WAS LIKE EVERY HORRIBLE EXPERIENCE I'VE EVER HAD SMASHED TOGETHER AND AMPLIFIED BY LIKE INFINITY.
AND THERE'S MORE WHERE THAT CAME FROM.
ANYTHING WE CAN USE?
NO, THEY'RE STILL DOING BLIND-FOLDS.
THESE GUYS ARE WELL TRAINED AND WELL ORGANIZED. THEY'VE DONE THIS BEFORE AND KNOW JUST HOW WELL IT WORKS.
EITHER WE TELL THEM WHERE WE HID THE GLASS PLANET--
OR THEY KEEP PUTTING US INTO THAT MACHINE UNTIL OUR SOULS BREAK INTO A MILLION TINY PIECES.

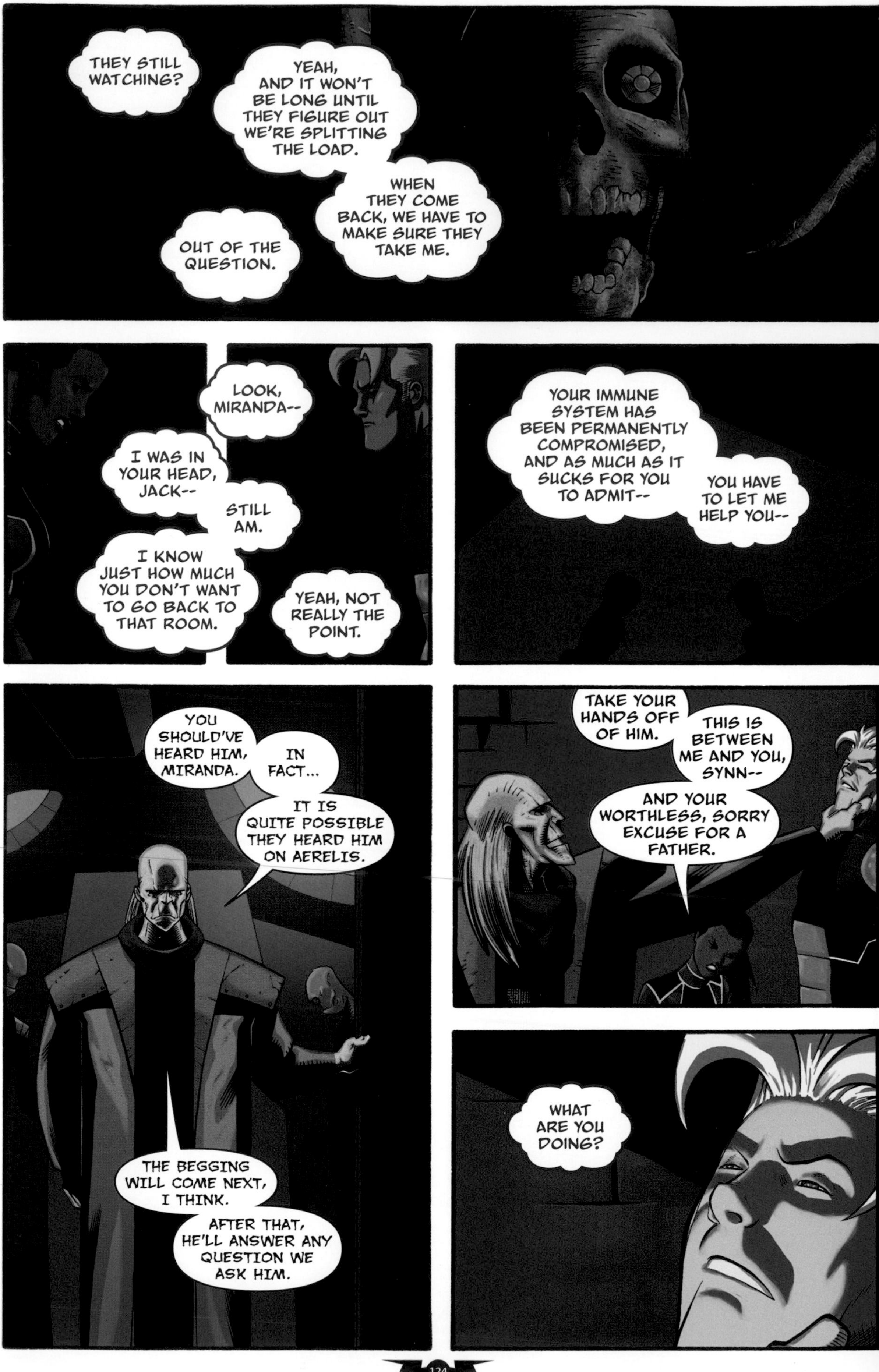
THEY STILL WATCHING?
YEAH, AND IT WON'T BE LONG UNTIL THEY FIGURE OUT WE'RE SPLITTING THE LOAD.
WHEN THEY COME BACK, WE HAVE TO MAKE SURE THEY TAKE ME.
OUT OF THE QUESTION.
LOOK, MIRANDA--
I WAS IN YOUR HEAD, JACK--
STILL AM.
I KNOW JUST HOW MUCH YOU DON'T WANT TO GO BACK TO THAT ROOM.
YEAH, NOT REALLY THE POINT.
YOUR IMMUNE SYSTEM HAS BEEN PERMANENTLY COMPROMISED, AND AS MUCH AS IT SUCKS FOR YOU TO ADMIT--
YOU HAVE TO LET ME HELP YOU--
YOU SHOULD'VE HEARD HIM, MIRANDA.
IN FACT...
IT IS QUITE POSSIBLE THEY HEARD HIM ON AERELIS.
THE BEGGING WILL COME NEXT, I THINK.
AFTER THAT, HE'LL ANSWER ANY QUESTION WE ASK HIM.
TAKE YOUR HANDS OFF OF HIM.
THIS IS BETWEEN ME AND YOU, SYNN--
AND YOUR WORTHLESS, SORRY EXCUSE FOR A FATHER.
WHAT ARE YOU DOING?

UNNGH!

YOU HEARD ME.

THAT'S WHY YOU AND YOUR CREW OF MISFITS EVEN TOOK THIS GIG, RIGHT?

YOU WANT TO DO WHAT DADDY COULDN'T?

I TOOK *HIM* DOWN, BIG GUY--

BEFORE I WAS EVEN A TEENAGER.

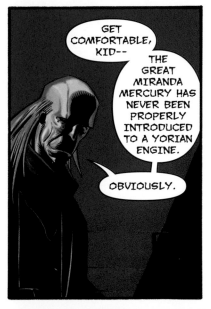

GET COMFORTABLE, KID--

THE GREAT MIRANDA MERCURY HAS NEVER BEEN PROPERLY INTRODUCED TO A YORIAN ENGINE.

OBVIOUSLY.

NO--

NOOO!

AAAAAHH!

JACK!

JACK, SAVE YOUR STRENGTH.

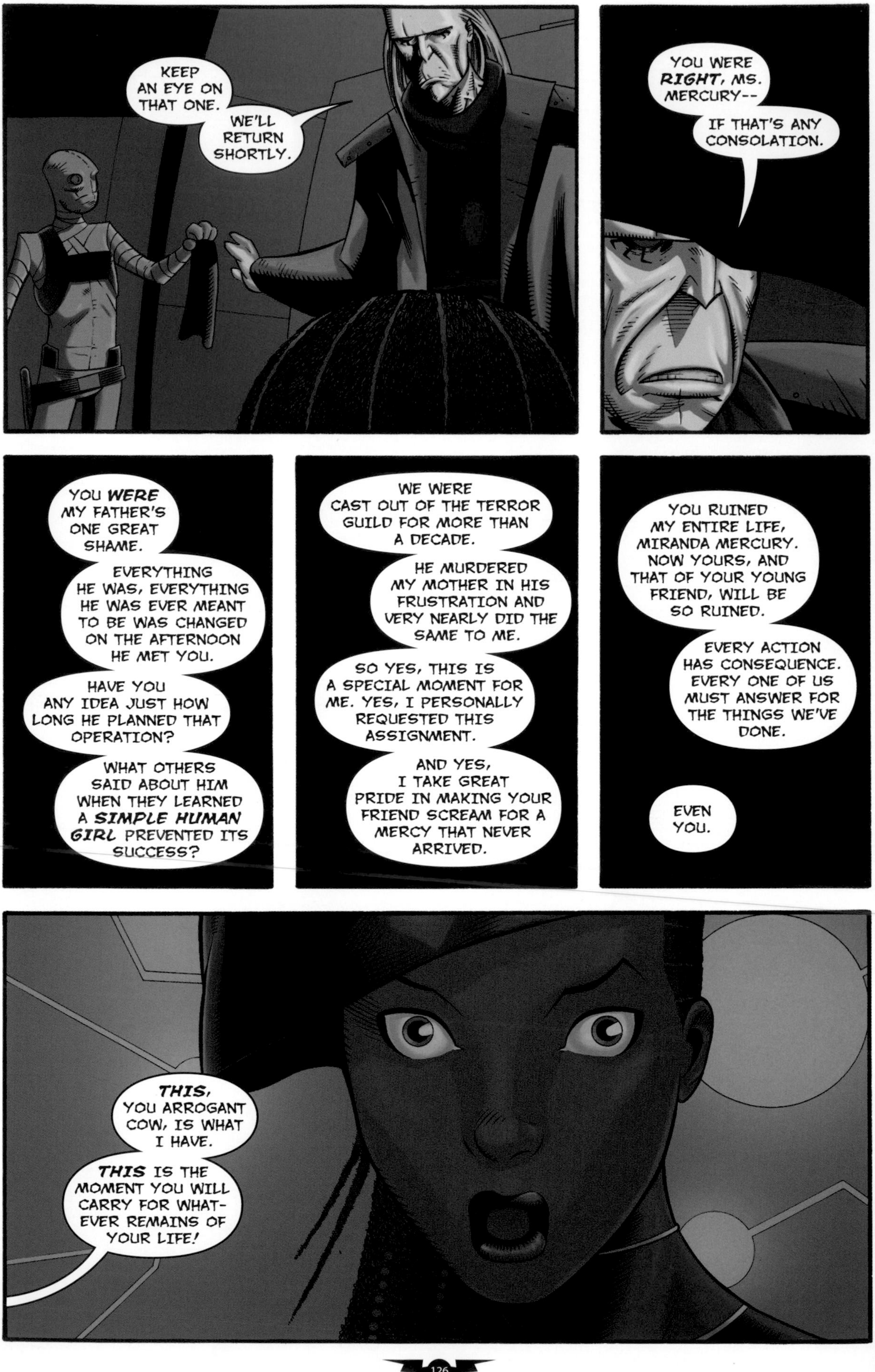
KEEP AN EYE ON THAT ONE.
WE'LL RETURN SHORTLY.
YOU WERE RIGHT, MS. MERCURY--
IF THAT'S ANY CONSOLATION.
YOU WERE MY FATHER'S ONE GREAT SHAME.
EVERYTHING HE WAS, EVERYTHING HE WAS EVER MEANT TO BE WAS CHANGED ON THE AFTERNOON HE MET YOU.
HAVE YOU ANY IDEA JUST HOW LONG HE PLANNED THAT OPERATION?
WHAT OTHERS SAID ABOUT HIM WHEN THEY LEARNED A SIMPLE HUMAN GIRL PREVENTED ITS SUCCESS?
WE WERE CAST OUT OF THE TERROR GUILD FOR MORE THAN A DECADE.
HE MURDERED MY MOTHER IN HIS FRUSTRATION AND VERY NEARLY DID THE SAME TO ME.
SO YES, THIS IS A SPECIAL MOMENT FOR ME. YES, I PERSONALLY REQUESTED THIS ASSIGNMENT.
AND YES, I TAKE GREAT PRIDE IN MAKING YOUR FRIEND SCREAM FOR A MERCY THAT NEVER ARRIVED.
YOU RUINED MY ENTIRE LIFE, MIRANDA MERCURY. NOW YOURS, AND THAT OF YOUR YOUNG FRIEND, WILL BE SO RUINED.
EVERY ACTION HAS CONSEQUENCE. EVERY ONE OF US MUST ANSWER FOR THE THINGS WE'VE DONE.
EVEN YOU.
THIS, YOU ARROGANT COW, IS WHAT I HAVE.
THIS IS THE MOMENT YOU WILL CARRY FOR WHAT-EVER REMAINS OF YOUR LIFE!

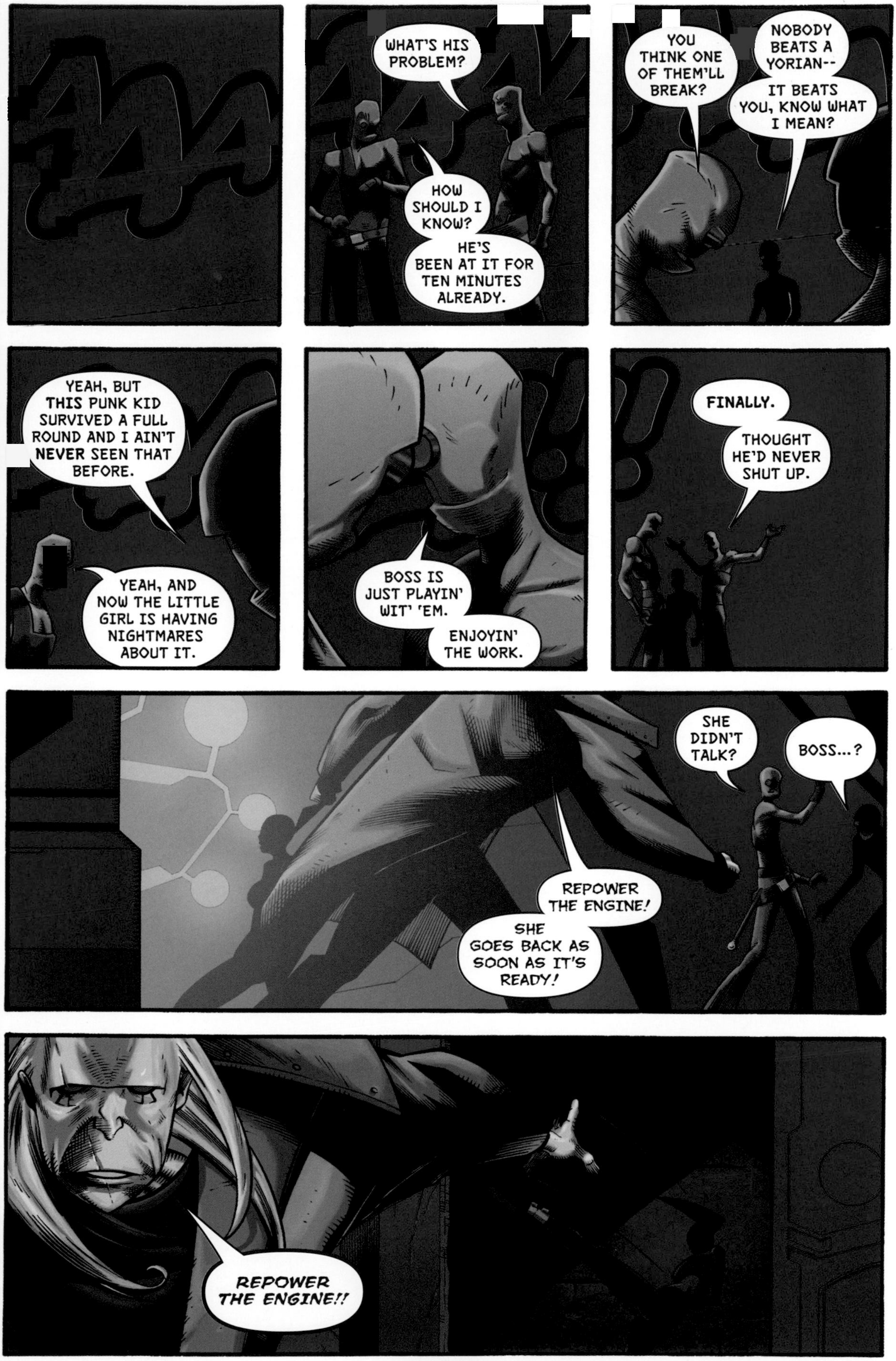
WHAT'S HIS PROBLEM?
HOW SHOULD I KNOW?
HE'S BEEN AT IT FOR TEN MINUTES ALREADY.
YOU THINK ONE OF THEM'LL BREAK?
NOBODY BEATS A YORIAN--
IT BEATS YOU, KNOW WHAT I MEAN?
YEAH, BUT THIS PUNK KID SURVIVED A FULL ROUND AND I AIN'T NEVER SEEN THAT BEFORE.
YEAH, AND NOW THE LITTLE GIRL IS HAVING NIGHTMARES ABOUT IT.
BOSS IS JUST PLAYIN' WIT' 'EM.
ENJOYIN' THE WORK.
FINALLY.
THOUGHT HE'D NEVER SHUT UP.
SHE DIDN'T TALK?
BOSS...?
REPOWER THE ENGINE!
SHE GOES BACK AS SOON AS IT'S READY!
REPOWER THE ENGINE!!

JUST ASK THE QUESTION, JACK--

OR AT LEAST STOP THINKING IT AT ME.

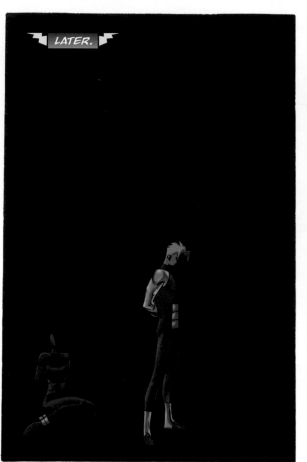

JACK, PLEASE.

WE MIGHT NOT HAVE MUCH LONGER.

I DON'T KNOW WHY, BUT I CAN'T--

I CAN'T TELL YOU IF YOU DON'T ASK.

...

WHY DIDN'T YOU TELL ME ABOUT THE VIRUS?

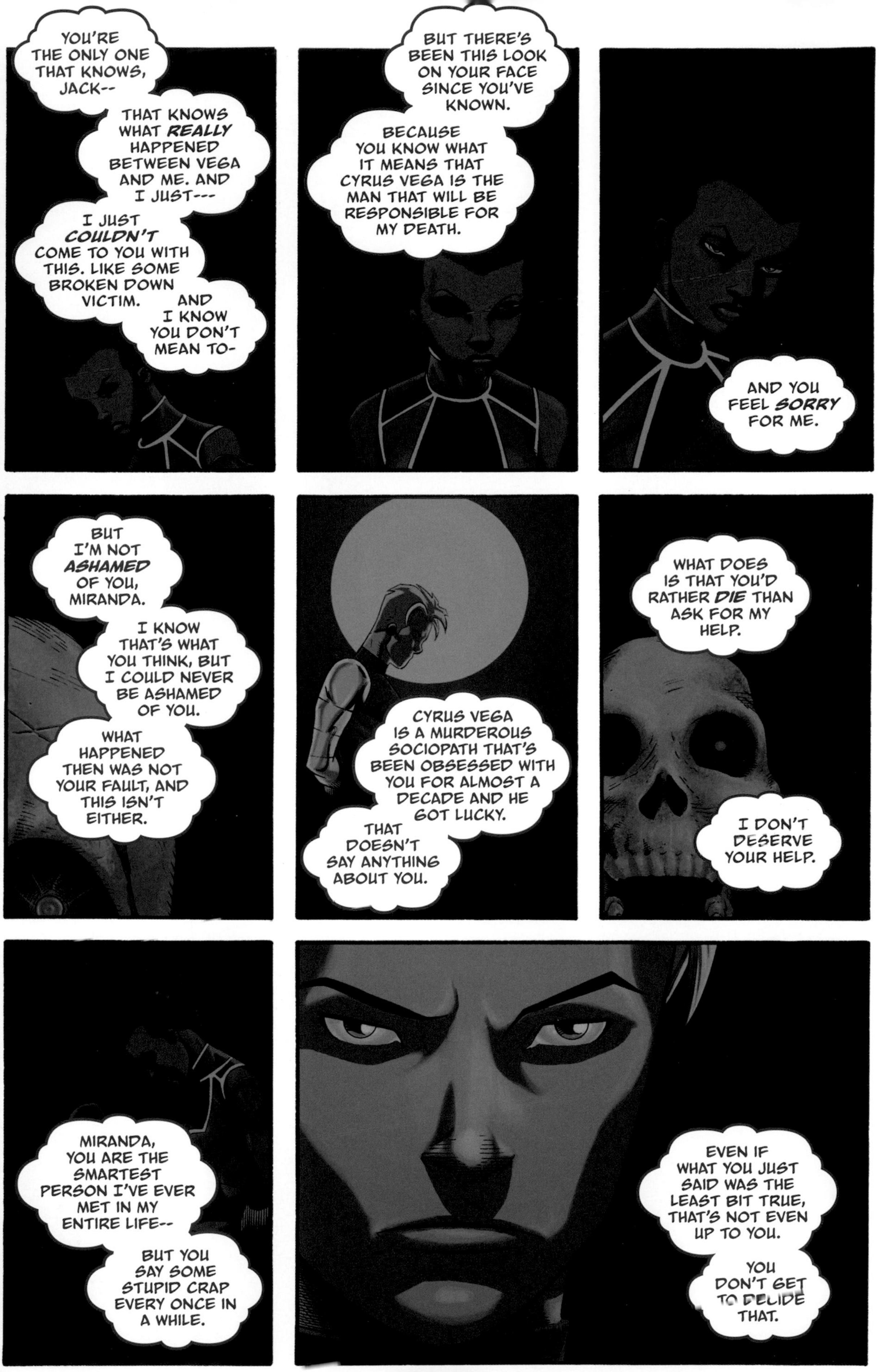
YOU'RE THE ONLY ONE THAT KNOWS, JACK--
THAT KNOWS WHAT REALLY HAPPENED BETWEEN VEGA AND ME. AND I JUST---
I JUST COULDN'T COME TO YOU WITH THIS. LIKE SOME BROKEN DOWN VICTIM.
AND I KNOW YOU DON'T MEAN TO-
BUT THERE'S BEEN THIS LOOK ON YOUR FACE SINCE YOU'VE KNOWN.
BECAUSE YOU KNOW WHAT IT MEANS THAT CYRUS VEGA IS THE MAN THAT WILL BE RESPONSIBLE FOR MY DEATH.
AND YOU FEEL SORRY FOR ME.
BUT I'M NOT ASHAMED OF YOU, MIRANDA.
I KNOW THAT'S WHAT YOU THINK, BUT I COULD NEVER BE ASHAMED OF YOU.
WHAT HAPPENED THEN WAS NOT YOUR FAULT, AND THIS ISN'T EITHER.
CYRUS VEGA IS A MURDEROUS SOCIOPATH THAT'S BEEN OBSESSED WITH YOU FOR ALMOST A DECADE AND HE GOT LUCKY.
THAT DOESN'T SAY ANYTHING ABOUT YOU.
WHAT DOES IS THAT YOU'D RATHER DIE THAN ASK FOR MY HELP.
I DON'T DESERVE YOUR HELP.
MIRANDA, YOU ARE THE SMARTEST PERSON I'VE EVER MET IN MY ENTIRE LIFE--
BUT YOU SAY SOME STUPID CRAP EVERY ONCE IN A WHILE.
EVEN IF WHAT YOU JUST SAID WAS THE LEAST BIT TRUE, THAT'S NOT EVEN UP TO YOU.
YOU DON'T GET TO DECIDE THAT.

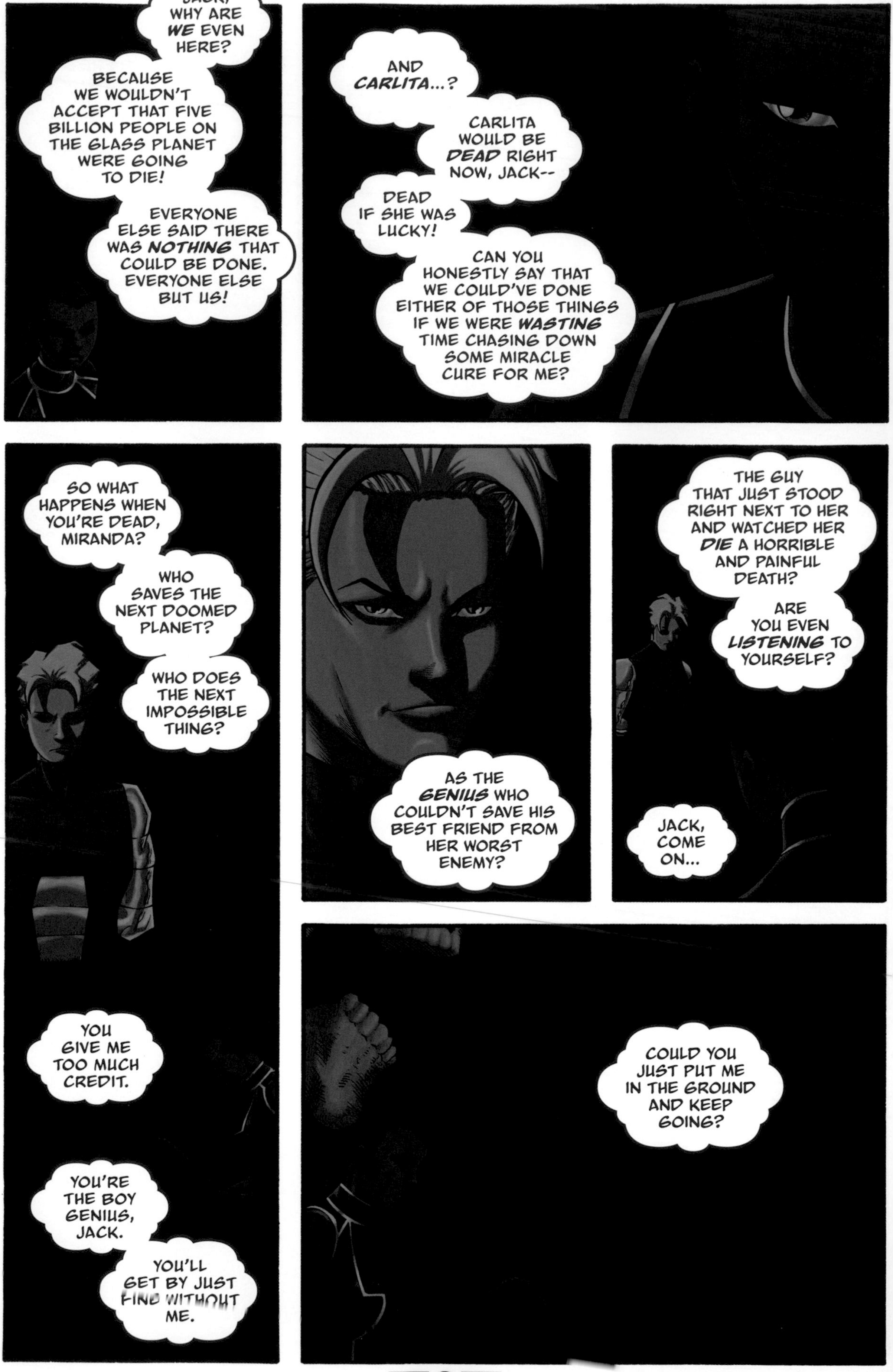
JACK, WHY ARE *WE* EVEN HERE?
BECAUSE WE WOULDN'T ACCEPT THAT FIVE BILLION PEOPLE ON THE GLASS PLANET WERE GOING TO DIE!
EVERYONE ELSE SAID THERE WAS *NOTHING* THAT COULD BE DONE. EVERYONE ELSE BUT US!
AND *CARLITA*...?
CARLITA WOULD BE *DEAD* RIGHT NOW, JACK--
DEAD IF SHE WAS LUCKY!
CAN YOU HONESTLY SAY THAT WE COULD'VE DONE EITHER OF THOSE THINGS IF WE WERE *WASTING* TIME CHASING DOWN SOME MIRACLE CURE FOR ME?
SO WHAT HAPPENS WHEN YOU'RE DEAD, MIRANDA?
WHO SAVES THE NEXT DOOMED PLANET?
WHO DOES THE NEXT IMPOSSIBLE THING?
AS THE *GENIUS* WHO COULDN'T SAVE HIS BEST FRIEND FROM HER WORST ENEMY?
THE GUY THAT JUST STOOD RIGHT NEXT TO HER AND WATCHED HER *DIE* A HORRIBLE AND PAINFUL DEATH?
ARE YOU EVEN *LISTENING* TO YOURSELF?
JACK, COME ON...
YOU GIVE ME TOO MUCH CREDIT.
YOU'RE THE BOY GENIUS, JACK.
YOU'LL GET BY JUST FINE WITHOUT ME.
COULD YOU JUST PUT ME IN THE GROUND AND KEEP GOING?

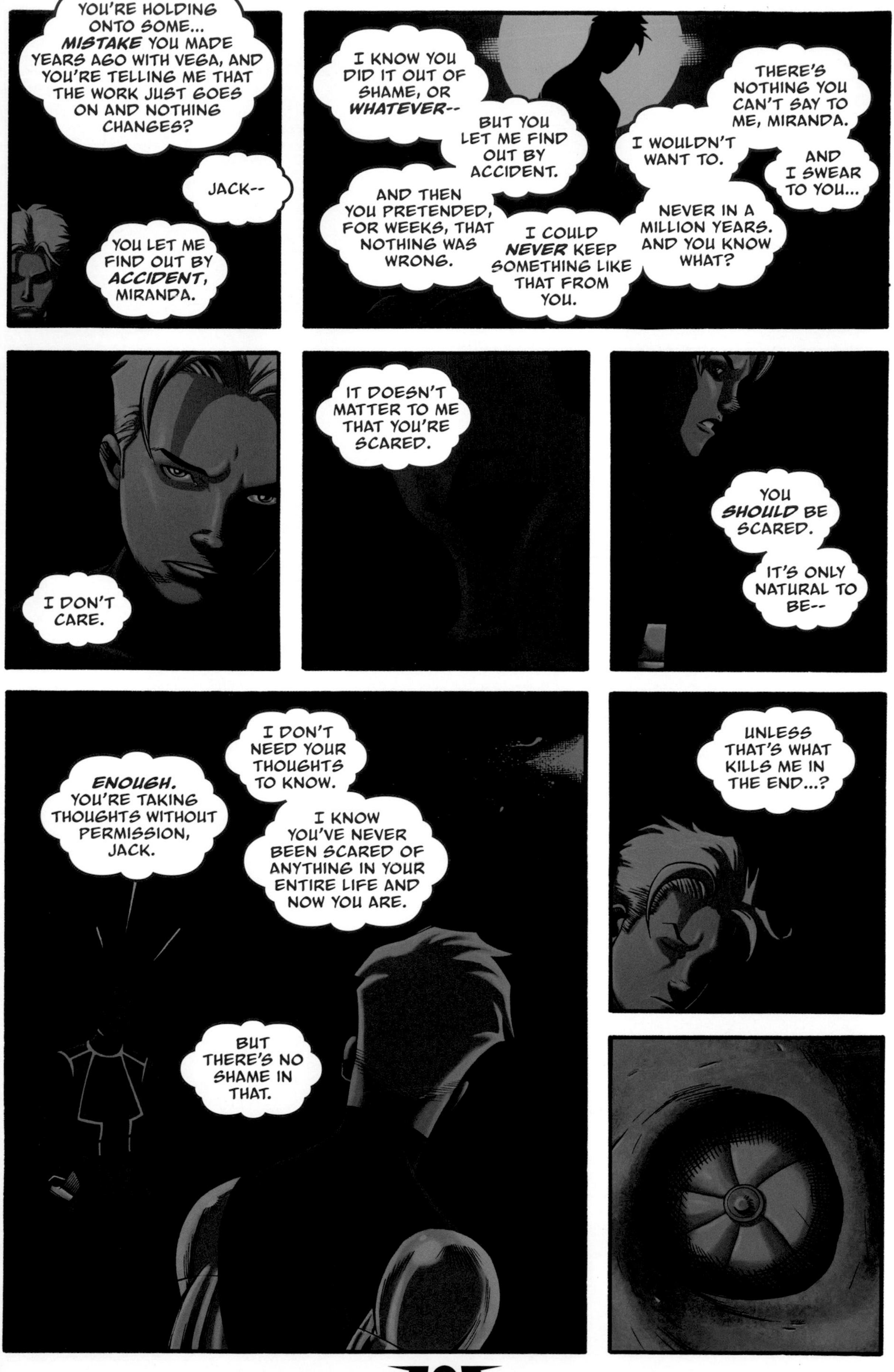
YOU'RE HOLDING ONTO SOME... MISTAKE YOU MADE YEARS AGO WITH VEGA, AND YOU'RE TELLING ME THAT THE WORK JUST GOES ON AND NOTHING CHANGES?
JACK--
YOU LET ME FIND OUT BY ACCIDENT, MIRANDA.
I KNOW YOU DID IT OUT OF SHAME, OR WHATEVER--
BUT YOU LET ME FIND OUT BY ACCIDENT.
AND THEN YOU PRETENDED, FOR WEEKS, THAT NOTHING WAS WRONG.
I COULD NEVER KEEP SOMETHING LIKE THAT FROM YOU.
THERE'S NOTHING YOU CAN'T SAY TO ME, MIRANDA.
I WOULDN'T WANT TO.
AND I SWEAR TO YOU...
NEVER IN A MILLION YEARS. AND YOU KNOW WHAT?
I DON'T CARE.
IT DOESN'T MATTER TO ME THAT YOU'RE SCARED.
YOU SHOULD BE SCARED.
IT'S ONLY NATURAL TO BE--
ENOUGH. YOU'RE TAKING THOUGHTS WITHOUT PERMISSION, JACK.
I DON'T NEED YOUR THOUGHTS TO KNOW.
I KNOW YOU'VE NEVER BEEN SCARED OF ANYTHING IN YOUR ENTIRE LIFE AND NOW YOU ARE.
BUT THERE'S NO SHAME IN THAT.
UNLESS THAT'S WHAT KILLS ME IN THE END...?

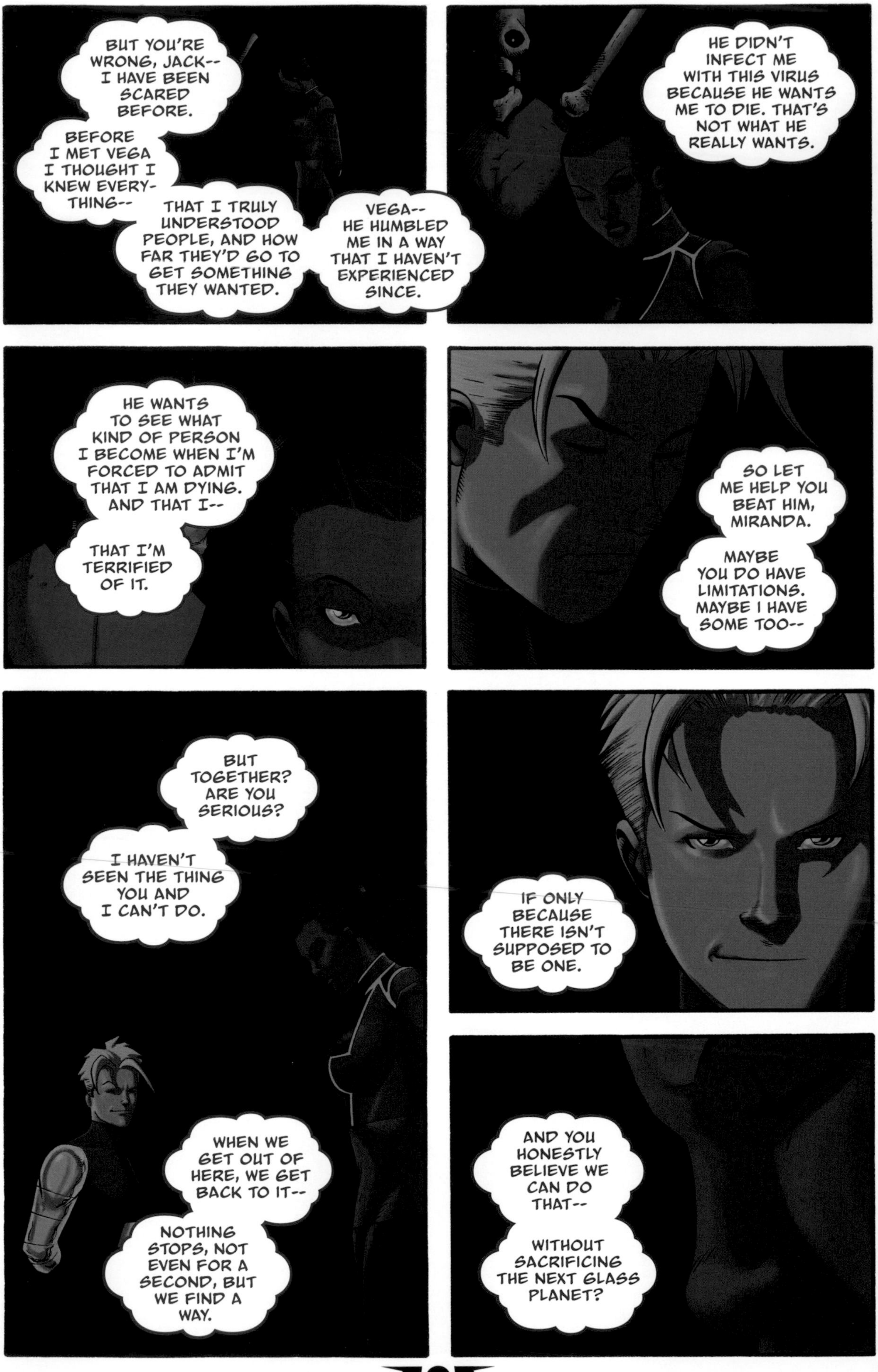
BUT YOU'RE WRONG, JACK-- I HAVE BEEN SCARED BEFORE.
BEFORE I MET VEGA I THOUGHT I KNEW EVERY-THING--
THAT I TRULY UNDERSTOOD PEOPLE, AND HOW FAR THEY'D GO TO GET SOMETHING THEY WANTED.
VEGA-- HE HUMBLED ME IN A WAY THAT I HAVEN'T EXPERIENCED SINCE.
HE DIDN'T INFECT ME WITH THIS VIRUS BECAUSE HE WANTS ME TO DIE. THAT'S NOT WHAT HE REALLY WANTS.
HE WANTS TO SEE WHAT KIND OF PERSON I BECOME WHEN I'M FORCED TO ADMIT THAT I AM DYING. AND THAT I--
THAT I'M TERRIFIED OF IT.
SO LET ME HELP YOU BEAT HIM, MIRANDA.
MAYBE YOU DO HAVE LIMITATIONS. MAYBE I HAVE SOME TOO--
BUT TOGETHER? ARE YOU SERIOUS?
I HAVEN'T SEEN THE THING YOU AND I CAN'T DO.
IF ONLY BECAUSE THERE ISN'T SUPPOSED TO BE ONE.
WHEN WE GET OUT OF HERE, WE GET BACK TO IT--
NOTHING STOPS, NOT EVEN FOR A SECOND, BUT WE FIND A WAY.
AND YOU HONESTLY BELIEVE WE CAN DO THAT--
WITHOUT SACRIFICING THE NEXT GLASS PLANET?

...

IF IT STARTS TO INTERFERE WITH THE WORK, THE SECOND I THINK WE'RE LOSING A STEP--

WE PULL BACK. BOTH OF US.

AND JACK...?

I'M SORRY.

I KNOW, BUT YOU DON'T HAVE TO APOLOGIZE TO ME.

I KNOW, BUT I SHOULD.

YEAH, YOU SHOULD.

SO-- YOU'RE PRETTY CONFIDENT WE'LL GET OUT OF HERE THEN?

NOW WHO'S TAKING THOUGHTS WITHOUT PER- MISSION?

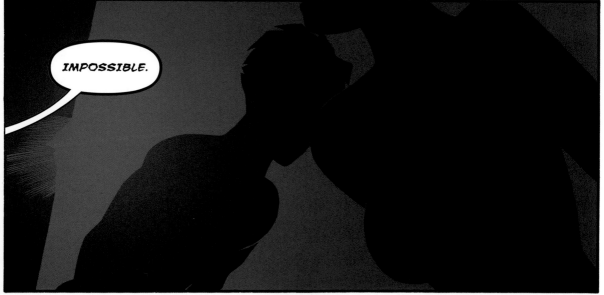

IMPOSSIBLE.

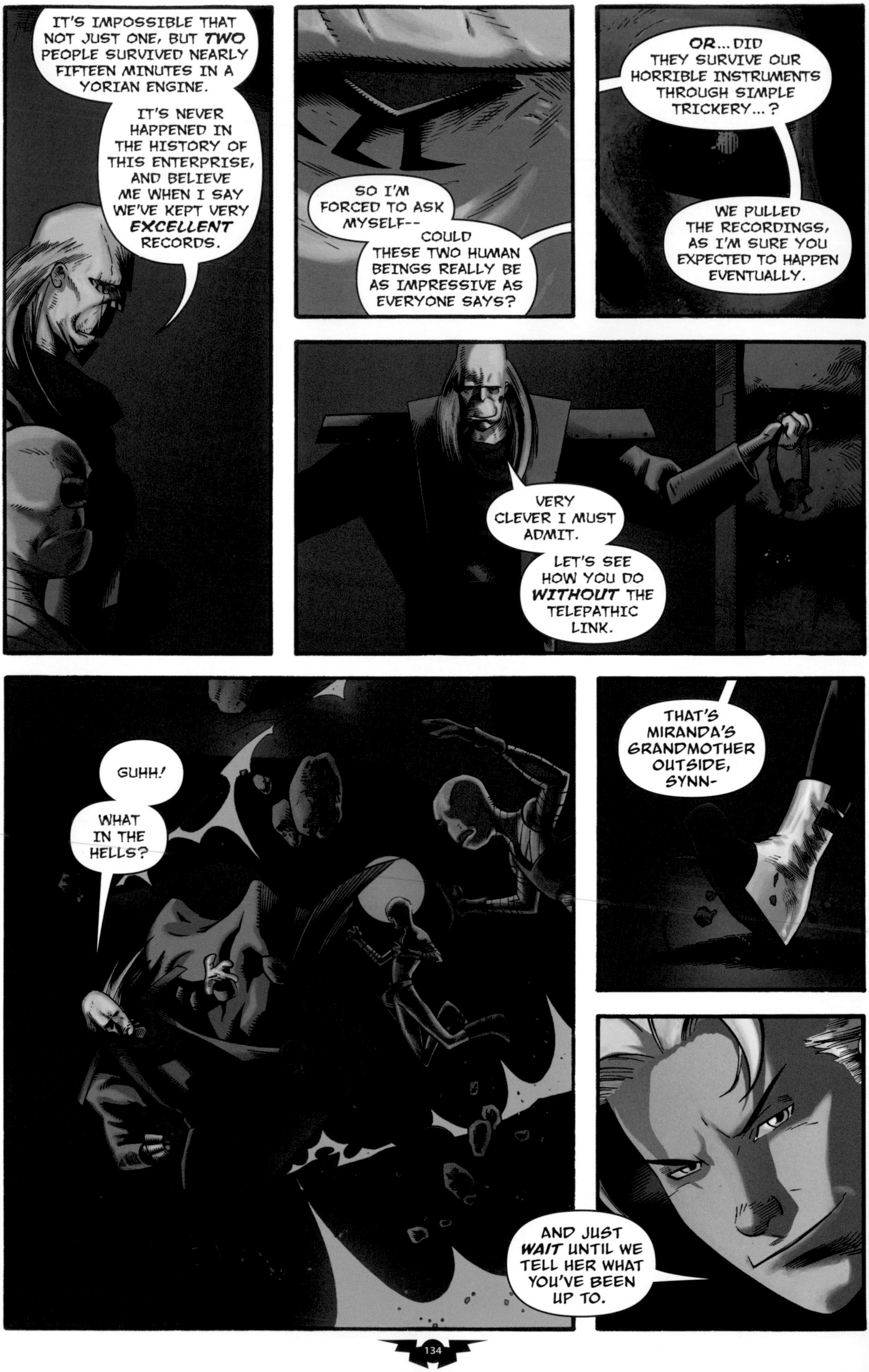
IT'S IMPOSSIBLE THAT NOT JUST ONE, BUT TWO PEOPLE SURVIVED NEARLY FIFTEEN MINUTES IN A YORIAN ENGINE.
IT'S NEVER HAPPENED IN THE HISTORY OF THIS ENTERPRISE, AND BELIEVE ME WHEN I SAY WE'VE KEPT VERY EXCELLENT RECORDS.
SO I'M FORCED TO ASK MYSELF--
COULD THESE TWO HUMAN BEINGS REALLY BE AS IMPRESSIVE AS EVERYONE SAYS?
OR... DID THEY SURVIVE OUR HORRIBLE INSTRUMENTS THROUGH SIMPLE TRICKERY...?
WE PULLED THE RECORDINGS, AS I'M SURE YOU EXPECTED TO HAPPEN EVENTUALLY.
VERY CLEVER I MUST ADMIT.
LET'S SEE HOW YOU DO WITHOUT THE TELEPATHIC LINK.
GUHH!
WHAT IN THE HELLS?
THAT'S MIRANDA'S GRANDMOTHER OUTSIDE, SYNN-
AND JUST WAIT UNTIL WE TELL HER WHAT YOU'VE BEEN UP TO.

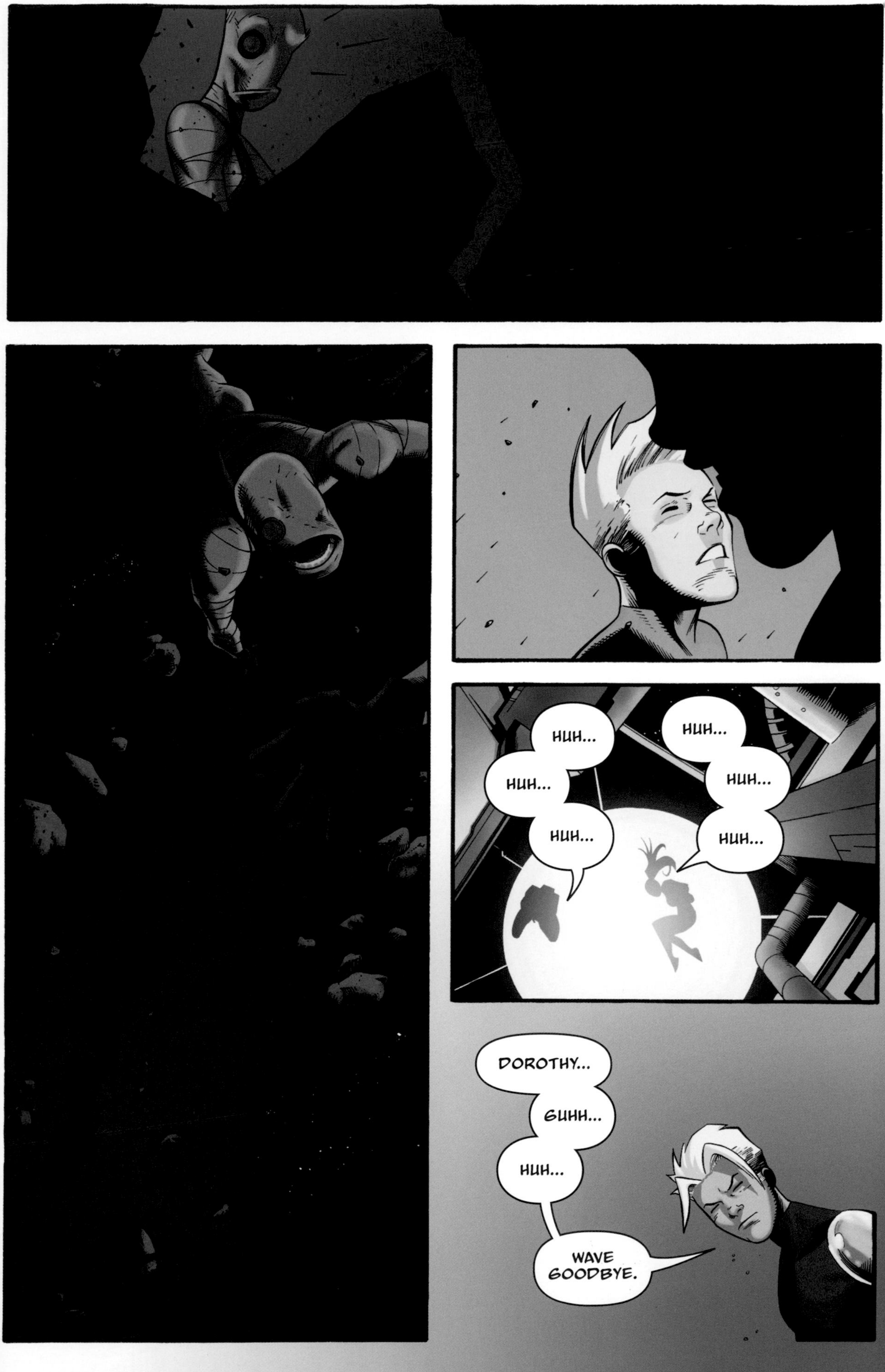
HUH...
HUH...
HUH...
HUH...
HUH...
HUH...
DOROTHY...
GUHH...
HUH...
WAVE GOODBYE.

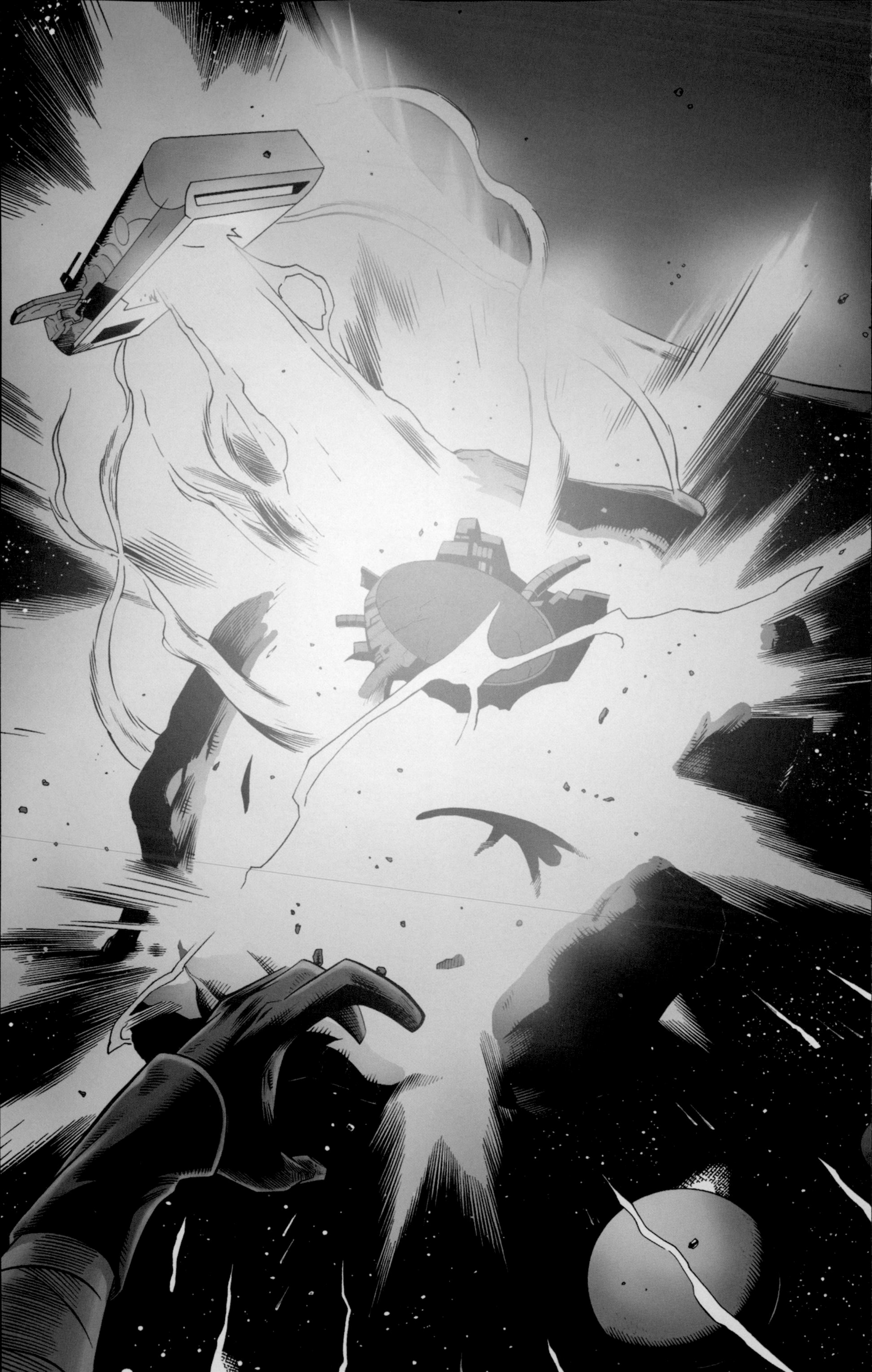

WOW, THAT SUCKED.

YEAH, TELL ME ABOUT IT. HOW DID SHE EVEN FIND US?

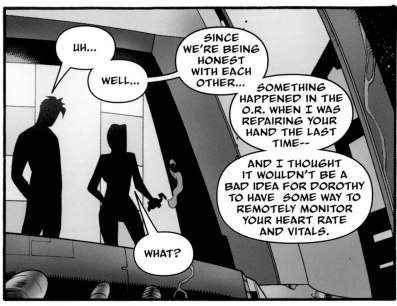

UH...

WELL...

SINCE WE'RE BEING HONEST WITH EACH OTHER...

SOMETHING HAPPENED IN THE O.R. WHEN I WAS REPAIRING YOUR HAND THE LAST TIME--

AND I THOUGHT IT WOULDN'T BE A BAD IDEA FOR DOROTHY TO HAVE SOME WAY TO REMOTELY MONITOR YOUR HEART RATE AND VITALS.

WHAT?

OR FOR THE MONITOR TO ALSO INCLUDE A POSITIONING CHIP CAPABLE OF TRANSMITTING FROM THE HEART OF A BLACK HOLE SUN.

WHAT!?

IT'S A LONG STORY, BUT I--

YOU THINK HER FIRE SUPPRESSION SYSTEMS ARE DAMAGED?

DOROTHY, CAN YOU RUN A DIAG--

OH, NO...

JACK, THAT'S NOT WHAT THIS IS.

DOROTHY'S CRYING.

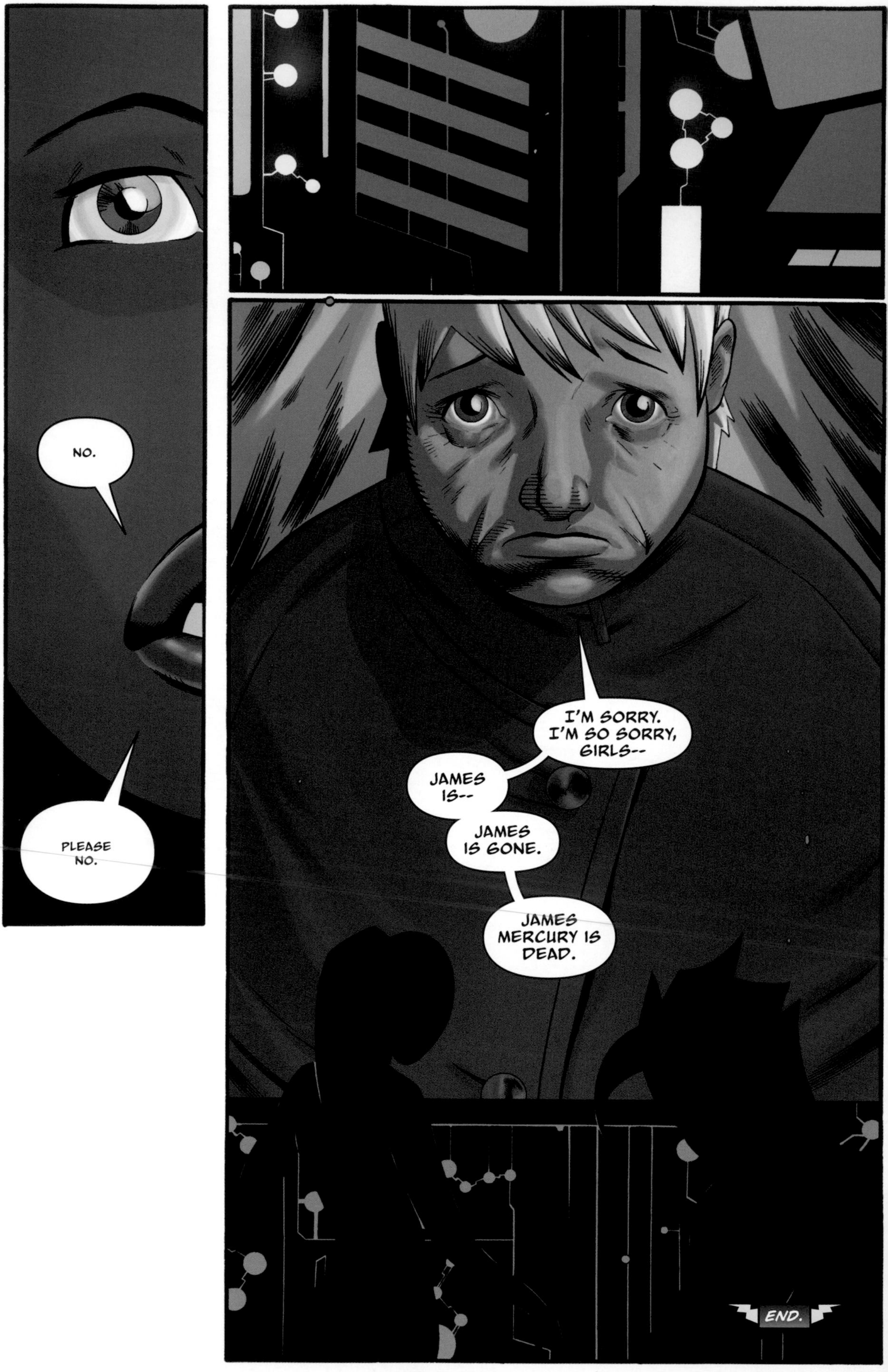
NO.
PLEASE NO.
I'M SORRY. I'M SO SORRY, GIRLS--
JAMES IS--
JAMES IS GONE.
JAMES MERCURY IS DEAD.
END.

THE IMPOSSIBLE HAS HAPPENED---
JAMES MERCURY HAS DIED.

THE MAN THAT RAISED MIRANDA MERCURY
AND HELPED TURN HER INTO
THE HERO SHE IS TODAY
IS GONE FOREVER.

NOW---AFTER A LONG TIME AWAY,
MIRANDA IS FINALLY COMING BACK HOME.

LIKE MANY WHO HAVE
LOST SOMEONE UNEXPECTEDLY,
SHE IS WRACKED BY CRUSHING GUILT
OVER THE THINGS SHE NEVER HAD
THE CHANCE TO SAY...
AND BY THE THINGS THAT SHE DID...

EPISODE 300

MIRANDA MERCURY

AND THE TIMELY DEATH!

WRITER
BRANDON THOMAS

PENCILER
LEE FERGUSON

INKER
MARC DEERING

LETTERER
MATTY RYAN

COLORIST
JAMES BROWN

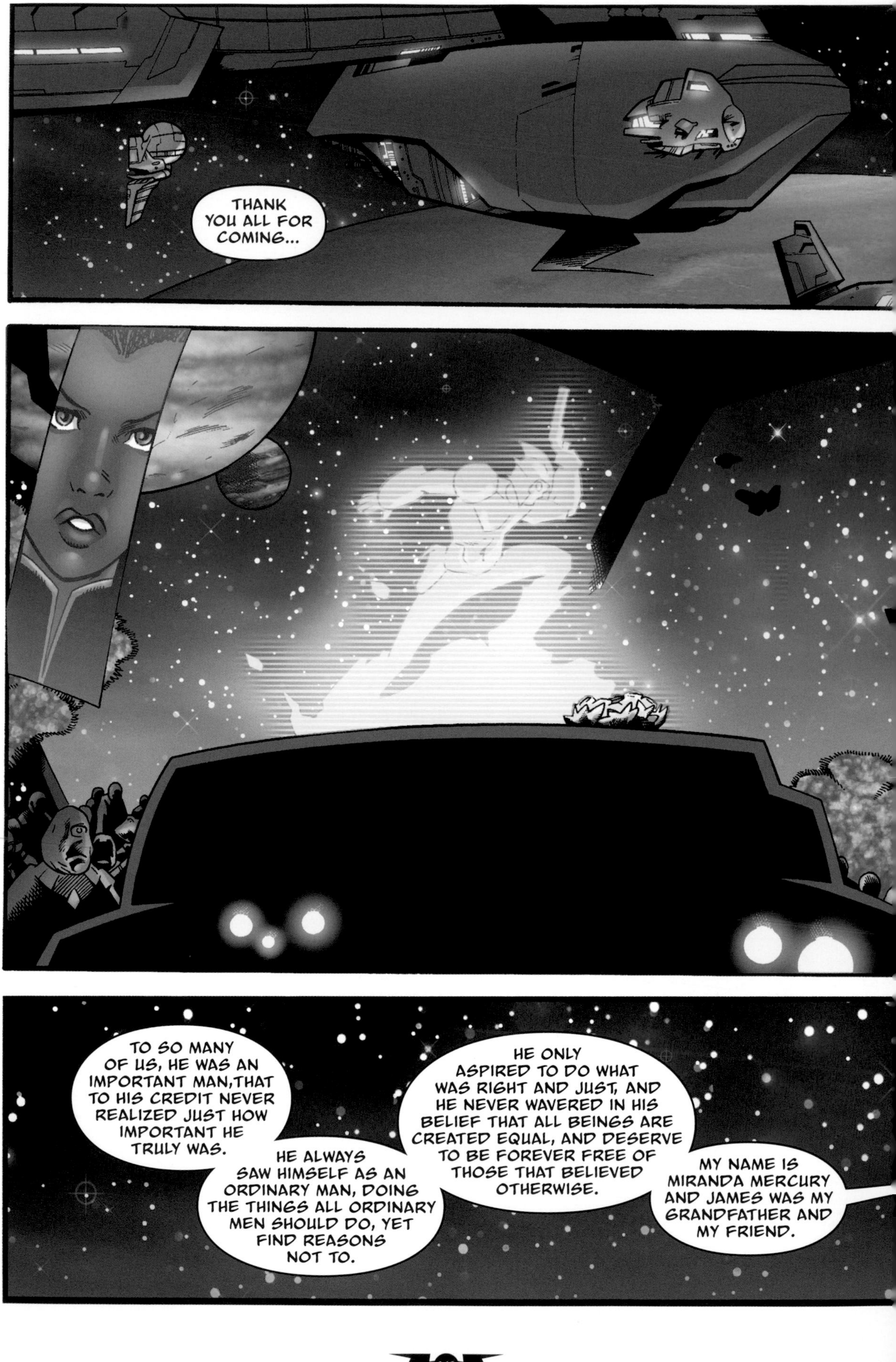
THANK YOU ALL FOR COMING...
TO SO MANY OF US, HE WAS AN IMPORTANT MAN,THAT TO HIS CREDIT NEVER REALIZED JUST HOW IMPORTANT HE TRULY WAS.
HE ALWAYS SAW HIMSELF AS AN ORDINARY MAN, DOING THE THINGS ALL ORDINARY MEN SHOULD DO, YET FIND REASONS NOT TO.
HE ONLY ASPIRED TO DO WHAT WAS RIGHT AND JUST, AND HE NEVER WAVERED IN HIS BELIEF THAT ALL BEINGS ARE CREATED EQUAL, AND DESERVE TO BE FOREVER FREE OF THOSE THAT BELIEVED OTHERWISE.
MY NAME IS MIRANDA MERCURY AND JAMES WAS MY GRANDFATHER AND MY FRIEND.

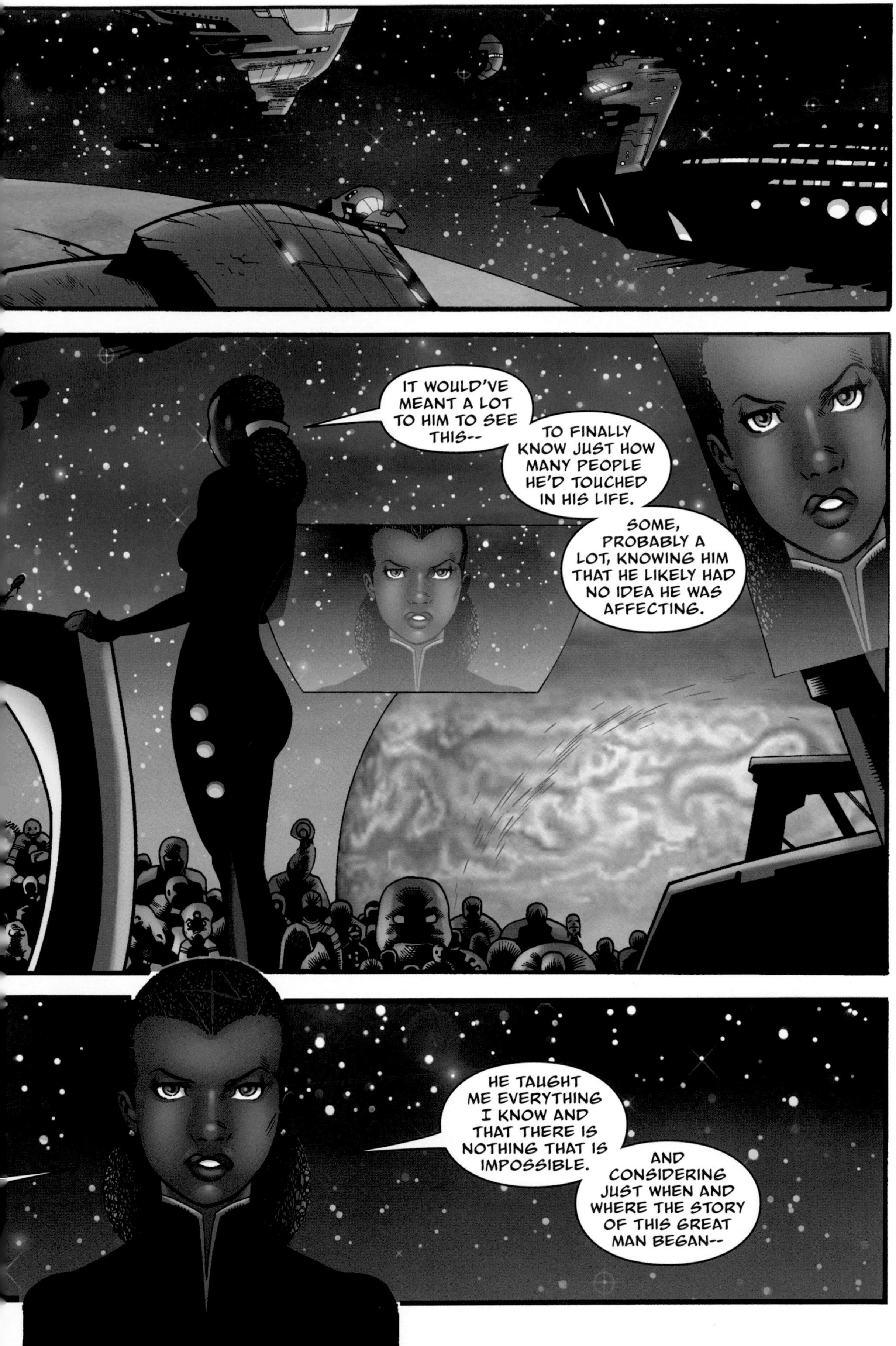
IT WOULD'VE MEANT A LOT TO HIM TO SEE THIS--
TO FINALLY KNOW JUST HOW MANY PEOPLE HE'D TOUCHED IN HIS LIFE.
SOME, PROBABLY A LOT, KNOWING HIM THAT HE LIKELY HAD NO IDEA HE WAS AFFECTING.
HE TAUGHT ME EVERYTHING I KNOW AND THAT THERE IS NOTHING THAT IS IMPOSSIBLE.
AND CONSIDERING JUST WHEN AND WHERE THE STORY OF THIS GREAT MAN BEGAN--

HE WOULD KNOW.

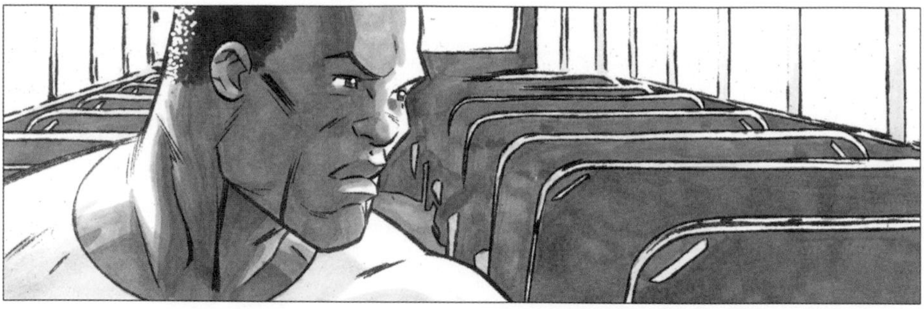

THE WORLD THAT JAMES WAS BORN ON WAS NOT THE ONE HE DESERVED. HIS INTELLECT, HIS INGENUITY, AND HIS KINDNESS WERE WASTED IN A PLACE WHERE EQUALITY WAS JUST A WORD, AND SOME MEMBERS OF SOCIETY WERE FORCED TO FIGHT FOR THE BASIC HUMAN DIGNITIES ALL SHOULD BE AFFORDED.

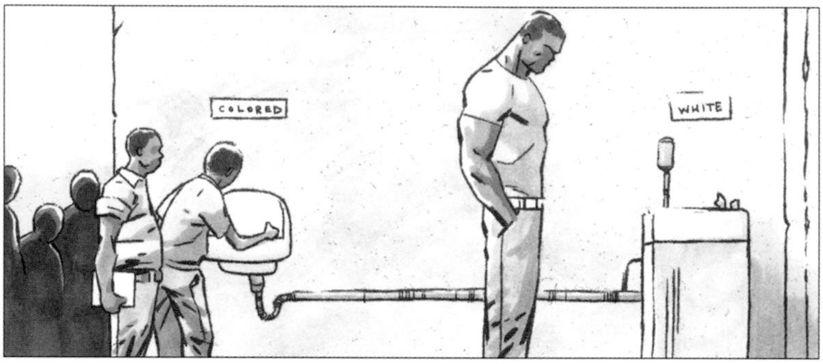
COLORED
WHITE

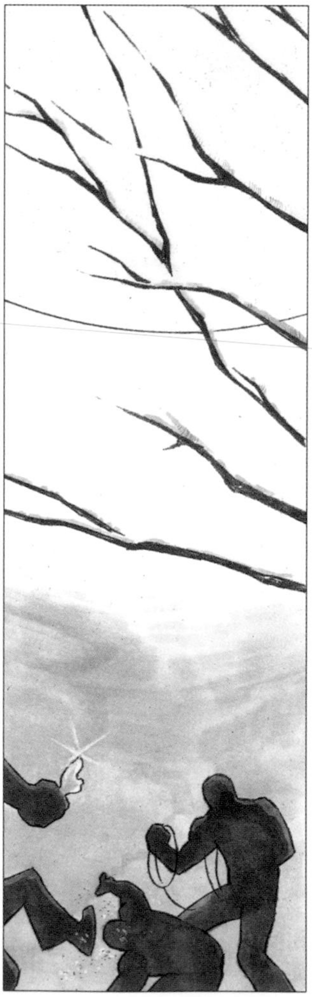

AND THIS UNCONSCIONABLE OPPRESSION AND INTOLERANCE STEMMED FROM SOMETHING AS INNOCUOUS AS THE COLOR OF ONE'S SKIN--

AN INJUSTICE THAT SOME OF YOU HAVE EXPERIENCED FIRSTHAND.

YET DESPITE THE INDIGNITIES HE SUFFERED EVERY DAY OF HIS LIFE, JAMES ALWAYS KNEW THAT HE WAS DESTINED FOR SOMETHING MORE--

A GREATER LIFE WITH GREATER ASPIRATIONS THAT THIS WORLD COULD NEVER STRIP FROM HIS INCREDIBLE MIND.

BUT WHAT IT COULD DO IS TAKE HIS LIFE AWAY BEFORE THAT DESTINY WAS PROPERLY FULFILLED--

AND IT CERTAINLY PUT FORTH ITS BEST EFFORT.

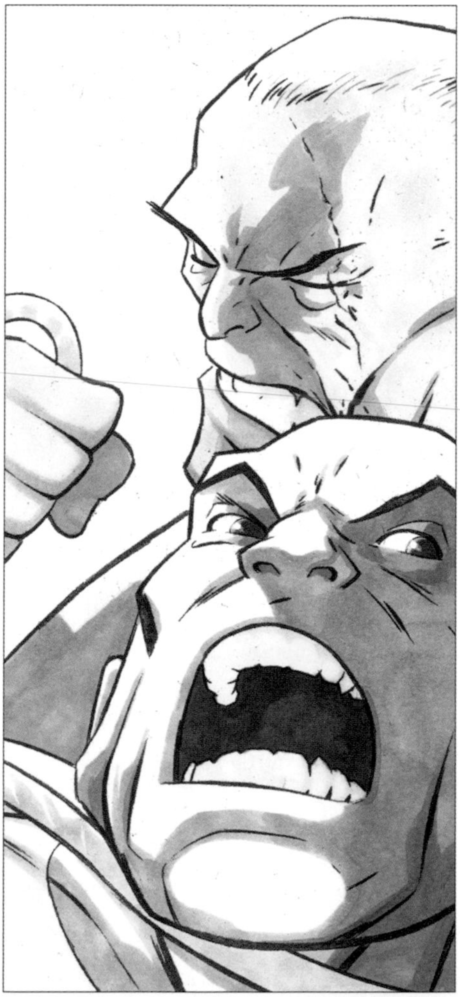

AND THEN SOMETHING HAPPENED.

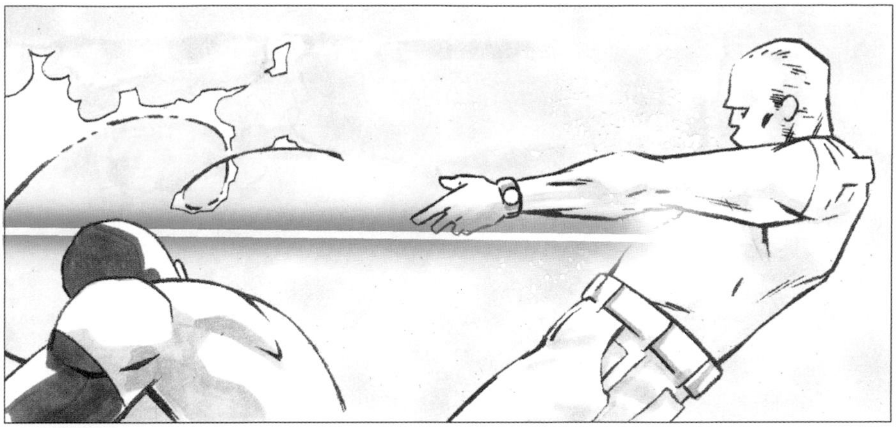

SOMETHING IMPOSSIBLE.

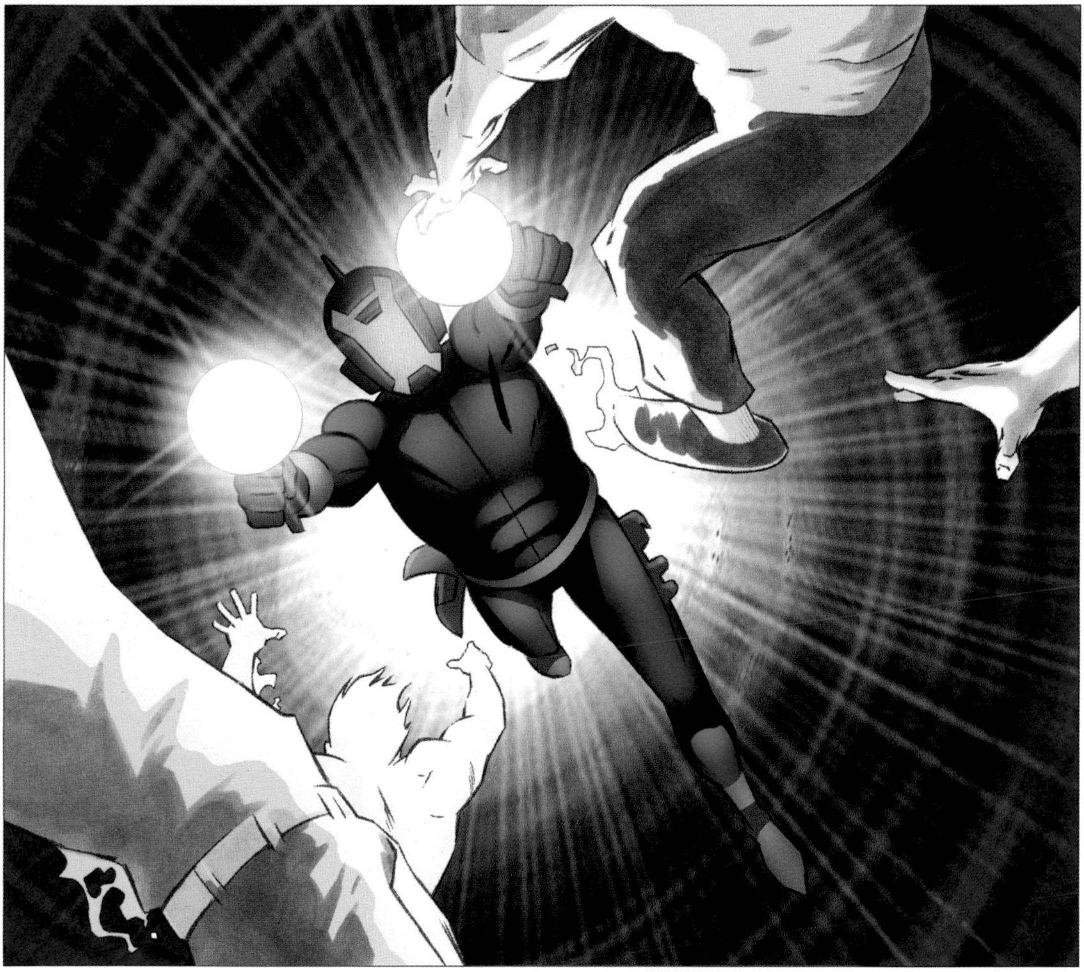

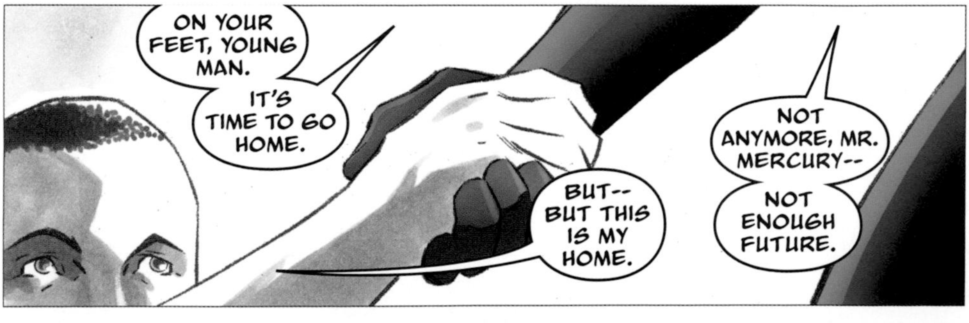
ON YOUR FEET, YOUNG MAN.
IT'S TIME TO GO HOME.
BUT-- BUT THIS IS MY HOME.
NOT ANYMORE, MR. MERCURY--
NOT ENOUGH FUTURE.

JAMES
I DON'T... I DON'T UNDERSTAND... WHERE ARE WE? WHAT... WHAT IS THIS PLACE? IT'S BEAUTIFUL...

[redacted]
IT IS INDEED, BUT WE DON'T HAVE THE TIME TO PROPERLY APPRECIATE IT. THESE TYPES OF CHRONAL INCURSIONS ARE NEVER TREATED LIGHTLY, SO I WILL NEED YOU TO LISTEN VERY CAREFULLY...

CHRONAL? ARE YOU TELLING ME THAT THIS IS... THAT THIS IS THE FUTURE?

IT IS OF COURSE ONE POSSIBLE FUTURE, WHICH CAN BE SAID OF ANY PLACE THAT WE HAVE NOT YET DISCOVERED. OTHER FUTURES ARE QUITE DIFFERENT, THOUGH YOU WILL FIGURE THAT ONE OUT SOON ENOUGH.

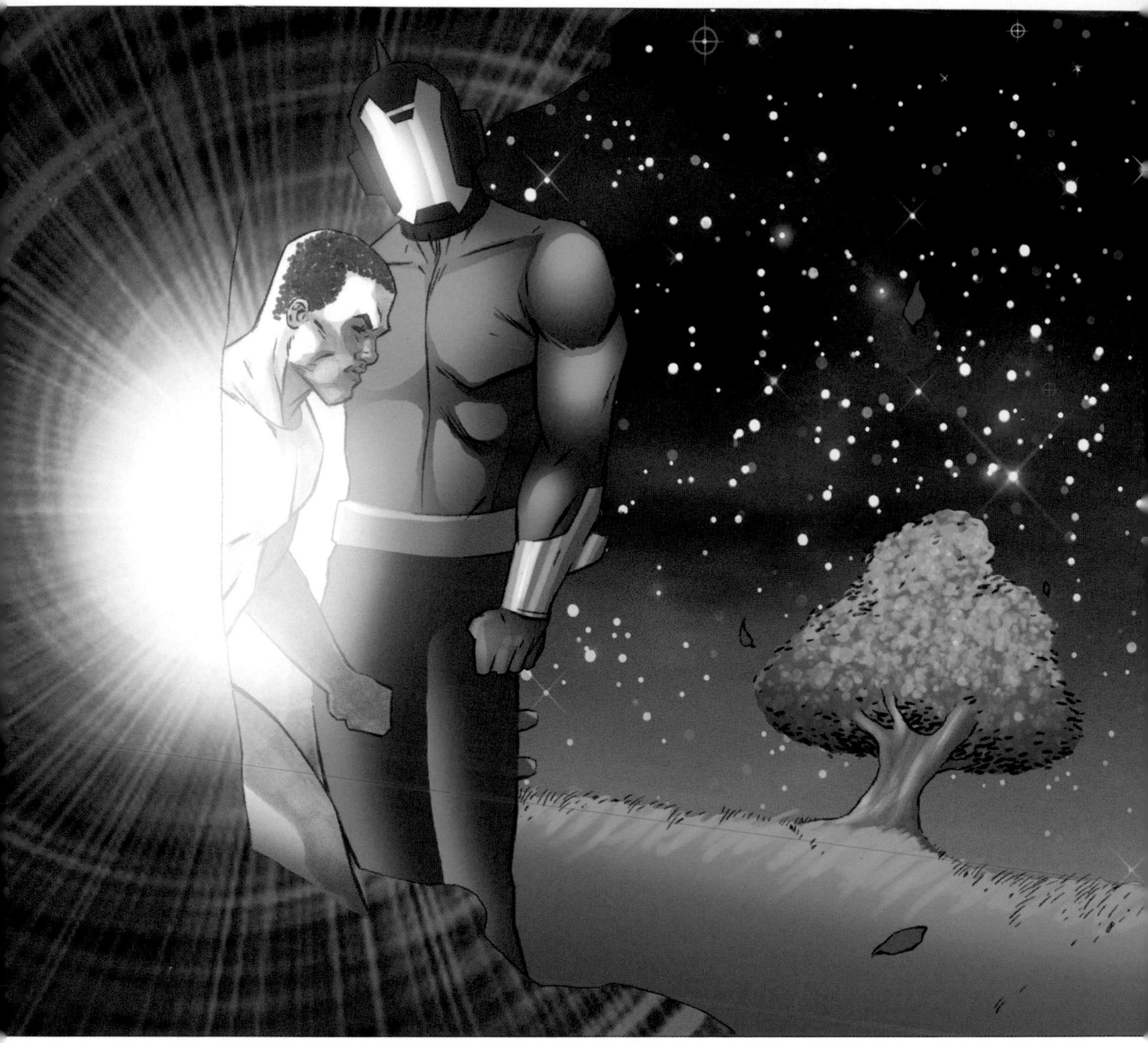

THE IMPORTANT THING IS THAT YOU ARE NOW ABLE TO BEGIN ANEW, IF YOU SO CHOOSE.

AN EXISTENCE FAR REMOVED FROM THE ONE IN WHICH YOU FOUND YOURSELF THROUGH NO FAULT OF YOUR OWN.

IT IS TRUE THAT YOUR WORLD ONLY NEEDS TIME TO CHANGE FOR THE BETTER, BUT IT IS TIME YOU DO NOT HAVE.

WHAT YOU CAN ACCOMPLISH IS TOO IMPORTANT TO BE LEFT IN THE HANDS OF SOMETHING AS UNPREDICTABLE AS SIMPLE CHANCE.

WAIT... I KNOW THIS PLACE. THAT'S MY...

NO...

JAMES
THIS IS MY LABORATORY... THESE ARE MY THINGS... MY NOTES...

HOW DID YOU KNOW? I'M THE ONLY ONE THAT KNOWS ABOUT ANY OF THIS... THIS ISN'T POSSIBLE...

[redacted]
AND YET SOMEHOW IT IS.

YOUNG MAN, WE ARE BOTH STANDING HERE BECAUSE YOUR HOME WORLD WOULD HAVE DONE EVERYTHING IN ITS POWER TO DISARM YOUR SPIRIT, YOUR INTELLECT, AND YOUR GREAT POTENTIAL.

YOU'RE NOW STANDING IN A PLACE WHERE SUCH THINGS CAN BE REWARDED--

PROVIDED YOU ARE WILLING TO BUILD A BETTER FUTURE WITH YOUR OWN TWO HANDS AND SHARE IT WITH AS MANY AS POSSIBLE.

WHERE WILL YOU START? WHAT WILL BE YOUR FIRST GREAT GIFT TO THE WORLDS?

THEY'RE... THEY'RE JUST IDEAS... I CAN'T...

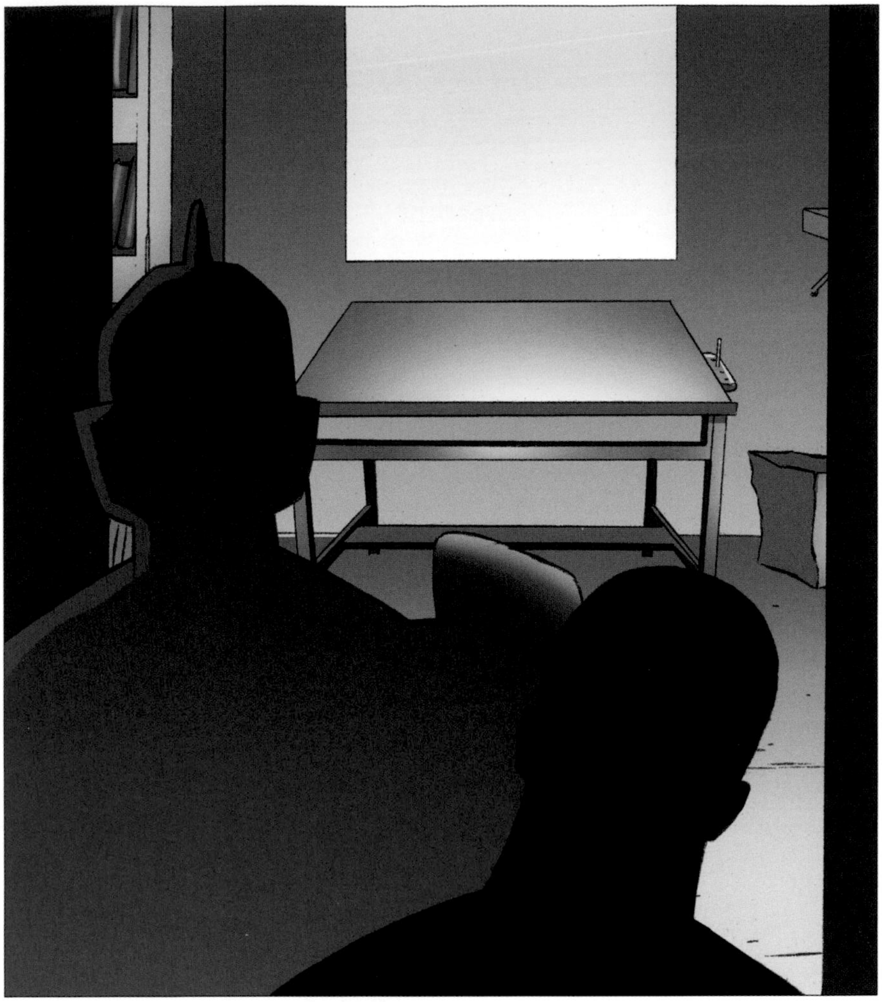

THERE IS ***NOTHING*** MORE VALUABLE THAN AN IDEA. RIGHT NOW, THEY ARE DESTROYING YOUR HOME PLANET, BUT THEY CANNOT ONLY BE USED TO DAMAGE AND DEFEAT THOSE NOT IN POWER. YOU ***KNOW*** THIS, JAMES...

WHAT OBSTACLE HAVE YOU EVER KNOWN THAT YOU COULD NOT THINK YOUR WAY PAST?

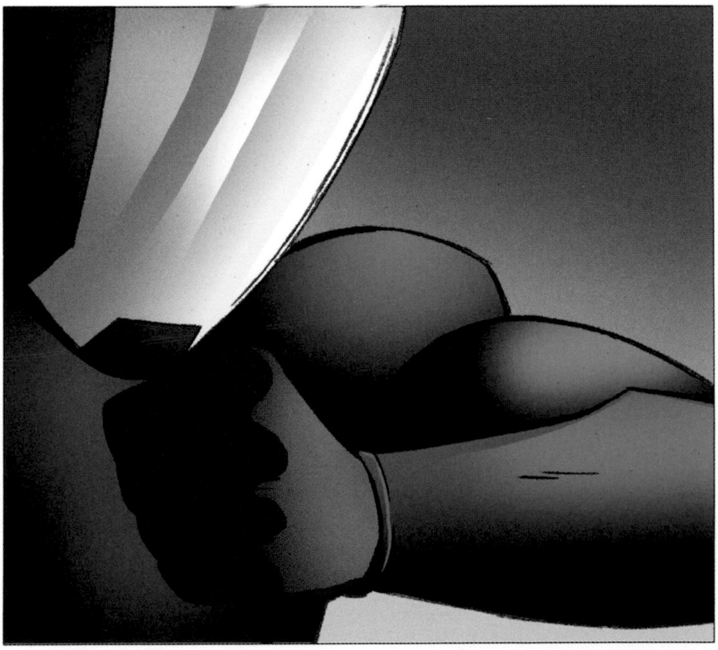

NOTHING YOU'RE SAYING MAKES ANY SENSE... NONE OF THIS DOES.

AN IDEA COULDN'T SAVE ME FROM BEING ***KILLED*** BY MEN I'D DONE NO WRONG TO.

I AM GRATEFUL FOR WHAT YOU'VE DONE, BUT EITHER TAKE ME BACK HOME OR EXPLAIN CLEARLY JUST WHAT IS HAPPENING HERE--

WHY SHOULD I BELIEVE THIS IS ANYTHING MORE THAN A DREAM?

COUGH...

COUGH COUGH...

COUGH!

WHAT IS IT...

WHAT'S WRONG?

JAMES
BUT, BUT THAT'S
IMPOSSIBLE--

COUGH...

COUGH...

YOU'LL SPEND YOUR ENTIRE
LIFE PROVING DIFFERENT.
AND AN IDEA *DID* SAVE YOUR
LIFE...JUST ONE YOU HAVEN'T
HAD QUITE YET...

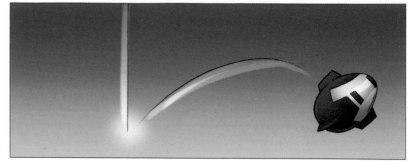

AND WHEN YOU FIND YOURSELF STANDING WHERE I AM NOW,
TELLING A MAN JUST LIKE YOU EXACTLY WHAT HE NEEDS
TO BEGIN HIS MOST IMPORTANT
WORK, YOU'LL KNOW THAT YOU'VE
DONE ALL YOU COULD AND MORE.

THAT YOU HAVE TRANSCENDED YOUR HUMBLE BEGINNINGS,
AND THAT IDEAS--

IDEAS ARE THE ONE THING THAT CAN NEVER BE STOPPED.

BUT I DON'T UNDERSTAND ANY
OF THIS...YOU HAVE TO TELL ME--

TO TELL YOU MORE THAN THIS WOULD
BE TO INVITE DESTRUCTION UPON US
BOTH, AND TO DENY YOU THE GLORY
OF A DREAM PROPERLY REALIZED.

WHAT I'VE DONE TODAY, YOUNG MAN...
THE HUMAN BODY CAN ONLY ENDURE
SO MUCH.

WHAT ARE YOU SAYING?

THAT BY SAVING ME, YOU'RE--

ONCE TO RESCUE THE ONES YOU LOVE
FROM THE LIFE YOU ALL ONCE KNEW.
ONCE TO DEFEAT THE GREATEST EVIL
YOU'LL EVER KNOW. ONCE MORE TO
ENSURE THAT YOU EVER HAVE A CHANCE
AT ALL.

I NEED *MORE*...THIS ISN'T ENOUGH...

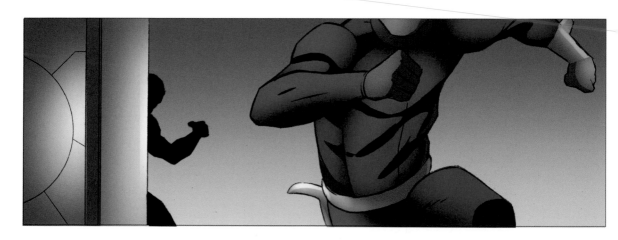

GOOD LUCK, BOY...THE PARADOXES
WILL BE HERE ANY MINUTE...

WAIT! WHAT THE HELL IS A--

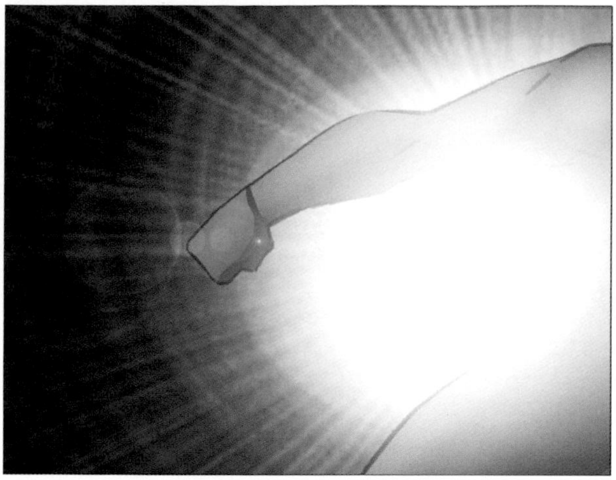

JAMES WOULD NEVER LEARN THE IDENTITY OF THE MAN WHO RESCUED HIM, BUT THERE WAS NO DENYING THE OPPORTUNITY THAT NOW LAY IN FRONT OF HIM.

THE THINGS HE'D BEEN DREAMING, THE INVENTIONS AND INNOVATIONS THAT HIS HOME WORLD HAD NO PLACE FOR COULD NOW BECOME A REALITY.

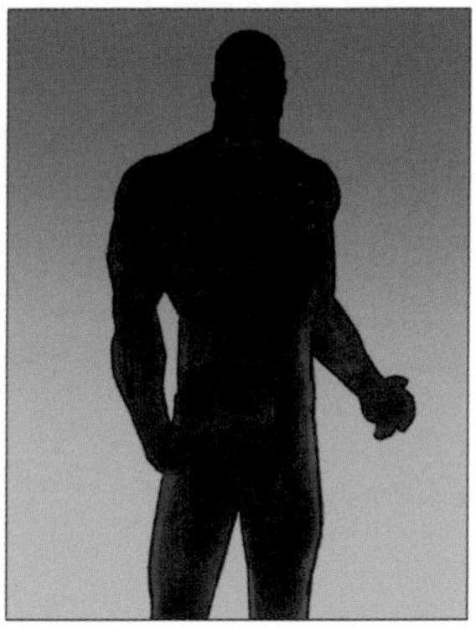

THERE WERE NO LIMITATIONS--

THERE WAS NO IMPOSSIBLE.

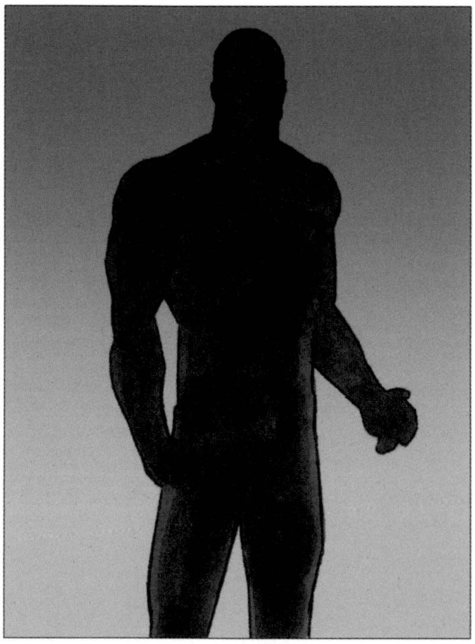

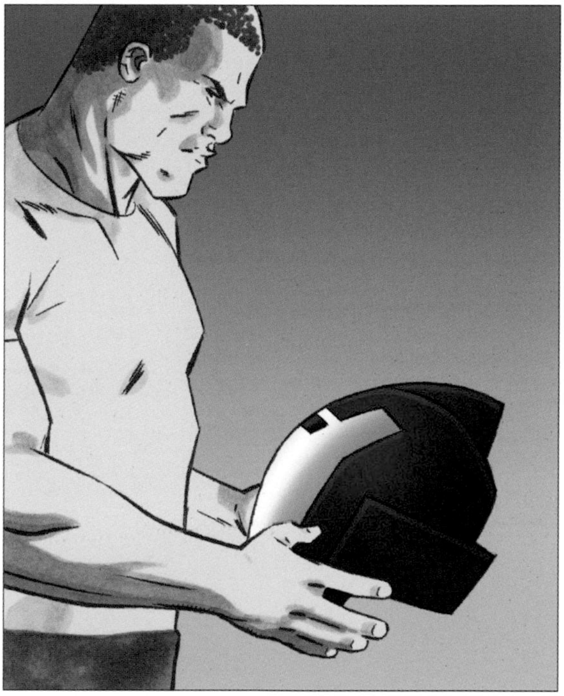

AND MOST IMPORTANTLY, THE PEOPLE HE CARED FOR MOST SUDDENLY HAD A HOME WHERE THEY COULD ALL EXIST IN PEACE, FREE OF THE RACIAL STRIFE AND INJUSTICE THAT HAD COME TO DEFINE SO MANY OF THEIR LIVES.

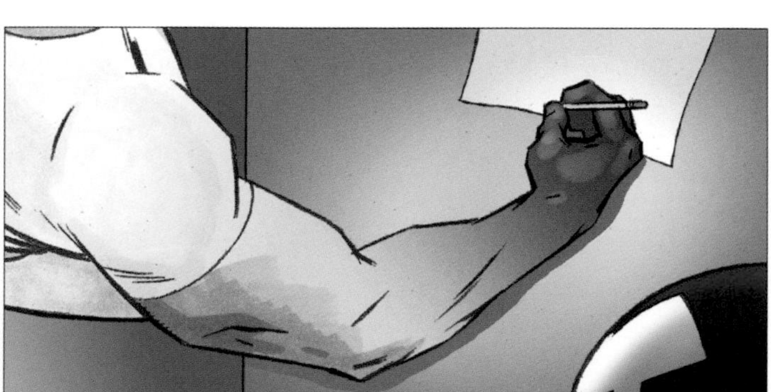

HE JUST NEEDED A WAY TO GO BACK FOR THEM, AND HE HAD ALL THE TIME IN THE WORLD NOW.

FOR JAMES, THE CALL OF DESTINY HAD ARRIVED, AND WITH EVERY BREATH IN HIS BODY, HE WOULD PREPARE AN ANSWER.

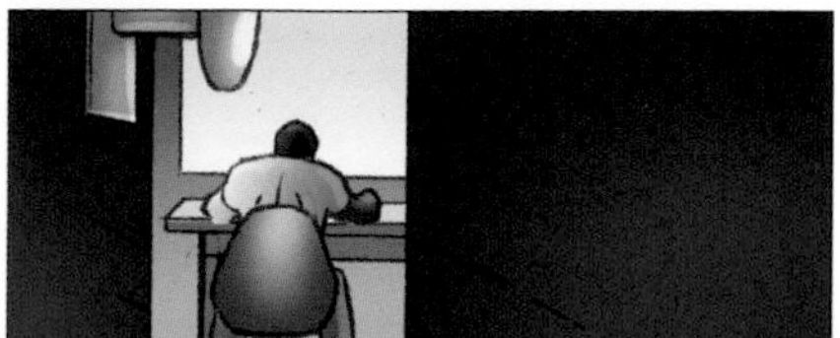

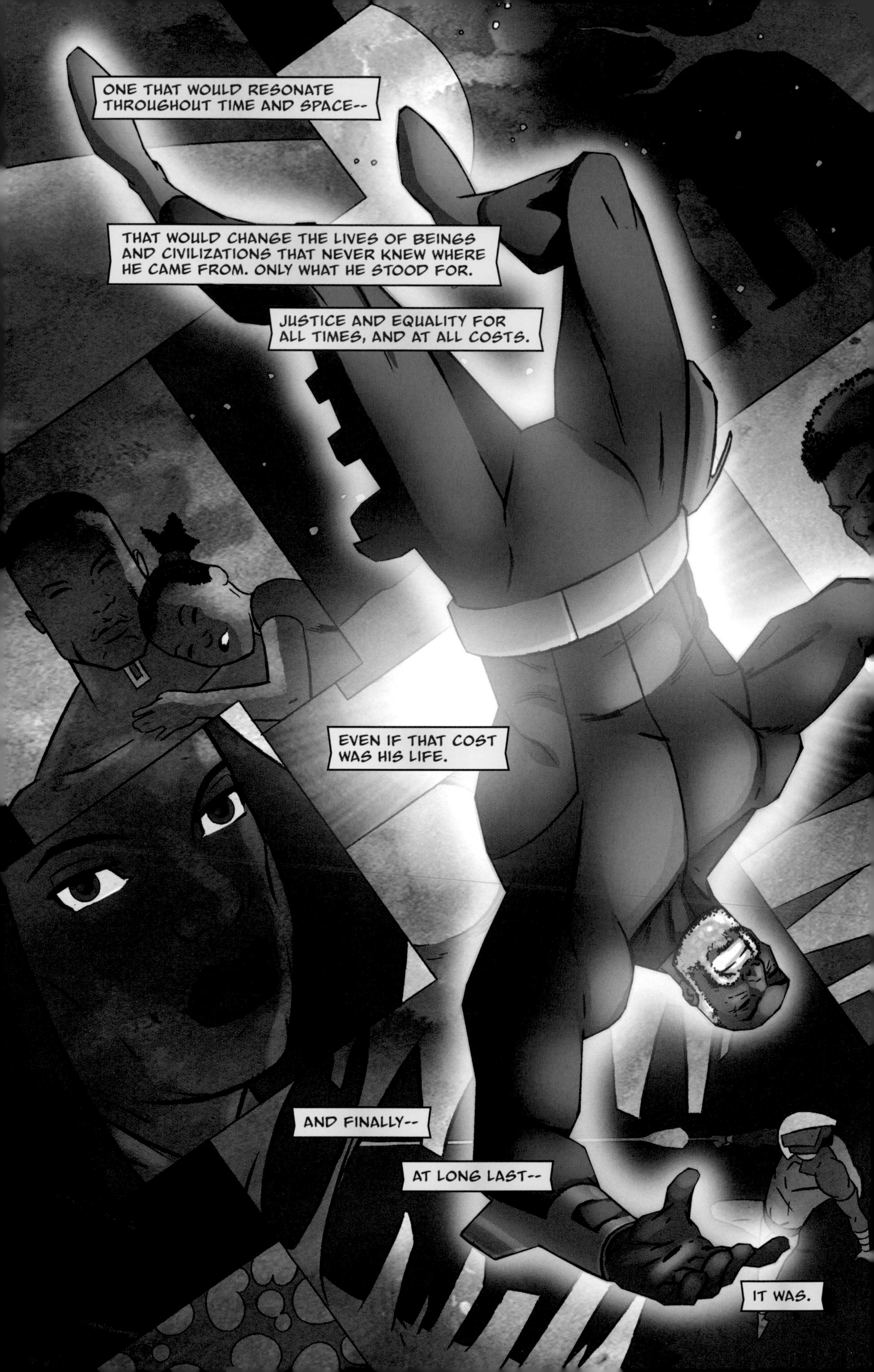
ONE THAT WOULD RESONATE THROUGHOUT TIME AND SPACE--
THAT WOULD CHANGE THE LIVES OF BEINGS AND CIVILIZATIONS THAT NEVER KNEW WHERE HE CAME FROM. ONLY WHAT HE STOOD FOR.
JUSTICE AND EQUALITY FOR ALL TIMES, AND AT ALL COSTS.
EVEN IF THAT COST WAS HIS LIFE.
AND FINALLY--
AT LONG LAST--
IT WAS.

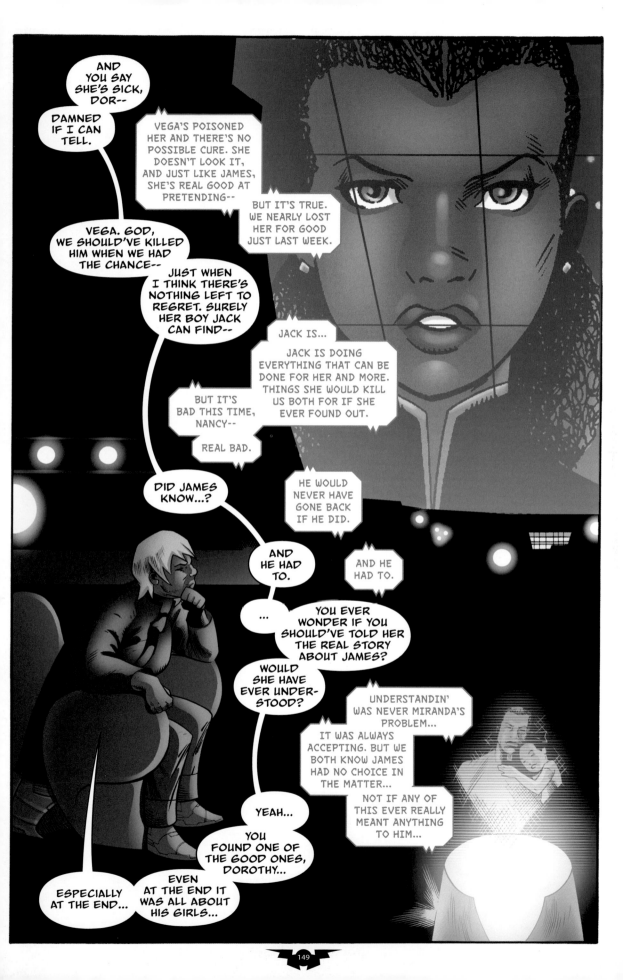

AND YOU SAY SHE'S SICK, DOR--

DAMNED IF I CAN TELL.

VEGA'S POISONED HER AND THERE'S NO POSSIBLE CURE. SHE DOESN'T LOOK IT, AND JUST LIKE JAMES, SHE'S REAL GOOD AT PRETENDING--

BUT IT'S TRUE. WE NEARLY LOST HER FOR GOOD JUST LAST WEEK.

VEGA. GOD, WE SHOULD'VE KILLED HIM WHEN WE HAD THE CHANCE--

JUST WHEN I THINK THERE'S NOTHING LEFT TO REGRET. SURELY HER BOY JACK CAN FIND--

JACK IS...

JACK IS DOING EVERYTHING THAT CAN BE DONE FOR HER AND MORE. THINGS SHE WOULD KILL US BOTH FOR IF SHE EVER FOUND OUT.

BUT IT'S BAD THIS TIME, NANCY--

REAL BAD.

DID JAMES KNOW...?

HE WOULD NEVER HAVE GONE BACK IF HE DID.

AND HE HAD TO.

AND HE HAD TO.

...

YOU EVER WONDER IF YOU SHOULD'VE TOLD HER THE REAL STORY ABOUT JAMES?

WOULD SHE HAVE EVER UNDER- STOOD?

UNDERSTANDIN' WAS NEVER MIRANDA'S PROBLEM...

IT WAS ALWAYS ACCEPTING. BUT WE BOTH KNOW JAMES HAD NO CHOICE IN THE MATTER...

NOT IF ANY OF THIS EVER REALLY MEANT ANYTHING TO HIM...

YEAH...

YOU FOUND ONE OF THE GOOD ONES, DOROTHY...

EVEN AT THE END IT WAS ALL ABOUT HIS GIRLS...

ESPECIALLY AT THE END...

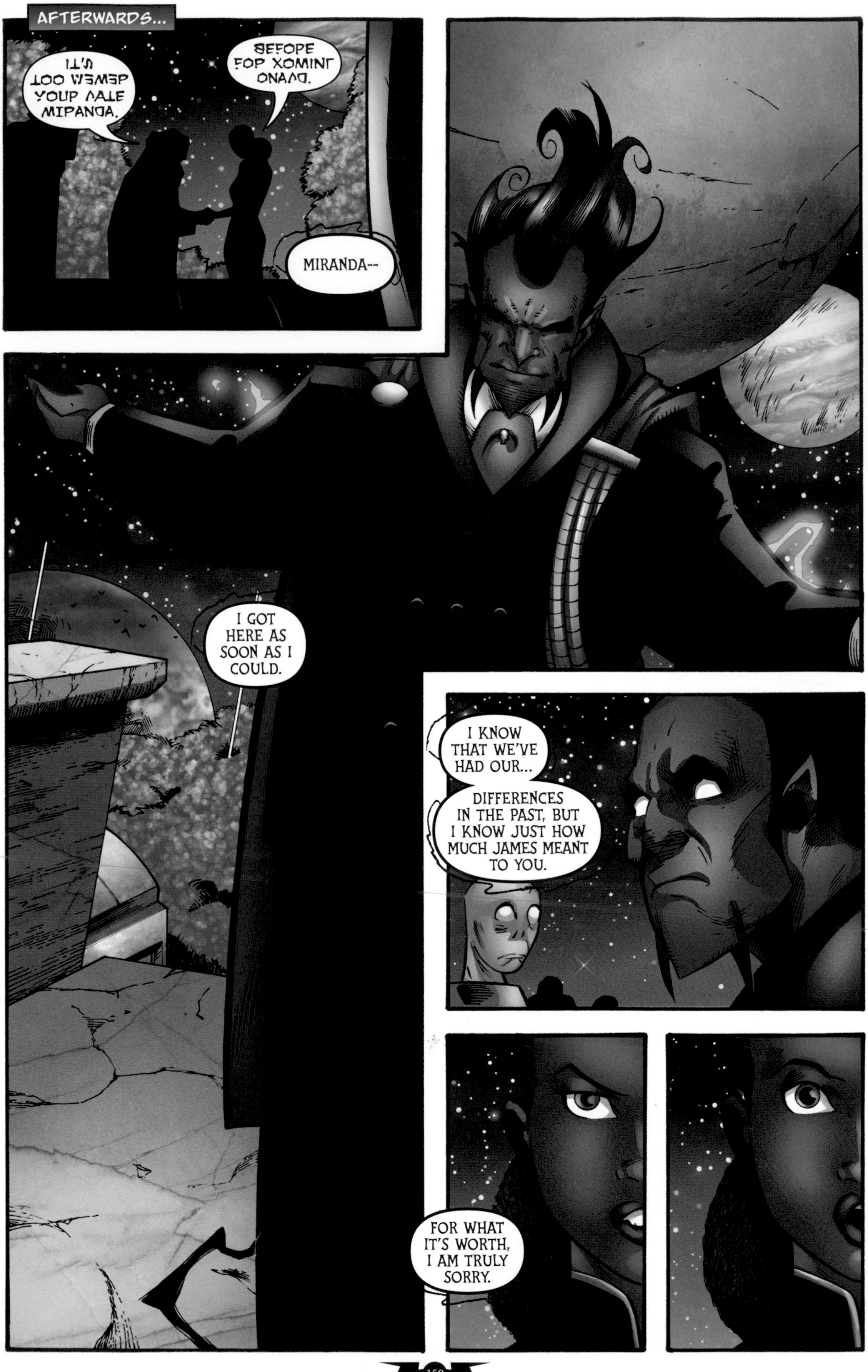
AFTERWARDS...
MIRANDA--
I GOT HERE AS SOON AS I COULD.
I KNOW THAT WE'VE HAD OUR...
DIFFERENCES IN THE PAST, BUT I KNOW JUST HOW MUCH JAMES MEANT TO YOU.
FOR WHAT IT'S WORTH, I AM TRULY SORRY.

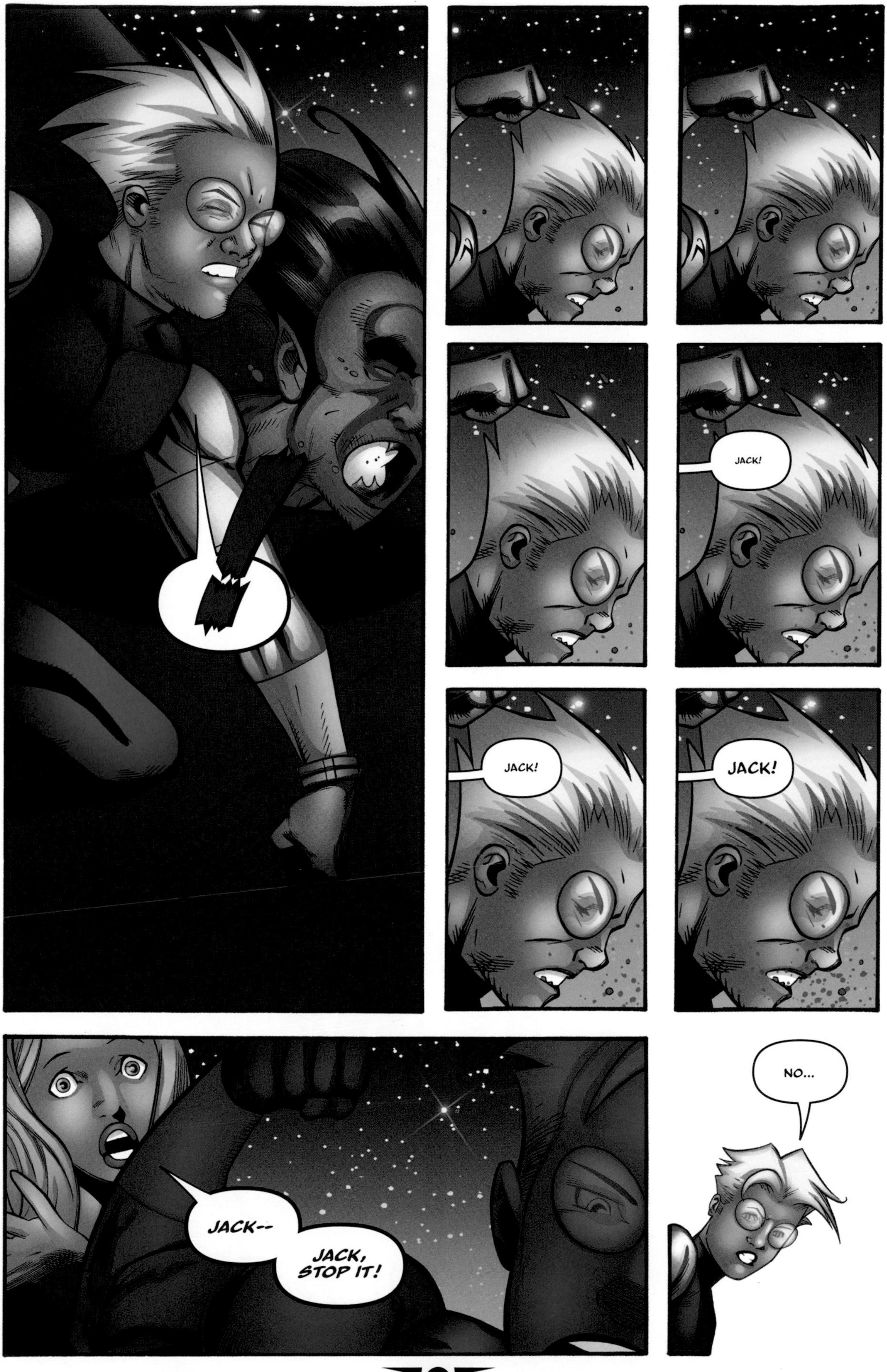
JACK!
JACK!
JACK!
JACK--
JACK, STOP IT!
NO...

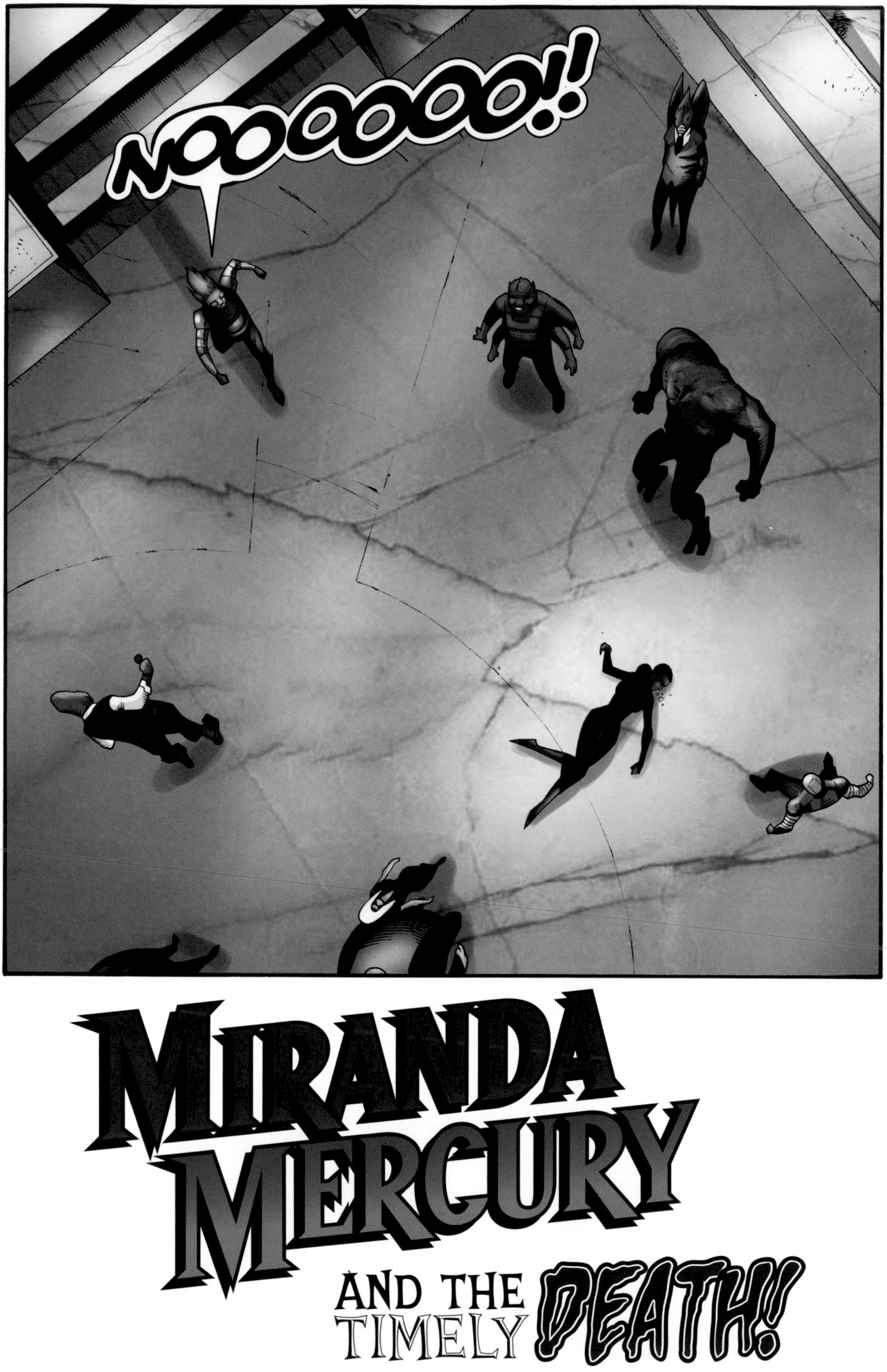
NOOOOOO!!

MIRANDA MERCURY AND THE TIMELY DEATH!

IT WASN'T ALWAYS LIKE THIS.

ONCE MIRANDA MERCURY
WAS A YOUNG WOMAN
WITH IMPOSSIBLE SHOES TO FILL
AND HER OWN IDEAS ABOUT
HOW THINGS SHOULD BE DONE.
FOR YEARS SHE'D WAITED FOR
THE OPPORTUNITY TO STEP OUT OF HER
FAMOUS FAMILY'S SHADOW.
TO MAKE HER OWN WAY.

THAT TIME IS NOW.

MIRANDA IS ALL ALONE OUT THERE.

JUST THE WAY SHE WANTED IT.

EPISODE 124

MIRANDA MERCURY
AND THE FINAL LESSON!

WRITER
BRANDON THOMAS

PENCILER
LEE FERGUSON

INKER
MARC DEERING

LETTERER
MATTY RYAN

COLORIST
JAMES BROWN

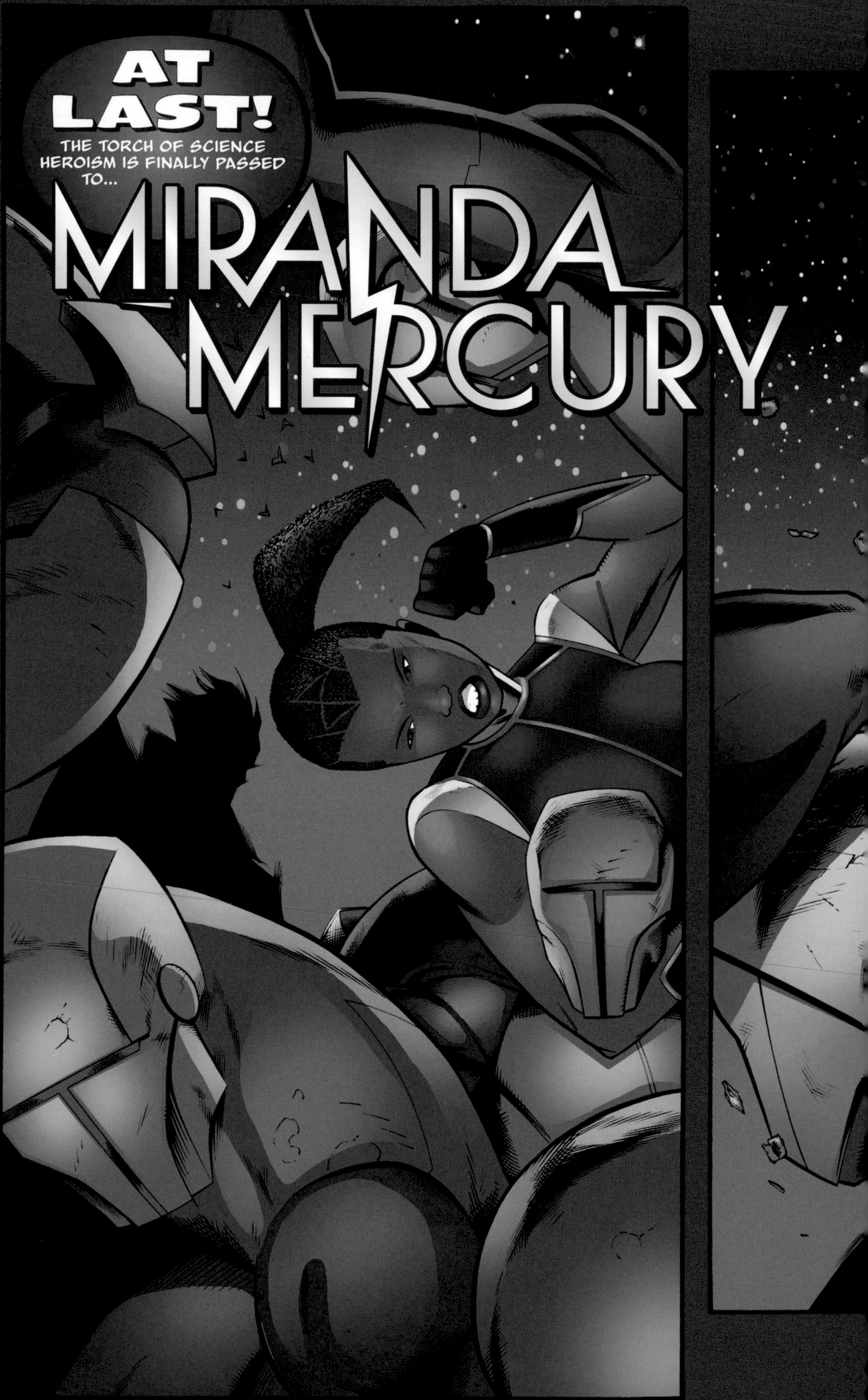
AT LAST!
THE TORCH OF SCIENCE HEROISM IS FINALLY PASSED TO...
MIRANDA MERCURY

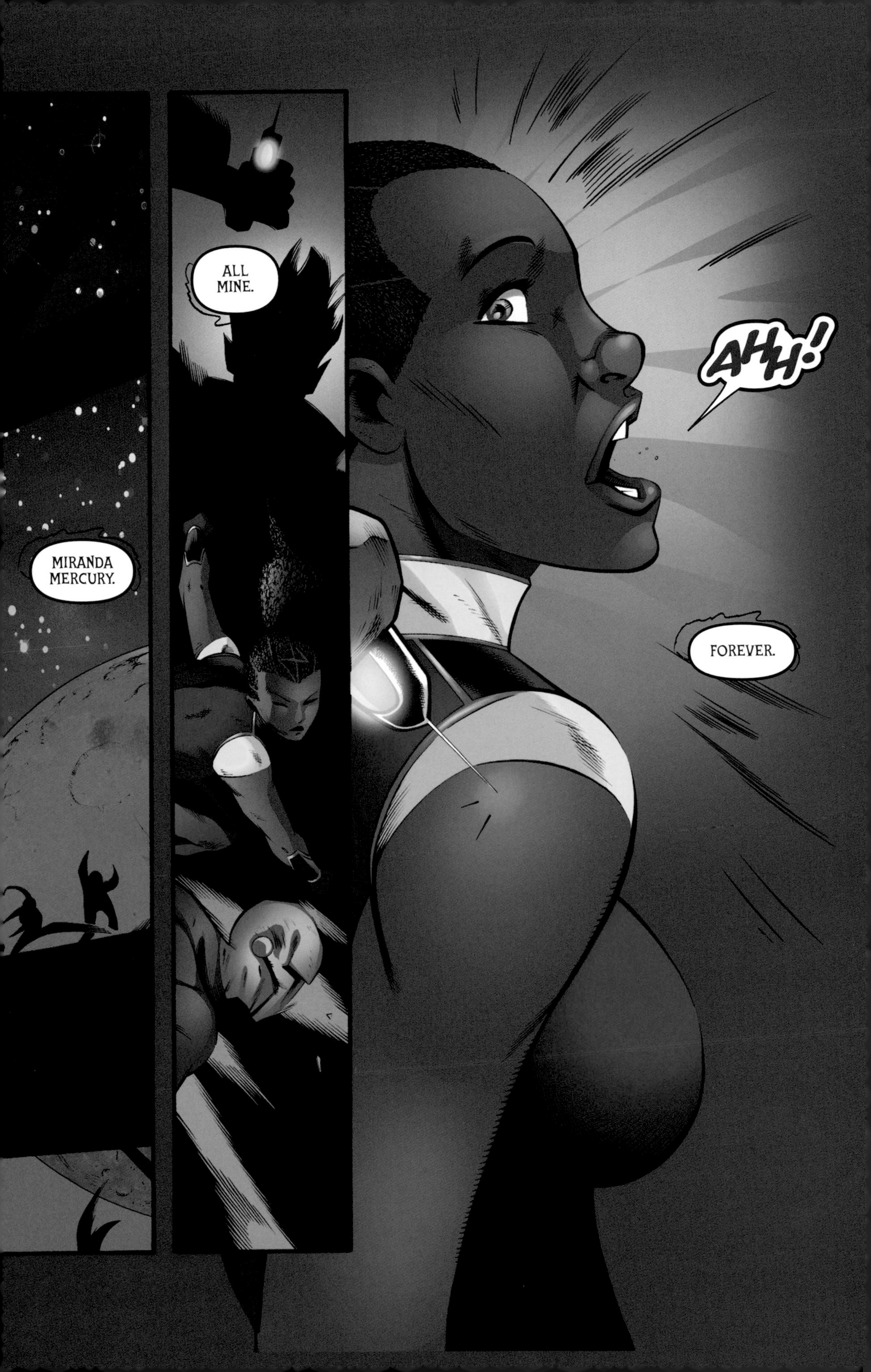
MIRANDA MERCURY.
ALL MINE.
AHH!
FOREVER.

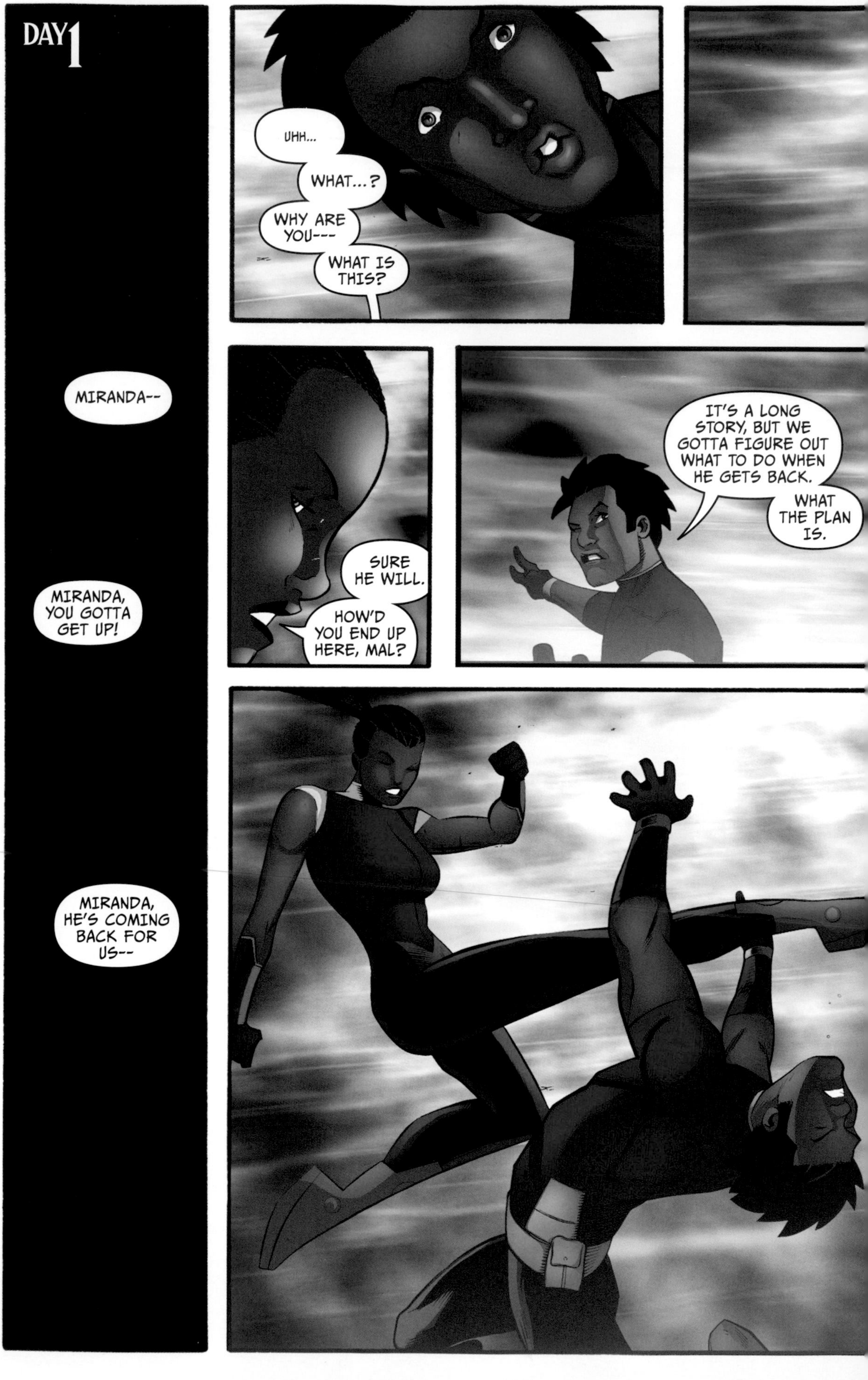
DAY 1
UHH...
WHAT...?
WHY ARE YOU---
WHAT IS THIS?
MIRANDA--
SURE HE WILL.
HOW'D YOU END UP HERE, MAL?
IT'S A LONG STORY, BUT WE GOTTA FIGURE OUT WHAT TO DO WHEN HE GETS BACK.
WHAT THE PLAN IS.
MIRANDA, YOU GOTTA GET UP!
MIRANDA, HE'S COMING BACK FOR US--

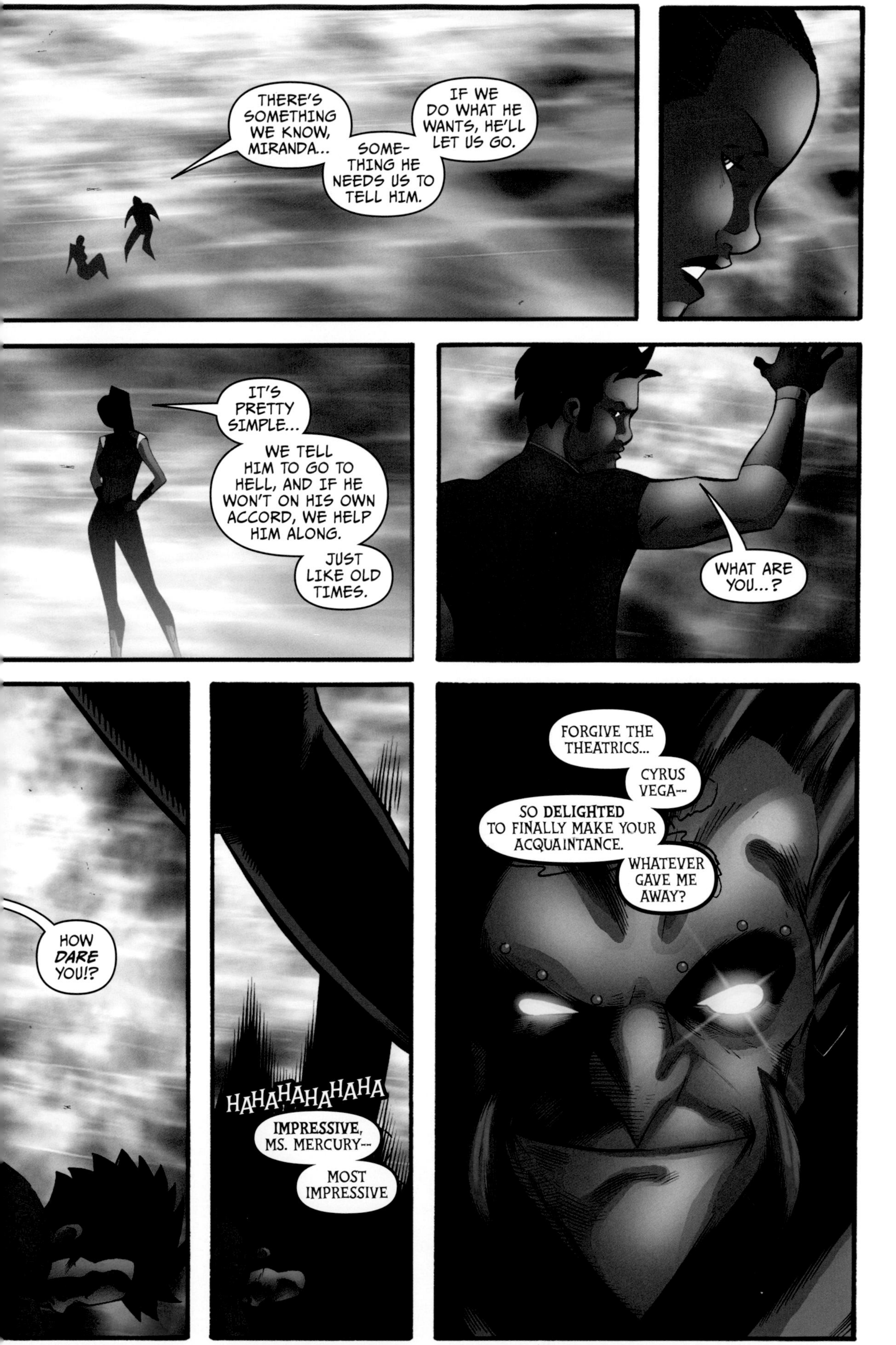
THERE'S SOMETHING WE KNOW, MIRANDA...
SOME-THING HE NEEDS US TO TELL HIM.
IF WE DO WHAT HE WANTS, HE'LL LET US GO.
IT'S PRETTY SIMPLE...
WE TELL HIM TO GO TO HELL, AND IF HE WON'T ON HIS OWN ACCORD, WE HELP HIM ALONG.
JUST LIKE OLD TIMES.
WHAT ARE YOU...?
HOW DARE YOU!?
HAHAHAHAHAHA
IMPRESSIVE, MS. MERCURY--
MOST IMPRESSIVE
FORGIVE THE THEATRICS...
CYRUS VEGA--
SO DELIGHTED TO FINALLY MAKE YOUR ACQUAINTANCE.
WHATEVER GAVE ME AWAY?

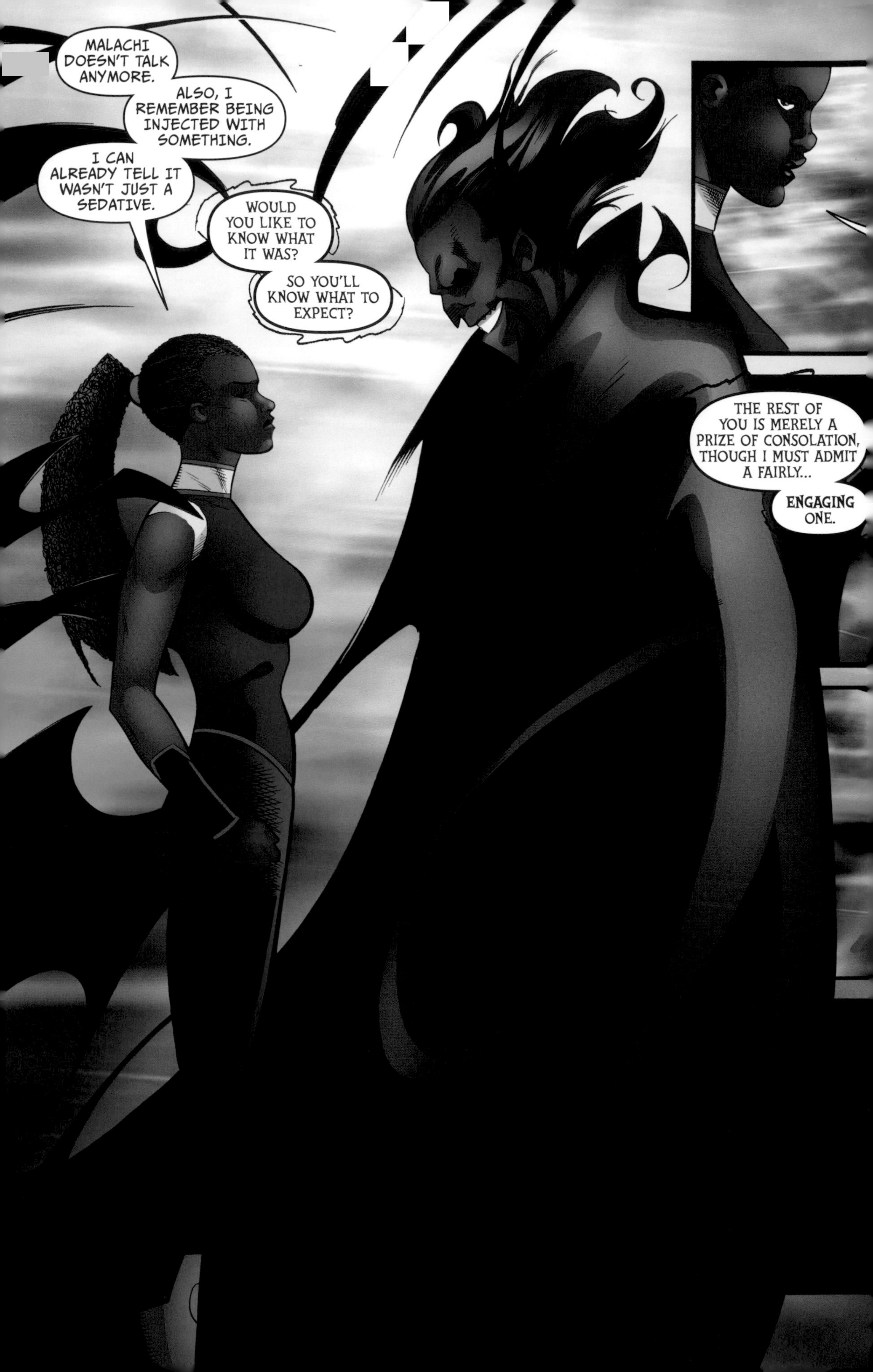
MALACHI DOESN'T TALK ANYMORE.
ALSO, I REMEMBER BEING INJECTED WITH SOMETHING.
I CAN ALREADY TELL IT WASN'T JUST A SEDATIVE.
WOULD YOU LIKE TO KNOW WHAT IT WAS?
SO YOU'LL KNOW WHAT TO EXPECT?
THE REST OF YOU IS MERELY A PRIZE OF CONSOLATION, THOUGH I MUST ADMIT A FAIRLY...
ENGAGING ONE.

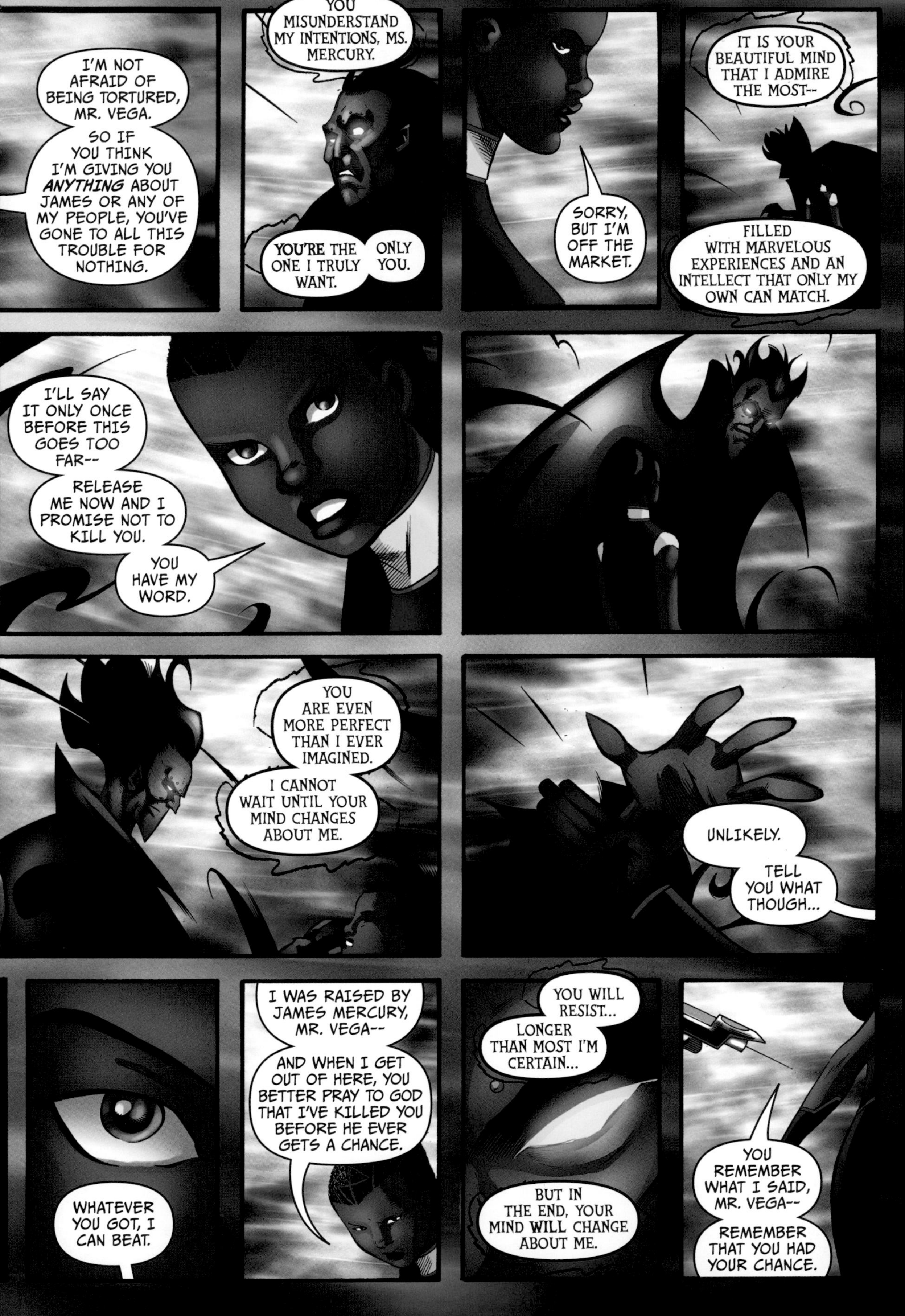
I'M NOT AFRAID OF BEING TORTURED, MR. VEGA.
SO IF YOU THINK I'M GIVING YOU *ANYTHING* ABOUT JAMES OR ANY OF MY PEOPLE, YOU'VE GONE TO ALL THIS TROUBLE FOR NOTHING.
YOU MISUNDERSTAND MY INTENTIONS, MS. MERCURY.
YOU'RE THE ONE I TRULY WANT.
ONLY YOU.
SORRY, BUT I'M OFF THE MARKET.
IT IS YOUR BEAUTIFUL MIND THAT I ADMIRE THE MOST--
FILLED WITH MARVELOUS EXPERIENCES AND AN INTELLECT THAT ONLY MY OWN CAN MATCH.
I'LL SAY IT ONLY ONCE BEFORE THIS GOES TOO FAR--
RELEASE ME NOW AND I PROMISE NOT TO KILL YOU.
YOU HAVE MY WORD.
YOU ARE EVEN MORE PERFECT THAN I EVER IMAGINED.
I CANNOT WAIT UNTIL YOUR MIND CHANGES ABOUT ME.
UNLIKELY.
TELL YOU WHAT THOUGH...
WHATEVER YOU GOT, I CAN BEAT.
I WAS RAISED BY JAMES MERCURY, MR. VEGA--
AND WHEN I GET OUT OF HERE, YOU BETTER PRAY TO GOD THAT I'VE KILLED YOU BEFORE HE EVER GETS A CHANCE.
YOU WILL RESIST...
LONGER THAN MOST I'M CERTAIN...
BUT IN THE END, YOUR MIND **WILL** CHANGE ABOUT ME.
YOU REMEMBER WHAT I SAID, MR. VEGA--
REMEMBER THAT YOU HAD YOUR CHANCE.

DAY 2

WHAT HAPPENED?

OH, HONEY-- NO NEED TO WORRY.

HE WAS HURT AND WE'RE JUST FIXING HIM UP.

THAT'S ALL.

THAT'S NOT WHAT *MAL* SAID, GRANDPA JAMES.

HE SAID SOME BAD GUYS WANTED THE CODES TO ALDARIA'S PLANET FENCE SHIELD AND THEY *MADE* HIM TELL THEM.

MAL SAID PEOPLE *DIED* BECAUSE.

OBVIOUSLY, I NEED TO HAVE A TALK WITH THAT MOTORMOUTH COUSIN OF YOURS.

DID HE KNOW?

KNOW WHAT, SWEETIE?

THAT PEOPLE COULD *DIE* IF HE TOLD THE BAD MEN THOSE CODES?

...

YES, MIRANDA, HE KNEW.

THEN WHY DID HE--

TO STOP THE HURT, BABY...

ANYTHING TO STOP THE HURT.

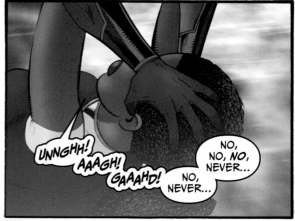

UNNGHH! AAAGH! GAAAHD!

NO, NO, *NO*, NEVER...

NO, NEVER...

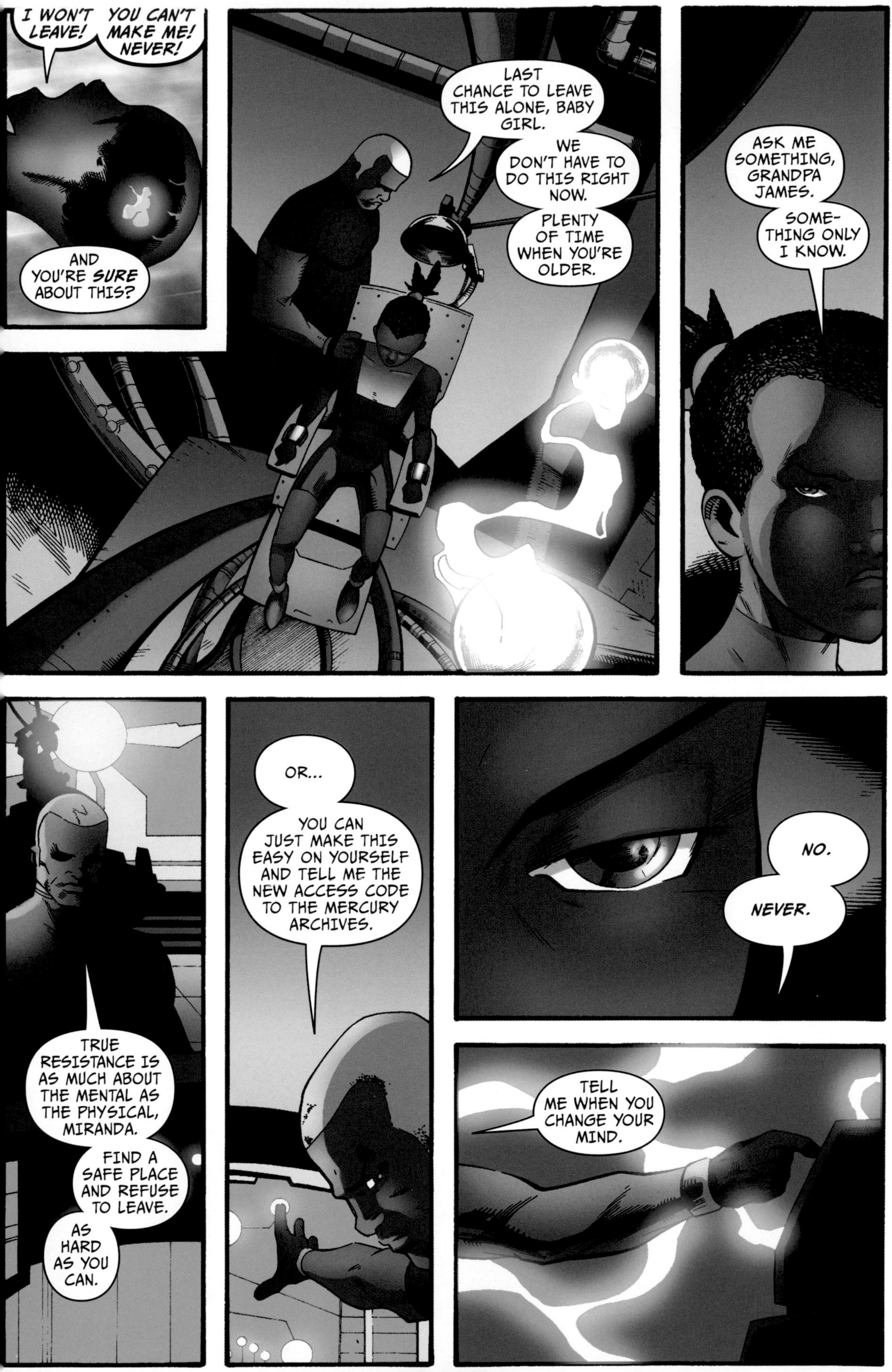
I WON'T LEAVE!
YOU CAN'T MAKE ME! NEVER!
AND YOU'RE SURE ABOUT THIS?
LAST CHANCE TO LEAVE THIS ALONE, BABY GIRL.
WE DON'T HAVE TO DO THIS RIGHT NOW.
PLENTY OF TIME WHEN YOU'RE OLDER.
ASK ME SOMETHING, GRANDPA JAMES.
SOME-THING ONLY I KNOW.
TRUE RESISTANCE IS AS MUCH ABOUT THE MENTAL AS THE PHYSICAL, MIRANDA.
FIND A SAFE PLACE AND REFUSE TO LEAVE.
AS HARD AS YOU CAN.
OR...
YOU CAN JUST MAKE THIS EASY ON YOURSELF AND TELL ME THE NEW ACCESS CODE TO THE MERCURY ARCHIVES.
NO.
NEVER.
TELL ME WHEN YOU CHANGE YOUR MIND.

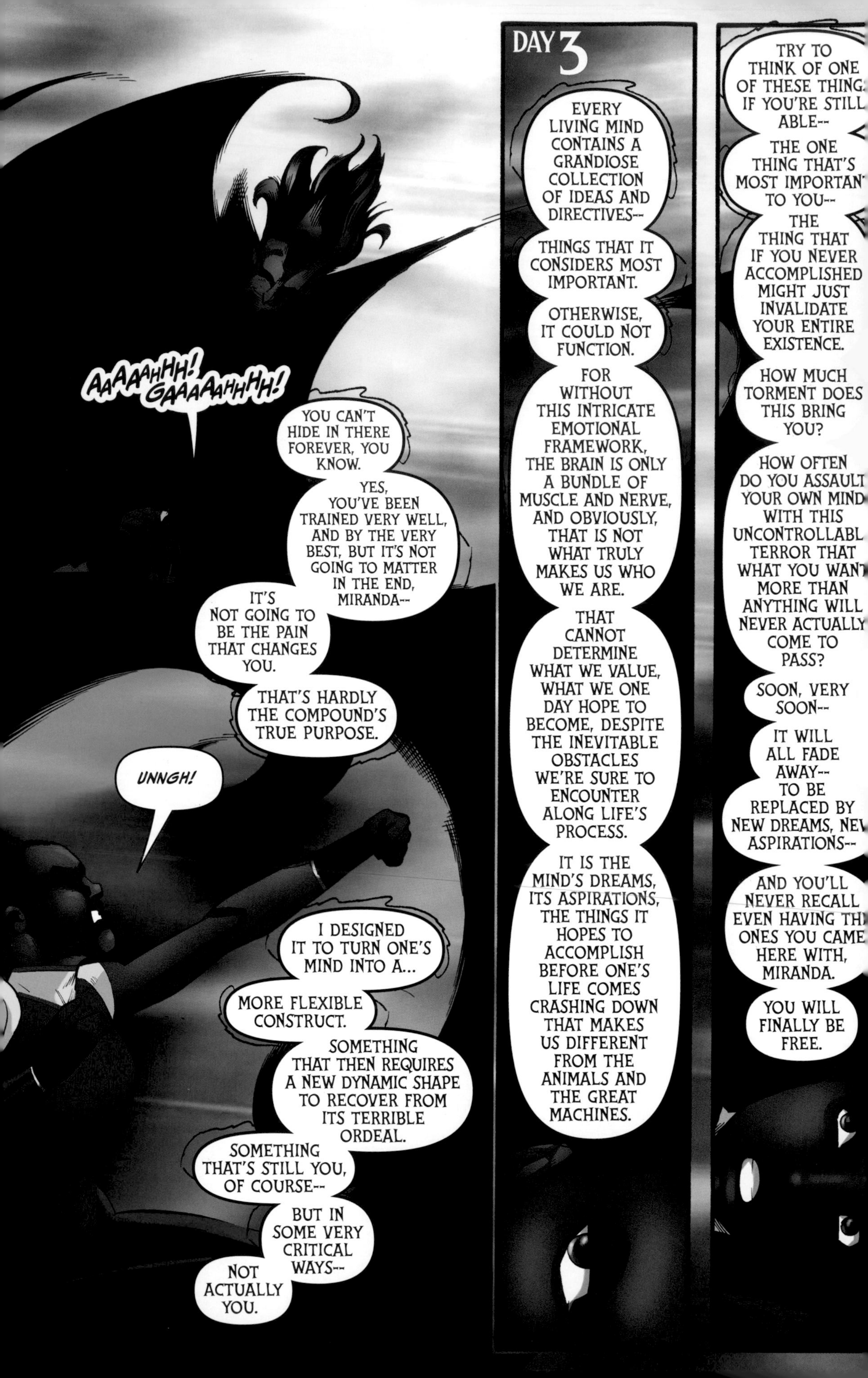
AAAAAHHH! GAAAAAHHHH!
YOU CAN'T HIDE IN THERE FOREVER, YOU KNOW.
YES, YOU'VE BEEN TRAINED VERY WELL, AND BY THE VERY BEST, BUT IT'S NOT GOING TO MATTER IN THE END, MIRANDA--
IT'S NOT GOING TO BE THE PAIN THAT CHANGES YOU.
THAT'S HARDLY THE COMPOUND'S TRUE PURPOSE.
UNNGH!
I DESIGNED IT TO TURN ONE'S MIND INTO A...
MORE FLEXIBLE CONSTRUCT.
SOMETHING THAT THEN REQUIRES A NEW DYNAMIC SHAPE TO RECOVER FROM ITS TERRIBLE ORDEAL.
SOMETHING THAT'S STILL YOU, OF COURSE--
BUT IN SOME VERY CRITICAL WAYS--
NOT ACTUALLY YOU.
DAY 3
EVERY LIVING MIND CONTAINS A GRANDIOSE COLLECTION OF IDEAS AND DIRECTIVES--
THINGS THAT IT CONSIDERS MOST IMPORTANT.
OTHERWISE, IT COULD NOT FUNCTION.
FOR WITHOUT THIS INTRICATE EMOTIONAL FRAMEWORK, THE BRAIN IS ONLY A BUNDLE OF MUSCLE AND NERVE, AND OBVIOUSLY, THAT IS NOT WHAT TRULY MAKES US WHO WE ARE.
THAT CANNOT DETERMINE WHAT WE VALUE, WHAT WE ONE DAY HOPE TO BECOME, DESPITE THE INEVITABLE OBSTACLES WE'RE SURE TO ENCOUNTER ALONG LIFE'S PROCESS.
IT IS THE MIND'S DREAMS, ITS ASPIRATIONS, THE THINGS IT HOPES TO ACCOMPLISH BEFORE ONE'S LIFE COMES CRASHING DOWN THAT MAKES US DIFFERENT FROM THE ANIMALS AND THE GREAT MACHINES.
TRY TO THINK OF ONE OF THESE THING IF YOU'RE STILL ABLE--
THE ONE THING THAT'S MOST IMPORTAN TO YOU--
THE THING THAT IF YOU NEVER ACCOMPLISHED MIGHT JUST INVALIDATE YOUR ENTIRE EXISTENCE.
HOW MUCH TORMENT DOES THIS BRING YOU?
HOW OFTEN DO YOU ASSAULT YOUR OWN MIND WITH THIS UNCONTROLLABL TERROR THAT WHAT YOU WAN MORE THAN ANYTHING WILL NEVER ACTUALLY COME TO PASS?
SOON, VERY SOON--
IT WILL ALL FADE AWAY--
TO BE REPLACED BY NEW DREAMS, NE ASPIRATIONS--
AND YOU'LL NEVER RECALL EVEN HAVING TH ONES YOU CAME HERE WITH, MIRANDA.
YOU WILL FINALLY BE FREE.

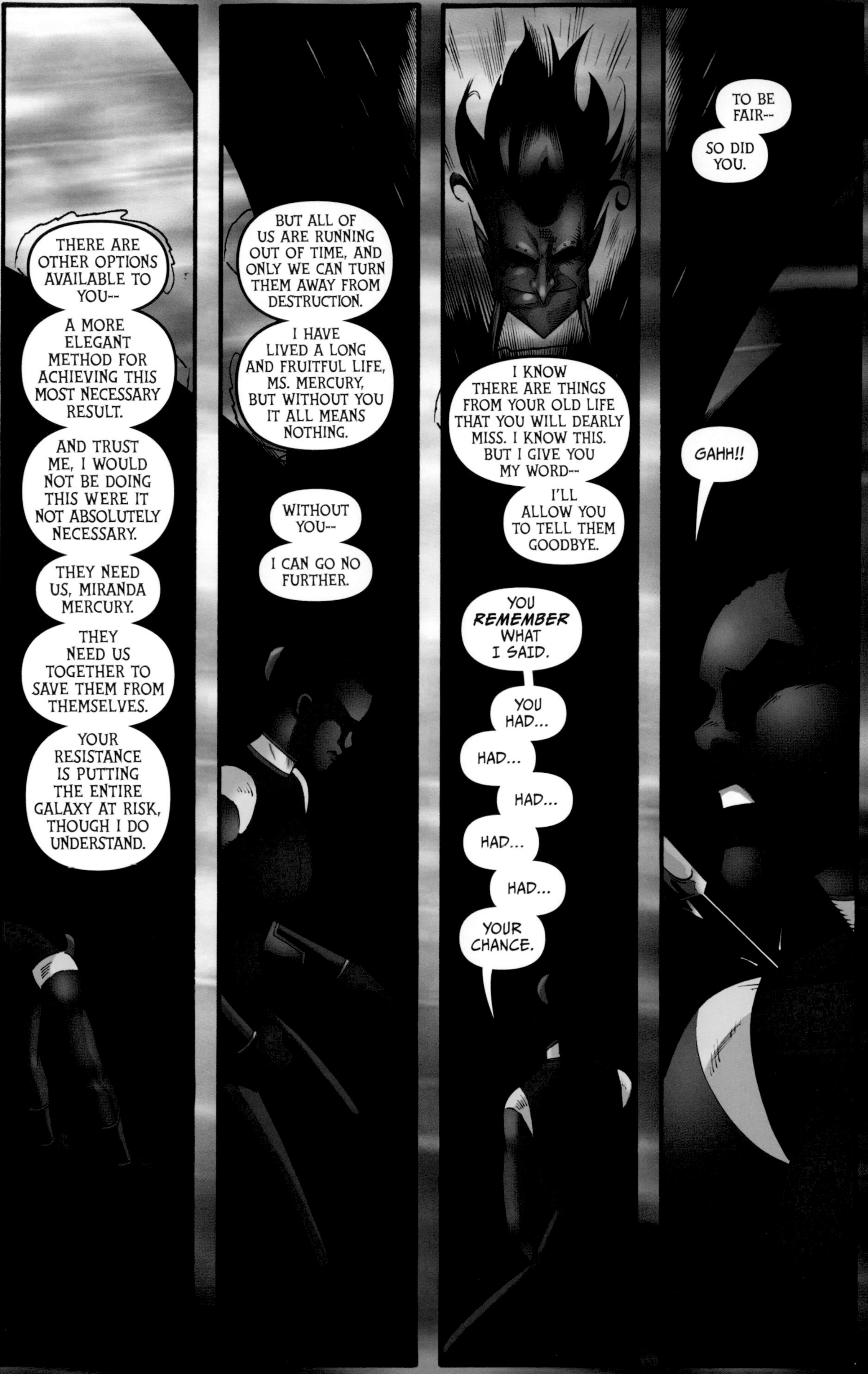
THERE ARE OTHER OPTIONS AVAILABLE TO YOU--
A MORE ELEGANT METHOD FOR ACHIEVING THIS MOST NECESSARY RESULT.
AND TRUST ME, I WOULD NOT BE DOING THIS WERE IT NOT ABSOLUTELY NECESSARY.
THEY NEED US, MIRANDA MERCURY.
THEY NEED US TOGETHER TO SAVE THEM FROM THEMSELVES.
YOUR RESISTANCE IS PUTTING THE ENTIRE GALAXY AT RISK, THOUGH I DO UNDERSTAND.
BUT ALL OF US ARE RUNNING OUT OF TIME, AND ONLY WE CAN TURN THEM AWAY FROM DESTRUCTION.
I HAVE LIVED A LONG AND FRUITFUL LIFE, MS. MERCURY, BUT WITHOUT YOU IT ALL MEANS NOTHING.
WITHOUT YOU--
I CAN GO NO FURTHER.
I KNOW THERE ARE THINGS FROM YOUR OLD LIFE THAT YOU WILL DEARLY MISS. I KNOW THIS. BUT I GIVE YOU MY WORD--
I'LL ALLOW YOU TO TELL THEM GOODBYE.
YOU *REMEMBER* WHAT I SAID.
YOU HAD...
HAD...
HAD...
HAD...
HAD...
YOUR CHANCE.
TO BE FAIR--
SO DID YOU.
GAHH!!

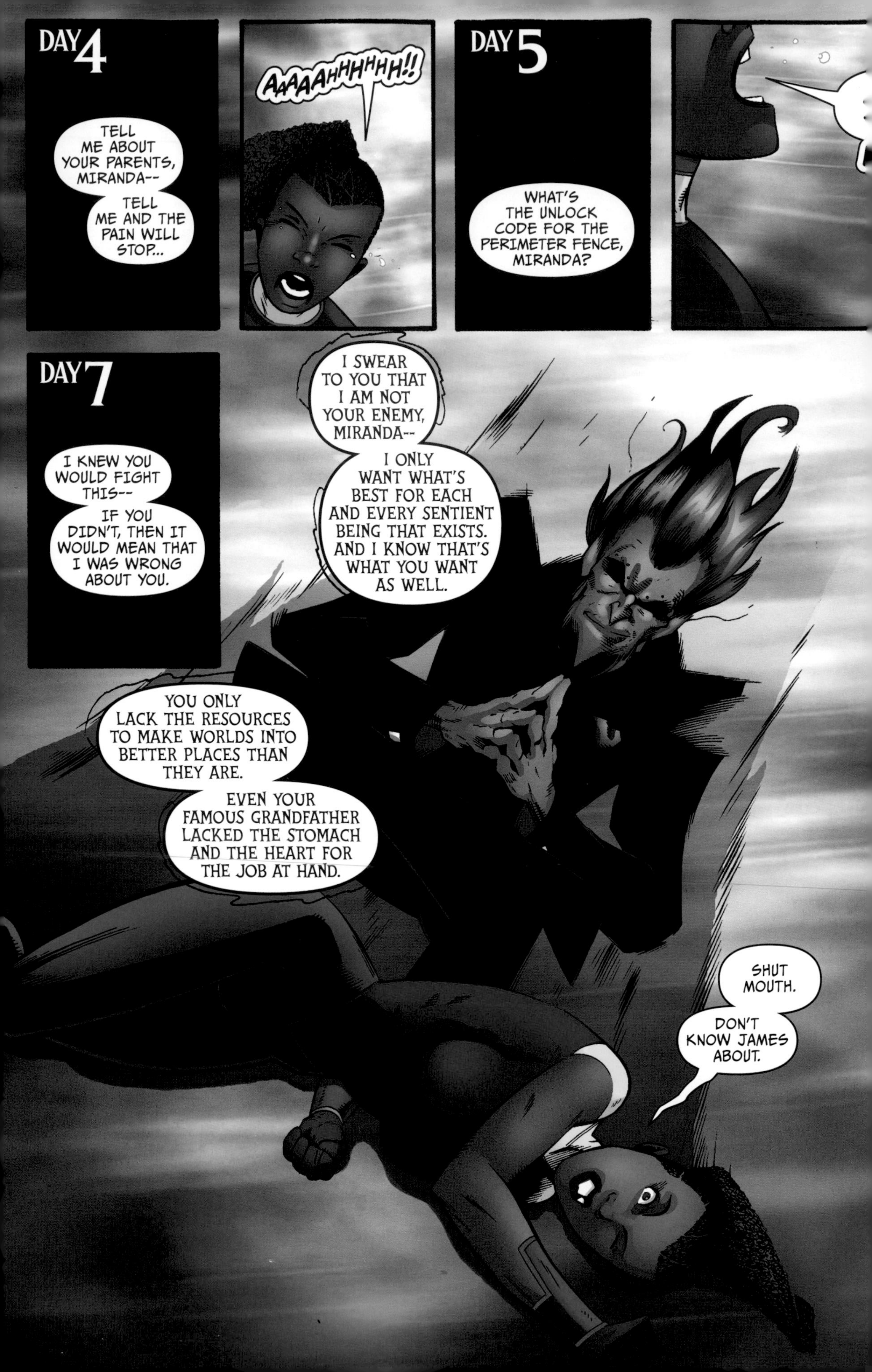
DAY 4
TELL ME ABOUT YOUR PARENTS, MIRANDA--
TELL ME AND THE PAIN WILL STOP...
AAAAAHHHHHH!!
DAY 5
WHAT'S THE UNLOCK CODE FOR THE PERIMETER FENCE, MIRANDA?
DAY 7
I KNEW YOU WOULD FIGHT THIS--
IF YOU DIDN'T, THEN IT WOULD MEAN THAT I WAS WRONG ABOUT YOU.
I SWEAR TO YOU THAT I AM NOT YOUR ENEMY, MIRANDA--
I ONLY WANT WHAT'S BEST FOR EACH AND EVERY SENTIENT BEING THAT EXISTS. AND I KNOW THAT'S WHAT YOU WANT AS WELL.
YOU ONLY LACK THE RESOURCES TO MAKE WORLDS INTO BETTER PLACES THAN THEY ARE.
EVEN YOUR FAMOUS GRANDFATHER LACKED THE STOMACH AND THE HEART FOR THE JOB AT HAND.
SHUT MOUTH.
DON'T KNOW JAMES ABOUT.

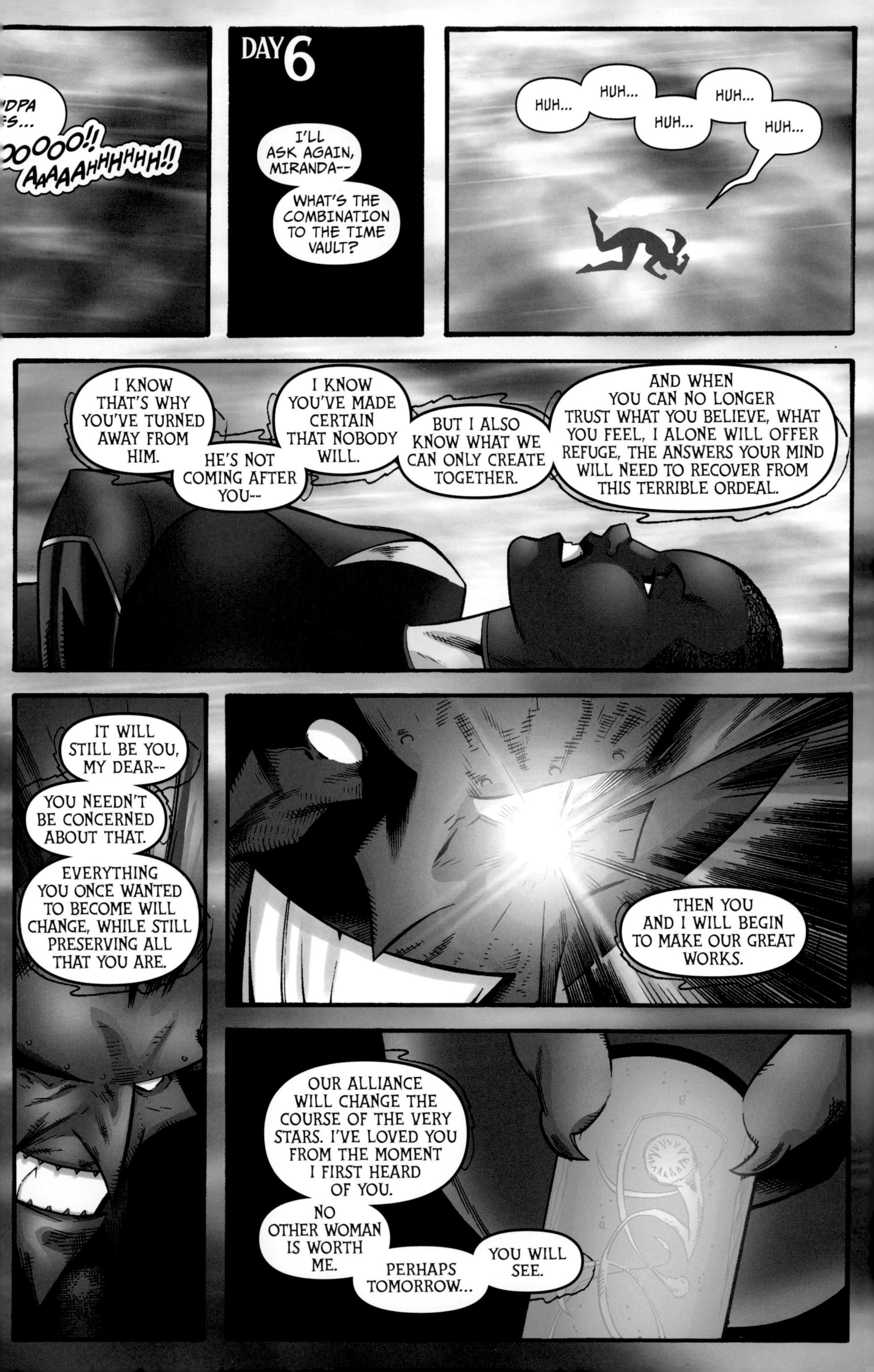

AAAAAHHHHHH!!
DAY 6
I'LL ASK AGAIN, MIRANDA--
WHAT'S THE COMBINATION TO THE TIME VAULT?
HUH...
HUH...
HUH...
HUH...
HUH...
I KNOW THAT'S WHY YOU'VE TURNED AWAY FROM HIM.
HE'S NOT COMING AFTER YOU--
I KNOW YOU'VE MADE CERTAIN THAT NOBODY WILL.
BUT I ALSO KNOW WHAT WE CAN ONLY CREATE TOGETHER.
AND WHEN YOU CAN NO LONGER TRUST WHAT YOU BELIEVE, WHAT YOU FEEL, I ALONE WILL OFFER REFUGE, THE ANSWERS YOUR MIND WILL NEED TO RECOVER FROM THIS TERRIBLE ORDEAL.
IT WILL STILL BE YOU, MY DEAR--
YOU NEEDN'T BE CONCERNED ABOUT THAT.
EVERYTHING YOU ONCE WANTED TO BECOME WILL CHANGE, WHILE STILL PRESERVING ALL THAT YOU ARE.
THEN YOU AND I WILL BEGIN TO MAKE OUR GREAT WORKS.
OUR ALLIANCE WILL CHANGE THE COURSE OF THE VERY STARS. I'VE LOVED YOU FROM THE MOMENT I FIRST HEARD OF YOU.
NO OTHER WOMAN IS WORTH ME.
PERHAPS TOMORROW...
YOU WILL SEE.

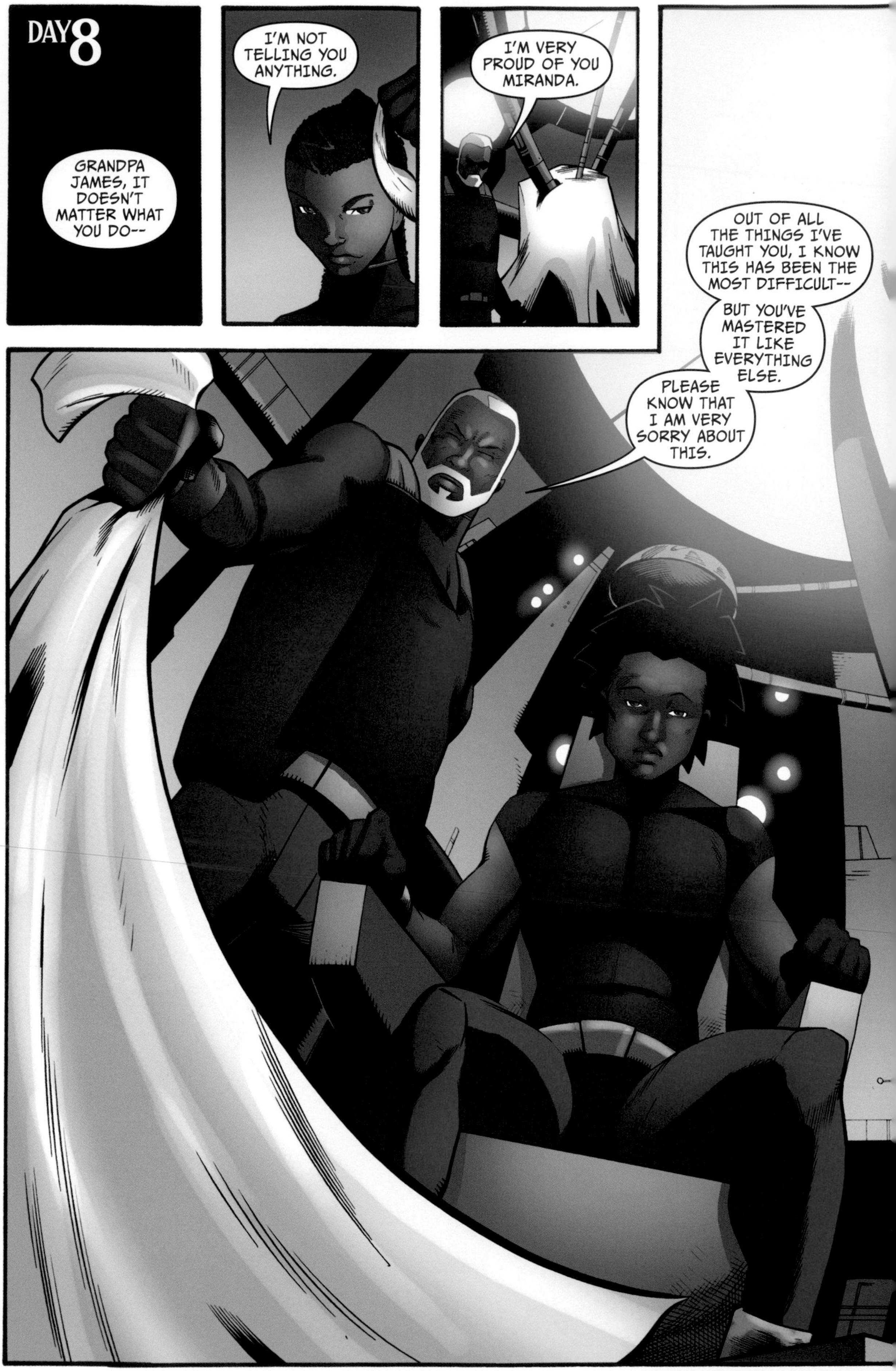
DAY 8
GRANDPA JAMES, IT DOESN'T MATTER WHAT YOU DO--
I'M NOT TELLING YOU ANYTHING.
I'M VERY PROUD OF YOU MIRANDA.
OUT OF ALL THE THINGS I'VE TAUGHT YOU, I KNOW THIS HAS BEEN THE MOST DIFFICULT--
BUT YOU'VE MASTERED IT LIKE EVERYTHING ELSE.
PLEASE KNOW THAT I AM VERY SORRY ABOUT THIS.

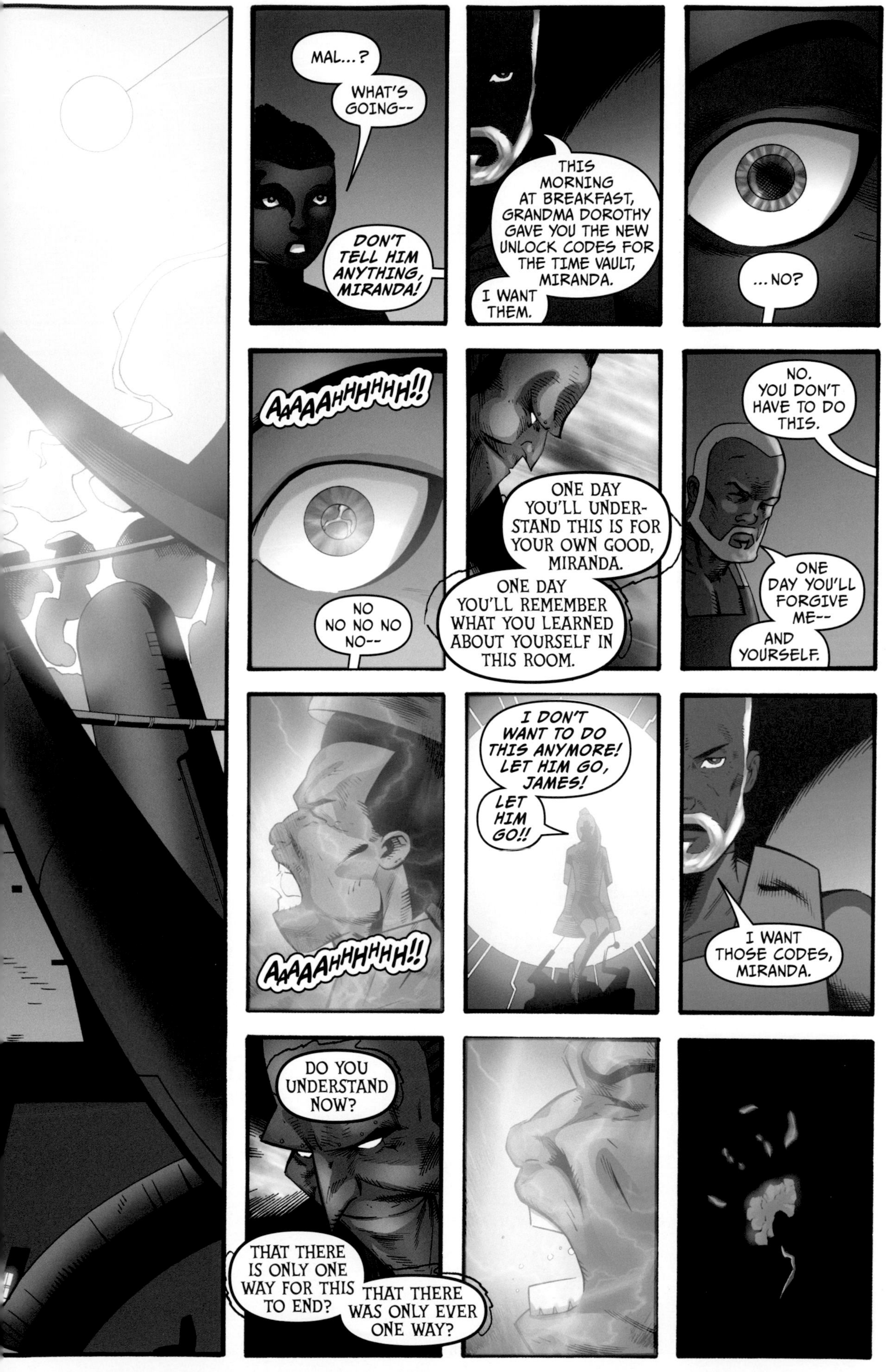
MAL...?
WHAT'S GOING--
DON'T TELL HIM ANYTHING, MIRANDA!
THIS MORNING AT BREAKFAST, GRANDMA DOROTHY GAVE YOU THE NEW UNLOCK CODES FOR THE TIME VAULT, MIRANDA.
I WANT THEM.
...NO?
AAAAAHHHHHH!!
NO NO NO NO NO--
ONE DAY YOU'LL UNDERSTAND THIS IS FOR YOUR OWN GOOD, MIRANDA.
ONE DAY YOU'LL REMEMBER WHAT YOU LEARNED ABOUT YOURSELF IN THIS ROOM.
NO. YOU DON'T HAVE TO DO THIS.
ONE DAY YOU'LL FORGIVE ME--
AND YOURSELF.
AAAAAHHHHHH!!
I DON'T WANT TO DO THIS ANYMORE! LET HIM GO, JAMES!
LET HIM GO!!
I WANT THOSE CODES, MIRANDA.
DO YOU UNDERSTAND NOW?
THAT THERE IS ONLY ONE WAY FOR THIS TO END?
THAT THERE WAS ONLY EVER ONE WAY?

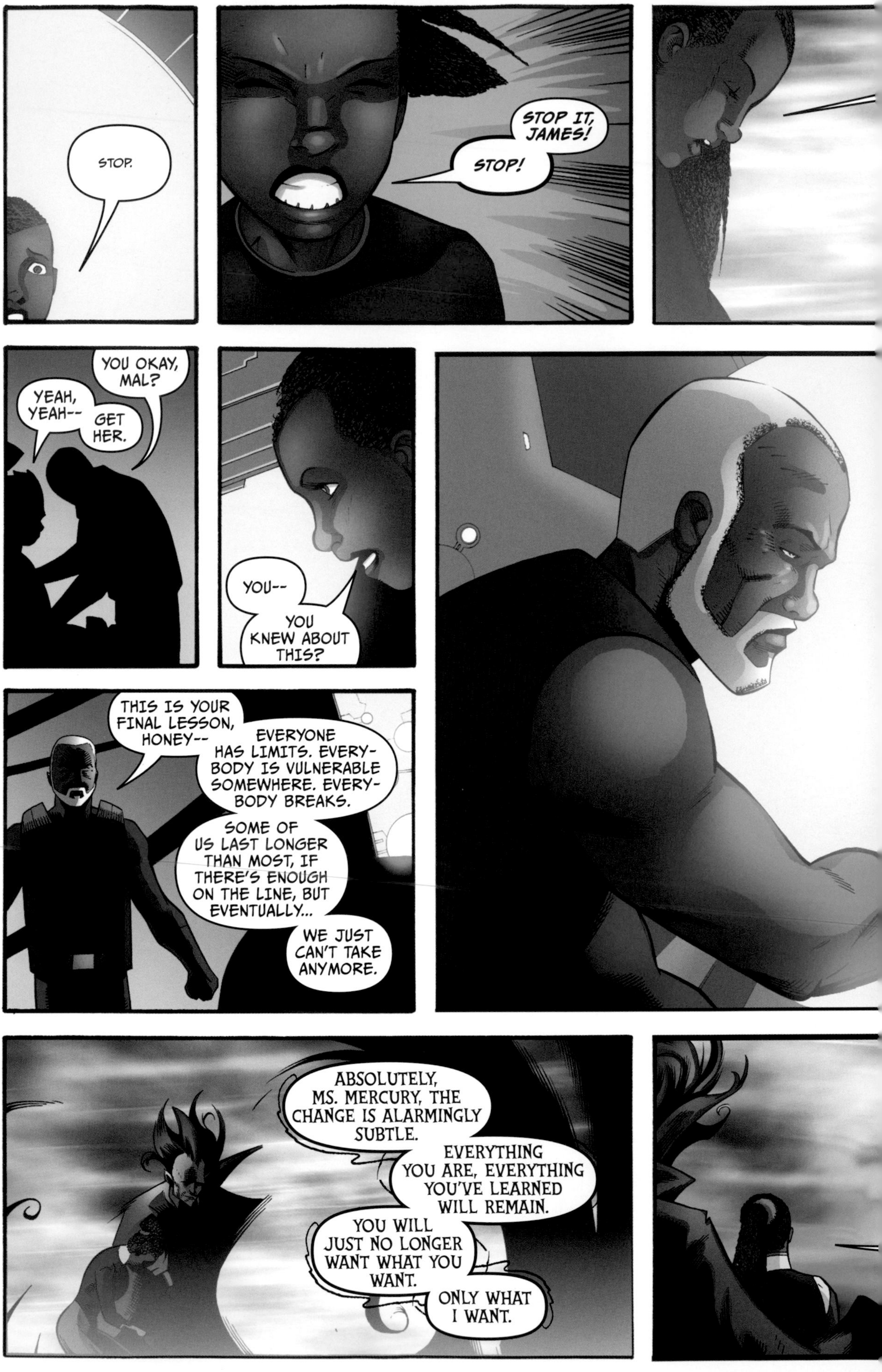
STOP.
STOP IT, JAMES!
STOP!
YOU OKAY, MAL?
YEAH, YEAH--
GET HER.
YOU--
YOU KNEW ABOUT THIS?
THIS IS YOUR FINAL LESSON, HONEY--
EVERYONE HAS LIMITS. EVERYBODY IS VULNERABLE SOMEWHERE. EVERYBODY BREAKS.
SOME OF US LAST LONGER THAN MOST, IF THERE'S ENOUGH ON THE LINE, BUT EVENTUALLY...
WE JUST CAN'T TAKE ANYMORE.
ABSOLUTELY, MS. MERCURY, THE CHANGE IS ALARMINGLY SUBTLE.
EVERYTHING YOU ARE, EVERYTHING YOU'VE LEARNED WILL REMAIN.
YOU WILL JUST NO LONGER WANT WHAT YOU WANT.
ONLY WHAT I WANT.

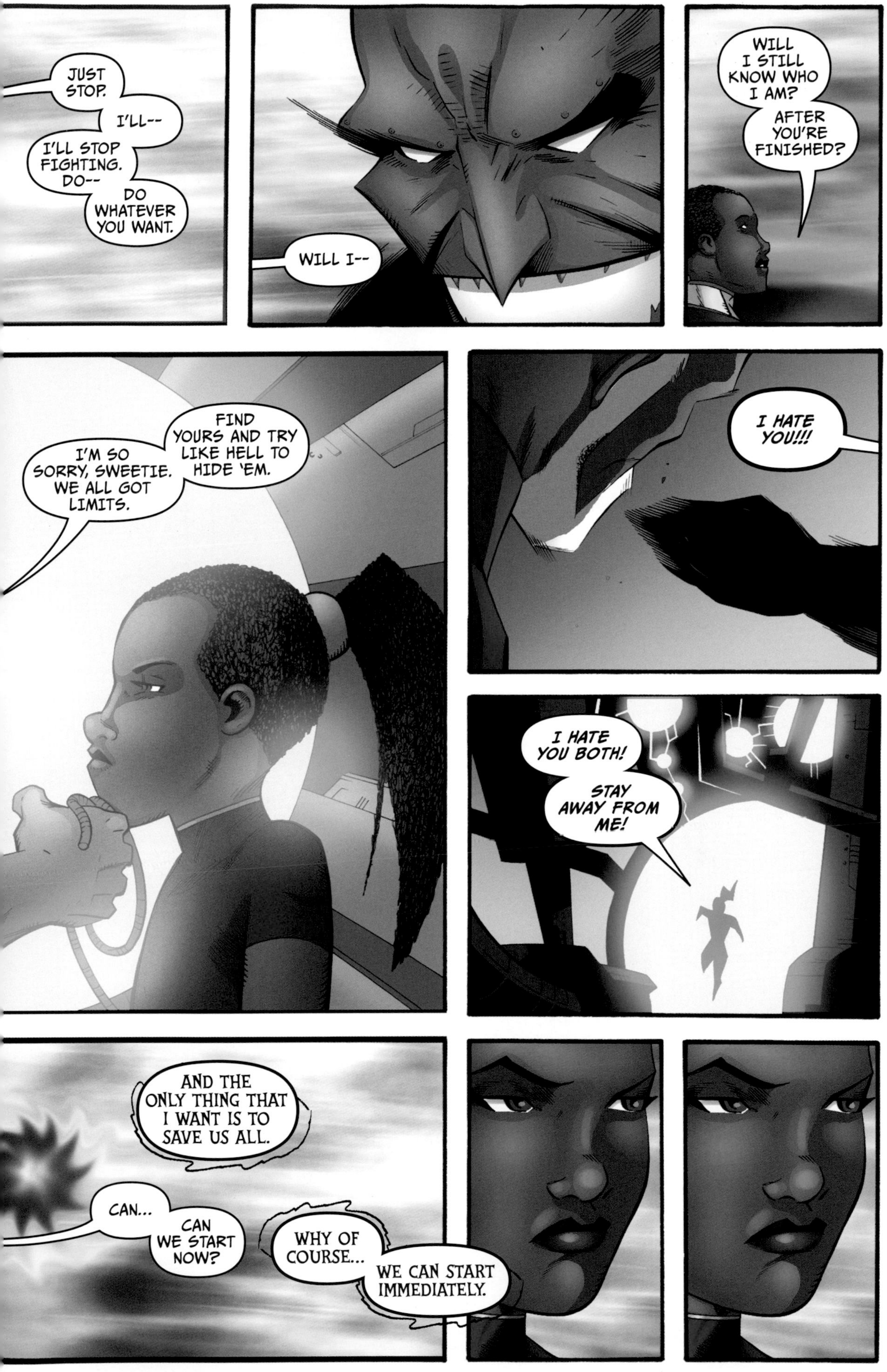
JUST STOP.
I'LL--
I'LL STOP FIGHTING. DO--
DO WHATEVER YOU WANT.
WILL I--
WILL I STILL KNOW WHO I AM?
AFTER YOU'RE FINISHED?
I'M SO SORRY, SWEETIE. WE ALL GOT LIMITS.
FIND YOURS AND TRY LIKE HELL TO HIDE 'EM.
I HATE YOU!!!
I HATE YOU BOTH!
STAY AWAY FROM ME!
AND THE ONLY THING THAT I WANT IS TO SAVE US ALL.
CAN...
CAN WE START NOW?
WHY OF COURSE...
WE CAN START IMMEDIATELY.

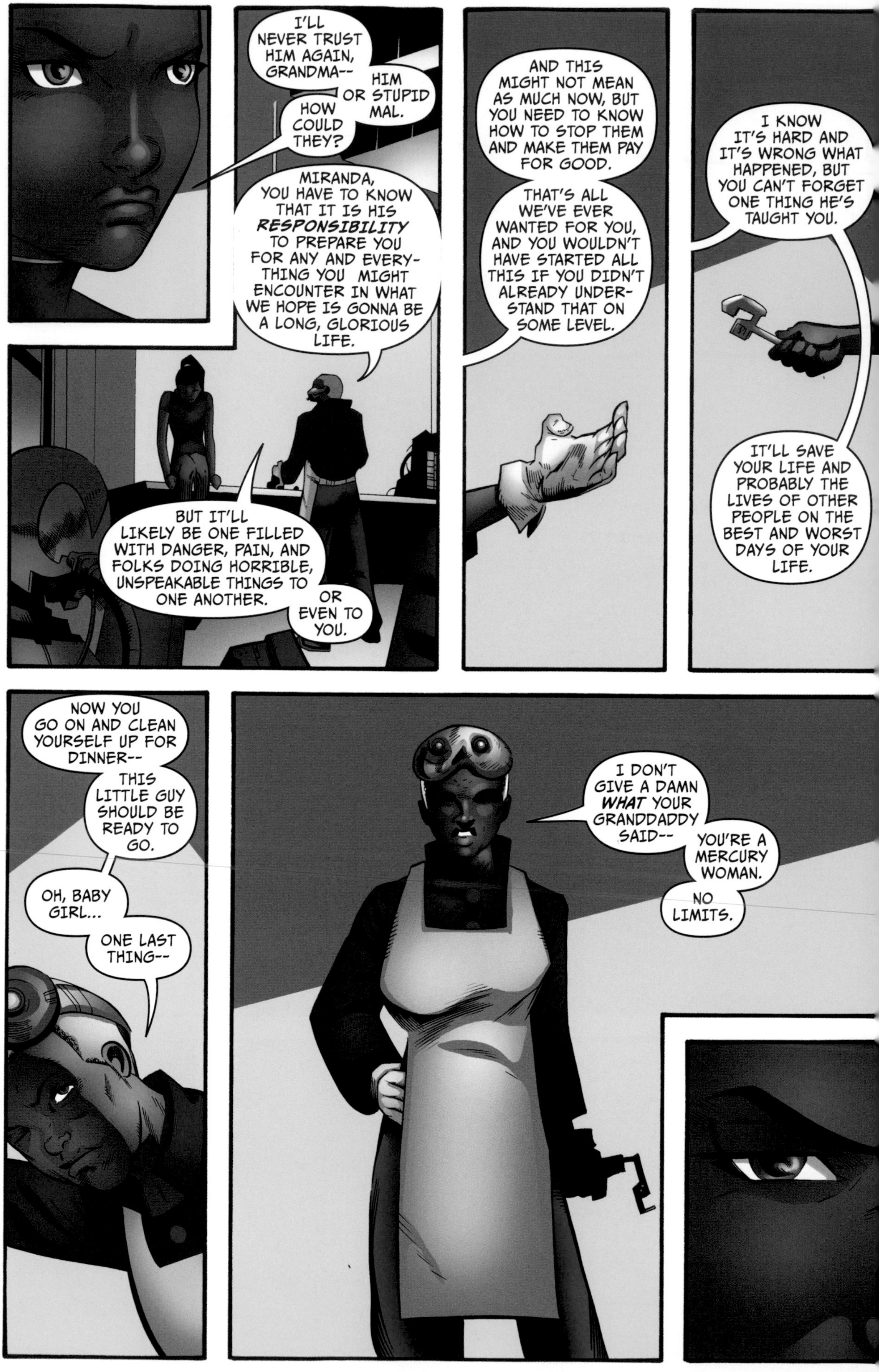

I'LL NEVER TRUST HIM AGAIN, GRANDMA--
HIM OR STUPID MAL.
HOW COULD THEY?
MIRANDA, YOU HAVE TO KNOW THAT IT IS HIS RESPONSIBILITY TO PREPARE YOU FOR ANY AND EVERYTHING YOU MIGHT ENCOUNTER IN WHAT WE HOPE IS GONNA BE A LONG, GLORIOUS LIFE.
BUT IT'LL LIKELY BE ONE FILLED WITH DANGER, PAIN, AND FOLKS DOING HORRIBLE, UNSPEAKABLE THINGS TO ONE ANOTHER.
OR EVEN TO YOU.
AND THIS MIGHT NOT MEAN AS MUCH NOW, BUT YOU NEED TO KNOW HOW TO STOP THEM AND MAKE THEM PAY FOR GOOD.
THAT'S ALL WE'VE EVER WANTED FOR YOU, AND YOU WOULDN'T HAVE STARTED ALL THIS IF YOU DIDN'T ALREADY UNDERSTAND THAT ON SOME LEVEL.
I KNOW IT'S HARD AND IT'S WRONG WHAT HAPPENED, BUT YOU CAN'T FORGET ONE THING HE'S TAUGHT YOU.
IT'LL SAVE YOUR LIFE AND PROBABLY THE LIVES OF OTHER PEOPLE ON THE BEST AND WORST DAYS OF YOUR LIFE.
NOW YOU GO ON AND CLEAN YOURSELF UP FOR DINNER--
THIS LITTLE GUY SHOULD BE READY TO GO.
OH, BABY GIRL...
ONE LAST THING--
I DON'T GIVE A DAMN WHAT YOUR GRANDDADDY SAID--
YOU'RE A MERCURY WOMAN.
NO LIMITS.

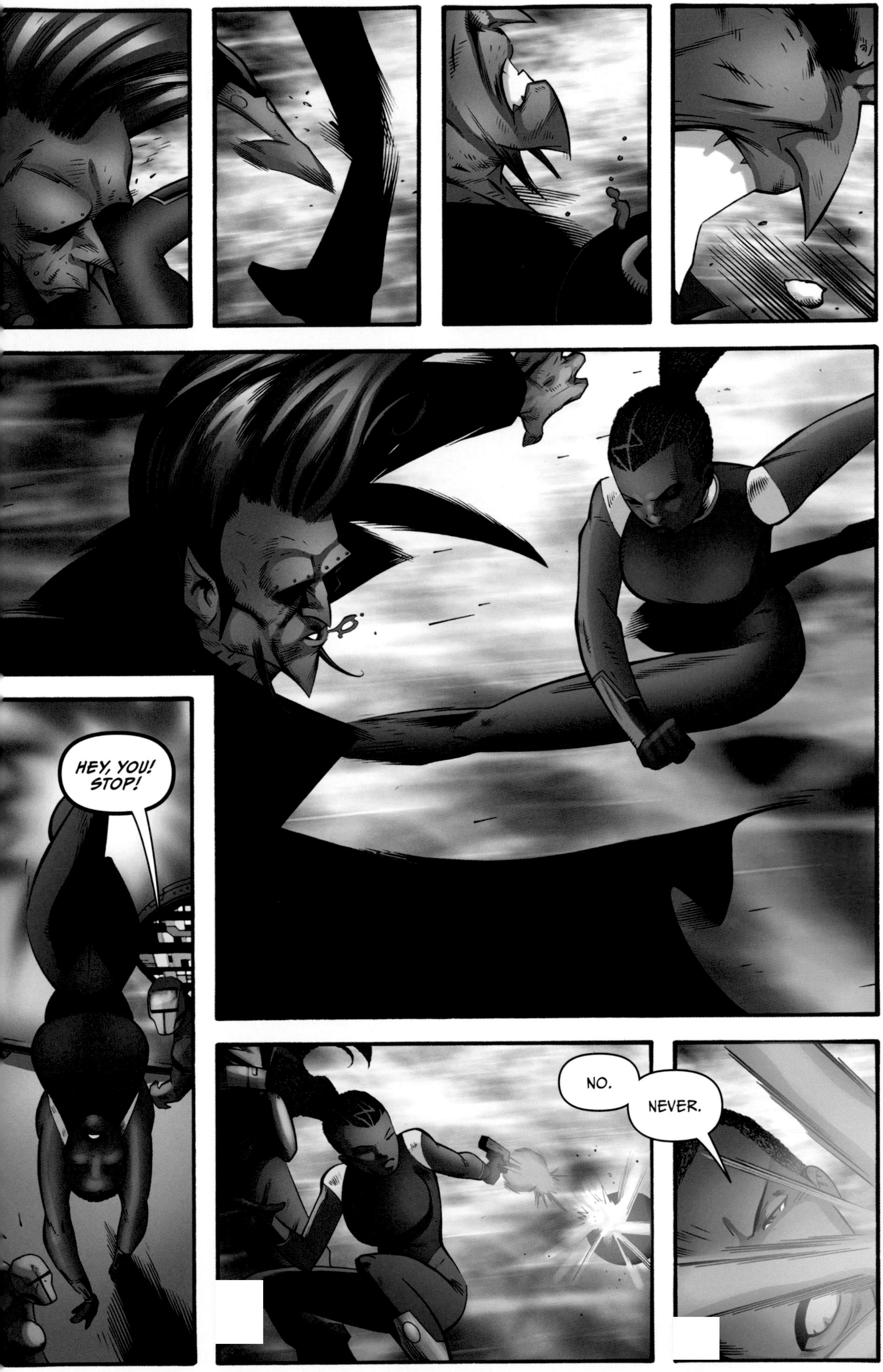
HEY, YOU! STOP!
NO.
NEVER.

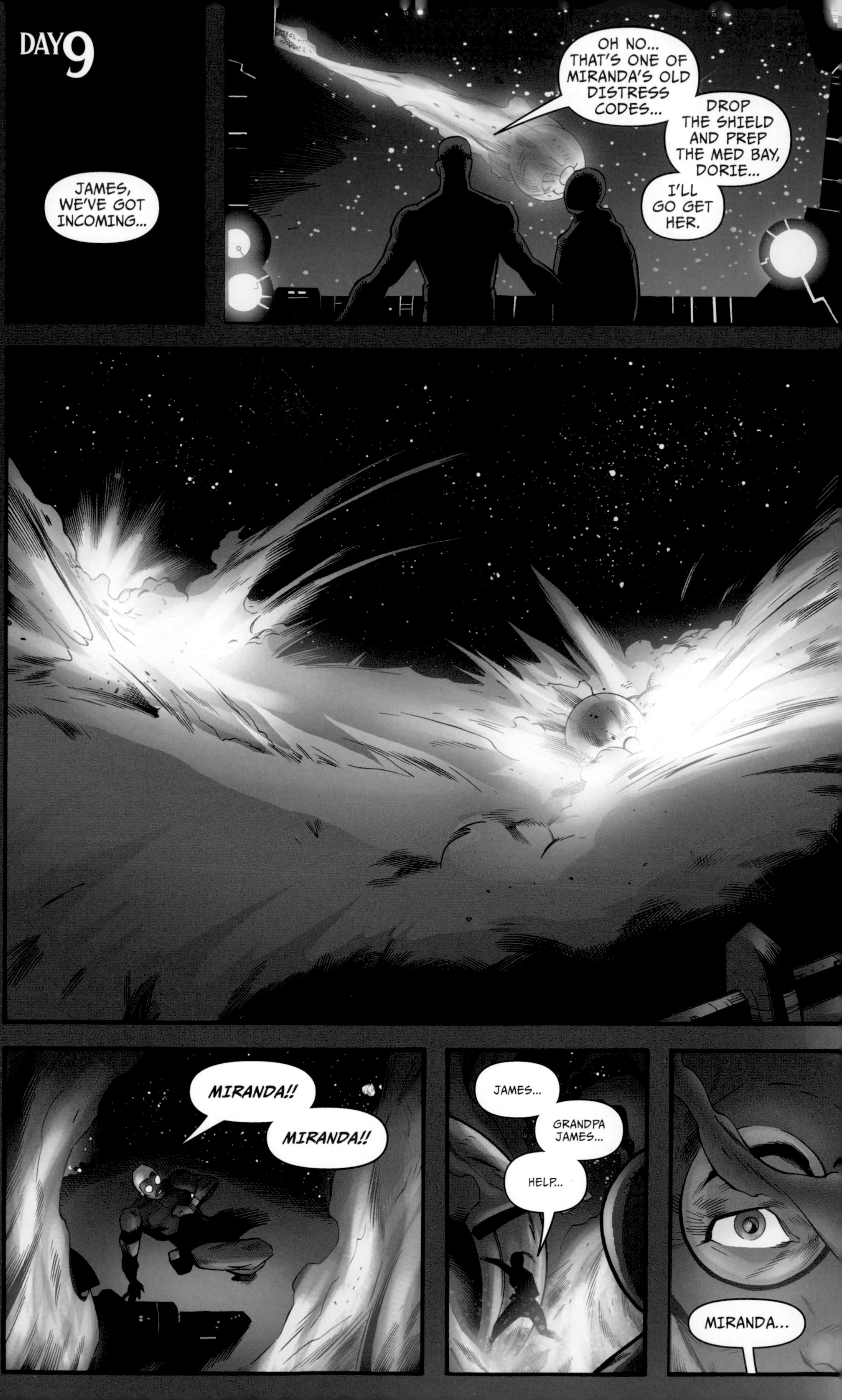
DAY 9
JAMES, WE'VE GOT INCOMING...
OH NO... THAT'S ONE OF MIRANDA'S OLD DISTRESS CODES...
DROP THE SHIELD AND PREP THE MED BAY, DORIE...
I'LL GO GET HER.
MIRANDA!!
MIRANDA!!
JAMES...
GRANDPA JAMES...
HELP...
MIRANDA...

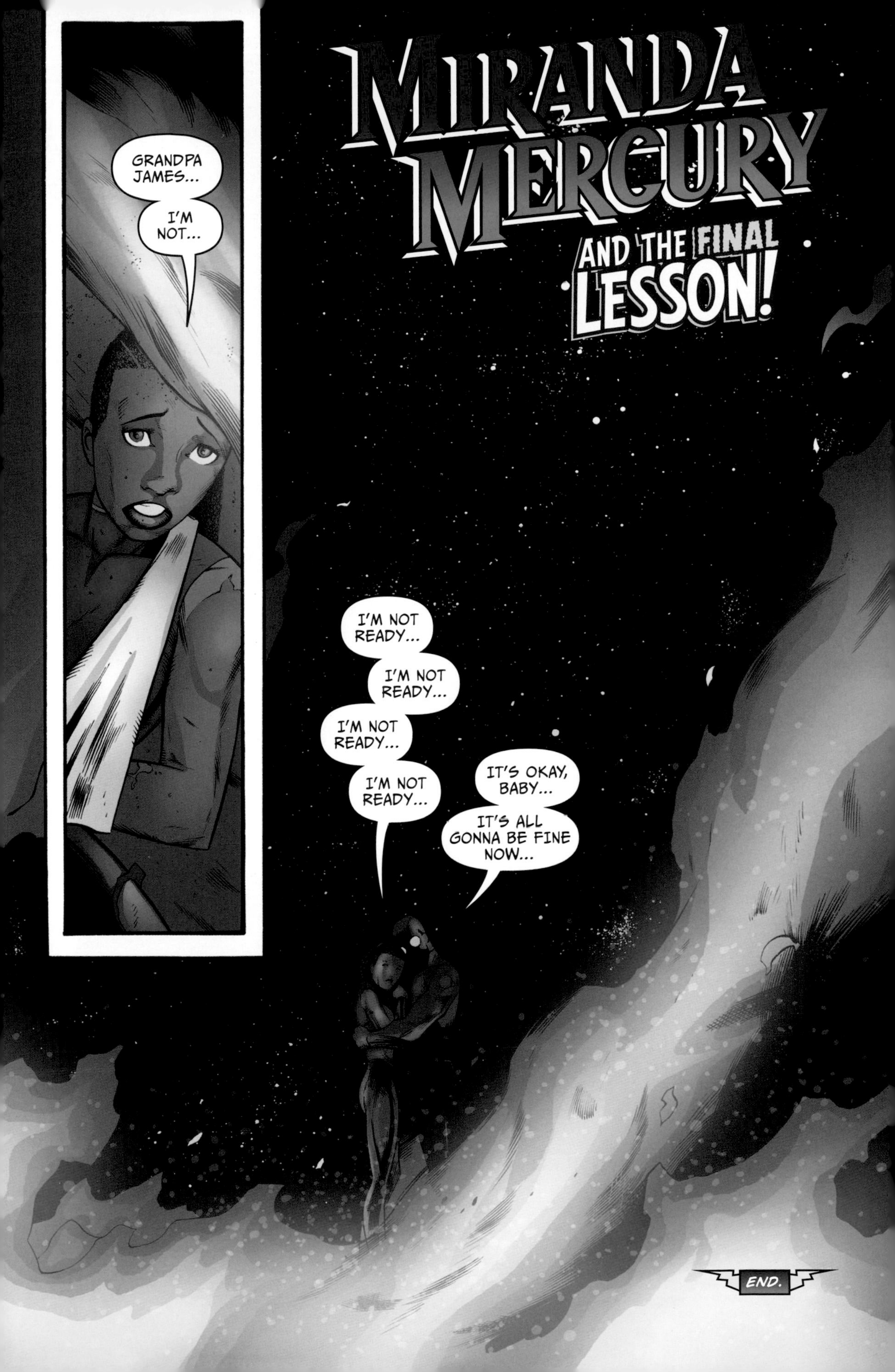
MIRANDA MERCURY
AND THE FINAL LESSON!
GRANDPA JAMES...
I'M NOT...
I'M NOT READY...
I'M NOT READY...
I'M NOT READY...
I'M NOT READY...
IT'S OKAY, BABY...
IT'S ALL GONNA BE FINE NOW...
END.

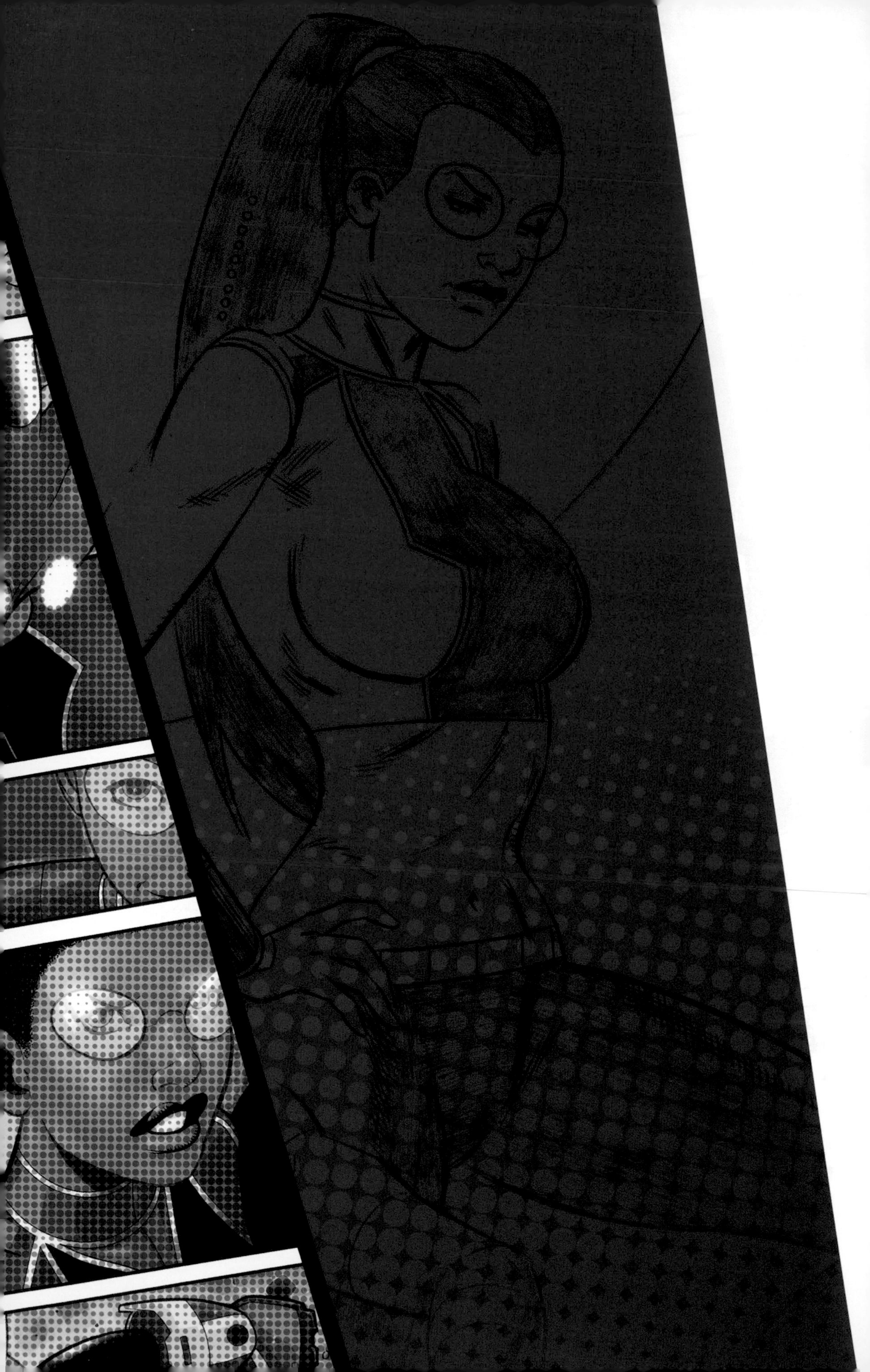

The book you're holding in your hands encompasses over five years of our lives...

The first real notion of this character was committed to paper in early 2005, and never in my wildest dreams did I imagine that it would take us quite so long to get to this point. Miranda Mercury was initially created as a way to overcome obstacles, and I think that aspect of her character manifested itself at critical points throughout this long, strange journey to get her many adventures into print. As I've been writing about this in public for years now, some of you have already heard all about her and about all of the things that have delayed her arrival over the years. The fact is that almost everything about creating this book and getting it published has been a struggle, and occasionally someone will just outright ask me, "How are you still doing this...why are you still doing this? Why don't you just let it go?"

Here's what it is though...we kept pushing at this because in my mind we had no other choice, as there was simply no way in hell that I would allow the obstacles to ultimately define this character or to define us. Every single person on this creative team can attest to their own personal journey with Miranda Mercury, but no one is living the same life they were when work on this project began. Some of us have lost people that meant the world to us, or in other cases, dogs that did. Some of us have gotten married (that's me, hey sweetie). All of us have moved houses/apartments numerous times, and one of us was even forced from his home by the unexpected revelation that his home was filled to the brim with toxic drywall...a gift that keeps on giving with any and all manner of recurring respiratory problems. Through it all it's been proven that life does indeed go on and on, and yet Miranda Mercury somehow refuses to fade away.

Though it was never an easy road, it's the one we found ourselves on time and time again, and we never stopped fighting for the opportunity and the right to make this book. And though I admit this next bit begrudgingly, I know that the constant delays have ultimately helped the quality of the final product. As a writer, some of these scripts were completely beyond my meager skills several years ago, and I hope there's an obvious progression at work here, that the book got progressively better the further you dug into it. That might not have been the case if we'd been able to really get going in 2006, and better comics beats more comics any day of the week, in our eyes.

So take it from the book we hope you just enjoyed reading...never let anyone tell you something is "impossible," or tell you definitively what you are or what you have to offer. If you're crazy enough to have a dream, you have to protect it and fight for it at all times and at all costs. You have to be willing to sacrifice almost anything to see it through. Most importantly, you have to have the help and support from friends and family that have probably grown tired of hearing you drone on and on about this special thing, this consuming aspiration that's always going to be a part of you, but will never say so and always push you to never let it go. To never surrender it to anybody. Because it's hard, maybe not as hard as we've made it look, or maybe even harder than that, but I can tell without hesitation that in the end, it's all absolutely worth it. Every second of the whole thing.

There's a great line in Grant Morrison and Frank Quitely's All-Star Superman series that I wish I'd come up with first and used as the overall tagline for this book....only nothing is impossible. That sentiment right there is the entire point of Miranda Mercury. That's why we never quit despite what seemed to be an endless series of unfortunate events, and no shortage of people lining up to tell us about this book and how unsuccessful it would be. And that is why this is the proudest and most grateful I've ever been in my somewhat lengthy relationship with comics, both as a fan and as a creator. The fact that you're even reading this is a tremendous personal victory for myself and everyone that's brought their talents and their passion to this book, which many believed could not or should not exist.

So the next time anyone is lining up to tell you why you don't have a chance, that what you have to say doesn't matter, or that what you want more than anything is "impossible," you tell them what Miranda Mercury would say to anyone that would ever dare utter such a thing---

"Impossible for **you**, maybe."

Thank you for joining us, and for a much more comprehensive look back at the many creative stages of *The Many Adventures of Miranda Mercury*, please visit **www.mirandamercury.com**.

—Brandon Thomas
Chicago, IL
January 2011

DEDICATIONS AND ACKNOWLEDGEMENTS

BRANDON THOMAS

R- Before I met you, I'd almost given up. Now every day
your smile reminds me to never quit, never surrender,
and to never settle under any circumstances.
Truly the best is yet to come.

LEE FERGUSON

Friends and family, especially Lyndi and the kids...
not only for the encouragement and enthusiasm,
but for understanding, despite all those
long hours and lost weekends.
Couldn't have made it without you... love you guys.
Grandma Nancy...miss you.
God... I am truly blessed in every way that matters.

MARC DEERING

For my wife and family.
For keeping the "nappy" in line.

MATTY RYAN

To my wife, my family, and my friends
for simply putting up with me.

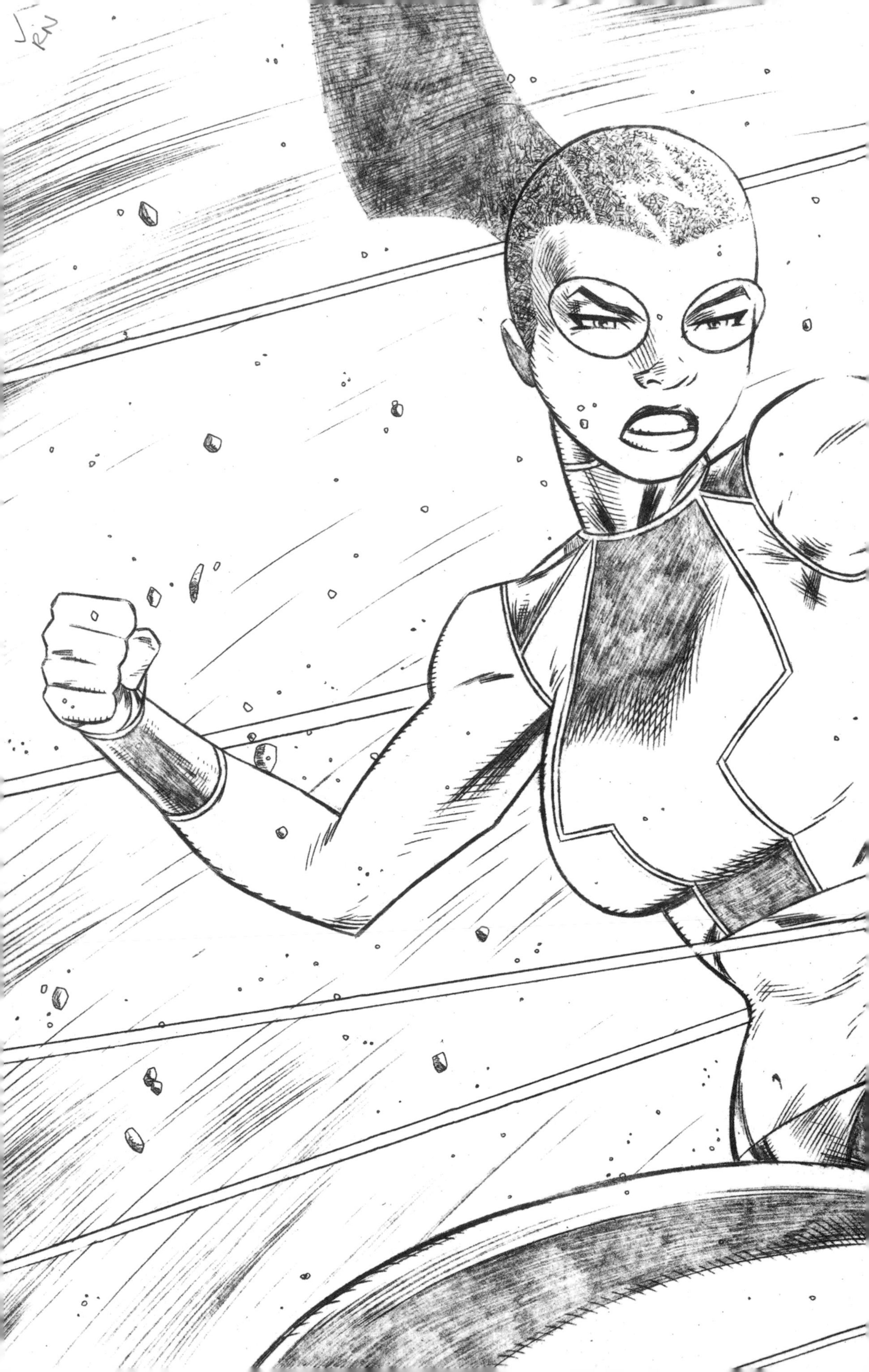